WE JUST KEEP RUNNING THE LINE

WE JUST KEEP RUNNING THE LINE

BLACK SOUTHERN WOMEN AND THE POULTRY PROCESSING INDUSTRY

LaGUANA GRAY

LOUISIANA STATE UNIVERSITY PRESS)|(BATON ROUGE

Published by Louisiana State University Press
Copyright © 2014 by Louisiana State University Press
All rights reserved
Manufactured in the United States of America
First printing

Designer: Barbara Neely Bourgoyne
Typeface: Ingeborg
Printer and binder: Maple Press

Library of Congress Cataloging-in-Publication Data

Gray, LaGuana, 1974–
  We just keep running the line : black Southern women and the poultry processing industry /
LaGuana Gray.
      pages cm
  Includes bibliographical references and index.
  ISBN 978-0-8071-5768-8 (cloth : alk. paper) — ISBN 978-0-8071-5769-5 (pdf) —
  ISBN 978-0-8071-5770-1 (epub) — ISBN 978-0-8071-5771-8 (mobi) 1. Poultry industry—
  Employees—Southern States—Social conditions. 2. African American women employees—
  Southern States—Social conditions. 3. Poultry plants—Management—Southern States—
  History. 4. Discrimination in employment—Southern States—History. 5. Industrial
  relations—Southern States—History. 6. Working class African Americans—Southern
  States—History. I. Title.
    HD9437.U63S684 2014
    331.4'8649308996073075—dc23
                                                                    2014011366

CONTENTS

Acknowledgments   vii

Introduction   1

1. "Arkansas's First Boomtown"   19

2. "I Was a Single Parent—I *Had* to Work"   43

3. "I Learned This—You Ain't Nobody!"   76

4. "They Don't Expect the Human Body to Break Down!"   104

5. "They Are about to Outnumber All the Different Races"   126

Conclusion   154

Appendix A. Biographies   163

Appendix B. Interview Questions   167

Notes   171

Bibliography   233

Index   267

ACKNOWLEDGMENTS

As with any work such as this, the time, effort, love, and patience of many people poured into it. I cannot, in this space, fully thank all of them—for everyone from research assistants to librarians across the country to encouragers from my small hometown played a part. So, please, charge any omissions to my head and not my heart! I do want, however, to express the most gratitude and admiration to the women and men poultry processing workers who opened up their lives, homes, and hearts to me and made this book possible. It could not have been without you. I hope that I did your stories justice.

To my colleagues at my alma mater, Louisiana Tech, particularly Drs. Stephen Webre, Elaine Thompson, and Dave Anderson, thank you for checking on the work (and on me) and for your support in giving me platforms to share and refine it. To my colleagues in the Department of History and the Honors College at the University of Texas at San Antonio, thank you for the advice and being both cheering sections and gentle taskmasters, according to my need. To the women senior faculty, including Landon Storrs, Bernadette Pruitt, Rhonda Gonzales, Kirsten Gardner, Ann Eisenberg, Sonja Lanehart, and Joycelyn Moody, who have taken the time to advise and mentor me and help me learn the ins and outs of academic life, I cannot thank you enough. I know that you all know how important that is to junior faculty, particularly underrepresented junior faculty. And to my poor department chair, Gregg Michel, who bravely suffered through a million questions, e-mails, and brief meetings from/with me as I worked through the book process, thank you. The support of my fellow junior faculty members during this process was absolutely crucial. So, Kinitra Brooks, Jerry Gonzalez, and Linda Benavides, I appreciate you so much.

My circle of women friends and family has been absolutely crucial in sustaining me, a lifelong task, though they went into overdrive while I was researching and writing. A-1, Becky, Coti, Diante, Keisha Grace, both my Kims, Melissa, Mrs. O, Sister, Tesha, Tessa, TeTe, TK, and Ms. Tosha, I love you and am so grateful for the gifts of your love, support, kindness, laughter, tears, and assistance. To my Louisiana School for Math, Science, and the Arts "Sweeties" and my larger LSMSA family, I love you.

To my family, particularly my aunts and uncles, first cousins, nieces and nephews, and brother, thanks for your enthusiasm for the project and always checking on me. I promise to be less of a poorly traveled hermit now. Thank you, Aunt Jo, for always being there, no matter what. For Jamari, Jakobe, Jalen, and Corey, who lived with a frantic, stressed me in the last stages of preparation of this work—I realize that old saying, "If Mama's not happy, no one is happy," is somewhat true. I'm sorry! I love y'all, though! My parents both inspired and financially and emotionally supported this project—I am forever in debt to them for their unconditional love and belief in me. Rest in Love, Daddy.

And, Mama, I will simply paraphrase something I said long ago: I know that I am a product of your labor of love. I hope you are proud of the fruits that I bear.

WE JUST KEEP RUNNING THE LINE

INTRODUCTION

In September 2009, after a little more than twenty-three years, my mother's tenure as a poultry processing worker in El Dorado, Arkansas, came to an end. She worked initially for ConAgra Poultry and ultimately for Pilgrim's Pride. She was mostly noncommittal about her job, dismissing the difficulty of the work by noting that processing chickens "will feed and clothe you." Still, there was always the unspoken knowledge that, though my brother was also a longtime poultry processing worker, neither of them wanted my sister or me to work at the plant. When my sister asked my brother to help her get a summer job there, he refused. My mother told her, "You don't need to work there." The reason, quite simply, is this: processing line work is hellacious. Poultry plants' rapid line speeds and extreme temperatures are linked to a number of physical ailments. Beyond the physical harm they endure, poultry processing workers confide in researchers that they labor in psychologically harrowing environments in which racist and sexual harassment are rampant.

I knew about the repulsive nature of the work from my mother, my brother, and many other relatives who made their way, every workday, through the steel gates of the El Dorado, Arkansas, and Farmerville, Louisiana, poultry plants. As a child, I quickly learned why my mother washed her clothes separately from the rest of the family's; we all understood that no amount of bleach would obliterate the scent of the plant. I was witness to the "chicken rashes" and boils that my family endured, which the com-

1

pany maintained had nothing to do with contact with chicken carcasses and repeated exposure to the toxin-laced water used to clean processing room floors and assembly lines. Many newly hired people quit within days or weeks. They complained that the work was too hard, too cold, too fast.

Just how fast was explained by Mark Simmons, chairman of Simmons Food. In 1999, at a reception in honor of his company's fiftieth anniversary, Simmons noted that when Frank Pluss and his father opened a plant in Siloam Springs, Arkansas, in 1952, "they could process 10,000 chickens a day." "Today," he boasted, "we can process 10,000 chickens in 30 minutes."[1] Although Simmons included himself in making this claim, his position as chairman of the company is not like jobs found inside poultry processing plants. According to one scholar, poultry processing workers labor in quasi–penal conditions, a result of the drive for low costs and high profits.[2]

Because of my family members' objections to my even considering temporary work in the industry, I was relatively ignorant of how poultry processing plants ran and the nature of poultry processing work. The messages I did receive were enough to make me wonder, what of the workers who have endured the phenomenal speed-up? Why did poultry processing have such a hold on this area? Why would anyone go into poultry processing work, and how did anyone stay? Those have been the guiding questions of this project. To try to answer them, I fashioned a history of one group of poultry processing workers, the black women who worked primarily in the poultry processing complex of El Dorado, Arkansas, and at the smaller complex in Farmerville, Louisiana.

This is a story of the rise of the poultry processing industry in El Dorado and the labor force upon which it came to rely, a labor force composed heavily of poor, rural black women, many of them from North Louisiana. To explore that rise, though the El Dorado plant did not open until 1955, I found it necessary to analyze the circumstances that brought the poultry industry to this region, circumstances that have their beginnings in the early twentieth century. The poultry industry thrives in part because it can keep labor costs low through tight control of its workforce. As David Harvey argues in *Justice, Nature, and the Geography of Difference*, that workforce is rendered controllable because it is composed of workers who are geographically isolated and typically "nonunionized and pliable."[3] Harvey's description was true of black women who worked in the El Dorado plant. An examination of these women's lives inside and outside the plant and of the factors that brought them to the poultry industry—roughly spanning the period from the Great Depression until the El Dorado plant stopped most production in 2009—is crucial to this study. A key source for the project is a set of oral and written interviews with black women poultry processing workers conducted between 2003 and 2012.[4] To recruit participants, I asked poultry processing workers whom I know to recommend interviewees. (Brief biographies of the interviewees and the questions that I asked them appear in appendixes A and B.)

Their stories led me to conduct electronic, written, and oral interviews with local school teachers, an English as a Second Language coordinator, and the executive secretary of the Georgia Poultry Justice Alliance and launch an e-mail correspondence with Reverend Jim Lewis, who has spent decades championing the cause of workers and farmers exploited by the poultry processing industry. Having used a snowballing method means that my sample was neither random nor geographically widespread. The approach allowed me to focus on workers in a particular town and to try to construct a story of how and why they came to the industry and how members of this community understood their relationships with the poultry industry and other workers.[5]

The poultry industry has dramatically changed the cultural landscape of portions of the South through its heavy recruitment of Latino workers since the end of the twentieth century. It was therefore important for this study to gauge longtime black residents' early reactions to the growth of the Latino population in the area and how the arrival and presence of this "new" group affected understandings of community and work. I distributed a survey for that purpose. I also included relevant questions in the interviews and explored the collections on Latino migrants to Union Parish and North Louisiana held by the now defunct Louisiana Regional Folklife Program at Louisiana Tech University.

My research supports earlier studies that maintain that a number of factors, including rigid class and race hierarchies and the post–World War II "selling of the South" by local and state governments and businesses, have created an exceptionally poor climate for labor in the South while simultaneously encouraging the rapid growth of southern industry.[6] Despite the poor working conditions and low wages, poultry processing workers remain largely unorganized, and their interests have been betrayed routinely by liberal and conservative politicians alike. Yet rather than finding a current of worker antipathy to unionization, I found people who had once been interested in traditional organization were dismayed by a union, the United Food and Commercial Workers, that they felt was out of touch. Like early union members, the poultry processing workers I interviewed understood themselves and their interests as in conflict with those of management. The pro-business stance of their union, then, rather than the union itself, was unacceptable to them.

Other studies have connected the economic vulnerability of poor people to their social vulnerability.[7] Especially in the case of African Americans, the suppression and violation of their civil rights in the South made them a prime target for low-wage industries. The social vulnerability of black women was more pronounced than that of poor whites or black men. In the mid-twentieth century custom barred black women from many of the jobs men could work and kept them from earning wages that men could. Popular sentiment begrudged their participation in the system of social provision that assisted poor white women, and the law assigned them to less generous programs, a fact supported by the records of the old Department of Public of Welfare held at the Louisiana State Archives. Thus, low-wage labor was often the only means of survival a black woman could hope for.

In other words, their location in the rural South, with its dearth of work alternatives, combined with the denial of their social and political rights, drew black women to the poultry processing industry. The industry capitalized both on their status as women, constructed as more compliant and docile than men, and on the historical defeminization of black women, which characterized them as fit for the dangerous, arduous, often grisly work usually reserved for men. For decades black women dominated poultry processing line work. But toward the end of the twentieth century, as they gained, at least legally, more rights and opportunities and developed a tradition of protest, their employers began to search for a new, exploitable labor force. Across the South processors turned to Latino workers. In southern Arkansas, however, the shift was not so pronounced. Black women, in the face of few prospects, held on to poultry processing jobs and in the process learned to work and live with people the industry had cast as their competitors.

In seeking to understand these black women's attitudes toward their work and what keeps them in their difficult, low-paying jobs, I came to recognize that they were able to stay not only because they had to but because they became skillful at negotiating with plant management and prioritizing their time and tasks. These negotiations occurred largely outside a collective body such as the union, with which many were so disillusioned. Instead, daily individual acts of negotiation, compromise, and sacrifice allowed black women to create a work environment more conducive to how they defined themselves as workers *and* family members.

To understand the working lives of black women in the post–World War II era requires a discussion of the nature of their labor in the first half of the twentieth century. Black women had long sought escape from the low pay and low status of domestic work because they perceived household work, even though it was paid, as reminiscent of slavery.[8] They loathed the stigma of domestic work and resented the demands white employers made on their time and their bodies. They sought to distance themselves from this "labor of sorrow" by identifying themselves primarily as wives and mothers and not as servants. This distinction was especially important in the 1930s. The Great Depression presented employers of domestic workers with the opportunity to lower wages and extend hours, benefits of which they eagerly took advantage. During these desperate times household workers were so exploited that the market for their services resembled a "slave market" characterized by meager pay, long hours, and hard work. The circumstances in which most domestic workers labored were so bleak that some organizations intervened in an effort to improve working conditions. The Young Women's Christian Association (YWCA) and the National Committee on Household Employment attempted to regulate the domestic service industry. These groups hoped to end the seventy-two- and eighty-four-hour weeks prevalent in household work; the YWCA even drew up model schedules. Neither organization had counted on the intransigence of white women employers or appreciated the severely circumscribed mobility of black women workers. The movement made no long-lasting gains. Despite the abominable conditions, black women remained concentrated in domestic service because racism and sexism excluded them from most other jobs.[9]

The other mainstay of black female employment, agricultural work, was just as problematic as domestic work. Although women on farms arguably had more autonomy (in the sense of freedom from close white supervision), black women, at the juxtaposition of racial, gender, and class prejudices, still rested at the bottom of the rural hierarchy.[10] The poorest black women rarely benefited from the gendered division of labor, which assigned the "hardest" jobs to men. These women had to work whenever and wherever they were needed. In addition, to help support their landless families, many black women had to take domestic jobs away from their own homes. This arrangement, in effect, created a "triple day" for black farm women: they farmed, cared for their own families, and did wage work in other households.[11]

The propertyless status of black farmers meant that most were sharecroppers, a system that rendered many black families overworked, poorly housed, and barely fed. In addition to farmwork responsibilities, black women often acted as negotiators with white landlords, a harrowing task in itself. The role of "helper" was not available to all farm women; in the absence of male relatives, black women provided all required labor in the home and in the fields.

Given the seemingly hopeless nature of their status as workers, it is no wonder that black women, like millions of other Americans in the Depression era, looked to Franklin Roosevelt's New Deal for relief. The New Deal did hold promise for workers. It pushed forth the National Labor Relations (Wagner) and Social Security Acts and set up various public works programs. The Agricultural Adjustment Act, designed to help farmers, including sharecroppers, was another product of the New Deal. Still, it was not until the era of full employment brought by World War II that black women managed to escape household work and farming by the thousands. During the war years the percentage of black women laboring as domestic workers dropped sharply as they entered industrial jobs.[12] The percentage of black females in farmwork dropped even more dramatically as farm women, too, headed for the factories. World War II represented a time of striking change for black women as workers.

Yet the character of that change proved problematic for several reasons. Although the number of jobs open to black women expanded, the type and quality of jobs did not change much. Black women were used disproportionately in janitorial work. Black women typically received the dirtiest, most arduous jobs in the factory. In many cases black women were confined to the same types of jobs and the same patterns of racial and gender discrimination that they had experienced before the war.[13]

Demobilization at the end of the war also demonstrated the limited nature of job opportunities for black women. Once the war was over, black women realized just how tenuous their hold on wartime occupations was. Women, and especially black women, were represented disproportionately in the postwar layoffs. Because much of their job expansion had come from increased production of durable goods, black women found themselves displaced when demand slumped after the war. Many black women reluctantly returned to domestic service.[14]

For black women the mixed legacy of federal legislation from the New Deal and World War II eras did not ease the problem of job displacement. The Agriculture Adjustment Act (AAA), for example, paid farmers to cultivate less land, reducing the need for tenants. Although the act provided that landlords share the payment with tenants, tenant eviction was widespread, and landowners literally stole the checks that the government made payable to sharecroppers. For black families on the verge of insolvency, the AAA provided little benefit.[15] Louisiana was among the states where this problem was especially acute.

Some New Deal policies operated against black workers by excluding them from their relief and recovery provisions. Union members celebrated the Wagner Act because it legalized closed shops and gave workers the right to bargain collectively. The act, however, also worried black workers. The historical exclusion of African Americans from trade unions made them wary that closed shops would "close" them out completely from many trades.[16] Other New Deal accomplishments were just as disappointing to African Americans: because local governments commonly administered public works programs and federal relief money, African Americans were typically offered little in the way of cash or jobs.[17] Perhaps the most striking exclusion of black women workers occurred in the context of Roosevelt's 1935 Social Security Act. The exclusion of domestic service and agricultural work from the social insurance provisions of the act and the popular image of the widowed white mother as the only mother deserving of welfare left black women with few alternatives as their job opportunities shriveled.

While much New Deal legislation had an unimpressive effect on the status and opportunities of black women workers, scholars debate the record of World War II's antidiscrimination legislation—notably Roosevelt's Executive Order 8802 and the subsequent Fair Employment Practices Committee (FEPC). Issued in 1941, Executive Order 8802, a response to the threat that disappointed black workers would "march on Washington," prohibited discrimination on the basis of race, religion, and nationality in war-related employment and created the FEPC. The FEPC was charged with ensuring employer compliance with antidiscrimination policies.

Historians recognize the limited capabilities of the FEPC; they disagree, however, about how well the committee worked within its confines. Jacqueline Jones dismisses the FEPC as ineffectual, insisting that the agency produced much talk and fanfare but few results. In a more generous tone, Karen Anderson admits that the FEPC did exert some pressure but stopped short of actually halting production to push racial equality. Anderson also contends that employers' unwillingness to hire black workers and the fact that the FEPC handled individual cases and complaints rather than attacking patterns of discrimination in hiring proved insurmountable obstacles.[18] In contrast, Eileen Boris argues that although the FEPC disadvantaged women by privileging race, religion, and nationality over gender, the committee made a concerted effort to contest employer discrimination and to go beyond individual cases. James Green asserts that the FEPC pressed for change in hiring practices and sometimes refused to back down in the face of white hate strikes.[19]

How much, then, had black women workers' status and opportunities changed by the end of the war? Given the unfavorable legacy of New Deal programs, the loss of wartime jobs, the return of many to domestic service, and the FEPC's mixed record, World War II could be interpreted, to borrow a phrase from Jacqueline Jones, as no great turning point in black women workers' history. That interpretation, however, is based largely on numbers and material gains. Although these measures are significant, they are inadequate for measuring the impact of the 1930s and 1940s on the lives of black women. It is important to note, however, that though many black women found themselves again in domestic service, they were never again as reliant on household work as they had been before the war. Black women workers had managed to gain a foothold in industrial labor—work that many more of them would occupy in the coming years. Industrial employment had drawn many black women out of the South, a move that almost unilaterally offered some improvement of status and expansion of opportunity. The Aid to Dependent Children program (ADC), as begrudging as it was, did offer some relief to single black mothers outside the South. Finally, some black women did benefit from the higher pay and somewhat improved working conditions that collective bargaining had secured in southern regions.

The status of black women workers after 1945 seemed improved, if tenuous. Yet in the South especially, job opportunities were scarce for unskilled workers. Southern officials, in their drives to recruit businesses to the region, recognized the vulnerable status of these workers. Boosters capitalized on southern workers' lack of alternatives, offering them up to industries as cheap and nonunion. Keeping poor workers in such weak circumstances allowed the South to make progress while simultaneously holding onto its hierarchical system.[20] One of the industries that decided to accept the offer was poultry processing. And by the 1960s one of the marginalized groups the industry depended on was poor black women.

My work is not without precedent. Historians have written about black workers in the related meat processing industry.[21] Through the lens of the United Packinghouse Workers of America (UPWA), Rick Halpern and Roger Horowitz trace the working lives of black and white meatpackers in the Midwest. Both groups faced poor working conditions and wages, but they were unable to organize together in the early twentieth century, separated by race and by the machinations of meatpacking employers. By the 1930s, however, black and white workers tried to bridge the gap, fashioning the UPWA into a powerful, vibrant union. The UPWA emerges as an exception to theories of union failure and decline based on the precept that workers cannot organize effectively around common class issues. The militancy of black workers in the UPWA prompted the union's strong pro–civil rights position and perpetuated its leftist stance.

Even the UPWA could not fully address the goals of black women workers. While the union may have had an exceptional record on race issues, it was not so progressive in matters of gender. Male unionists sabotaged women's efforts and tried to silence outspoken black women of the UPWA. This false separation of "race" and "gender" issues limited the advancement of black women meatpackers in the industry.[22]

Within academia few scholars outside of science and animal studies departments have written extensively about the poultry processing industry in particular. By contrast, journalists have produced many exposés of the industry. In 1987 the television newsmagazine *60 Minutes* aired a segment pointing out that a lot of processed chicken was infected with salmonella. Twelve years later *60 Minutes* revisited the industry, documenting the plight of chicken catchers.[23] In 1989 *Southern Exposure,* the magazine of the Institute of Southern Studies, published a special issue, "Ruling the Roost: A Special Report on the Poultry Industry."[24] The issue detailed how minimally regulated poultry processors exploited chicken farmers, poultry processing workers, and consumers. Two years later, during a fire at an Imperial Foods "cook plant" in Hamlet, North Carolina, twenty-five people perished, primarily because the fire doors were locked.[25] The tragedy brought a moment of national attention to the working conditions and lack of regulation in the industry, but, according to David Harvey, it was a woefully brief and insufficient moment because Americans were unwilling to explore deeply why such a catastrophe could happen and who shared the blame for the "murderously negligent event."[26]

Journalist Eric Schlosser's hugely popular *Fast Food Nation* also provided an insight into the industry. In examining the popularity of Chicken McNuggets, Schlosser details how the drive for more chicken has hurt poultry growers, turning them into "little more than serfs."[27] More recently, Human Rights Watch published a report that alleged that very little has changed since *Southern Exposure*'s special issue.[28] In the same vein, in February 2008 journalists at the *Charlotte Observer* produced a series of articles and images, ominously entitled "The Cruelest Cuts," that described the dangerous and demanding work done every day by poultry processing workers in North Carolina. The series editors vowed to reveal "the human cost of bring poultry to your table."[29]

Anthropologists have penned more scholarly works about the industry. David Griffith has written at length about poultry processing, most significantly in *Jones's Minimal*.[30] Griffith analyzes poultry processing as an example of an industry that thrives upon low-wage labor, delving into how companies recruit Latino labor—using the kin networks of the most disadvantaged workers and establishing plants in areas where labor costs have historically been low—and how workers supplement the inadequate income. I argue that though this model is true for Latino workers, poultry processors first used it successfully to recruit black workers in South Arkansas/North Louisiana, an area that lacked industries requiring unskilled labor.

Angela Stuesse's anthropological dissertation focuses on an area of Mississippi in which the economy is dominated by the poultry processing industry. She studies the effects of transnational migration on the area and on the racial and social hierarchies long in place. As an activist-scholar, Stuesse examines the reasons for the difficulties faced in organizing poultry processing workers by unions and other associations.[31] Sociologist Helen Marrow also looks at the experiences of Latino immigrants once they have made it to the "new destination" areas of the South. Her book *New Destination Dreaming* unfolds in a poultry producing section of North Carolina. Among other issues Marrow studies how working in the poultry processing industry shapes immigrants' opportunity for economic stability and mobility and how encounters and relationships between ethnic/racial groups are influenced by competition (or lack of competition) over the low-wage, low-skilled rural jobs typified by poultry processing.[32]

Steve Striffler, also an anthropologist, argues in *Chicken: The Dangerous Transformation of America's Favorite Food* that chicken, favored by Americans because they perceived it to be inexpensive and healthier than red meat, is not necessarily cheap or healthy.[33] The genetically engineered chicken, the farmers robbed of autonomy by the contract growing system, the workforce that labors in grueling conditions, all pay heavily for our demands. The popular value-added products are typically high in sugar and fat. Lack of effective oversight means that the innocuous-looking chicken in the grocer's refrigerated case may be from diseased chickens or unsanitary plants. In one chapter Striffler paints a vivid "ethnographic portrait" of work inside a processing plant. My work builds on this approach. Using the stories of poultry processing workers, I construct a picture of their working lives but also of how their work affects their lives away from the plant.

Historians are less represented in studies of the industry. In his study of the Amalgamated Meatcutters and Butcher Workmen of North America (AMBW), David Brody describes how the union became interested in the industry—the AMBW sought to expand just as poultry processing was taking hold.[34] By the 1940s the AMBW recognized how important organizing the industry would be in the struggle to unionize meat processing workers. Brody's study ended in the early 1960s; my work begins where his left off, continuing the story of the AMBW's struggle to organize poultry processing workers.

A more recent work, Leon Fink's *Maya of Morganton,* is a community study in an international context. Fink chronicles the stories of the Guatemalan Mayas who organized to protest work conditions at a Case Farms poultry processing plant in Morganton, North Carolina. Globalization has created a "nuevo" South, one in which rapid Latino immigration, sparked partly by poultry processors' use of transnational kin networks, has changed the cultural landscape. In studying the "sending community" in Guatemala, Fink finds continuity too. One example, the Mayans' valuing of cooperation and reciprocity cultivated in various community associations, was undoubtedly a factor in the Mayans' ability to come together in the Laborers' International Union of North America (LIUNA). Cooperation and reciprocity sustained the Maya of Morganton in the face of employer obduracy and native residents' hostility.

In contrast to Fink's focus on processing plant workers, Monica Gisolfi's work on the industry focuses on poultry farmers in Upcountry Georgia. She traces the rise of the poultry industry and the hopes it instilled in poverty-stricken cotton farmers.[35] In an effort to escape desperate impoverishment, these farmers abandoned their small cotton farms to grow chickens for rapidly expanding poultry firms. But the outcome was not all they hoped for. Gisolfi notes that "Georgians came to depend on chicken in the way their ancestors had depended upon cotton, a dependence that begot poverty and indebtedness."[36]

Brent Riffel's 2008 dissertation, "The Feathered Kingdom," looks at the phenomenal growth of industry giant Tyson Foods and its relationship with people who work for the company in and outside of the plants.[37] Like Gisolfi, he examines the significance of poultry processing to post–World War II agribusiness development and the plight of once-independent poultry farmers. Riffel also discusses company efforts to block and disrupt unionization and the role of the industry in transforming the labor force in the South: jobs once worked by rural native southerners are increasingly the domain of Latino immigrants.

In terms of processing plant work, the works of Griffith, Marrow, Striffler, Fink, and Riffel all primarily examine the experiences of Latino immigrants.[38] While the role of Latino workers in the poultry industry is clearly significant, that focus is not as relevant to the area of South Arkansas / North Louisiana I study because Latinos did not arrive to the industry in noticeable numbers until the first decade of the twenty-first century, and the major plant at El Dorado ceased most operations in 2009. Thus, I focus on black women both because I believe their story deserves greater attention and because the labor force along the central portion of the South Arkansas / North Louisiana border have remained primarily black.

A number of articles center on black poultry processing workers. In 1983 Ken Lawrence and Anne Braden provided a look at the struggles of two groups of black workers.[39] "The Long Struggle" tells first of the Mississippi Poultry Workers' Union (MPWU), which formed after sixty workers walked off the line at a Forest, Mississippi, plant in 1972. The MPWU refused to join the AFL-CIO because its members feared that they would lose control of their local. Instead, they reached out to create a broader-based coalition of labor groups and civil rights organizations. The MPWU was successful, winning the strike and recognition from the National Labor

Relations Board (NLRB). Seven years later, in Laurel, Mississippi, two hundred Sanderson Farms poultry plant workers struck. They copied the MPWU's model and built a coalition only to find themselves sabotaged by their union. Lawrence and Braden's work is an early critique of the shortcomings of union organizing that is divorced from other social justice issues.

Lawrence and Braden mention that the Sanderson Farms strikers were mostly black women, but Linda Cromer's "Plucking Cargill: The RWDSU in Georgia" focuses on "the 22" black women who walked out of the Buena Vista plant where they worked.[40] Their protest led to Cargill's becoming, in 1987, the first unionized plant in the county. Cromer notes that Cargill signed the contract with the Retail, Wholesale and Department Store **Union** but refused to comply with its terms. The fight to stay union was an industry-wide problem.

Building on the efforts of Lawrence, Braden, and Cromer, my work is an attempt to situate the story of black women in the history of the poultry processing industry. Examining the story of black women helps us understand that the labor force in poultry plants and other rural southern industries is not simply a matter of which workers are available. Instead, these workforces are constructed, built to satisfy the needs of an industry that relies heavily on a large supply of cheap, unskilled workers in dire need of jobs. It is difficult to understand the current dynamics in processing plants, their primary location in the U.S. South and Southeast, the nature and speed of line work, the relationship between management and line workers, and the ongoing racial and ethnic segmentation in plants with multiracial workforces, for example, without knowing the history of how the industry developed and changed and the way work was constructed in raced and gendered ways within plants almost from the beginning. Thus, telling this story necessitated that I address two other questions that extend the story further into the past. The first is how and why did the poultry processing industry come to thrive in an area in which black women were both available to become the predominant workforce and symbolic of what processors most wanted in their laborers? To answer that question, chapter 1 briefly describes the story of the rise of the industry in Arkansas and then narrows its focus to discuss how it grew, nurtured by town boosters and local residents, in El Dorado, Arkansas. El Dorado was transformed from Arkansas's first oil boomtown into a poultry processing headquarters. The decline in plant agriculture, drying up of the oil wells, and incentives offered by the government, combined with an aggressive industrial recruitment program, opened El Dorado to poultry processing.

Tracing the development of the poultry industry allows insight into the processes by which southerners remade their economies via an aggressive post–World War II campaign to industrialize the South. Studying the industry over time reveals significant changes in agriculture, including the rise of agribusiness and new models of food production. From poultry processors we learn that demand does not always drive an increased supply: by making chicken cheaper and offering an ever-expanding variety of products, the poultry industry helped change consumption patterns and consumer demand. And just as it forever changed chicken, the industry has also continually changed the rural, southern countryside in economic, physical, and social terms.

A closer examination of the early years of southern industrialization also reveals how the racial, class, and gender hierarchies honed in the "old" plantation South set a precedent for the "new" industrialized South. The status of poultry farmers, largely poor white men who had little besides their land and their labor and typically had to rely on credit to get into the industry, and of overwhelmingly poor and black processing plant workers, who were often in desperate need of work, gave processing plant owners a clear advantage and meant that the industry developed in a manner predicated on a structured inequality. The determination to uphold old hierarchies would determine how black women, desirable as workers because of their social and economic vulnerability, would be treated in the industry for years to come.

The second question that I endeavor to answer here, to contextualize the lives and labors of the women whom I study, is how did black women in the South Arkansas / North Louisiana region come to work in the poultry industry? That processors may have eventually considered black women suitable workers does not automatically translate into their entry into the plants. To answer this question, in chapter 2 I examine life in Bernice, Louisiana, and explore why many of the town's black women crossed the state border to work in poultry processing in El Dorado. Agricultural jobs in the postwar period declined just as politicians placed Louisiana at the forefront of rising anti-welfare sentiment, aimed particularly at black women, whose mothering had long been regarded with suspicion and disdain. Additionally, Bernice was a sawmill town. Much of the work available there, and in the towns and cities surrounding Bernice, was categorized as men's work, leaving job-seeking women with few alternatives. As they made their way into the labor-intensive work required in the plants, black women developed strategies to balance work and family lives.

This chapter also investigates an interesting conundrum: poultry processing work was in a sense one of few paid-work alternatives for black women, who were begrudged public assistance, who sought to leave domestic work, and who were pushed out of traditional agricultural work. Thus, for many women a dearth of opportunity drove them into this unpleasant work. Yet it was desired by some black women as a step up from the domestic and agricultural labor they had done for generations. Poultry processing work represented both the dirty, toilsome industrial labor reserved for African Americans *and* a move toward the goal of greater access to employment opportunity for which so many had campaigned in the middle of the twentieth century.

The story of the poultry processing industry in South Arkansas illustrates southern black women's entry into industrial labor and the benefits and costs of that move to these women's lives. It also supplements literature on the global pattern of women's, and particularly colored women's, integral role in the food system and those women's economic and social vulnerability.[41] Southern progress rested on the regressive treatment of marginalized workers. This treatment is considered in detail here in chapters 3 and 4. Chapter 3 analyzes the emotional and psychological conditions under which poultry processing workers labor. Poultry processing workers report laboring in psychologically harrowing environments and being subjected to racist and sexist harassment. Their attempts to humanize their work environment and themselves, via individual and collective strategies, are often denied by management. I look at these strategies, including the promise and failure of unionization and the ways in which black workers express solidarity outside of unions. The chapter also explores other organizations' and associations' attempts to promote collective action among poultry processing workers.

Chapter 4 examines the environment of poultry processing plants and the physical demands made upon employees. There is an often unspoken demand that line workers perform as if they are machines, impervious to the rate of work, the insulting words and actions of people around them, and the painful toll on their bodies. The rapid line speeds and temperature extremes are linked to a number of ailments, from physical exhaustion to musculoskeletal disorders. Chapter 4 also documents the gendered division of labor in poultry processing plants and the manifestations of sexism in the industry. Given the nature of work in the plants, I also try to discern why workers stay and what techniques they develop to make the work bearable. The decline of labor unions prompts poultry processing workers to employ other forms of organization and resistance. No matter how poor the treatment or how automated the industry has become, black women have resisted becoming cogs in the poultry processing machine.

This book makes a straightforward contribution to the historical record—the literature is by no means oversaturated with descriptions of poultry processing in South (versus Northwest) Arkansas or by the stories of working-class black women in rural North Louisiana. But this book intervenes in another way as well. Black women are commonly constructed negatively, painted, among other things, as lazy and irresponsible, disconnected or otherwise bad mothers, and decidedly vulgar and aggressive, thus outside the bounds of femininity (and the delicacy that the feminine is sometimes accorded). Poultry processors have both benefited from and extended that narrative; they demand that black women work difficult jobs for long hours with little regard for their health and as if "paid laborer" constitutes the entirety of these women's identities. Yet despite the fact that black women did, and still do, this strenuous work, as more Latino laborers joined the workforce (a phenomenon discussed in chapter 5), processing plant management recycled familiar tropes to explain the shift.[42] They dismissed black workers as habitually tardy or absent, unwilling to work hard, and insubordinate. Telling the story the way that I do allows black women, at least momentarily, to disrupt this unflattering narrative and take control of their stories. Through their words we see a more accurate glimpse of the whole of who they are, their roles in their communities and families, what they prioritize, and their often conflicted feelings about their paid work.

This work is also motivated by the sort of spirit evidenced in the *Charlotte Observer*'s "Cruelest Cuts" series, whose subtitle is "The Human Cost of Bringing Poultry to Your Table." The benefits of the poultry industry have been much more readily visible to the public eye than the costs.[43] Over and over, as a longtime resident of South Arkansas / North Louisiana, I heard about how the poultry industry "saved" our small towns and the people in them. Indeed, saving us is the "noble mission" of poultry companies, according to Bo Pilgrim, the founder of the poultry industry giant Pilgrim's Pride. Governor Bobby Jindal and the state government of

Louisiana demonstrated that belief in rural salvation–through–industry in 2009, after Pilgrim's Pride shuttered the Farmerville complex. Louisiana's political leaders offered Foster Farms around fifty million dollars in taxpayers' money to buy, upgrade, and operate the poultry processing plant.[44] Once Foster Farms accepted, Jindal proclaimed it "a major victory for the people of Northeast Louisiana and our entire state."[45] When Jindal and Foster Farms CEO Ron Foster came to Farmerville for the ceremonial reopening of the plant, they were greeted, according to a local journalist in an article entitled "Resurrected," with a hero's welcome.[46] Indeed, so "noble" was Foster Farms that the company was awarded the "2010 Corporate Investment and Community Impact CiCi Award by *Trade & Industry Development Magazine* on behalf of its contributions to Farmerville, Louisiana."[47] Virtually elided from the discussion of the company's beneficent acts was the fact that Foster Farms had received generous incentives from the people of Louisiana, not to mention the costs to the more than eleven hundred people who were simultaneously grateful for the work but aware of the toll it took on them.

Just as the inhabitants of Louisiana were grateful for the work and the benefits resulting from employment, so it was for me. Even though the benefits to the community had been more visible to me than the costs, I was cognizant of the toll on a personal level. Money made from poultry processing helped keep me clothed, sheltered, and fed; allowed me the room to explore my interests via financial support from my mama; and kept me afloat when I went away to Louisiana's premiere boarding school. Most significantly, my undergraduate education was financed by a four-year, full scholarship sponsored by Con Agra. Only when I was older could I see the costs, the disheartening comparisons. I had to reflect on all the nice clothes I was careful to keep separate from my mother's, which bore the indescribable smell of freshly slaughtered meat; my carefully manicured fingers that sometimes had to rub my mother's aching and swollen ones; the fact that, in terms of paid work, I have largely been able to do what I *love* to do because Mama did what she *had* to do. I wanted to learn more about the costs to her and women like her, how they felt about their work, their lives, their sacrifices. I wanted to make those costs visible in the same ways that the benefits and our ongoing, obedient gratitude to the poultry industry were.

My desires were bolstered when I approached veteran poultry processing worker Janet Strong about this project. "Somebody should write about this," she told me, "should help us. Should tell somebody what they do to us." But before this "somebody" could write about it, I had to collect and listen to the stories of women who had been connected to the industry. As numerous scholars have noted, such testimonies, "whether directly to the reader or through the offices of a collaborating writer," have been crucial in bringing the stories of marginalized groups into the center.[48] Although she speaks of a different type of exploitation, Danielle McGuire argues that "African America women reclaimed their bodies and their humanity by testifying. . . . [They] loudly resisted what Martin Luther King, Jr., called the 'thingification' of their humanity."[49] Over and over the women with whom I spoke did just that—they insisted that they were human, valuable, and worthy of decent treatment. In response to Janet Strong's assertion that someone "should tell somebody what they do to us," my answer became that there was no better somebody than the women themselves.

CHAPTER 1

"ARKANSAS'S FIRST BOOMTOWN"

THE EMERGENCE OF THE "GREATLY BENEFICIAL"
POULTRY PROCESSING INDUSTRY

On October 23, 1954, the Alexandria, Louisiana, *Town Talk* announced that, "Louisiana Poultry Co.'s plant . . . has been leased to two Chicago businessmen—J. H. [Herb] Johnson and J. C. [Jess] Merkle." The plant had recently been abandoned by Cudahy Packing, the second time it had closed in its two-year history. According to *Town Talk,* Jess Merkle and Herb Johnson were untroubled by the operation's less-than-stellar past. They had "confidence in the development of commercial processing in Louisiana and the successful operation of the plant."[1] As employees of Swift & Company, one of the "Big Four" in American meat processing in the first half of the twentieth century, Merkle and Johnson trusted in their own expertise. They were also willing, according to Merkle, to take the significant risk of leaving Swift to "see if we couldn't go into business for ourselves."[2]

Their confidence was well placed. The plant in Alexandria thrived, and Merkle and Johnson began to think about expanding. In 1955 the Greater El Dorado Committee (GEC), from nearby South Arkansas, visited the Louisiana plant and returned home impressed with Merkle and Johnson's work. The GEC was El Dorado's official "booster" and the visit part of a "planned program to obtain new industries" for the south-central Arkansas city.[3] The committee offered to build a poultry plant in El Dorado, 150 miles from Alexandria, if Merkle would agree to operate it. The GEC made an offer "that we just couldn't turn down," recalled Merkle.[4] The two businessmen accepted, and on July 19, 1956, J-M Poultry Packing Company opened in El Dorado. Fewer than one hundred employees processed about two thousand birds per day.[5] By 2008 more than sixteen hundred employees were processing well over one million chickens per week.

Over the next fifty years El Dorado's stake in poultry processing expanded from a modest, individually owned plant to the poultry processing headquarters for the transnational giant ConAgra. In 2003 ConAgra sold the old J-M Poultry to Pilgrim's Pride, then the second largest poultry producing company in the United States and the largest employer in all of Union County, Arkansas. In this relatively small southern city, growing and processing poultry became a multimillion dollar industry.[6]

In tracing the expansion of El Dorado, Arkansas, from oil boomtown to poultry processing center, this chapter examines the ability of citizens and boosters to redefine a town economically and socially.[7] First, I situate that shift more broadly via a brief history of the early growth of the poultry industry throughout Arkansas. The explosive growth of chicken processing in El Dorado in the last half of the twentieth century was a result of numerous factors. The story of the development of El Dorado's poultry processing industry fits into the larger southern story of post–World War II industrialization of agriculture in which significant transformations in traditional agriculture, changes in consumer demand, the lucrative process of vertical integration, and dedicated support from agricultural agencies, local boosters, and various levels of government encouraged phenomenal growth. Also important are the unrealized hopes of agriculturists, farmers, and plant workers that poultry processing would lessen the economic vulnerability of dispossessed farmers and displaced workers. There is, in other words, a less benign reason for the industry's development: southern boosters attracted business to the South by promising a low-paid, low-skilled workforce. In the middle of the twentieth century former agricultural workers sought new crops and new jobs. The vulnerable status of these "women, minorities, and other marginal groups in rural areas" would prove a great benefit to the industry.[8]

BUILDING AN INDUSTRY FROM (CHICKEN) SCRATCH

In the early 1900s there were few indications that poultry processing would become the South's largest agribusiness or that El Dorado would be essential in that development. Arkansas's commercial broiler industry began quietly, with efforts in the extreme northwestern corner of the state. Brent Riffel recounts the story of M. L. Price, an employee of Aaron Poultry and Egg Company, who came to Fayetteville in 1914 "in search of farmers who would raise poultry as contract growers." Price, described by a contemporary historian as "one of the alert, energetic and farsighted business men of the city," would help establish Ozark Poultry and Egg Company, branching out to the towns of Rogers and Fort Smith as well.[9] Ultimately, the difficulties of continuing to expand the industry there and persuading farmers to grow chickens led Price to sell his interest. But his Arkansas-based partners, Jay Fullbright and Richard Clark, pressed forward.[10] Nevertheless, the poultry business managed to be "little more than a 'break even proposition.'"[11]

Two years after Price's initial effort, the Glover family of Benton County made an unexpected foray into the industry. J. J. Glover had watched his daughter's 4-H project with interest. "Young Miss Glover" had kept and tended eggs in a commercial brooder house until they hatched, then raised the chicks until it was time to take them to market. She received fifty cents per pound for her flock of twenty broilers. Glover, an apple farmer whose orchard had almost been destroyed by disease, decided to try the project on a larger scale. Eventually, he marketed and sold his "Arkansas Broilers" for a little over one dollar each. Encouraged by Glover's fortune, a few farmers ventured into poultry growing but with little success. Disease, poor nutrition, and inappropriate housing shortened chickens' life spans and lessened the quality of their meat.[12] The "few birds farmers managed to produce," argues Riffel, "were virtually worthless."[13]

In response to these difficulties, the Arkansas Agricultural Experiment Station (known as the Station), based at the University of Arkansas, Fayetteville, began working in earnest on the problems of poultry husbandry in the 1910s.[14] Charged with the task of improving and expanding agriculture in Arkansas, the Station began breeding and housing programs with the goal of opening poultry farming to Arkansas farmers. Just as important as making poultry farming possible was the Station's effort to make it profitable. In his study of the industry's growth in the state, Stephen Strausberg contends that Arkansas farmers viewed poultry growing as unattractive because in addition to the birds' high rate of mortality, "the farmers had no knowledge of market information."[15] This lack of knowledge was problematic when "farmers failed to understand the demand for chickens and eggs and their value."[16] Scientists and agriculturists at the Station believed poultry farming promised to be a lucrative endeavor, with the potential to elevate some Arkansas farmers above the desperate poverty in which they lived. Thus, Station employees worked throughout the 1920s to help a growing number of Arkansas farmers reap the maximum benefit from fledgling poultry efforts.[17]

Nevertheless, only a few farmers in Arkansas, or any other part of the country, could see the potential in raising chickens in these early years. Before 1950 "farmers viewed poultry raising as a way to put spilled grain, grass, and insects around the farm yard to productive use."[18] The devastating effects of pullorum, a widespread, infectious disease of young chicks, in particular, limited participation in poultry farming despite the promise of increased income. Arkansas, like most of the South, "lagged behind the rest of the nation in poultry husbandry."[19] Chickens roamed freely in farmyards all over the state, with few attempts made to strengthen flocks through selective breeding or to enter poultry farming seriously. Farm households were likely to profit more from eggs than the chickens that produced them. The production of chicken meat remained largely an outgrowth of egg production. Well into the century, quality chicken remained a delicacy of sorts, a symbol of prosperity, as evidenced by Herbert Hoover's promise of "a chicken in every pot."[20]

Chickens' susceptibility to disease was only one reason poultry farming remained small scale. Many male farmers initially shied away from poultry growing, according to LuAnn Jones, because it was considered "woman's work." In the Arkansas Ozarks, for example, "farm women usually cared for chickens and turkeys."[21] Melissa Walker quotes a journalist who opined that "women are more adapted to the care of poultry than is the average man," a belief rooted in what Walker describes as "stereotypical notions about women's attention to detail and their careful nurturing of living creatures."[22] Women were indeed the primary caretakers of chickens on their family farms. Carolyn Sachs notes that before the rise of the agribusiness poultry industry in the United States, and presently in other areas of the world, women took on the work of raising chickens because they could "easily raise a small number of chickens on minimal land without capital investment, credit, or the assistance of men, and usually they control the income from their chicken enterprises."[23] Thus, many farm men regarded chickens as little more than a source of "grocery money to the farm housewife."[24]

That money, however, could be crucial to a family's well-being. As Ila J. Blue of North Carolina remembered, "We survived because . . . we did things besides just the farm."[25] One of those "things" was her mother's practice of selling eggs and other farm products to a local sanatorium. Another North Carolinian explained that her family kept chickens not for pets but "for our livelihood."[26] A Georgian woman dismissed the difficulties of chicken growing by noting that "the joy and happiness of being the means of saving our home . . . and my family having a decent living pays for all the discouragement."[27] Psyche Williams-Forson describes how black women used chickens and the skills of preparing and cooking them to earn money to take care of their families. These women "purchased their home[s] 'with chicken legs.'"[28] Walker sums up the importance of poultry and poultry products to some farm families: "For women whose families were toiling on marginal farms, poultry production often made the difference between paying property taxes or losing the farm; between keeping children in school or not; between calling a doctor in case of illness or not; indeed, between survival or starvation."[29] Arkansas women undoubtedly realized the benefits of poultry income as they attended a U.S. Department of Agriculture (USDA)–sponsored demonstration that taught them "to cut waste and spoilage in eggs and poultry sent to market."[30] Poultry raising and tending could provide a woman with far more than a little pocket money.

Despite the fact that white men are credited with "pioneering" the industry, Jones argues that it was women who paved the way for later development.[31] Studying farm women in North Carolina, Jones finds that women researched and improved breeding within their own flocks, conducted much of the early-twentieth-century marketing of eggs and chicken meat, and encouraged their husbands to build chicken houses and invest in new flocks. Similarly, Walker notes that white farm women, in particular, enjoyed access to "proper feeds" and the "latest scientific production advice disseminated by farm magazine editors and by extension agents" to increase their poultry profits.[32] It is no wonder, then, that women, though rarely mentioned, were significant in the early commercial broiler industry. One particularly industrious Baltimore, Maryland, woman, who raised and sold her prize flock of five hundred, is credited with beginning the poultry industry on Delmarva, a peninsula comprising Delaware and eleven counties along the Eastern Shore.[33] Similarly, Mrs. Hoyt Chitwood of Magazine, Arkansas, built her hatchery into a thriving business despite financial hardship and the death of her husband.[34]

It was only as poultry concerns expanded and required more capital that men became integrally involved, in line with the desires of "poultry scientists and cooperative extension services [who] hoped to shift poultry production from women's small flock production to larger-scale, male-controlled enterprises."[35] Men could enter poultry farming because it was becoming sufficiently "masculinized." Rather than improvements being the product of women's experience and know-how, they now bore the mark of scientific study and experimentation. Instead of popular notions that held chicken and egg farming as a sideline activity and the source of "pin money," poultry farming was set to become the dominant activity and primary source of income on farms across the South. Farmers would have to seek out credit, access to which was denied to married women, who could not acquire credit in their own names. Women farmers, described in gendered terms as "tending" and "raising" and "nurturing" chickens, were increasingly replaced by male farmers, who "grew" them.[36] Nevertheless, as Monica Gisolfi argues, the appropriation by men of poultry farming as it became the primary source of a family's income meant "women ceased being the lords of their flocks, but they by no means ceased working with broilers."[37]

These stories, and others, of poultry farming success were enough to tempt more Arkansas farmers living in desperate conditions in the 1920s and 1930s to try poultry farming. Most of Arkansas's traditional crops and the people who grew them were in trouble. Their ability to marshal resources to continue their struggles was dramatically lessened by the fact that they had suffered through economic decline steadily in the aftermath of World War I. Their situation was further worsened by continued overpopulation of farmland, overreliance on cotton (despite the fact that the price of cotton had declined almost steadily after 1923), and a series of natural disasters.[38] Nan Woodruff notes that through the 1920s cotton farmers "had experienced . . . fluctuating . . . prices, under-production and over-production, indebtedness and foreclosures, an increase in tenantry, and the almost total collapse of the rural banking structure."[39]

The collapse of the banking system, combined with the other misfortunes, devastated Arkansans. "Such a combination of economic and climatic disasters had never before coincided," suggests Pete Daniel, and no person or governmental body was equipped to deal adequately with the disasters.[40] Farm families, in particular, faced complete destitution as state and charitable resources dwindled and President Herbert Hoover and local elites balked at offering direct federal relief.[41] The late 1920s and 1930s saw a marked decline in land ownership and the rise in sharecropping among poor farmers, who found themselves simply unable to pay their debts. These landless farmers were particularly vulnerable as "fewer of them than ever owned horses mules or implements."[42] Yet even given the struggles of cotton farmers, Arkansas fruit farmers, according to Carl Moneyhon, were "perhaps" the hardest hit. Apple farmers had been plagued by problems for some time, from the San Jose scale disease to infestation by codling moths, which had "nearly wiped out" the state's apple orchards.[43] Moneyhon also recounts the difficulties faced by rice and corn farmers. He summarizes the agricultural losses in Arkansas during that time: in 1920 the collective value of the state's farms was "over $753 million dollars. . . . By 1930 the collective value . . . had fallen to approximately $547 million, a loss of over 27%."[44]

As the economy plunged and prices dropped, Arkansas officials continued to try to persuade farmers to diversify. Desperate fruit and cotton farmers began to pay attention to the Station's and poultry promoters' suggestions to grow chickens.[45] A number of other events in the late 1920s increased the attractiveness of poultry growing to Arkansans. The first successful train shipment of broilers from Springdale, in Washington County, occurred in 1926. Around the same time, poultry scientists finally understood the importance of vitamin D in chickens' diet, making possible year-round poultry confinement and production. In 1927 the Arkansas Poultry Improvement Association was developed. It worked closely with the Station to train and send out poultry inspectors to assist and advise poultry farmers. That year also marked the first time that Arkansas farmers "shipped" their poultry to market via cars.[46] Chicken increasingly seemed a viable alternative to farmers who were searching for one.[47]

Modest poultry farming gains continued into the Depression years. The Depression actually stimulated the poultry industry by encouraging farmers to raise chickens both for supplemental income and for food. Because egg and chicken prices had already been low, poultry farmers did not lose as much, proportionally, as other farmers.[48] Outside Arkansas the 1930s also brought the establishment of the National Poultry Improvement Plan (NPIP). While responsible for a number of accomplishments in poultry farming, perhaps the NPIP's most significant contributions (in conjunction with university and pharmaceutical scientists) were the eventual eradication of pullorum and typhoid, the implementation of sanitation procedures, and spreading the practice of poultry inspection. Arkansas farmers in the 1930s watched as poultry farming and processing became a viable, profitable enterprise on the Delmarva Peninsula.[49] They also saw the burgeoning success of some their own. John Tyson of Springdale, who had established his business in 1931, began hauling chickens over long distances to large cities such as Chicago, Detroit, and Houston, where demand was high. Tyson made enough money to expand his fledgling business to include a hatchery and feed mill.[50] The success of other hatcheries and poultry farms in and near Springdale prompted one journalist to claim in 1937 that the area's "fruit industry has a recent rival in the poultry industry which . . . has reached vast proportions in this part of the country." The journalist suggested that "the rapid growth of the poultry industry here opens up many new avenues of profit for local men. The farmer with small acreage often does well to turn his attention to poultry farming and the man with proper location and interest in the young industry may find it a profitable one."[51] Encouraged and supported by scientists at the Station, white, male farmers in Arkansas explored the possibilities of raising poultry. They also benefited from government assistance; the Works Progress Administration, for example, allocated funds for the construction of Highway 71, allowing poultry farmers in northwestern Arkansas to reach markets in Kansas City, Missouri, more easily.[52]

Arkansas's traditional agricultural system was shaken hard during the Great Depression. Cotton's status as "king" had been challenged by enforced crop reduction and the decline of the plantation system of cotton farming, marked by the movement of farmers, particularly tenants, away from the land.[53] This movement off the land would intensify in the aftermath of the Depression, as mechanization spread and industrial work opened. Landowners came to depend more and more upon mechanical help. Machines such as tractors and the Rust cotton picker slowly made cotton farming a less labor-intensive endeavor. The lure of industrial work drew farmworkers out of rural areas and sometimes out of the South, further eroding the South's agricultural system, in which planters were used to exerting almost complete control over their "employees."[54]

Many Arkansas farmers who did stay on the land looked to other agricultural pursuits and continued to make small strides into the poultry industry. Poultry growing presented an increasingly attractive opportunity to white farm men, who were more likely than their black counterparts to be landowners, to have access to the credit and capital needed to sustain a poultry farm and remain on the land. In 1940 the Northwest Arkansas Broiler Show, a well-attended and publicized event, brought together many of the pioneers of Arkansas's poultry industry.[55] It was American participation in World War II, however, that would spark the phenomenal growth of northwestern Arkansas's poultry industry and entice cities in the southern counties to give poultry growing and processing a try.[56]

In 1943 the Office of Price Administration, concerned with the widespread shortages of the war years, decided to ration beef. The federal government encouraged the expansion of the chicken industry by providing subsidies. Poultry growers, universities, and various associations began the drive to make a "meatier" breed of chicken. In the space of months, poultry became a viable, cheap substitute for red meat. Annual per capita consumption of chicken was 30.5 pounds in 1943, up from about 17 pounds in 1938.[57] The more organized industry in Delmarva could not meet the growing demand for chicken because the whole of its production was under government contract for the U.S. Army. Southern poultry producers stepped into the gulf created by this sudden demand and the short supply.[58]

Arkansans joined other parts of the South in trying to meet the new demand for chicken. Arkansas farmers copied John Tyson and used their cars to deliver poultry products to surrounding areas. Poultry growing spread from its northwestern Arkansas roots throughout the state. Between 1940 and 1945 poultry meat production in Arkansas increased by 48 percent, and 17.5 million pounds of broilers were produced for commercial sale.[59] By the end of the war poultry farming in Arkansas was no longer a supplemental activity of farm women. Poultry had become "the second largest source of agricultural income in the state."[60] The business of poultry production was being taken over by a new class of "poultry men," white businessmen who were not necessarily farmers and who could see the potential of poultry beyond the barnyard.

Having made significant progress in improving nutrition and fighting disease, poultry growers concentrated in earnest on improving breeds.

Their efforts were facilitated by A&P supermarkets, which held a "Chicken of Tomorrow" contest to encourage breeders to produce a broad-breasted chicken for commercial sale.[61] Arkansas borrowed the idea and held its own annual state contest beginning in 1946, in advance of the first national competition of 1948. The University of Arkansas–Fayetteville was host to the second national contest in 1951.[62] While Arkansas farmers did not win either of the national competitions, the Chicken of Tomorrow contest was significant to Arkansas farmers for two major reasons. First, it taught the poultry men much about chicken breeds and successful breeding. After having a barbecue "featuring large helpings of Chicken of Tomorrow broilers," the American Association of Agricultural College Editors adopted a resolution acknowledging the "significant improvement" in taste and quality represented by the contest's chickens.[63] Seizing the opportunity to posit Arkansas as an important chicken growing region, UA-Fayetteville president Lewis Jones theorized that "the climate here permitted the birds to grow so much larger than those in former . . . contests."[64] Second, the extra funds raised through these contests were used to build new facilities for the Station and establish the Arkansas Poultry Federation (APF).[65]

Poultry production was big business in Arkansas. The Agricultural Extension Service reported that Arkansas farmers produced more than forty-nine million birds in 1950, making the state fourth in broiler production in the nation.[66] Poultry processing plants began to appear all over Arkansas, replacing the small, private slaughterhouses, a response to the millions of chickens being grown for sale. Within little more than a decade after the war, John Tyson had expanded the company that carried his name to include a poultry processing plant. That expansion moved Tyson further into the process of vertical integration, launching the company on its way to becoming a global giant.[67] Several other companies emerged, trying to make a profit in the still unstable poultry industry. Despite postwar expansion, most of them were still centered around Benton and Washington counties in northwestern Arkansas. Jess Merkle and Herb Johnson would help spread the burgeoning industry across the state.

FROM BOOMTOWN TO POULTRY CAPITAL

When Jess Merkle settled in El Dorado, the southern part of the state was just beginning to participate in the industry in a significant fashion.

While northwestern Arkansas farmers were making hesitant forays into poultry growing, the people of El Dorado were engaged in other economic pursuits. From the town's founding in 1843, El Dorado's residents, like most citizens of Union County, relied on subsistence agriculture and initially small-scale timber/lumber operations for income and survival. Although it was slowly exhausting the soils of Arkansas, cotton remained Union County's "great" commercial crop, "grown all over the place."[68] The arrival of railroads near the end of the nineteenth century, however, elevated timber to a veritable "cash crop" as companies could now move their product from its source to market with greater ease and in larger quantities. As a result, El Dorado's population and economy underwent a modest boom in the first decades of the new century. Historian Ben Johnson maintains that "the construction of railroads in the 1890s led to the county's greatest economic transformation between the Civil War and the 1920s oil boom. . . . The railroads created the local timber industry."[69] Lumber companies established a number of sawmills and built worker camps close by. These camps would later become the cities and towns that dot southern Arkansas.[70]

Although the timber industry allowed the people of Union County to become "prosperous and comfortable," the most notable boost to El Dorado's economy was the oil boom that began when the Busey oil well blew in the city on January 10, 1921.[71] Entrepreneurs had been drilling for oil since 1914, and the citizens reacted to this first significant strike with jubilation. "The first emotions of the natives," notes Union County historian Juanita Green, "was that of amazed surprise . . . some of them fairly wallowing in the grimy, greasy mess." El Dorado residents called their little city "Arkansas's First Boomtown," a title still used by the city's chamber of commerce. Within weeks of the Busey's blowout, the population of four thousand swelled to over twenty thousand, as "oil operators, field men, drillers, roughnecks, geologists, lease hounds, hotel, café, soft drink, barber, shoe shine, and other types of proprietors" swarmed to the city.[72] Successive strikes brought more new residents to the overcrowded town.

El Dorado was initially ill equipped to deal with the population explosion. Union County historian Anna Cordell describes one area as "a bawdy spot . . . where murders went unsolved and bootleg liquor went unstoppered."[73] Historians of the city describe the hastily erected tent cities and shacks along the notorious Hamburger Row, where new arrivals went for everything from burgers to brothels.[74] The timber and railroad town was suddenly an oil town. Never, according to A. R. and R. B. Buckalew, "would the town or its people . . . be the same again."[75]

Once it worked out the worst of the bugs, El Dorado fashioned itself appropriately for a newly wealthy town. Oil money made El Dorado one of the richest places in Arkansas and fostered its growth into a "city of the first class."[76] Millions of dollars were invested to develop Arkansas oil fields, and the influx of money soon showed. El Dorado was suddenly home to Lion Oil, Murphy Oil, and related industries. People wearing "diamonds and costly furs rubbed elbows with [those] in oil soaked khaki." John Ragsdale, a petroleum engineer who grew up in the area, remembers the vast improvements in the city's infrastructure in his autobiographical history *As We Were in South Arkansas*.[77] Shacks soon gave way to a "building spree" that included the construction of ornate, well-preserved public buildings such as a new courthouse, elegant churches, and an eight-story "skyscraper" that housed one of the new companies—Lion Oil.[78] The buildings stood as "a testament to the cosmopolitan atmosphere found in El Dorado during the oil boom era."[79] As J. Scott Parker describes: "In the span of just four years, El Dorado went from a town where chaos reigned and only four roads were paved to a cosmopolitan city filled with sprawling homes, a thriving business community, modern conveniences . . . and an active social calendar."[80]

The "boom" times would not last, however. Production decreased significantly, partially a result of over-drilling and exploitation of oil reserves and other resources. And as the Great Depression took its toll on the economy, the drop in prices and credit difficulties took their toll on the industry.[81] Of the 1930s Cordell surmises, "It almost seemed as if [El Dorado's] prophetic good fortune had deserted it."[82] The oil money would remain important to the city's economy, boosted by a 1937 strike at Shuler Field. But El Dorado's citizens recognized the need for other industrial pursuits.

The people of El Dorado looked at their local economy, determined the need for diversification, and developed plans to recruit industry to their area. James Cobb has written famously about the "selling of the South," the practice whereby southern cities and states offered a "prodigious array of incentives and gimmicks" such as tax exemptions, industrial bonds, capital for building and operations, and other forms of subsidization to attract businesses to the South.[83] The boosters who sought to "sell" El Dorado and Arkansas would be crucial to the growth of the poultry processing industry in the state.

In the immediate postwar period much of Arkansas was caught up in the industrial recruitment drive that had its roots in the 1943 founding of the Arkansas Economic Council by prominent state business leaders. The council sought to encourage postwar economic growth and stymie the significant outward migration of Arkansans by enticing established businesses to open industrial plants in Arkansas. Over the next couple of years council members persuaded the state assembly to create the Arkansas Resources and Development Commission, charged with showing interested manufacturers the wealth of "Arkansas opportunities."[84] In 1949 the state elected Governor Sid McMath, who was determined to show companies Arkansas's "natural advantages of the climate, availability of natural resources, and the potential skill and productivity of our workers."[85]

The boosterism of politicians and business leaders indeed seemed beneficial. Ben Johnson points out that "the Arkansas manufacturing boom did take off after the founding of the Arkansas Economic Council and accelerated during the 1950s. Between 1946 and 1959 the state's manufacturing employment rose by 44 percent in comparison to the 11 percent rise throughout the nation."[86] In 1955 booster efforts culminated in the state assembly's passage of Act 404, the Arkansas Industrial Development Act. The language of section 40 of the act recognized the urgent need for increased employment opportunities "to stop the further loss of population."[87] Toward this end the act provided for the creation of the Arkansas Industrial Development Commission (AIDC). The state assembly charged the AIDC "with the dual role of securing more industrial and agricultural jobs."[88] A relatively new Arkansan, Winthrop Rockefeller, initially chaired the AIDC.[89] Although Arkansas officials had been working for quite some time to recruit industry and improve agriculture—efforts symbolized, for example, by the 1945 establishment of the Arkansas Resources and Development Commission—Rockefeller and his staff were notably successful.[90] Under Act 404, cities could form their own industrial development corporations (IDCs), and many of them did, encouraged by the growth of industrial interests throughout the state.

Concerned about the city's dependence on the oil industry, the El Dorado Chamber of Commerce had created the GEC in accordance with Act 404 in 1955 to "diversify in order to have a more balanced economy."[91] The El Dorado boosters were an active, determined group. Businessman Thomas Reynolds, who would soon serve as chairman of the GEC's Executive Committee, wrote Governor Orval Faubus about El Dorado's "organized effort to obtain new industry" and urged the governor to choose some of El Dorado's most dedicated boosters to represent the state in its quest to recruit industry.[92] Merkle credited the "forefathers" for their foresight: "they could see this economy of El Dorado had to change."[93] El Dorado boosters sought to raise money from local businesses and residents to "finance qualified industry." With those funds the El Dorado IDC purchased land to create an industrial area southeast of town.[94]

The first project undertaken by the GEC was the establishment of the poultry processing plant. The GEC believed the plant symbolized "a real step in industrial diversification."[95] Chicken was a promising cash crop, according to Merkle, able to be grown on land that was "all timber land or oil land."[96] El Dorado business recruiters had to lure Merkle away from the competing city of Ruston, Louisiana.[97] They agreed to construct a building comparable to the Alexandria plant and equip it according to Merkle's specifications, an endeavor that would cost a bit over $200,000.[98] The GEC raised $120,000 in "donations from the public" with "the balance being supplied by loans from . . . local banks."[99] In return, J-M Poultry would pay a nominal rent and have the opportunity to buy the plant at a later date.[100] Merkle accepted the deal, and, though the GEC hoped to have the plant ready by May 1, the plant opened in July 1956.

Initially quite small, the plant began growing soon after opening. Within two years the University of Arkansas's Industrial Research and Extension Center described it as an "efficient, large-scale operation."[101] The number of employees had more than doubled.[102] El Dorado was part of the fastest-growing broiler producing area in Arkansas.[103] As one newspaper columnist observed, "This oil capital is . . . fast becoming a South Arkansas poultry center . . . [it] is an industry that means much at the present and can be made to mean much more."[104] An advertisement in one of the local newspapers estimated that the plant would add around "$3 million annually to the economy of El Dorado and South Arkansas."[105]

Related businesses soon appeared. In 1957 the El Dorado Poultry By-Products Company was established to recycle the plant's poultry waste into feather meal and poultry feed supplements. The Corn Belt Hatchery built a facility "capable of hatching approximately 80,000 chicks a week." In nearby Junction City "a new veneer plant for making boxes for shipping poultry" was installed.[106]

The city's leaders worked to make the plant an important part of the community and to encourage residents to feel invested in it and understand the way it functioned in a basic sense. Shortly after it opened, the plant held an open house, featuring talks to emphasize the potential importance of the industry to the El Dorado area and guided tours of the plant's interior. A local newspaper ran images illustrating the whole process, the lines staffed overwhelmingly by diligent white women overseen by smiling white men. Their white clothing and the lines and belts themselves were markedly clean, devoid of the blood and gore spatter common in processing plants.[107]

Of symbolic significance residents proclaimed a new agricultural "king"—chicken—and, beginning in 1958, celebrated an annual "King Chicken Day."[108] Community reaction to El Dorado's first poultry festival also provided evidence of the desire to support the plant and the industry. From the time the GEC wooed Jess Merkle to El Dorado, the city's business and civic leaders recognized the potential of the fledgling industry. In 1962 a writer at the *El Dorado Daily News* noted that the APF decided to host its annual poultry festival in El Dorado because of "the rapid progress of the poultry industry in Union County." Subsequent editions of the paper encouraged residents to show their appreciation and gratitude for the industry by getting "the festival spirit early." Eager to support the new industry and "assure other such festivals," businesses bought tickets to the events in bulk and continued to do so in later years. Anna Cordell expressed residents' appreciation of the efforts of the GEC and the success of the plant: "The Greater El Dorado Committee . . . has accounted for considerable industrial diversification including a large chicken processing plant. . . . The poultry industry has grown to be an important part of the economy in the area . . . and has done much to develop allied businesses."[109]

The state government echoed the city's encouragement of the industry. Governor Orval Faubus exempted feed, seed, and fertilizer from a much-hated 2 percent tax. In 1959 the Arkansas legislature determined that poultry companies were eligible to receive financial assistance from the state.[110] Despite continued volatility within the industry, the people of El Dorado, and Arkansas generally, were determined to see the industry succeed. The "tremendous promotional effort on the part of leading citizens and major organizations" in the state was crucial in stopping out-migration and increasing opportunities in manufacturing employment.[111]

"IDEAL GEOGRAPHIC LOCATION, SUFFICIENT PRODUCTION LABORERS"

Boosterism was not the only factor that led to the growth of El Dorado as a "poultry center" and the phenomenal expansion of the poultry industry overall.[112] There were other, seemingly innocuous reasons. The simplest was consumer demand.[113] Although Americans returned to beef as the primary meat choice in the aftermath of World War II, consumption of all types of chickens continued to climb. The growth in per capita broiler consumption—the three- to five-pound, young chicken preferred by processors—was especially striking, rising from about 2.0 pounds in 1940 to 29.9 pounds in 1965.[114] Consumer demand continued to soar as the real price of chicken fell. A long-term decline in the price of chicken reduced its cost from "one-half that of beef to about one-sixth." The development of processing plants, whose lines and belts facilitated faster processing, also made possible a drop in the cost of poultry products.[115] The Arkansas poultry industry worked hard to help meet this growing demand. By 1965 the state was second only to Georgia in broiler production and, according to the Resources and Development Commission, was "challenging Georgia for the top position."[116]

Perhaps the greatest boon to poultry production was the advent of vertical integration, a process that began in Arkansas in the early 1950s and was firmly in place by the 1970s. The transformations it engendered permitted poultry processing's growth into an industry with sales of several billion dollars per year.[117] Vertical integration allowed the emerging poultry companies to control production from the egg to the grocery display. Before it was instituted, each phase in growing and processing chickens was distinct, with different businesses and farmers controlling the production and price of feed, the number and availability of eggs and chickens, the processing of poultry, and the delivery to stores. This "intensive segmentation," according to Ben Johnson, was a "critical inherent weakness."[118] Worries about feed prices, chicken quality, and small profits led entrepreneurs such as Tyson, feed companies, and the emerging poultry processors to buy hatcheries and feed mills. Newly integrated companies supplied chicks and feed from their own hatcheries and feed mills to growers (chicken farmers) under a system of contract growing. After a number of weeks the company returned to pick up the young chickens and carried them to the processing plant to be slaughtered and prepared for sale. Then the company delivered the birds to grocery stores.[119]

Merkle described vertical integration as "the greatest thing that ever happened to the chicken business. Because it immediately took the risk away from the farmer. The farmer didn't have any risks about whether to buy this chick or that chick because the chicks are now owned by the company and you know they are going to put the best chick they can on the operation. . . . It also brought about stability to the farmer cause he had a cash crop that he could depend on."[120] Before integration, chicken processing had been a largely haphazard, poorly regulated, inefficient industry.[121] Plants were hastily constructed to process the chickens being grown in ever increasing numbers. The industry ran much more smoothly after integration, and some of the improvements, coupled with the USDA's new poultry inspection mandates, increased the quality of birds offered to consumers. The system, and the chickens, became more standardized. Vertical integration also fostered significant increases in the number of chickens grown and processed. One sociologist in the 1950s found that "due to this type of integration, broiler production . . . expanded from only 34 million in 1934 to 1.3 billion in 1956."[122]

J-M Poultry began its process of vertical integration in 1966 with the acquisition of a hatchery. Shortly afterward, the company built its own feed mill and bought the operation that had provided its live chickens. The company celebrated and defended integration, maintaining that exerting such "strict controls over all phases of production . . . assure[s] our customers of the very highest quality." Vertical integration heralded a period of even more growth for J-M Poultry.[123]

Another significant reason for J-M Poultry's success is the city's geographical location. Before it became increasingly industrialized, poultry processing had occurred close to major cities—like most livestock slaughter—so that the product would be closer to major markets and near the "egg basket" of the Midwest. Advances in transportation and technology, fostered by government investment in the burgeoning "Sunbelt" during and after World War II, meant that proximity to markets became less important, and poultry meat production became an industry in its own right. The South's milder climate, coupled with the accomplishments of poultry science, permitted year-round chicken growing. In addition, the majority of the nation's small farmers were in the South. They could grow chickens in large numbers with less labor than was required for more traditional crops. It made economic sense to locate poultry processing plants near the source of the chickens. The exhausted, poor soils and farming troubles of the South meant that farmers were desperate for new crops, and pro-cessors could buy up land for less than the price of the Midwest's "prime farm land."[124] In Arkansas, where the "great commercial crop" was falling victim to boll weevils and being altered by mechanization, small farmers were increasingly willing to try new forms of agriculture to keep their farms.[125] Processors realized that the South had "unmatched comparative advantages" when compared with other regions of the United States.[126]

As noted earlier, the move south by many industries was facilitated by the efforts of booster clubs and organizations. Even the National Planning Association (NPA) joined the effort. In 1946 the NPA formed the Committee of the South on the Location of Industry, on the belief that "the develop-ment of the South is a matter of major national policy."[127] The Committee of the South published its first report in 1949, a glowing appraisal of the South's open markets, available materials, and pleasant climate. Constant comparisons to the North found the South "as good . . . or better" on a number of measures.

Buried near the back of the report is a section on labor. Workers were plentiful, the committee noted, the surplus a result of the closing of war plants. Many industries found this labor pool attractive and heeded the committee's call to locate part of their business in the South. The commit-tee claimed that these newcomers were generally pleased with southern workers and paid them "roughly the same wage rates" as their northern counterparts. The industries that came south after World War II chose southern communities because of "low turnover and lack of competition for workers." The report emphasized that new industries were *not* fleeing northern unionization and pay rates.[128]

In painting such a rosy picture, the committee denied that southern labor was markedly different from northern labor. The report disregarded the fact that southern workers were typically paid less and did not address why unions had been the victims of such decisive defeats in the South. "Available labor and satisfactory labor attitudes were more important to these companies," claimed the report, "than the South's allegedly cheap labor."[129] New industries were worried not about unions per se, accord-ing to the committee, but about the troublemaking tendencies of "some of their leaders."[130] But Paul Aho and Allan Rahn argue that the Midwest lost ground to the South as the broiler industry grew because the its "combi-nation of higher wage rates and liberalized state government-mandated fringe benefits" gave the South an advantage.[131] Similarly, Chul-Kyoo Kim and James Curry contend that "the availability of low cost labor" was one of the key factors for the industry's location in the South. [132] As for Arkansas specifically, a study commissioned by booster organizations bluntly announced that "Arkansas is a backward state in labor relations," a problem brought on by industry leaders' unwillingness to acknowledge, much less cooperate with, organized labor.[133]

The committee's attempt to conceal some of the more questionable aspects of the state of southern labor actually illuminated another element that helped the industry grow in El Dorado. The industry has profited from its employment of a vulnerable workforce inside and outside the plants. Poultry companies and farmers have, for example, viewed vertical integration in rather different terms. As a result of vertical integration, the poultry men triumphed over the farmers. Male farmers' usurpation of their wives' autonomy as chicken farmers "prefigured the erosion of independence [they] would experience when they began growing broilers on contract."[134] The system by which farmers were free to sell their chickens to the highest bidder virtually disappeared. In the contract growing system, farmers agree to grow chickens for one company. While vertical integration allowed poultry processing farms to "insure better chicks, more standardized management practices and better disease control," it also increased poultry farmers' vulnerability.[135] Some farmers claim they have no job security beyond the number of weeks it takes them to "grow out" the chicks. The company may or may not renew their contracts by delivering new chicks. The more established farmers in Delmarva resisted the contract-growing system for years, fearing the loss of their autonomy and tenancy-like conditions.[136] Whatever qualms Arkansas farmers may have had, the problems that continued to plague Arkansas farms—such as the dependence on plant (rather than animal) agriculture in the face of increasingly exhausted soils, pest infestations, and declining prices—left them unable to rebuff the system.[137]

The loss of independence was accompanied by the assumption of serious debt. From the beginning, capital-strapped small farmers had to rely on credit to ease their way into the industry. Many Arkansas farmers were only able to try poultry growing after the owners of feed companies extended them credit for feed and chicks. According to C. Curtis Cable: "In 1929 and 1930 a new method of financing was introduced by local feed dealers and hatcherymen. . . . Farmers obtained both chicks and feed, or feed alone, on credit, and the total amount due was payable when the broilers were marketed. . . . This financing method was one of the major contributions to the early growth and steady expansion of the industry."[138] Monica Gisolfi considers credit arrangements such as this the first move toward the controversial contract growing system.[139] It was a shift from the tradition of poultry raising that was not particularly capital intensive. Gisolfi and William Heffernan describe the ingenuity of farmers who fashioned housing and watering supplies out of readily available material and buildings on their farms.[140] But the demands of integrators changed that, mandating that farmers invest in expensive farm equipment, chicken housing, and supplies. In response, according to Heffernan, "poultry growers . . . [were forced to] mortgage their homes and incur large debt to secure the capital necessary to meet these demands."[141] The result has been the creation of a power imbalance that disadvantages the farmers, one in which, argues Heffernan, the poultry firms are allowed to make all the most important decisions. If the farmers do not please the firms, then the farmers may receive no more chicks and therefore no more income to pay their large debts. Farmers' dreams of independent economic success go commonly unrealized as their futures rest on the decisions of the poultry processors.[142]

The early years and structure of the poultry industry represent one of the most successful attempts at basing a "modern" industry on an "old" plantation model. An elite class of white men were able to exert their authority and ability to control poorer whites, who were still farmers, and African Americans, who were now industrial workers, rendering both groups economically dependent on the "upper" classes. Arkansas workers, especially agricultural workers, were indeed familiar with this system of economic dependence, as planters in the state had sought to keep them tied to the land at "starvation wages" even as the country became industrialized. Nan Woodruff recounts that during the early Depression, when planters were given rations to distribute to their tenants, "they used the rations to control their labor force."[143] Throughout the 1930s and 1940s planters had a strong ally in the federal government. Government policies were instrumental in "limiting southern farm workers' economic possibilities as well as restricting their civil rights."[144] Local branches of government agencies and commissions were staffed with elites who had a vested interest in ensuring the continuation of the status quo. Thus, government programs and interventions favored the "political elite."[145] In Arkansas examples were plentiful, stretching from the planters' usurpation of Red Cross authority during the Great Flood of 1927 to the predominance of local elites on New Deal agency boards to the 1943 passage of Public Law 45 and the Pace Amendment, which guaranteed that the government would not intervene in agriculture, as it had in other occupations, to set minimum wages and maximum hours.[146]

The legacy of social control was reflected in southern hostility toward organized labor as well. Compared to other southern states, Arkansas had a higher percentage of unionized workers, but Arkansas was not exactly friendly to organized labor. By 1944 Arkansas had a right-to-work law that encouraged and protected open shops and discouraged union membership.[147] Further, according to Ben Johnson: "In 1962, the University of Arkansas's Bureau of Industrial Research published a reassuring analysis for its business clientele: 'A concentration of high-wage, highly-organized industries in a labor surplus area does not raise the levels of wages and union organization for other manufacturing industries of the area.'"[148] The boosters who so heavily engaged in industrial recruitment, most often white men drawn from the upper socioeconomic classes, derived some benefit from the paternalistic system based on racial, economic, and gender hierarchies. Thus, according to David Goldfield, "the booster, a rhetorical proponent of change, is actually afraid of and opposed to change; *progress* has been a euphemism for *tradition*."[149]

Indeed, boosterism was fueled by paternalism and white racism, according to historian Michelle Brattain, creating a system in which southern elites managed to subordinate both white and black labor. While boosters posited industrialization as the salvation of poor white southerners, they consciously engaged in attracting labor-intensive, low-wage, anti-union industries that gave the South "little opportunity to experience the rapid self-sustaining expansion that might have generated the capital and demand needed to attract more desirable firms" and offered poor white people little chance of escaping poverty or their dependence on the paternalistic overtures of the white elite.[150] Boosters and the industries they attracted also circumscribed the opportunities for African Americans by initially excluding them from new industry and then later labeling the most undesirable jobs in factories as "black jobs."[151] The continued subordination of the working class was crucial to the industrialization process in the South; boosters promised "friendly" labor relations and a docile workforce, and they were determined to deliver on that promise.[152] Cobb notes that boosters "lost no time" in promoting their right-to-work laws to any industry that might potentially establish itself in their states.[153]

The poultry industry capitalized on the South's labor climate. Like other manufacturers, poultry companies moved away from the growing organization and pay scale in the North. The poultry industry's search for "cheap, non-militant labor" led processors south or kept them there, where "uneducated, unskilled workers were abundant."[154] The industry, with its own history of problematic reinforcement of hierarchies—"poultry men's" assumption of control from women, the wealthier processors' triumph over the small farmers, the system of credit and capital intensive farming accoutrements that made poultry farmers' position reminiscent of that of their cotton growing foreparents—seemed a natural fit for the area.

The racism and paternalism that had weakened the position of southern labor for decades worked to the advantage of the growing poultry industry. Unskilled and seeking work, former tenants and dispossessed small farm owners made ideal labor forces for the new industries. These industries, according to Cobb, "were concerned primarily with getting maximum productivity out of work forces consisting largely of ex-sharecroppers, females, and children, none of whom were likely to complain about wages and working conditions."[155]

In El Dorado poultry processors soon had competition for the city's vulnerable labor pool. For its size El Dorado had established an impressive industrial complex in the 1950s and 1960s. Prescolite Manufacturing, Chase-Grocord Rubber Company, and Engineered Wood Products were but a few of the companies that had plants in the city, in addition to the longtime oil and timber concerns. These plants tended to hire men, however, leaving the job-seeking women with few alternatives. Like most southern poultry plants, J-M poultry eventually welcomed these women by the dozens. Indeed, jobs that required working "on the line" were filled predominantly by women. In El Dorado these women tended to be black.[156] By drawing black women into these jobs, Merkle came to be a "much-reviled figure in upper-class El Dorado households accustomed to inexpensive domestic workers."[157]

Black women may have exemplified the type of worker southern boosters promised.[158] In the middle of the twentieth century they were in a uniquely vulnerable position. Agricultural jobs were fast disappearing, "the most striking change in patterns of black women's work."[159] They had lost most of the occupational gains they had made during World War II, and many were forced to return to the domestic service they deplored. Large numbers of black women and their children lived in poverty, but they were initially ineligible for governmental assistance because social insurance programs excluded agricultural and domestic work and because welfare caseworkers insisted they find employment.[160]

The story of black women's struggles played out in the El Dorado area much as it did elsewhere in the South. Ella Fields, who lived her young life between El Dorado and Bernice, Louisiana, experienced many of the problems black women did in the postwar years. Born in 1919, she spent most of the 1940s and 1950s "picking and chopping cotton for Mr. Tommy Green." After Mr. Green invested in a mechanical cotton picker, she lost her source of income. She began keeping house and working as a nanny for a white family in Bernice until diabetes and hypertension rendered her unable to work. Because she had never paid into the social security system, she received a monthly "welfare" benefit from the Old Age Assistance program.[161] Ms. Fields's illness had a profound effect on the life of her daughter, Tavia Wright. Instead of pursuing higher education, Mrs. Wright went to work immediately to help her mother care for her younger brother. Mrs. Wright ended up at the poultry processing facility in El Dorado. The poultry processing industry was glad to have the hundreds of women like her, with limited education and job skills and few alternatives.

It is those women who worked inside the plants—who labored long, hard hours in difficult conditions, sacrificing their time, their health, and even their lives to make a better product faster—who are the focus of this study. The rise of "big chicken" may have pushed women out of their primary role in chicken raising, but it by no means removed them from poultry production altogether. "Their labor," argues Sachs, "remains essential to the success and profitability of the poultry industry."[162] For black women that labor has largely been on the lines inside the plant. To study these women and their work is to examine how gender, racial, and socioeconomic hierarchies shaped the development of an industry and the selection of its labor force. It is also to observe how the devaluation of black women's labor has allowed the United States to ignore their plight for decades. The preponderance of black women workers in the poultry processing plant of El Dorado, Arkansas, affected the internal environment, conditions, and operation of the plants and the lives of the women who work in them. Americans have their chicken in every pot but at an extraordinary cost to the people who produce them. "They'll make you question yourself," says former line worker Kenya Drayton of poultry processing companies, "make you wonder if you are a person or not because nobody would even treat a *dog* like this."

CHAPTER 2

"I WAS A SINGLE PARENT— I *HAD* TO WORK"

As it grew, the poultry processing complex in El Dorado did not draw all its employees from that city or even from the state of Arkansas. Union County's southern border comprises part of the northern border of Claiborne and Union parishes in Louisiana.[1] Many Louisianans have crossed the border to find employment in the poultry industry. Bernice, located in Union Parish, is one community that supplied a number of workers; one of them was Vivian West. Born in 1947, West had lived her whole life in Union Parish, first in Spearsville, then in Bernice. She knew of the poultry plants in El Dorado and lived not so far from a chicken farm. Even though the farm was not visible from her parents' place, the stench of the chicken houses hovered in the air, serving as a daily reminder of the farm's proximity. Despite the fact that she knew people who farmed chickens or processed them, she never imagined herself "going to the poultry" to work.[2] She wanted to be a full-time wife and mother. In the early 1960s she left school to pursue that dream. West married her childhood sweetheart, and they had three daughters in quick succession. Yet reality was a lot less smooth than her dreams imagined it would be. After a few rocky years, West found herself divorced and the primary caretaker of her young girls. To survive, she had to transition to paid work.

She began working at J-M Poultry Packing Company in the late 1960s on the evisceration line. She did not enjoy the work. Evisceration was a particularly bloody process that caused line workers much pain.[3] Employees of a Mississippi plant noted their company's acknowledgment of the difficulty of eviscerating: "The gut pullers get paid more money than other workers. The company seems to think they have a more strenuous job than everybody else."[4] Whether she found it unpleasant or not, West felt it was a job she had to take. In the aftermath of her divorce, she had few marketable skills and no high school diploma. In her opinion working at J-M was one of the few options she had: "A lot of these places—I don't know if they just said it—but they weren't hiring women. Not us, anyway. But the poultry would. So I went, but only because I *had* to work. What else could I do? . . . We didn't have child support like now. . . . Welfare . . . they'd be in your business so much and trying to talk to you any kind of way. I wasn't going to fool with that. It was hard, but I did it."[5]

West's experience highlights factors that drew black women from Louisiana into the El Dorado industry. As a black woman and a single mother, her economic options were limited. Louisiana, like Arkansas and most other southern states, had experienced dramatic changes in agriculture, lessening the need for the kind of farmwork that West's parents had done. The industries in Bernice and the nearest cities, El Dorado and Monroe, primarily hired men. Finally, West did not feel the system of social provision, to which single mothers should have been able to turn, was truly accessible. Her dismissal of the welfare system was based on the very real experiences of poor black Louisiana women in the first half of the twentieth century. As part of a preexisting trend of excluding African Americans from government services and assistance, the state government circumscribed or denied welfare benefits to black women. This measure was an attempt to try to control the allegedly promiscuous behavior of black women, as evidenced, they claimed, by the growing number of mothers and children of color represented on welfare rolls.[6] Limiting welfare benefits was also a method of curtailing black agitation for civil rights, because many poor African Americans used the program, and keeping African Americans available for menial work. Segregationists in Louisiana, in their efforts to maintain Jim Crow in the face of a growing movement for change, created a political, economic, and social climate hostile to poor black women, restricting many of them to arduous, dirty, low-status work.

THE "BIG WOODS" OF BERNICE

Since its founding, Bernice has been linked to El Dorado. Established in 1899 as a stop for the Arkansas Southern Railroad, on a route that began in El Dorado, Bernice lies thirty miles south of El Dorado on Highway 167. Despite the fact that it is the second largest town in Union Parish, its population has never exceeded two thousand people. Located in North Louisiana's Piney Woods, the plentiful supply of towering pine trees led people to refer to the new town and the surrounding area as the "Big Woods." Bernice's economic life historically centered around this natural resource, and the parish once led the state in timber production.[7] Bernice is a sawmill town, having been home to Hageman's, G. E. Lindsey Lumber Company, and Courtney Reed Lumber Company. Louisiana Pacific, a producer of finished lumber, had a plant there for a number of years. Just north of the town, the village of Lillie hosted a now-defunct particleboard plant, and to the west, between Bernice and Lisbon, is a chip mill. Like many of the businesses in El Dorado, Bernice's timber and lumber companies chiefly employed men. Black women in Bernice who needed to earn wages labored on farms and as domestic workers well into the twentieth century.

An examination of Union Parish's history reveals that although it was sometimes secondary to wood industries, agriculture, particularly cotton farming, was an important source of income throughout the late nineteenth and into the first half of the twentieth centuries. "Cotton," explained one resident, "was the only cash crop farmers could rely on."[8] A 1935 report by the Federal Emergency Relief Agency (FERA) noted that Union Parish residents were abandoning "lumbering" to return to farming.[9] Another study described cotton as the "chief source of support" and noted that "everything has been built around the cotton farm and cotton market."[10] Cotton was not the only crop grown in Union Parish. Farmers throughout the parish tended cattle, soybeans, corn, and watermelon.[11]

Making a living as a farmer proved difficult in the parish. Poor soil, erosion, alternate floods and drought, and the depressed price of cotton troubled farmers in the 1920s and 1930s, making them symbolic of other farmers in what FERA had labeled a "problem area."[12] Additionally, farmers in Union Parish engaged in "too much one-crop farming and too little utilization of the resources for subsistence."[13] They also resisted adapting to new farming techniques and practices.[14] Moving away from cotton, the crop upon which they most heavily depended, must have seemed too daunting a task. Thus, the troubles that affected their neighbors to the north, in Arkansas, also visited North Louisiana's farmworkers in the 1920s and 1930s.

"ALL HAD TO LEAVE THEIR HOMES"

Black farmers in Louisiana struggled throughout the 1930s, finding only pockets of relief through New Deal policies that left the planter class in control. The denial of welfare benefits in the middle of the century was part of a long-standing trend in Union Parish in which African Americans were excluded from governmental provision and protection, a trend on prominent display during the Depression years. As Union Parish historian Truett West notes of African Americans in the parish in the 1930s, the winds of change represented by government programs "must have seemed to be blowing past them without effect." The parish made few provisions for the education of black children, running black schools sometimes for six months a year and sometimes during winter months only.[15] The pattern for these children's education was set by agricultural needs. Union Parish native Pearl Adams Harris remembers that some black boys in the parish could not begin school until after the cotton harvest. John Quincy Watley left school after sixth grade to help his father farm and "support the family."[16] In a study of education in Union Parish between 1927 and 1937, Laval Taylor reports that white schools typically operated 178 days, while black schools operated between 80 and 116 days. Taylor also records the differentials between per-pupil expenditures, construction and upkeep, teachers' salaries, and teachers' training in black and white schools, finding that less was spent on black schools, black students, and black faculty.[17]

The school board made the attempts to educate black children more difficult by providing no transportation for black children, even after buses were made available to white children.[18] But black parents and black children were determined to have the younger generation educated. Black families on the outskirts of Bernice, whose children would have had to walk several miles, founded a school in their community because "they didn't want their children to have to walk all the way to Bernice to go to the colored school."[19] Other families found places for their children to board to be closer to the one black high school.[20]

Schooling was not the only area in which black families were neglected. The administrators of New Deal agencies in Louisiana seemed to care little about black small farm owners and tenants who were simultaneously being pushed off the land and barred, by local practice and threats of violence, from relief. V. H. Sonderegger, state forester for Louisiana, noted the impossibility of putting the black men who worked for the Civilian Conservation Corps to work in North Louisiana, writing that "it was not permissible or possible to work such colored men in the piney woods section of the state."[21] Despite desperate poverty, African Americans in Union Parish were underrepresented on relief roles.[22] Planters feared losing control of their black labor force, a threat represented by the U.S. government because federal relief payments were commonly more than what black workers earned in agricultural or domestic work.[23] Planters complained that relief would erode African Americans' work ethic. An interview with a white Union Parish resident reflected the common paternalistic notion that the economic arrangement set up by her father and his oversight were needed by the black sharecroppers on his farm to make them work and help them prosper. The arrangement, she claimed, "encourage[d] them to work harder."[24]

In 1933, frustrated by the ongoing exclusion from social programs and provisions, some black residents of Union Parish joined in a "conspiracy," led by Walter and Houston Burnside, two brothers who were not from the area. The Burnsides, white con men, identified themselves as government agents who had come to ameliorate the suffering of African Americans. From October to November 1933 black citizens paid to join the Burnsides' secret organization, receiving shotguns and details of a plan to seize Farmerville, the parish seat, and to demand more food, more land, civil rights, and the right to intermarry with whites. The last demand was the one most discussed by contemporary local newspapers and by a number of interviewees four decades later, who dismissed the desperate conditions in which black residents had lived.[25]

White citizens retaliated by dragging African Americans suspected of participating from their homes and whipping them. The black secretary-treasurer of the organization was shot and killed by police as they attempted to "save" him from lynching. Greta de Jong recounts that white men in Union Parish beat and killed a number of black men in 1933 and 1934, violence connected directly to the conspiracy by the author of an anonymous letter sent to the Justice Department.[26] The outcome of the conspiracy for many black farmers, according to the anonymous letter writer, and to West, was not the increased autonomy for which they hoped but greater loss, as many were simply run off their land. The letter said: "9 men . . . all had to leave their homes, wives and children . . . to keep white people from killing them. Some has 80 a[cres] of land, some 40 a[cres] some 200 a[cres] some as much as 400 a[cres]." This property was later bought up by local white residents. White men also used the conspiracy to further exclude African Americans from relief. According to the letter writer, after a number of black men were beaten, the white perpetrators "forbid the men to work on relief or to sign up for work."

White men could not beat all hope of a more just society out of African Americans. African Americans in Union Parish and across Louisiana continued to demand greater social and economic equality in the mid-twentieth century. In Union Parish advocates for African Americans focused most notably on the old problem of unequal access to quality education, bringing suit against salary differentials in teachers' pay in 1948 and ongoing segregation in the schools in the 1960s.[27] As the movement for civil rights spread across the state, so did a backlash among white citizens determined to preserve Jim Crow and the privileges the system afforded to them. This backlash would have serious negative effects on black citizens and particularly on poor black mothers such as Vivian West. In the 1950s and 1960s Louisiana legislators used welfare policy as a weapon against black women to deny access to social services in hopes of discouraging civil rights activism and further undermining any chance for economic stability.

BACKLASH

It is important to note two factors that shaped the context in which state legislators denied social assistance to black women: the volatile circumstances surrounding ongoing civil rights agitation and the status and perception of poor black women. First, the atmosphere around civil rights issues was particularly charged by 1960. White southern recalcitrance had remained firm in the face of a movement that had by then been growing for some time. By the time the Supreme Court handed down its 1954 decision in *Brown v. Board,* challenging, ideologically at least, the very basis of the South's segregated world, white southerners were ready to mount what Virginia senator Harry Byrd rightly called a massive resistance to the dismantling of southern apartheid. Louisiana's segregationists mobilized to protect Jim Crow. The state legislature established the Joint Legislative Committee to Maintain Segregation (JLC) in 1954 and busied itself passing bills intended to circumvent and obstruct the Supreme Court's decision.[28]

Segregationists identified the continued disfranchisement of African Americans as the most effective tool for thwarting desegregation and upholding white supremacy. The dismal statistics for Louisiana indicated that less than a third of eligible African Americans were registered to vote in 1956. In four majority black parishes (East Carroll, Madison, Tensas, and West Feliciana), not a single black person was registered.[29] The Citizens' Councils, organizations of white supremacists, determined that getting rid of registered black voters was the "key to victory in the segregation struggle."[30] With the help of Willie Rainach, chairman of the JLC and a Citizens' Council member, the Citizens' Councils of various North Louisiana parishes purged parish rolls of black voters.[31] They began in Ouachita Parish, which borders Union on the southeast, successfully challenging 3,420 of the parish's 5,700 black voters.[32] The purges that swept across North Louisiana drew the attention of the Department of Justice (DoJ), sparking an investigation by the FBI. The bureau found that the Citizens' Council, using allegations of technical errors, accusations of misspelling, and subjectively administered literacy tests, had wrongfully purged thousands of black voters. Despite the evidence, grand juries sitting in Louisiana refused to return any indictments.[33]

The continued violation of African Americans' civil rights led to the passage of the Civil Rights Act of 1957 and the establishment of the Commission on Civil Rights. One of the express duties of the commission was to investigate charges that U.S. citizens were being denied the right to vote because of their race or color. From black Louisianans the commission received a "continuing stream of affidavits alleging denial of the right to vote."[34] Although it could make recommendations and seek federal injunctions to prevent voter intimidation in federal elections, the commission acted slowly and with great caution.[35] It thus proved ill equipped to deal with the southern obstinacy exemplified by the white power structure of Louisiana. The Louisiana purges continued. Union was one of the parishes in which the Citizens' Councils "enjoyed considerable success."[36] In October 1956, 1,099 "nonwhites" in Union Parish were registered to vote. Three years later, despite the establishment of the commission, that number had dropped to 377.[37]

While the Citizens' Council kept busy purging black voters, Louisiana's legal system also stymied the work of the commission. The state's registrars, on advice of counsel, denied the commission's requests to examine their records. Louisiana attorneys attacked the validity of the commission, based on the fact that the commission protected the identity of complainants, and argued that the Civil Rights Act of 1957 was unconstitutional. In July 1959 the commission planned a hearing to address the complaints it had received from citizens of North Louisiana, only to have a federal judge issue an injunction barring the hearing. July also marked the culmination of a purge in Washington Parish in which 1,377 black voters (out of a total of about 1,500) were removed from the voting rolls based largely on the challenges of four white residents.

Congress noted the commission's lack of success. In its two years the commission findings had only prompted the Justice Department to bring three suits—including the Washington Parish case. "It would appear that few, if any, Negro citizens have been able to vote as a result of Justice Department enforcement of the 1957 Act," observed Representative John Dingell of Michigan. In fact, the percentage of eligible "nonwhites" who were registered to vote in Louisiana fell from 31.7 percent in 1956 to 27.5 percent in 1959.[38] "Is it not strange," taunted Louisiana senator Allen Ellender, "that the enactment of a so-called right-to-vote law has actually had the opposite effect?"[39]

In its 1959 report the commission suggested that the real problem lay with the Civil Rights Act of 1957. It simply could not secure and protect the right to vote. The commission recommended more forceful legislation that would, among other provisions, empower a federal officer to step in to register black voters when local registrars would not. The requested legislation materialized in 1960.

Thus, by the spring of 1960 Louisiana was on the defensive, despite its triumphant stance in the late 1950s.[40] New civil rights legislation was imminent, even with the participation of Ellender, Louisiana, senator Russell Long and sixteen other southern senators in a record-breaking filibuster. On February 29 the Supreme Court affirmed district judge Skelly Wright's order that the Washington Parish voters be placed back on the rolls. Judge Wright dealt segregationists another blow on May 16, when he handed down an integration plan for New Orleans schools that would be initiated that fall. Such was the political climate as the state legislature prepared to convene in the summer of 1960.

The second circumstance that facilitated the legislature's actions was the vulnerability of black women who turned to "welfare" rather than social insurance programs as their job opportunities declined and disappeared. This vulnerability is predicated on at least two factors. The first is the stereotypical characterization of black women that portrays them as promiscuous and immoral and their mothering as unnecessary and, in the worst cases, damaging. The second is the nature of the welfare system in the United States. The characterization of black women as hypersexual has a long history in the Western world, borne, according to scholar Janell Hobson, of white men's othering and eroticizing of Africa, so that "any body that emerges from the continent is constituted as an oversexed body."[41] This image, typically called "Jezebel," serves as a foil for white women's presumed purity and a justification for the sexual exploitation of black women in and out of slavery.[42]

Deemed immoral and cast as the opposite of the devoted white mother, black women commonly have the value of their mothering questioned and dismissed.[43] Legal scholar Dorothy Roberts, who has written on this subject in numerous books and essays, notes that throughout American history "social discourse [has] condemn[ed] African American mothers as deviant."[44] It is a condemnation rooted in the slavery-era valuation of black women in terms of property rather than in terms of humanity: "It [was] necessary to assume that black women were promiscuous and fickle and gave no more thought to their offspring than pigs did to their litter," writes Michele Wallace. "Therefore, whites might sell black children with impunity and do with them what they pleased."[45] Slave owners, who effectively had complete control and ownership over enslaved black children, commonly disrupted the relationships between black mothers and their children. Mainstream beliefs did not recognize their relationships as sacred and necessary in the same way that relationships between white mothers and their children were believed to be. "Slavery," according to Roberts, "could only exist by nullifying black parents' moral claim to their children."[46] Long after the institution of slavery had ended, the practice of systematically abrogating black parents' rights to their children and the assertion of white people's control over black families persisted. Roberts reveals what the very real consequences of such practices are: poor black mothers are more likely than other groups to have their families interrupted and their children taken by the state.[47]

Just as the attempted negation of the parent-child relationship persisted, the cultural degradation of black motherhood did not fade away with the end of slavery. Black motherhood, particularly single black motherhood, is constructed as the cause and effect of a number of socio-economic problems in black communities. Thus, it is always in need of reform and oversight.[48] The Moynihan Report of 1965 gave these assumptions about the "pathological" nature of black motherhood perhaps their most famous platform, positing single black motherhood as the cause of poverty, criminality, and dysfunction within black communities.[49] But these ideas did not come out of nowhere; politicians, social workers, and journalists across the country had been exploiting them long before the report came out, arguing that poor black mothers did not "deserve" to be rewarded with "handout[s]" for their destructive behavior, which "transfer[s] a deviant lifestyle to their children that dooms each succeeding generation to a life of poverty, delinquency, and despair."[50] Perhaps black mothers' biggest transgression has been that they literally and figuratively "transfer" blackness to their children. Melissa Harris-Perry engages W.E.B. Du Bois's contention that to be black in the United States is "to be a problem," finding it still relevant and characteristic of the way that black people are regarded in the present day.[51] Given this context, it is no wonder that poor black women's pregnancies continue to be described as "epidemic," "irresponsible," and "poor choices" and that the families they head are described as "broken" and "fragile." White Louisianans were able to exploit this familiar, deeply entrenched image of selfish and negligent black mothers.

These notions of deservingness and the definition of welfare as a handout are tied up in the very founding of the U.S. welfare system.[52] Many scholars have discussed the construction of the Social Security Act of 1935 as a two-tier, and thus inherently unequal, system.[53] The first tier was originally composed of the "honorable" programs, a well-organized system of unemployment, old age, life, and disability insurances. These programs were considered honorable because they benefited people—usually men and their wives and children—who had once been active in the workforce. "Welfare" programs made up the second tier, most notably Aid to Dependent Children (ADC), a program that offered assistance to single mothers and their children. Because social insurance was designed as a contributory system, it was more acceptable to the American public than ADC. In receiving social insurance benefits, citizens supposedly reaped a return on their mandatory investments. In receiving welfare, citizens were living off the funds of hardworking taxpayers. These programs were less respectable in a society that valued paid work highly and regarded poverty as a sign of moral failing.[54]

Agriculture and domestic service, the workplace domains of black women, were left out of the occupations that enjoyed the first-tier benefits.[55] The exclusion was purposeful, a blatant attempt to placate the southern congressmen whose support Franklin D. Roosevelt desperately needed in order to pass the Social Security Act of 1935. Excluding African Americans from social insurance programs in which the federal government determined benefits would allow southern whites to continue to control black income and labor. "Minimizing poor mothers' access to welfare," argues sociologist Ellen Reese, "ensured a ready supply of cheap female and child labor."[56] The exclusion also meant that when black families needed assistance, they had to turn to the so-called charity programs, perpetuating the stereotype of African Americans as lazy and in search of handouts.[57] This image fueled Louisiana's reluctance to aid poor black mothers.

African American women who lacked access to the honorable programs were commonly denied access to the charitable ones as well. Phyllis Palmer notes that southern welfare boards often would deny the eligibility of black domestic workers for programs such as ADC. These boards argued that domestic work was readily available and that black women could call on family and community networks to watch their children.[58] L. M. Montgomery, a child welfare worker in Claiborne Parish, which borders Union Parish on the west, defended the underrepresentation of African Americans in the program by arguing, "If a [black woman] has an illegitimate child, it will be cared for or supported by the parents or sisters or some other relatives." She also relied on the stereotype of black mothers as ambivalent toward and neglectful of their children. "We get more response from whites," she said, "because they seem to be more vitally concerned with children."[59] In 1943 Louisiana became the first state to initiate work requirements for welfare applicants. If the welfare administrator determined that the mother could work, especially in the fields, then she was summarily denied aid. One Caddo Parish grand jurist, charged with examining the increase in welfare costs, demanded to know "why you have so many Negro women on your payrolls. Why can't they go back to the country and work?"[60]

That seemed to be the sentiment of the Union Parish Welfare Board in the case of Ella Fields, the mother of Tavia Wright, one of the women featured in this book. For Fields ADC was "a little hard to get on." Once she left the fields for domestic work, she did not earn enough to support her small family. She had few skills, having only attended the Old Shiloh Black School for three or four years.[61] She applied for ADC but was initially rejected. Her daughter remembers that "when she did get on it, what she had to do was dress us up like we were really poor. She had to put us on raggedy clothes, had us looking like anything, like we were thrown away before we could get on ADC because there were so many people talking against her. They didn't want her on it."[62] Fields seemed to fear, quite accurately, that any indication that her family lived above a level of sheer survival would give the welfare board reason to turn her down.

Former poultry processing worker Aarica Jones has similar recollections of the unpleasant nature of dealing with welfare authorities. In a sense, Jones contends, love got her "into trouble." At sixteen she fell in love with a local boy. "You know what go along with that," she says, and in 1956, at the age of eighteen, she found herself pregnant and unmarried. For a while she and her boyfriend had a rather tense relationship, as he was not the father she hoped he would be: "We wasn't ready to be grown, wasn't ready for that kind of responsibility." Nevertheless, she loved him and wanted to make a future with him. By twenty-one she had her second child. Her patience with her children's father had expired. She ended the relationship. Eventually, she applied for ADC to help care for her children: "I wished I didn't need it. They talk to you so nasty and wanted to come check up on you just like you was a child. Them was some nasty people, and my nerves would just be up when I had to see them. But I had to take care my kids." In her interview Jones was careful to combat prevalent stereotypes of black women. She was not "fast"; her children's father was her first sexual partner, and she had been faithful to him. Welfare was only one way in which she had provided for her children. She also worked "on the side, mostly cleaning after white folks." She had to choose these jobs carefully, lest the "welfare office" found out and terminated her benefits. In addition to her paid work, Jones remembers, "I kep' a clean house, and I cooked all the time!"[63] Yet stories such as Jones's did not represent the popular image of those receiving welfare and were not highlighted enough to help overcome resentments toward black welfare recipients.

Despite state resistance, the number of black parents and children who received ADC in Louisiana continued to grow in the postwar period, from 31,000 in 1947 to over 100,000 in 1959, in part because of federal government efforts to ensure a more democratic system of administering the program.[64] Nationally, after 1942, the number of black and the number of non-widowed ADC recipients increased sharply, while the number of white widows in the program, those historically perceived by taxpayers as most "deserving" of aid, fell.[65] These changes made the program progressively more vulnerable to attacks.[66] Louisiana politicians were at the forefront in launching these attacks, complaining that white taxpayers should not subsidize black illegitimacy or the alleged sexual promiscuity of black women.[67] To their benefit their attacks were timely, as the popularization of the "subsidization of illegitimacy" myth had by this time spread quite widely.[68]

Attacking the character and citizenship of black Louisianans served at least two major purposes for segregationist politicians. First, it helped maintain a social hierarchy predicated in part on the continual shaming and stigmatization of African Americans. As Melissa Harris-Perry argues, "Systematic state-sponsored racial shame was central to Jim Crow."[69] The backlash against welfare was, and is, rooted in the basic premise that poor black women ought to be shamed *and* ashamed of themselves. They should be ashamed of having babies while unmarried, ashamed of needing what is construed as a handout, and ashamed of their inability to control their overly sexual natures.

Popular sentiment held that black communities, with their deficient moral compasses, did not adequately shame these women and that these women did not feel the shame that could lead to repentance and improved behavior. According to Rickie Solinger, "Black women, illegitimately pregnant, were not shamed . . . There was no redemption possible for these women."[70] Even those who were supposedly sympathetic to poor black women accepted notions of their cultural inferiority. In 1959, for example, Pennsylvania Department of Public Welfare employee Margaret Thornhill wrote an article that asserted that the department should expend more effort to bring about "a shift in thinking and attitude" among African Americans; many social workers despaired of helping them, she averred, because "illegitimacy carries no stigma among Negroes . . . [and] all Negroes love children, it matters not who gives birth to them." Thornhill recommended that "the demands and expectations of white middle-class culture" be imposed on African Americans.[71] Because black people did not efficiently shame each other, the state, with its problematically crafted welfare system, took on the tasks of shaming and behavior modification.

Nancy Fraser and Linda Gordon argue that the ADC program, with its "means-testing, morals-testing, moral and household supervision, home visits, extremely low stipend . . . humiliated [and] infantilized" recipients.[72] The state, as exemplified by Louisiana in 1960, also made black welfare recipients responsible for a number of social problems. According to Solinger: "Black women [were] blamed for the population explosion, for escalating welfare costs, for the existence of unwanted babies, and blamed for the tenacious grip of poverty on blacks in America."[73] Their behavior and their lack of remorse about it clearly justified and evidenced their social inferiority and the need for a segregated society.

The ongoing defamation of the character and denial of citizenship of black Louisianans also garnered, for segregationists, support for their second purpose: the ongoing efforts to disfranchise African Americans and keep them impoverished and subordinate. Conservative politicians "found it politically profitable to associate Black illegitimacy in their constituents' minds with the rising cost of public welfare grants."[74] This is exactly what Louisiana's segregationist politicians did. Once the connection had been made, legislators could punish African Americans for their "aberrant" behavior and their work to end racial segregation. Welfare was an effective tool. If the state removed the only source of income from thousands of black families, "funds that [were] admittedly needed to provide the basic essentials of life itself," African Americans' focus would shift from civil and political rights to mere existence, and they would remain readily, even desperately, available for low-wage, low-status work.[75] At the same time, Louisiana took a strong stance against the increasingly unpopular single black mother and her supposed licentious nature. After all, according to K. Sue Jewell, "African American women who are recipients of social welfare services are also defined as contributing to the social, cultural, and economic degeneration of American society."[76] This episode highlighting black women's alleged lack of morality and self-control could serve to validate white southerners' fears that an integrated society would spell doom to their morally and culturally superior way of life.[77]

In 1960 the Louisiana state legislature amended Revised Statute 14:79.1 with Acts 73 and 75. Act 73 made entering into common law marriage a crime. Act 75 prohibited "conceiving and giving birth to two or more illegitimate children." The violation of Act 75 could result in a one thousand–dollar fine and a year in jail. These acts specifically targeted African Americans, who had higher rates of cohabitation and out-of-wedlock births than whites.[78] The legislature also amended the State Constitution, through Act 613, to strengthen the "good character" and literacy requirement of voting laws. These acts worked together to circumvent the repeal of poll taxes and the new restrictions on white citizens' challenges of black voters.[79]

Individuals guilty of defying Act 73 or 75, whether criminally charged or not, were considered not of good character and were thus ineligible to vote. But Acts 73 and 75 worked in another, more immediately harmful manner. Louisiana was a strong supporter of "suitable home" guidelines for ADC recipients, rules that required caretakers to provide a home that met predetermined standards before the state would grant assistance. The passage of Acts 73 and 75 led to changes in the laws regulating welfare. Act 251 amended Louisiana Revised Statute 46:233: "In no instance shall assistance be granted to any person who is living with his or her mother if the mother has had an illegitimate child after a check has been received from the welfare department, unless and until proof satisfactory to the parish board of public welfare has been presented showing that the mother has ceased illicit relationships and is maintaining a suitable home for the child or children." In a single paragraph Louisiana had laid the groundwork to deny thousands of children aid to meet their most basic needs.[80]

Suitable home laws, as conceived, could have worked to protect children from abuse and neglect and to raise their standard of living.[81] The way they worked in many cases, however, changed the laws into a form of social control, effectively used "in such a racially biased manner that they virtually became proxy for racial exclusion."[82] Judgments of suitability were left to the discretion of the social worker, making it a highly subjective guideline. Suitable home laws allowed social workers to visit the homes of ADC recipients at any time and question friends, family, and neighbors about the household. Ella Fields's daughter was so ready to graduate high school and escape ADC because "they wanted to know everything about you and all your business. If you had a friend, like a boyfriend, you had to tell them who he was. You couldn't have company like you wanted to because they didn't really want you to have a man friend around or nothing like that."[83] Anna Marie Smith supports this claim, arguing that "African American women were particularly singled out for the worst of AFDC's sexual policing. . . . The AFDC programs operated by the southern states were particularly harsh; they routinely subjected African American women to the most aggressive forms of moral policing."[84] Because of the way the program was administered, in accepting ADC, families virtually forfeited their right to privacy.

Any law that affected welfare disproportionately affected Louisiana's black communities. By 1960, despite white protest and the vilification of black single mothers, 66 percent of approximately 100,000 ADC recipients in Louisiana were black, yet African Americans composed only 31.9 percent of the state's population. Louisiana legislators and welfare administrators went to work immediately to implement Act 251. The Department of Public Welfare notified 5,991 families, 5,582 of them black families, by letter in July that, as of August, they would no longer receive ADC because they had failed to provide a suitable home for their children.[85] The letters failed to mention any means of appealing to the state's Department of Public Welfare. The department justified the exclusion by claiming that those removed from the rolls might have their cases acted upon sooner by local boards than by the state office, ignoring local boards' history of denying black families access to welfare programs.[86] Further efforts led to the termination of 290 more cases. These 6,281 families included 23,459 children, 95 percent of whom were black.[87] These acts were a triumph for segregationists. The new laws further undermined poor black families' political equality—guaranteed by the Constitution and new legislation— by erasing any possibility of social equality afforded by some degree of economic independence.[88]

African Americans in Louisiana and across the country mobilized quickly to aid Louisiana's poorest children. Black churches, the National Association for the Advancement of Colored People, and the Urban League all endeavored to clothe, feed, and shelter the black families cut so abruptly from ADC. Aarica Jones, whose family was affected by the cuts, remembers that while the termination of her benefits occurred quickly, so did the response of family and friends: "I was glad we lived in the country. Wasn't nobody gone let my babies be hungry or in them streets. It did get tight on me. But people fed us and didn't [ex]change no word. I worried about how we was gone make it, but God saw fit that we did. God and the people who helped us."[89] Black newspapers denounced the cuts as spiteful, racially motivated, and an obstacle to civil rights agitation. Acts 73, 75, and 251 were, according to Lindhorst and Leighninger, "a blatant effort to punish and control African-American women."[90]

Having been aware for some time of the hostility toward ADC recipients, the Louisiana Department of Public Welfare did try to mount some defense. In the first half of 1960 State Commissioner of Public Welfare Mary Evelyn Parker circulated an article that equated attacks on ADC with a campaign against "helpless children" and issued a press release noting the relatively slow growth of the ADC caseload when compared to the growth of the population. Parker gave speeches that talked about the need for ADC, the fact that 75 percent of children who received benefits were "legitimate," and the narrow focus on what she called "the bad cases."[91] The chairman of the Alexandria, Louisiana, welfare board contended that "while it is true that the actual number of illegitimate births has been increasing, only a small change in the proportion of live births [from 7.9 to 8.2 percent between 1950 and 1959] which are illegitimate has occurred."[92] Parker and her staff hoped to refute the notion that the ADC program had become a respite for what one social worker called the "hard cases," women who bore more than one child outside of marriage.[93]

Years of bad press and centuries of the devaluation of black women's "motherwork" had a much more profound effect than the department's efforts. As black families made their way onto ADC rolls, according to Reese, the program "was subject to greater controversy."[94] The slow response of white media and citizens was testament to the growing effect of antiwelfare propaganda. Ten years of reporting on welfare fraud cases and rising costs, along with conservative politicians' steady claims that the majority of black mothers on welfare had never been married and regarded their children as a "business asset," further tarnished welfare and poor black mothers in the view of the white general public.[95] Louisiana governor Jimmie Davis called the mothers of the children removed from the ADC rolls "a bunch of prostitutes."[96] One state senator expressed the hope that Louisiana's legislation "would get rid of the whole program completely."[97] Eventually, the U.S. Department of Health, Education, and Welfare (HEW) intervened, holding hearings to determine the validity of Louisiana's suitable home policies and threatening to withhold federal funding.[98] In January 1961 HEW secretary Arthur Flemming decided that suitable home policies "impose a condition of eligibility that bears no just relationship to the Aid to Dependent Children program" and issued a statement effectively voiding suitable home policies everywhere.[99]

Despite the repudiation of their position, found in the Civil Rights Act of 1960 and Flemming's ruling, Louisiana's segregationists did not give up. They established a state sovereignty commission, dedicated to defending the state's rights to maintain its own school system, establish voting qualifications, and preserve its "traditional culture."[100] In Union Parish the school board resolved that it would refute any efforts at "race mixing," reassuring white parents that it stood for complete segregation.[101] Parish residents sent a letter to Governor Davis, urging him to "use every power at [his] command, including the Legislature, interposition, or any other means to retain segregation."[102] Both the *Gazette,* the newspaper of the parish seat of Farmerville, and the *Bernice News-Journal* posted an essay above their banners about the school desegregation "tragedy of New Orleans."

Thus, black women in Bernice faced the dilemma of living in a town clinging to segregation, where old job opportunities were fading and others were the domain of men, and living in a state where social provision was a much-maligned system. From 1950 to 1960 the number of black farm operators in Louisiana dropped by more than 56 percent.[103] In that decade the number of acres in cotton production in Union Parish shrank from 14,748 to 3,720.[104] The *Bernice News-Journal* commented on the "slim prospects of securing work" that Louisiana's professional farmworkers faced in 1960. Closer to home, the paper reported that only one cotton gin would operate in the area, as Bernice's cotton production was insufficient to require more.[105] Just as prospects for agricultural work in the parish were falling, Union Parish responded to the 1960 suitable home laws by cutting 36 of its approximately 228 welfare cases. Of 155 children who lost benefits in Union Parish, 147 were black.[106] The cuts came at a time when almost half of Union Parish families earned income below the Social Security Administration's defined poverty level.[107]

Throughout the 1960s black women in Bernice sought employment in varied places. The fact that the parish had "no substantial industry that offer[ed] employment to unskilled women workers" complicated their search.[108] New garment factories hired a number of women, black and white, but residents considered the income from garment manufacturing below average.[109] Black women also found work in the local hospital and nursing home, but it was the low-status, low-paying work as nurse's aides, kitchen workers, and housekeepers in which women of color historically have been overrepresented.[110] The two small garment factories, one hospital, and one nursing home provided a limited number of jobs.

Meanwhile, the proximity of a number of poultry processing plants to Union Parish drove parish boosters to explore the possibilities of the industry. The Union Parish Development Board recognized the appeal of a poultry processing plant to the parish's increasing number of chicken growers and as a source of employment for its unskilled laborers. The board expressed the belief that "a chicken processing center would pay a good dividend."[111] Small farmers in Union Parish were apparently persuaded—by1969 Union Parish was home to the greatest number of chicken farmers in the state and still produces the most poultry of any of the parishes.[112] Although the board's dream of a "chicken processing center" would be delayed for a few more decades, unskilled laborers from the parish still found employment in the industry in nearby plants.

In terms of work available to black women from Bernice, poultry processing was an acceptable alternative. It paid more than garment manufacturing, and while it was hard, dirty work, it seemed not to have the stigma, the similarity to domestic service, attached to institutional service work. In many cases, observed Angela Stuesse, "chicken plant work was *the* job opportunity for African Americans, to whom other factory work was still largely unavailable."[113] North Carolina poultry processing worker Donna Bazemore supported this idea in testimony before Congress, noting that for "minority women" poultry processing work was often "the only alternative to welfare and minimum wage jobs."[114] Indeed, in terms of wages and types of jobs available to them, black women in the 1960s did benefit from a civil rights platform that demanded greater economic access and opportunity.[115] But civil rights legislation was not enough to overthrow completely the historical practices and beliefs that often restricted black women to "devalued" labor, and frequently jobs that represented a "move up" for black women were the same types of jobs that white people and black men eagerly left behind.[116] As Irene Browne and Ivy Kennelly note of the post–civil rights era, "Opportunities for success in the U.S. labor market remain linked to gender and race and African American women continue to be among the most severely disadvantaged."[117] Thus, the move into work such as that available in the poultry industry could simultaneously represent a step forward and a continuation of old patterns. The rural Louisiana black women who made their way into the J-M Poultry Packing Company in the 1960s remembered, for example, being pleased with their starting wage of about $1.25 an hour.[118] But within the plant they discovered many of the same old problems—demands on their time and effort that conflicted with their family work, a structure built on the historic practices of racial and gender subjugation, and harsh physical labor that would forever change their bodies and their employment prospects.

THE MORE THINGS CHANGE . . .

Despite black women's hopes that factory jobs would represent a significant change in their lives and economic well-being, poultry processing
work fit well into a historical pattern that relegated black women to certain
kinds of work. Given black women's history of working in food preparation
and production in private homes in the South, their experiences inside
poultry processing plants were not as different from their old domestic
work as they hoped.

One of the most rigorous tasks that black women undertook as domestic
workers was the preparation and cooking of meals.[119] Hot, arduous, dirty,
and often bloody, food preparation could require significant physical
strength and consume quite a bit of time. Psyche Williams-Forson offers an
excerpt from Gwendolyn Brooks's novel *Maud Martha* (1953) to illustrate
how difficult food preparation—appropriately, dressing a chicken—could
be: "The nasty, nasty mess. [The chicken] had been given a bitter slit with
the bread knife and the bread knife had been biting in that vomit-looking
interior for almost five minutes without being able to detach certain
resolute parts from their walls. The bread knife had it all to do, as Maud
Martha had no intention of putting her hand in there. Another hack—another hack—STUFF! Splat in her eye. She leaped at the faucet. . . . People
could do this! People could cut a chicken open, take out the mess, with
bare hands or a bread knife, pour water in, as in a bag, pour water out,
shake the corpse by neck or by legs, free the straggles of water."[120] Scholar
Rebecca Sharpless discusses in depth how intricate and exhausting the
work of cooking could be, noting that for some live-in cooks "the workday
was de facto 24 hours."[121]

Cooking, and domestic service in general, was not only physically exhausting; it was also emotionally exhausting. Scholars who have studied
the relationships between black domestic servants and their white employers note that the relationship, in its most basic form, is predicated upon inequality—the power of the employer enhanced by the exploitability of the
worker.[122] "The personal relationship between employer and employee,"
argues sociologist Judith Rollins, "allows for a level of psychological exploitation unknown in other occupations."[123] White employers traditionally
dictated both how employees' work should be done and how employees'
demeanor should be while doing that work. Employers' demands rested
heavily on raced notions, so that they expected black women to be capable

of doing much more rigorous work than that expected of white women and to act in deferential ways that showed adherence to the rules of racial etiquette. Thus, employers policed domestic workers' labor and their personalities, often acting as disciplinarians or terminating employees for offenses as ambiguous as having a disagreeable temperament. In response to the vast, arbitrary power wielded by white employers who sought to mold black women into what white people wanted them to be—as employees and inferior beings—black women often engaged in the processes of "dissembling" or "shifting," in which they hid their true selves.[124] The persona presented to white employers was most often a polite, docile facade, but the maintenance of that persona could be taxing.

One of the most difficult demands made of black women engaged in domestic work was that they subordinate the needs of their own families to their paid employment. Cooking and caring for white women's children often prevented black women from doing those tasks for their own. Live-in black domestic workers might see their children once every week or two weeks, a fact that they lamented.[125] Black women sometimes challenged this erasure of their existence outside white people's homes. Sharpless maintains that "cooks negotiated for shorter hours, better pay, and better quantity and quality of foodstuffs to take home."[126] But the reality of needing the work limited, and sometimes negated, their ability to negotiate. Thus, black women faced a painfully ironic conflict: their paid work, in which they worked to ensure the welfare of other people's families, demanded they neglect their family work, causing many of them to agonize over their own children's welfare.

Domestic service would eventually loosen its grip on black women's lives, given legal gains and greater educational and economic opportunity. The work that "reproduced" families changed too, with increasingly more of it done outside the home in institutional settings as more women moved into remunerative work. Scholars Evelyn Nakano Glenn and Mignon Duffy point out that the least pleasant part of this labor, however, including food preparation and production, is still more likely to be done by people of color; such was the case for black women in North Louisiana who went into poultry processing plants.[127] Nakano Glenn and Duffy use a definition of food preparation that encompasses work as cooks, servers, and related occupations in restaurants, hotels, and institutional settings.

The American reliance on processed foods and the increasingly expanded work of processing plants means that poultry processing workers are engaged in a form of food preparation and production.[128] Some processing complexes, for example, contain "cook plants," in which marginalized workers prepare value-added foods such as chicken nuggets and flavored chicken wings. These facilities are adjacent to the old "kill plants," where their counterparts engage in the work of slaughtering and "dressing" of poultry—including rendering progressively more specialized cuts of meat—that used to be done in the home. Yvonne Liu and Dominique Apollon also suggest a broader view of the processes by which food is made ready and available for consumption. They look at the food system as a chain, linked from production all the way until food becomes available in retail outlets. Along each step of the way, black women and Latina workers are more disadvantaged than any other group.[129] Thus, black women who went into poultry processing not only saw the continuation of themselves in time-consuming, low-wage food preparation; they also saw the hierarchical structure characteristic of their relationship with their white employers in private homes replicated in public plants.

This is not to imply that factory work was exactly the same as domestic work or that black women did not benefit from the move out of domestic work. To be sure, factory work paid more, left black women a little less vulnerable to the whims of one individual, and, in theory, had legal protections and collective bargaining rights long absent from domestic work.[130] But poultry processing work shared many of the characteristics of their previous work: difficult, dirty labor in food production; a physically and psychologically abusive workplace; and the demand that black women subordinate the needs of their families to the demands of their employers.

"IT'S YOUR LIFE VERSUS THIS ONE"

When black women first began entering poultry processing work, they encountered circumstances in which "nearly all the foremen and supervisors were white men. Nearly all of the workers [were] black women."[131] Working with white male supervisors exacerbated the conflict black women experienced between paid and family work. Nakano Glenn argues that white employers are able to exploit minority women workers by denying their employees' womanhood—their responsibilities as mothers, wives, and caretakers. Similarly, in her pioneering study of black women's private and public work, Jacqueline Jones contends that employers tend to define black women solely in terms of their role as laborer, making few allowances for women's lives outside the workplace.[132] The experience of women throughout poultry processing plants echoes this analysis. "They didn't care if we had kids at home, a husband at home," remembered Neysha Mallory, "It's your life versus this one. It was bad."[133]

Mallory was acutely aware of how bad "this" life could be, as she knew she could have had a wholly different one. She had lived in Bernice her whole life, reared by a single mother who cared for seven children, in large part by working at the plant. Determined to escape her mother's struggles, she was serious about her studies. She graduated high school as an honor student and matriculated at a local university. But the school was not for her, or, she reflects, "Maybe I just wasn't ready." She left school with the intention of going back at some point in the future. In the interim she began working at the poultry plant and grew accustomed to the full-time work and wages: "Yeah, it was supposed to be temporary, never thought I would stay there like I did. I was just like, 'I'll stay here for a year so I get back in school,' but once you go out and you get your own place and the bills get to coming you know you have to have something to pay the bills, so I had to keep working, I just couldn't quit and go to school, I couldn't afford to do it like that."[134] She could afford it even less when she became a mother herself. Mallory was torn between her need to work to complement her husband's income and her desire to spend more time with the beloved daughter she had waited so long to have.

Echoing the "your life versus this one" comparison, workers also remembered supervisors' refusal to inform them of their children's illnesses when those supervisors were alerted by family members outside the plant. Alice Musgrove, a Mississippi poultry worker, recounted such a time: "One of my children called to tell me . . . another of my children was sick. They didn't tell me right away." When she indicated that she was leaving work, "the foreman [said] I shouldn't be so concerned about my own blood. They tell me, 'What's more important, your child or your job?'"[135] Of her days in the El Dorado plant, former processing worker Sylvia Martin remembered: "[If your] kid got sick, they really didn't wanna let you go home. My son had got hold to some seizure medicine and my supervisor let me work all day till it was time to go home [then] tell me my baby was in the emergency room and couldn't wake up. The *whole* shift."[136] Mothers are often faced with a difficult choice, according to former Union Parish teacher Lillian Gafford: "Do you want your job or do you want to be here to see about your children?"[137]

Vivian West explained that working at the plant "cut into the little time I did have with my kids; by the way I had to work, I neglected my children."[138] West made that complaint of her work in the 1970s, and it was echoed by women who worked processing poultry thirty years later.[139] When asked how she balanced her family and work lives during her two-year stint at the plant, from 2007 to 2008, Janae Earl said, "It was very hard, and I really couldn't. I didn't give my kids enough time like I should have."[140] Earl is a biological mother of three and caretaker of two more. She worked for the school district and had grown used to a schedule that mirrored her children's. Working in the poultry plant altered that schedule dramatically. Earl encountered the same dilemma many mothers in the industry do: the pay is better than most of the other low-wage, low-skilled work available, but it comes at a high cost.

Erratic work, exhausting labor, and company policies that penalize "taking a day" are some of the factors that infringe upon the multiple roles women in poultry processing fill away from work. The uncertainty of their work hours, in particular, made scheduling childcare, attending school events, or even spending time with their children hard. "Go in at 7:30," explained Sylvia Martin, "ain't no telling what time you might've come out."[141] Several women recounted their own and others' stories of having to call daycare to say they would be late to pick up their children or desperately search for rides for their children. From her time working for the school district, Earl recalled that "some kids were sick, and their parents couldn't come pick them up" and would have to try to find another way for their children to get home. "It's just hard when you work at the plant," she said.[142]

Gafford, once a teacher at Bernice's sole high school and married to a longtime processing plant employee, also saw the effect poultry processing had in the area of parental involvement:

> You could argue that working anywhere affects parental involvement, but not like this. Parents just cannot come to the school. Only when the problem is severe will they take off. And that's usually elementary. By the time they get to us [high school], I think there's even less involvement. Whether they work night or day, there's a problem. I mean, this isn't the kind of job

where you go announce "I'm taking a personal day." Please. So this is the story I get from my kids. If their parents work night shift, they are probably up when the kids are at school, trying to take care of home. By the time the kids get home, the parents have gone back to sleep or are getting ready to go to work. If their parents work day shift, a lot of the time, they are too tired to cook or clean, much less look over homework or sit down and just . . . have a conversation. Some of my kids feel like they are raising themselves.[143]

Gafford's former boss Eleanor Holloway observed some of the same difficulties during her thirty years in the Union Parish school system: "One of the things that I always noticed about the parents who were employed at the local poultry industry was the time constraint. And by that I mean . . . I never felt that they did not want to take a part in their children's school activities. I just felt that they were restrained from doing so."[144]

The problem Gafford identifies, the difficulty in taking time off, was exacerbated by Pilgrim's Pride's much-maligned point system. Under this system employees received a point or a half-point for missing work. Accumulation of ten points over the course of one year resulted in immediate termination. The company lauded the system for allowing employees freedom, the ability to miss a day with little explanation and without seeking approval. But employees decried the lack of subjectivity in the system. They received the same penalty for simply skipping a day of work as they did for caring for a sick relative. The desire for greater regard for each individual's situation may be indicative of the fact that black women realized that within the paternalistic atmosphere of the plant, such subjectivity might be benefit them. Throughout their interviews they routinely described Pilgrim's Pride as a worse employer than ConAgra, in part because of Pilgrim's Pride's stricter, less subjective treatment. Leon Fink also noted workers' disdain for companies' "brusque hire-and-fire approach," which replaced earlier "paternalism or personalistic approach[es] to the employees."[145]

Veteran workers admitted that the various companies that had owned the plant never instituted policies allowing personal or sick days, a source of discontent among employees. Nevertheless, arranging days off for family reasons used to be a much more personal process. "You'd just go to your supervisor," explained Tavia Wright, "tell him why you needed to be off, and he could let you off. Now you couldn't miss a lot of days, but they didn't try to punish you either."[146] Neysha Mallory illuminated how the point system worked against parents:

[There] wasn't a point system at first, and maybe you could go to your supervisor, and maybe you could get off. But as time went on, it's like things went downhill. . . . If we had to work over, people had to actually get off the line, ask somebody to get in their spot to call, especially if their child is at a daycare and the daycare was closing at five . . . a lot of them daycares will start penalizing you after a certain time, extra money, people couldn't afford that. . . . They could hold us there till seven thirty or something like that, and they had started doing that. And if you left, they started off [penalizing you] like a half a point . . . but after they got to see that people didn't care about the half a point, they started saying that if you leave an hour before time to get off, they were gonna give you a whole point. . . . If you get up to so many points, that's automatically a termination, ten points. And just say, you never know when you gonna have a sick child, you might wake up sick, but you done got a whole point just 'cause you got to leave one day an hour before they get off, and they done gave you a whole point like you done missed the whole day.

Some employees want the reason for their absences validated by the company, a distinction made between absences for family duties and "missing just for the sake of missing."[147] Given the fact that women are often the primary, and sometimes sole, caretakers of their families, the point system tends to work to their disadvantage in a way that it does not for men.[148]

And there were any number of family and community duties, in addition to mothering, that required missing work. Women reported that the hours and the nature of poultry processing work circumscribed time and effort allotted for nonwork activities such as socializing and maintaining relationships with significant others. Plant demands also interfered with religious practices and ceremonies, a particularly bothersome conflict. Southern black women's participation in and activism through their churches is a long-standing, well-documented tradition, and many of the women who processed poultry chaired church committees, organized functions, and offered assistance to church officers and infirm members.[149] When her hours varied widely, Wright often missed Wednesday night prayer service and was late for choir rehearsal. In her last years at the plant, her work schedule allowed her to "rush home and get ready for Wednesday night service, but I c[ould]n't cook or eat or do anything else until after nine."[150]

The mothers who work processing poultry are not the only ones who judge how it affects their parenting. Kenya Drayton, whose mother, Tavia

Wright, went to the El Dorado plant in 1985, when Drayton was eight, re-calls that it was hard for her to adapt to her mother being gone at night. Drayton missed everything from sleeping with both parents to having her mother comb her hair and cook meals. "Some things I missed, Mama couldn't help," she acknowledges, "but . . . still, it's just something."[151] And Trinity Mays simply noted of her mother, Ruth James, "I know it had to have been so hard for her."

Hard or not, being perceived as a good mother is extremely impor-tant to these women. Like most American women, black women are not immune to the widespread ideology of traditional "womanhood." It is a standard that uses, as one measure, women's efficiency at keeping house and rearing children. While feminist theories have tried to move women away from this intractable image, black women have not been so eager to abandon the ideal. White feminists, especially, have linked family work to oppression because of the historical relegation of women to the separate, inferior domestic sphere. Yet for black women family work, and especially childcare, signifies resistance to oppression because it is work whites can-not appropriate for their benefit.[152] The ability of black wives and mothers to stay at home has historically been a symbol of high status within black communities. Historians of middle-class black women maintain that these women have had to justify, within their communities and families, work-ing outside the home.[153]

The often backbreaking nature of black women's labor has impressed upon them the knowledge that working outside the home does not neces-sarily imply liberation.[154] Rather than prioritizing paid employment, many black women dream of taking care of family and home full-time. It is this work "that affirms their identity as women, as human beings showing love and care, the very gestures of humanity white supremacist ideology claimed black people were incapable of expressing."[155] For these reasons current and former employees of the poultry industry repeatedly noted that they "really didn't have to work," "didn't start till [their] kids went to school," and that their partners "didn't want [them] working that kind of job."[156]

Women in the poultry processing industry worked the same double day as millions of other women. The demands of poultry processing, coupled with the fact that women still bear the responsibility for most domestic work, mean that the double day of female poultry processors can be par-ticularly long and difficult. Nevertheless, especially given the decidedly "unfeminine" nature of their paid work, black women poultry processors take pride in their domestic work and resent the encroachment of their paid work.

While the passage of time did not ease the plant's demands on its working mothers, women with families to care for continued to seek employment in the industry. More and more of them were single mothers, going to work in the industry for the sake of their children. Bazemore, who left an abusive husband, said she ventured into the plant because she had to buy a dress for her daughter to wear in a play.[157] More often, the need was long term. As Lydia Martin described: "I got pregnant early. The daddy disowned her. I went to work to take care of my child."[158] Separated from her husband, Janae Earl related a similar story: "My husband wasn't doing what he should've been doing, so I went over there to make up the money to put in my household."[159] The dilemma of being solely responsible for their families' financial and emotional needs places these single mothers in an especially tenuous position.[160] Statistically younger, less educated, and poorer than married black women, single mothers tend to need their jobs most but are least able to tolerate the inflexibility of company policies.[161] Within the poultry industry unexpected demands for overtime and weekend work strain the sometimes limited childcare resources of single mothers. Illnesses, problems at their children's schools, and any other number of emergencies threaten the family's emotional well-being and its economic status. Despite these challenges, single mothers made up a substantial portion of the labor force in El Dorado.

The plight of single mothers is illustrated by the story of LaDonna Island. At fifteen she gave birth to her first daughter. Exactly one year later, she welcomed the arrival of her second child. She knew the dismal statistical predictions of what her life chances and those of her daughter were; when she performed well on the ACT test, her high school home economics teacher opined that it would do her no good, given her status as a teenaged mother. But Island was nothing if not smart and confident. She finished high school as an honor graduate. Within a couple of months she moved twenty miles down Highway 167 to Ruston, Louisiana, to pursue her education at Louisiana Tech University. Times were hard—she shared a cramped, problem-ridden home in a trailer park near the school. But Island persevered and earned her bachelor's degree in sociology.

Despite her attitude and determination, the reality of the dearth of economic opportunity in her rural southern environs, coupled with her own lack of mobility as a single mama of two young girls, pushed her through the doors of the plant. At the time of her first interview for this study, she had borne a third child, a son, and was expecting her third little girl. She was grateful for her job at the plant, noting the camaraderie with her coworkers in a fond tone, but did not like the ways in which her job intruded upon her other responsibilities as a mother:

> You just don't have enough time to be with your kids. Especially the weeks we work all seven days. I have to provide, but sometimes I think, what am I missing? Is it worth it? You leave before they go to school, and you get back when school is out. I used to have to wake my kids up and take them to daycare before school, and they'd have to go after. Now that my girls are older, I can leave them by themselves a little bit, but their godmother hates that. She gets them after school and some weekends. She said I was making them grown too fast, that they'd have boys over. I mean, she had a point, but I want to scream sometimes, ask somebody what I'm supposed to do. I have to work. I have to take care of my kids. But how, when I see them just a few hours before we fall asleep?[162]

Island admitted that she felt like a "full-time employee and a part-time mother."

The passing of time brought another obligation: the women who once worried that they neglected their children suddenly feared that they were neglecting their elderly parents. Tavia Wright recalled how her paid work conflicted with her perceived duty to her mother: "My problem came when Mama got sick. I was never one to miss work, not back then. I was too scared I was going to lose that job! But anyway, Mama got real sick one time, and I wanted to be off with her because she was going back and forth to the doctor. My brother was sick too, and [my stepfather] couldn't do everything. Plus, people look to a lady to help her mama. And I wanted to be with her. I went and asked my supervisor, and he flat out told me no! He said, 'We all have a job to do.' Like a job was as important as my mama! But I knew I couldn't afford to lose my job."[163]

After "crying and praying," Wright decided to go further and approach her union stewardess. The woman helped her arrange a leave of absence and avoid any penalties. But the short leave and her mother's lengthy illness meant that Wright nevertheless experienced a sense of guilt, of failing to meet her obligations as a daughter: "After a while, I had to put her in a nursing home. I had said that was something I would never do, that

I would take care of her. But I couldn't keep being off with her, and my children couldn't see about her. I couldn't work that job and see about her, but I never wanted her to go. I felt so guilty. . . . I felt real bad she had to go. I visited her all the time, and [my stepfather] would go sit with her, and my brother was there too, but it just wasn't right. But that job, that job."[164]

The stories of black women who worked processing poultry in El Dorado are full of strife, missed events, and days that seem too short. Still, there are also accounts of victory, of successfully balancing work and family despite the obstacles. While the low pay and "dirty" work involved in processing poultry did not invoke much satisfaction in black women, their other work—for family, community, and self—has been an important source of pride. It is this work, in the words of Jacqueline Jones, that constitutes black women's "labor of love." One employee echoed this sentiment: "The stuff you do for your kids, you don't mind it as much as work. I want to do everything with them, help them all I can, because they are *not* going to sling chickens for a living."[165]

Interviews of black women poultry processing workers reveal that a significant part of their self-perception is derived from who they are outside the workplace. While they described their working conditions in great detail, these women usually referred to their work in terms of the effects it had on their personal lives. Few discussed whether or not they considered themselves "successful" or "good" at their jobs; these terms were reserved, instead, for their family work, especially mothering. This is a common phenomenon. The low status of black working-class women's paid work renders it much less important, in their estimation, than their roles in their homes and communities.

This resistance to being defined by others is sometimes overt, as in the cases of Sherry Carter and Trinity Mays. Carter felt that the demands of her plant work meant that, with regards to her family, "everybody was getting short-changed." Primarily for that reason, she knew her days at the plant were numbered: "I think because I had graduated high school and I had some college by the time I got there, I knew that I could get a better job. I had enough confidence in my ability to know this was not something I was going to do long term. It was the best money I could find at the time, so I did it."[166] Like Carter, Mays worked at ConAgra shortly after giving birth to a baby boy, but, she explained, "he had to be at the babysitter's too long. And I was so tired, I couldn't play with him like I wanted. So I quit and took some time with my baby." Her situation was more flexible than that of many women in the industry. Mays had recently earned a bachelor's degree, and her husband supported their family while she searched for more suitable employment. "I needed that job, but I didn't *need* it," she explained.[167]

What of the women who did *need* these jobs? How did they manage to balance their double day in a way that helped them avoid "censure or criticism as mothers and/or as employees"?[168] The first step, according to many, was to speak up and speak out. Aarica Jones said she let her supervisors "know from jump . . . I'm all my babies got, so when they need me, I'ma be there. I didn't care if they didn't like it, I was gone see about my children." But she also admitted that she rarely missed work and established herself as a dependable, hard worker. Natalie Davis echoed the importance of speaking up to the supervisors. "You can't let people run over you in my job," she observed, or "you'll be crying every day." Speaking up often meant negotiating with supervisors over leaving early or coming in late to take care of family responsibilities. Jones recalled, for example, "If they asked me to show somebody how to do something or help get a bin down or stay a little late, I didn't mind helping them out." Davis, a single mother of two, scheduled her children's medical appointments on the same days, in the morning, so that she could report to work in the afternoon. Her supervisor did not necessarily like the situation, but "he deal[t] with it" because she was a good employee. She "gave" a little, too, by occasionally volunteering to work overtime or come in on weekends when her supervisor requested.[169]

In addition to honing their bargaining skills, women with paid and nonpaid work obligations become adept at managing time and living by strict schedules.[170] These skills are especially important for women who work nights at the plants. Sherry Carter, who worked the night shift for a short while, explains that after working all night, "you weren't able to come in and go to sleep. I'd stay up probably three or four hours." She spent that time doing housework and tending her newborn. Similarly, Tavia Wright noted, "I tried to do everything before I laid back down." That meant she started dinner, ironed clothes, cleaned the house, and tried to take care of her errands between eight in the morning and noon. Ruth James, too, said she managed to get some sleep, then she would "get up and cook and do my housekeeping and prepare for the night's work."[171] While women who work the night shift often feel they do not get enough rest, that lack is mediated by the fact of "d[oing] right by my kids."[172]

Black women also call upon the extended kin network long recognized as an important support mechanism for their families. West acknowledged the importance of her mother's help to her single-parent family. "I would have to take my children to my mother," she said. "My mother seen about my children."[173] And when West could no longer work in the plant, she helped her best friend and next door neighbor, Tavia Wright, who still worked there, by keeping her friend's daughters some nights, combing the girls' hair, and preparing meals for them. Other women remarked on the importance of friends and relatives in helping them fulfill their parenting duties: "I really didn't have no problems working because Mama was here with [my son]"; "Mostly my aunt . . . would tend to them for me."[174] Sisters Lydia and Sylvia Martin remembered their now deceased father with a smile. "Daddy was the baby sitter" was Lydia's simple remark. "Thank God my daddy was living for a little while," said Sylvia, "'cause family took care of my kids."[175]

In prioritizing their family work over the demands of poultry processing, black women contest the perceptions of employers who view paid work as the most important part of these women's identities. Eleanor Holloway lauds the efforts of mothers who worked in the industry who did their best to lessen the effects of what she calls "time restraints": "I did . . . on occasion a couple times say to a parent it doesn't make any difference whether you have your boots on and the hairnets and all the paraphernalia you wear to your job, just come on, because your child wants you there. And sometimes they would come in their work clothing, and that was perfectly okay, the important thing was not the clothing but the fact that they were there with their child. . . . Outwardly the parents would say, would talk about their struggles. But from being an outsider, from an outside perspective, you could never really see the difference in their struggles because their children came dressed like everybody else's kids, and that might have been due to uniforms, but they had neat, clean uniforms."[176]

And although Kenya Drayton noted the hardships she and her family faced, she also bore witness to how hard her mother worked to ease them and to prioritize her family work: "As far as cooking and cleaning, she still did most of that. Daddy tried, but we got tired of eating wieners and pork and beans and chicken that was burned on the outside and red by the bone. Mama started cooking before she lay down. We ate a lot of stuff out of the Crock-Pot and a lot of stuff that was warmed up, but that was okay. And you know, we belonged to everything . . . band, FHA [Future Homemakers of America], FBLA [Future Business Leaders of America], the church choir, Delta Teen Lift. I can't remember her missing one thing. She'd take her vacation around the time we had our state meetings and stuff, and she would go. Mama came to everything. I just don't know how she did it. But I could thank her every day for it now. I didn't appreciate it then, but I could thank her now."[177] This insistence on self-definition, these acts of caring as resistance, are perhaps the most profound statements Drayton's mother and women like her can make against the racism and sexism they face in the plant.

CHAPTER 3

"I LEARNED THIS— YOU AIN'T NOBODY!"

When Sherry Carter walked into the El Dorado plant to begin work in 1977, she was taken aback by the way she was addressed by her white supervisors: "I wasn't accustomed to being given orders in that manner." It was a difficult adjustment for her. As a black Louisiana native, she was familiar with the racial mores of her southern home, but the Jim Crow–era segregation of her youth, even though it was created out of the worst impulses and beliefs, had allowed her parents to protect her from some of the daily viciousness of racism. "The Bernice that we grew up in was better than the one you grew up in," she opined, recalling the close-knit relationship "between the teachers and the parents and the community" that had nurtured her and her cohorts. She grew up in a "black world," where she learned to be proud of the hard work and sacrifices of her father, a World War II veteran and schoolteacher, and her mother, who ran her own business. Despite the hostility of the outside world, they taught her that she had an inherent value and the potential to do anything. But her worth as a human being, as someone deserving of respect, seemed to be lost on her supervisors. "Your value was, 'you show up on time and get on the line!'" she said. "I didn't always feel the employees were respected. . . . Some of the supervisors didn't care how they talked to you. I mean, it could get almost violently nasty."[1]

That Carter chose the description "violently nasty" is fitting. Poultry processing is, by its very nature, violent work. Industry workers capture, stun, slaughter, and quickly dismember birds in a grisly, dirty process. The end result, pieces of various chickens wrapped into neat little packages, somewhat obscures the brutal reality of this transformation. What also remains largely unseen is another attempted transformation: the process by which poultry processing companies come to regard their employees as little more than pieces of a large processing machine. Discounting their roles as family and community members is not the only means by which management denies the humanity of poultry processing workers. Plant employees described the systemic disregard for their emotional and physical health, the insistence that they be little more than machines. "You weren't a person," contended Kenya Drayton. "You didn't matter."[2]

In their drive for increased productivity and profit, poultry processing firms have over the years engaged in techniques designed to render their employees infinitely complacent and controllable.[3] These largely southern industries have taken the racial, gender, and power dynamics of Old South plantations and brought them into New South factories. The attempted reduction of people into something less than human, in the words of poultry workers, justifies employees' exposure to physically debilitating conditions such as widely variant temperatures, inhumane line speeds, and toxic chemicals and to emotionally debilitating circumstances, including a workplace in which racism and sexism are central features in the organization of work and in the plant's very structure. Repeated exposure to such environments creates not only temporary physical discomfort for these workers but can cause chronic, irreversible ailments.[4] Poultry workers described a number of practices used in the process of dehumanizing them, including management's pattern of maintaining a climate of fear at the plant, its regular reminders to workers that they are "disposable," and its efforts to disrupt community building and attempts at collective action, particularly via unionization.

"OUR GUIDING PRINCIPLE—THE GOLDEN RULE"

Bo Pilgrim, cofounder of the country's largest poultry producer, Pilgrim's Corporation (formerly Pilgrim's Pride), smiles from the cover of his 2005 book, *One Pilgrim's Progress*. The book shares Pilgrim's vision for "how to build a world class company." The guiding principle of Pilgrim's Pride, according to the book is: "However you want people to treat you, so treat them."[5] Similarly, a representative of another poultry company, House of Raeford, proclaimed that the company "would never allow anyone to mistreat" its employees.[6] Given the experiences of workers inside poultry plants, this principle has not been effectively communicated—unless, of course, Bo Pilgrim wants to be intimidated, degraded, and pushed to his physical and emotional limits, which is what workers describe.

The process by which a rigidly gendered and raced hierarchy is maintained uses a number of techniques. One of them is the instillation of fear and the maintenance of an atmosphere of intimidation in efforts to suppress any expression of worker discontent and foster worker complacency. Almost a quarter-century ago Donna Bazemore expressed the opinion that "there is so much fear" at poultry processing plants.[7] Former employee Robert Ruth remembered that women would "stand there and cry" after encounters with their supervisors.[8] For many workers little changed since Bazemore and Ruth gave their descriptions. Intimidation is reinforced via the maintenance of a racial and gender hierarchy in the plant and the constant, disdainful yelling of supervisors. The legacy of racial etiquette, of black passivity in the face of white authority, has not completely disappeared from the rural southern areas in which most poultry processing plants are located. White male supervisors have been able to exploit and perpetuate this tradition and the related fear it provokes. "When I started at J-M, the women, especially the older women who had been saying 'Yes, sir' and 'No, Sir' to white men all their lives, they was scared. They wouldn't do nothing unless that white man said okay," explained Vivian West.[9] Coworkers cautioned Gloria Jordan in Mississippi to "be careful when you talk to that white man, or you'll be burned out tonight!"[10] Of her attempts to address workplace issues in North Carolina, Bazemore observed, "It was real intimidating to go to a bunch of white men and say, 'I've got this problem and your job caused it.'"[11]

The actions of plant owners and supervisors reinforced the power disparity between themselves and line workers. The condescension with which white employers treated black workers often had overtly paternalistic tones, with plant owners lauding workers' gratitude and loyalty. Joe Sanderson, of the poultry company Sanderson Farms, called black plant workers "my people," a "plantation phrase," according to Gloria Jordan. Many of the black workers at Sanderson Farms, steeped in an old tradition that required they acknowledge their dependence on the kindness of their white "superiors," expressed loyalty to Sanderson, despite abysmal work conditions.[12] Poultry companies such as Tyson also played up their "generosity" to employees, mandating that employees' gratefulness be shown via their refusal to join a union.[13] Bo Pilgrim, in a section of his book in which he describes the "hallmarks of a winning" employee, told the story of "Bill": "You can't buy or train loyalty and faithfulness. It's not a matter of intelligence or education. We have a Partner that everyone knows . . . [named] Bill and he is not a highly educated man. I am not sure he can read. But this man is a dedicated worker. . . . He is a faithful and loyal employee. I consider him highly valuable." Never does Pilgrim acknowledge that Bill's lack of education, and possibly illiteracy, significantly reduced his economic options, a factor that may have played a much bigger role in Bill's "loyalty and faithfulness" than Pilgrim's beneficence.

In the relationship between supervisors and line workers, the maintenance of a dominant-subordinate relationship does not necessarily have the facade of benevolence that frames owners' actions. Supervisors' paternalism is displayed in a much more hostile, disciplinarian stance, as supervisors "treat [workers] like children or step-children."[14] Of her brief time as an employee and her subsequent visit to a processing plant, Lillian Gafford said she heard "verbal abuse . . . I wouldn't wish on anyone."[15] Former employee Kenya Drayton agreed, recalling that supervisors made some employees "ill at ease" and that "the way some supervisors talked to people on the line was worse than the way you would give a command to a dog."[16] Angela Stuesse found that "Hispanic and Black workers point to mistreatment at the hands of their immediate supervisors as one of the most egregious problems they face at work."[17] Most of the former poultry workers interviewed for this study remembered this glaring lack of respect from some, though not all, of their supervisors. In 2003 a number of black employees from the El Dorado plant brought a class action suit against ConAgra and Pilgrim's Pride. One of the allegations was that they had been "addressed with profanity, yelling, and other demeaning communication."[18] Supervisors, it seemed, had not been made aware of Bo Pilgrim's assertion that he did not "want anybody in my company to be afraid of management."[19]

Even when black men did join the ranks of supervisors, according to Bazemore, "they get the whipping style, too. They want to keep those positions because it makes their life a little easier." In the same vein Bella

Dawes found black supervisors harder to work with because "they were so glad to get a title till it's something to them." LeeAnn Johnson said of the black male supervisors she encountered, "When black men think they have more seniority, they start thinking they're better than . . . our kind, the black kind." When asked why she thought this may be so, her theory paralleled Dawes's: "They were so happy to be head of something."[20] In her study of Mississippi poultry plants, Angela Stuesse observed that Latino workers also felt that black supervisors were particularly harsh.[21] Through the lens of the plantation analogy, promoting black men to supervisory positions still benefits the white owners, as it may be viewed in light of slavery-era practices in which the planter class fostered "divisive hierarchies" that "promoted the identification [of 'elite' African Americans] with their masters' interests."[22]

The comparison to plantation life and the existence of the race and gender hierarchy is strengthened by yet another issue in poultry plants: the sexual harassment and exploitation of black women by their primarily white male supervisors.[23] Ten percent of workers surveyed on the Delmarva Peninsula indicated, for example, that their supervisors had requested sexual favors.[24] In the case of El Dorado, Tavia Wright remembered a time when the problem seemed much worse: "There was a time when supervisors had their way of trying to get up next to the ladies. They act like they're playing, they say, 'Ooh, you look . . .' this way or that, just to get their way with the women. They would say things out of place, and the ladies didn't like it. But now they have this thing where if anybody says anything you don't like, touches you in a way you don't want to be touched—it should've been that way all the time—they can be dismissed from the plant. But there was a time when women went along with it because they were afraid because the supervisor was in control."[25]

The prevalence of sexual harassment may create an environment in which the objectification and harassment of women is seen as acceptable. LeeAnn Johnson, who worked in the industry for two years, recalled that it was not just supervisors who engaged in harassing behaviors: "Men patt[ed] on women's behinds and grabb[ed] at them. I was harassed; a man was telling me what he was going to do to me and all this mess. Some of the men was rubbing me on my butt. It made me feel uncomfortable."[26] Trinity Mays spoke of the plant atmosphere more succinctly: "The looks, the touches, that talk. You can't turn [move] for somebody bothering you."[27] Bazemore claimed that supervisors told female employees to wear tight, revealing clothing to distract visiting poultry inspectors "so [they] won't be stopping the line."[28] And employees of a Sanderson farm plant in Mississippi noted that "many of the mainly white male supervisors and foremen make sexual advances . . . fostering loyalty to management and attempts to cater to the supervisors. . . . Foremen would put their arms around them, caress them, or play up to them sexually as a way of countering resentment of discipline or persuading workers to accept orders. [Employee Gloria Jordan said,] 'They hug and pet on them . . . and then they forget the grievance.'"[29] Thus, supervisors also reap nonsexual benefits from sexual harassment.

It is no wonder, then, that many of the plant's former employees describe the atmosphere in the plant as hostile, particularly in terms of race. Although the plant had some people of color as supervisors and line coordinators, workers there nevertheless felt that the few white employees had an unfair advantage. The 2003 class action suit described the way in which work in the plant was "raced":

(17.) The total work force of the plant has consisted of more than 1000 persons, approximately 80 percent of whom have been African American persons.

(18.) The top level of management in the plant has included a plant manager. No black person has served at this level of management.

(19.) The plant has had an administrative office consisting of approximately 10 to 15 employees. Through the years only one African American person has worked in the administrative office.

(20.) The plant has had . . . numerous lower level supervisors. . . . The racial make-up of these supervisors has been majority white.[30]

"[Whites] had a better chance than we did," observed Tavia Wright. "They can come off the street, the blacks train them, and then [when whites are promoted] they pressure us to forget that."[31] Several employees agreed with her. Vivian West claimed that "they would allow the black to train the white and then they would get a white the job and move you to another position." "I was always the one," noted Bella Dawes, "who had to teach the supervisors who was over me!" Donna Bazemore described her mother's experiences in a North Carolina Perdue plant: "People like my mother have been working in the plant for 15, 20 years. And they bring in kids fresh out of college or high school, white kids, and they make these young white men the foremen who tell *her* what to do. And here she's been in that plant and knows everything a chicken ever had to offer you." When asked to remember an event that stood out from her tenure in the industry, negative or positive, LaDonna Island chose "the way the Supervisors and Plant managers were selected. The company would often hire Caucasian men and women, as opposed to offering these or better-paid positions to an African American individual that has been with the company for several years. The person getting hired would have no agricultural background and would have to be trained by the production workers on 'how to' perform the job."[32]

Such experiences left black workers hesitant to trust whites, afraid of eventual betrayal via the elevation of white people at their expense. Of his white supervisor DeShaun Lowe said: "I have had some ups and downs with him. Right now, we are in the up mode, but I don't know how long that's gon' last. Not being racist, but I just don't trust white. And his color is not gon' change. Right now he might be grinning in my face, but the next minute he may be stabbing me in the back."[33]

There are physical manifestations of a racially hostile atmosphere other than the skewed number of white people in supervisory positions. A former employee remembered seeing black dolls hanging from nooses in the plant. Another testified that he was invited to be the prey on a Ku Klux Klan hunting trip.[34] Many describe the racist graffiti that dotted the plants inner walls.[35] Plant workers also recounted stories of racial epithet–laced tirades. Many of them returned to the issue of the way supervisors talk to them, even when no overtly racist language is used. "It's a question of human dignity," Jordan contended. "They order you in a loud tone of voice."[36] It is not just the tone, though that "*is* hard to deal with" when you are not used to "people . . . talk[ing] to you any kind of way," said Drayton. It is also the content of the messages. "[Supervisors tell you,] 'If you leave this job today, I'll have somebody in here within thirty minutes.' And they could have somebody. They had people ready to get on the line, people needing jobs ready to get there," Drayton continued.[37] This "fear of job loss in an area where there is an extreme lack of viable employment" is a major component of the power imbalance inside the plants.[38] In an affidavit submitted to Congress, former industry worker

Marion White explained: "Since many single mothers like myself can't support our families on the minimum wage jobs that are the only other choice, and we don't want to go on welfare, we do what we're told. That's the rule. You can't defend yourself."[39]

When Bazemore began reaching out to workers through her work with the Center for Women's Economic Alternatives, individuals would request that she "tell my story, but not use my name." "They don't want to lose that job," she said.[40] The *Charlotte Observer* journalists who wrote "The Cruelest Cuts" series about the poultry processing industry in North and South Carolina found the same sentiment. It is one that management exploited, according to Neysha Mallory: "[Management] knew a lot of them older people, they had been there for a long time . . . they looked at them like they can't go nowhere, they looked at it like they didn't have another resort, another way out . . . they're gonna stay here and they're gonna put up with it, so, yeah, we gonna do them like that."[41]

Kenya Drayton also spoke specifically about the ways management exploits employees' fear of losing their job: "In South Arkansas and North Louisiana, there aren't many places that African American females can work and make a decent living trying to raise a family. . . . Where else were they going to work? . . . They had to go to ConAgra. I feel like they know we had to work, that's the number one reason they exploit us. Hispanics too. There aren't enough job opportunities for African American females and Hispanics . . . we're easy to exploit because we need work."[42] For a number of the Latino workers whom Drayton mentioned, the situation is even more tenuous because many of them are undocumented. "They are compulsively compliant," writes journalist Rick Thames, "ever-conscious that one complaint could lead to their firing or arrest or deportation."[43] It is a complacency "learned," in the words of Drayton, by some of their African American counterparts: "You'd just have to go in there and learn, 'Well, I need my job. I have to deal with that.'"[44]

Thus, poultry processing workers learn that they are a "disposable workforce." Maryland's Public Justice Center (MPJC) defines this category as meaning "that if workers become sick, disabled, or elderly, management 'disposes' of them."[45] To the MPJC's definition, workers add that companies dispose of them if they challenge the conditions in which they work. Rev. Jim Lewis, an Episcopal priest and poultry worker advocate, gives this disposable workforce a more human face: "If someone is hurt along this poultry production line, new hands are needed to step in and pick up the slack. Workers are expendable in this process. When injured workers are no longer capable of working, they are disposed of and replaced by new workers and a new work force, largely made up of immigrants."[46] Because the industry has a historically high turnover rate, as much as 100 percent in some plants, the company is not bothered by having to replace workers. Poultry processors, in the words of Rev. Jesse Jackson, have long "hired in, broken down, used up, and thrown out" their workers.[47]

"I don't know how people work there years and years and years because it is an experience," Drayton observed. Interviews with employees revealed that one of things they do to improve the "experience" is to try to build community.[48] Some of them reported initial success. "We had the best time at ConAgra," described Margie Young of her early days in the plant in the late 1970s and early 1980s. Deena Shine, who began around the same time, echoed her opinion: "When I first went there to the plant, it was nice. We had groups that worked together, we had dinners, like certain holidays they would allow . . . so many of us to get off the line and fix the dinners . . . to do the tables or whatever we had to do to make it an enjoyable day . . . you know, me and certain ladies, and I was one. . . . I wanted to make sure we got the decorations, even if I had to take whatever from home to make sure there was . . . if it was a baby or something coming we might would do them a shower, you know, different stuff enjoyable 'cause we all worked close and saw about each other and stuff, so it basically was okay." Neysha Mallory noted a similar ethos: "If you done been there for a minute, then you pretty much done got you your group that's on your side, and y'all gonna work together as a team. . . . Ya'all laughing and talking and mak[ing] the day go by. Girl, it had got . . . where you . . . got people that can sing, and we have church on the line."[49]

Black women in the El Dorado plant continued a long history of black female factory workers singing together. Jacqueline Jones recounted how black women in tobacco factories a century earlier "sang together. In this way they established a rhythm to make the repetitive tasks more bearable." Their singing also represented an attempt to "transcend" the unpleasant conditions in which they worked.[50] Tavia Wright remembered how the events that Shine and Mallory described sometimes overlapped: "We would have these little lunches. Everybody would bring . . . potluck, and we would put it together. Then we would pray and sing."

Wright also recalled an informal mentoring system in which older employees would try to teach new employees about the line, help them set a pace to keep up with the work, and teach them "techniques . . . to make the work easier." One of those techniques was attempting to slow the line. If the pace was too grueling, older workers instructed those new to the plant simply to "let the meat fall. Let it hit the floor. They'll slow down."[51] Drayton was grateful for the assistance of longtime employee "Monica": "There was this one woman, Monica, who'd be singing and working, singing and working. She was fast, and she stayed in a good mood. She'd look over and see some of our bins were getting too full, and she'd say, 'Hold on, baby. I'll be over there in a minute to help you.'"[52]

There was genuine love there, Wright believed: "Every morning, every lady would hug each other and say good morning. Try to make people feel like they were somebody. . . . We showed love toward one another. We learned to be a family."[53] But the push to suppress human expression meant that management eventually tried to disrupt these examples of community building. "Things started tightening up," said Deena Shine, of her last decade in the plant. "Everything was out of whack." Supervisors forbade the celebrations she and her coworkers enjoyed on their breaks. Of their mini–church services Mallory noted: "They had got where they didn't even want that to take place. They wanted you to be quiet." Mallory also observed the effects of the erosion of the system of building bridges between older and newer employees: "Older workers gone work together . . . they just come in there, and they be to themselves."[54]

Plant management would also test and try to break that sense of family, the human bonds, that develops among poultry processing workers. According to employees, El Dorado plant managers expected workers to keep laboring while coworkers suffered and even died. "If you do stop," said Wright, "they keep on you about getting back."[55] West recounted a particularly disturbing incident: "This lady got sick on the line. She was working where the inspectors work. She was calling for someone to come help her, but nobody came to help her. And the lady sat up there and slumped over. She was sitting on a stool; they pulled her back. A lady supervisor had walked up to her, and the lady fell back in her arms, and she died in her arms. She died on the line. They pulled her back from the line sitting on the stool, and another person walked up in her position. They never stopped the line. They kept on running the line, and this lady was dead. They did get her to the office. They took her by ambulance. But by the time she got to the hospital . . . she was already dead before they left the plant. They didn't even pay that no attention."[56]

It is not just that they had to watch coworkers suffer and die; it is that they had to do it without acting to help or save the very people they had come to care about. In all the stories recorded for this study, that fact is the one that workers lament most. The stories abound, with the common thread the workers' horror that *the line never stops.* Sylvia and Lydia Martin shared some of these stories:

> I saw a man fall down, had a heart attack on the line. Fall down dead. They wouldn't stop the line. They kept the line moving. Told them they *better not* cut the line off. The chickens just falling all over the man, the man lying on the floor dead. Laying on the floor in a puddle of bloody water, chickens everywhere. Saddest thing I've seen aside from my injuries. They opened the back door and rolled him out like a pile of trash. . . . Everybody better keep on working or you're going to personnel. You *better* keep on working.
>
> This man was up on the roof working. The leak was a little bit further over so they kept hollering for him to move over. He fell through. Come down on the inside of the plant. Everybody just keep working.[57]

Bella Dawes recalled her frustration at the slow response time to a coworker's distress and how she had to hide her own efforts to help the woman: "You gotta sit there and look at them die. Yep, now that's the truth. There was this lady that fell out, and she was under this skinner, and this water was draining in her nose. . . . I knew that I wasn't allowed to move the woman, and I took my foot, and I kind of pushed her, and I kept looking around to see if anyone was watching me. I kept pushing her until I got her head from under the skinner."[58]

Tavia Wright saw a coworker collapse after being caught up in a machine. "They never stopped the line," she said. "They would rush you to keep on working even though a person was in need." She also recounted the story of a woman who collapsed and was "laid on the wet catwalk," where people stepped "over her" because they had to continue working. Again, she noted, "they never did stop the line." Neysha Mallory's disgust for the devaluing of human life came through clearly in her description of a similar event: "One day a man fell off the line, said he had asked . . . to go to the nurse 'cause he was feeling funny. That man died right there in Pilgrim's Pride on the floor in front of cone line 6. They had the ambulance to come in 'cause that man did not have a pulse, and when they took him out of there . . . do you know they made them lines keep running? This man laid out, didn't even have a pulse. But they had wanted us to go back to work when they know they should have took all them birds off that line and waited till the ambulance came in there and removed that man."

In somber, striking detail, Sylvia Martin recalled how no amount of danger to employees, in her experience, had ever stopped the line for long: "I done seen the place blow up. Keep on working. The whole building shook. And we did not stop working that day. They cleaned up out back. We kept working. By-product blew up. . . . Keep working. We have had ammonia leaks . . . so bad where you can't even hardly get through the front door. . . . Keep working."[59] According to DeLores Biles, if coworkers did react by trying to shut down a line in response to an injury, supervisors tried to determine who did it, confronted the "guilty" parties, asking, "Who gave you permission to shut it down?" and had the discretion to issue disciplinary warnings.[60]

After repeated exposure to yelling, to condescension, to racism, to sexism, to the devaluing of their work and their lives, plant workers naturally conclude what these tactics are meant to teach them: "They don't think you are human," explained Drayton. "They don't," surmised West, "expect the human body to break down." Rita Eason, a North Carolina worker, realized that it amounts to the attempted reduction of living, breathing people into "machine[s], plugged in, running on electricity." Dawes remembered the moment she "learned" this reality: "You ain't nobody. You just a machine getting done what they want done." In testimony written for Congress, Bazemore acknowledged that this dehumanization is often effective: "You do what you're told. There's no such thing as thinking. After a while, you get out of the habit."[61] Denying workers' humanity allowed plant management to push workers to their physical and emotional limits and to be "more interested in the meat" than in the people who process it, according to Wright.[62] Perhaps she is right. After all, the one thing that will stop the line immediately is concern over the safety and quality of the chicken. "Indeed, the industry's obsession with building a better bird," noted one journalist, "stands in sharp contradiction to its blatant disregard for its employees."[63]

When told of Bo Pilgrim's repeated invocation of his Christian faith and his claim that the guiding principle of the company is the golden rule,

Wright expressed skepticism: "They said we have an employer [Pilgrim] with a spiritual background. My spirituality doesn't go that way. You'll be concerned about other people if you're rooted in the Lord."

The emphasis on controlling and repressing the heavily black workforce might follow the tradition of old southern mores, but it is also rooted in a very modern concern: producing as much chicken as possible. Steadily increasing the line speeds, extending hours, and ignoring workers' physical and emotional limits allow poultry companies to turn out more and more "product." To that end, according to those who have labored in the poultry processing plants, on top of the insistence that they work at a breakneck pace, plant management also tried to reclaim the bit of time allotted for workers' personal use.[64] Poultry workers across the South and over time have complained that companies' policies leave little time for an actual break. In Laurel, Mississippi, Pressie Clayton complained in the 1970s that her company shaved the ten minute breaks down to "4 or 5 minutes . . . once a day." Rigid supervision means that even the ability to go to the bathroom is curtailed. At Clayton's Sanderson Farms plant, management allowed "three toilet breaks a week outside of [the already truncated] normal breaks."[65] Another poultry worker commenting in 1989 remembered that "if you had to go the bathroom more than once in two or three hours, they would threaten to write you up."[66] In the 1990s Delmarva workers revealed that some of them alternately urinated on the line or refused to drink, hoping to avoid the need to use the bathroom, as did Guatemalan workers in North Carolina.[67]

Drayton described her frustrating experiences in the El Dorado plant in the early 2000s: "It was like standing on your feet for 4 hours at a time, and you had to try to hold . . . you couldn't just go to the bathroom. If you had to go to the bathroom, you had to wait for somebody to come relieve you off the line. So there you were, standing on your feet up high working in a bin, and you're cold, and you might have to use the bathroom, but you had to stand there until somebody could get to you and let you go to the restroom."[68] Mallory's account supports Drayton's: "If I wanted a break off the line to go to the bathroom, I just couldn't get down and go to the bathroom—I had to work till somebody came and relieved me. . . . If everybody busy, you know you constantly having to wait and constantly having to call your lead person to tell them, 'Look, I have to go to the bathroom!' That's just how it was."[69]

Other El Dorado employees described the problem quite vividly as well. They received ten minutes for non-lunch breaks. If they needed to use the bathroom during that time, they had to strip out of all their work gear and get in line. The line was the result of hundreds of workers going on break at once but only two bathrooms with approximately seventeen stalls each being available. If they were fortunate enough to use the bathroom, they had to then go back to the hallway, get back into gear, and be back on the line "by the time the first chickens come by."[70] The danger of this rushed pace was realized in 1990, according to Vivian West: "We were running one day to get back on the line, and this lady fell. And nobody could stop to pick her up because they were trying to get on the line to keep from getting written up. So, they stepped on her, over her, and she was trampled by us trying to get on the line. I was down there packing, running the party wing machine. I looked through the line, and she was laying on the thing, and they were stepping on her, over her. . . . When they got her to the hospital, she'd messed up a disc in her back. So, she never was able to come back to work. She tried, but she couldn't work. She left there with a *disability* because of that incident."[71]

The limitations and infringement on break time is symbolic of the industry's effort to control labor strictly. The pressure to keep production and, consequently, line speeds high "creates an environment in which control over workers' time and movement is central to time and production."[72] Or as one former supervisor explained, "When someone goes to the bathroom at a time when the line isn't shut down . . . it's a loss for the company."[73]

"WE HAVE MET STRONG RESISTANCE"

The attempts to render poultry processing workers controllable and vulnerable are not just bolstered by sentiment inside the plants. Located in the South, poultry processing companies have been able to capitalize on strong regional antiunion sentiment to obstruct and disrupt workers' attempts to join together and press for better conditions. The climate, both geographical and political, has been a boon to poultry companies. According to historian David Brody, "Southern workers were exceedingly hard to organize," the result of "employer and community resistance, small towns, race antagonisms, and violence."[74] The poultry industry fits into broader regional patterns of worker-management relations.

But why, given the fact that they are the lowest-paid workers in food processing and despite numerous efforts by unions, have poultry processing workers remained largely unorganized? The answer lies in at least four circumstances. First, in the broadest sense poultry processors have benefited from their location. The poultry processing industry operates largely in the South, a region historically unfriendly to unions. From the time the industry was getting established there, southern politicians worked to ensure that the companies that came south found the docile and unorganized workers promised to them. Second, poultry processing expanded during a time of resurging legal and sentimental hostility toward unionization. The 1947 Taft-Hartley Act, especially, further bureaucratized labor unions, silenced truly militant unionists, and imposed an ideology of neutrality on the National Labor Relations Board (NLRB), a body that initially acted in favor of labor. Unions are still suffering the legacy of that hostility.

Third, narrowing the view from the regional and national politics allows one to see how poultry processors capitalized on antiunion sentiment by perfecting techniques to impede organizing by workers. They frequently used unfair labor practices and purposefully relied on a vulnerable workforce. While such techniques are not unique to the industry, they are particularly effective given the industry's high turnover rate (which makes it hard to sustain union certification) and low wages.

Finally, unions have been unable to maintain relationships with the poor people of color who have historically worked processing poultry. The AMBW has repeatedly pushed to organize these workers, but few unions have been equipped to battle racism within the organization and in society in general effectively. The AMBW was affiliated with the American Federation of Labor (AFL), long the domain of skilled, white male workers, which rarely acted on behalf of low- and unskilled workers, especially in the South. The methods it used to organize skilled white men would not serve it well in organizing an industry dominated first by low-skilled black women, then by Latino immigrants. Black workers often understood unions as vehicles for civil rights agitation and first-class citizenship, but union officials accepted and even joined the denunciation of the leftist "labor radicals" who appealed to black workers.

Historian Michael Honey contended that when unions "purged . . . leaders most interested in organizing such workers, it cut off promising possibilities for union expansion and left the . . . working class prey to increasing stratification by race, gender, and occupational status."[75] This feeling of abandonment occurred in the El Dorado plant among the women who contributed their stories to this book. In its final years of operation, workers there felt the union no longer represented them. In other words, for them antiunion sentiment and business unionism had triumphed, and the shortcomings of union tactics in reaching workers of color were left largely unaddressed.

Historians have proposed a number of reasons for the South's reputation as virulently antiunion.[76] The problems of religious fundamentalism and single-party politics contributed to the failures of unionism in the South. The uniquely southern heritage of elite social control, the rigid divisions of race and class, and the hard lessons poor southerners had learned from poverty and domination thwarted unionization attempts. The uncontested power of the planter elite and later of business owners helped create an atmosphere of fear that engulfed workers and hindered their attempts to organize.[77] Perhaps no event embodies all these factors and is as emblematic of southern intransigence toward labor unions in the post–World War II period as the spectacular failure of "Operation Dixie," a drive by the Congress of Industrial Organizations (CIO). The CIO undertook a "Holy Crusade" in 1946 to organize recalcitrant southern industries. The federation sought to circumvent southerners' accusations of "radicalism" by enlisting southern organizers, denouncing communism, and prohibiting interracial union meetings.[78] Operation Dixie was nevertheless met almost immediately with vitriolic attacks from southern elites. Likened to a Communist invasion and a second Reconstruction, CIO organizers went to work with public opinion already against them. Managerial obduracy, racism, and paternalism made organizing textiles and woodworking (the South's largest industries) impossible. Religious leaders cast union membership as antithetical to Protestant Christianity, virtually forcing their congregants to choose between being a "Christian or a CIO man," a choice that had a "disastrous effect" on the CIO's recruiting efforts.[79]

The fate of Operation Dixie served as an omen for the fate of labor organizing in the postwar era. Southern antilabor sentiment became codified in measures such as the Taft-Hartley Act and right-to-work laws. The Taft-Hartley Act prohibited sympathy strikes and secondary boycotts and strengthened the influence of the National Labor Relations Board. Taft-

Hartley changed the course of unionism by changing the function of the NLRB. Initially charged to protect the right to organize, the NLRB now had to safeguard the rights of employers as well. Thus, the board, which had encouraged the spread of unionism, was now to play the role of "impartial referee."[80] Employers, on the other hand, no longer had to remain neutral. Taft-Hartley recognized management's right to "free speech" against unions and unionization, speech that by its very nature was imbued with the threat of job loss.[81] In an effort to diminish organized labor's influence, the act gave employers greater leeway in dissuading union membership and made it illegal for unions to contribute to political campaigns. The act also allowed states to draft so-called right-to-work laws that encouraged and protected open shops and discouraged union membership. Southern states that did not already have such laws in place quickly hurried to do so.[82]

By 1947 both Georgia and Arkansas, soon to be leaders in the production of processed poultry, had right-to-work laws in place that further hampered union organizing. Although scholars continue to debate whether or not right-to-work laws have significant effect on union membership, union efforts to organize seem to decline substantially in the wake of the passage of such laws.[83] Right-to-work laws also have a psychological effect. Workers may be hesitant to join a union and face harassment and job loss in right-to-work states, where unions are perceived as less powerful.[84] As Sanderson Farms poultry worker Verlina Forthner explained of her decision to break a strike and go back on the line, "I think unions are okay, but I don't see any sense in having a union in Mississippi with the right-to-work law."[85] Even researchers who assert that such laws have little actual effect on membership acknowledge that the laws send a very real symbolic message to companies too. According to economists David Ellwood and Glenn Fine, "A state's adoption of such a law might be viewed by firms as a signal that future wage levels in that state will be lower than they would otherwise be."[86] Southern boosters in the mid-twentieth century quickly framed right-to-work laws as another incentive to move industry south.[87]

Unions have not just been hampered from the outside, however. Labor organizations have been unable fully to overcome wariness on the part of racial-ethnic workers who were excluded from early visions of unionism and thus learned to distrust unions.[88] Jacqueline Jones observed that "the vast majority of southern black women had no role to play in trade unions dominated by white men." By the 1960s the poultry processing industry had begun the shift from white workers to a workforce that would be largely black and female. These women existed at the intersection of three categories of workers that historically had been excluded by unions: they were black, female, and unskilled. For such women membership in organizations that had historically cast people of color, immigrants, and women as enemies of the working-class white man offered little promise of improving work conditions and compensation.[89]

Defeatist attitudes and "pragmatism" have also hampered unionization in poultry processing. Union organizers often expressed frustration, via word and lack of deed, at the difficulties of organizing poultry processing workers, particularly given management's hostility and workers' distrust. The Amalgamated Meatcutters and Butcher Workmen (AMBW) opened its ranks to poultry workers in 1936, but the International did not begin a strong organizing effort until the 1940s. A 1943 conference delineated the poor circumstances in which poultry workers labored.[90] Fourteen years later the AMBW's poultry department was still trying to bring the physical environment up to the level of the Fair Labor Standards Act, noting that the conditions poultry processing workers faced were far below the standards for similar work in other industries.[91] Improving the economic situation would be just as difficult; the union's poultry department director, Shirley Barker, wrote of the Swift Company in particular: "We have met strong resistance on the guaranteed week, on a strengthened seniority clause, on the changed vacation clause; even on the 8-hour day. . . . When we came to talk about money, most of the plant managers almost refused to discuss the subject."[92] Resistance to such measures was common on the part of meat processors. As a result, Barker suggested that some "drastic steps" would have to be taken.

To date, drastic measures have rarely been taken. Instead, for the sake of pragmatism, unions often have not intervened on behalf of poultry processing workers or have done so only halfheartedly. Lawrence and Braden described that despite union efforts, in poultry processing "wages remained low and conditions poor. Sometimes, out of embarrassment at their inability or unwillingness to fight for these members, the unions would suspend their constitutions to permit lower dues for poultry workers."[93] In Center, Texas, in the mid-1950s, the AMBW refused to call a strike despite the support of most employees of the town's two poultry processing plants, Eastex Company and Denison Poultry. Instead, the union called for a national boycott of the companies' products. A strike would be futile, the AMBW argued, given the antiunion sentiment in eastern Texas and the ready supply of unskilled replacement labor. In April 1954 union members at both plants took the initiative and walked off the lines. The union organizers followed their lead and came to support the strikes.[94] Forty years later unions were still caught up in that reluctance and sense of futility. In North Carolina the "Maya of Morganton" organized themselves and staged walkouts and protests for some time in the mid-1990s before the Laborers' International Union of North America decided to become involved.[95]

This cautious, allegedly practical outlook has further distanced people of color from unions. The ascendancy of the American Federation of Labor's (AFL) vision in the post–World War II period meant that labor organizing in the United States would develop a narrow, somewhat conservative focus, one that was often at odds with the goals of workers of color.[96] The pitched battle against radical, leftist unionists, fought by the AFL, anticommunist unions within the CIO, and the federal government, alienated people of color.[97] It was the Left-led labor organizations, embodied in the middle of the twentieth century by certain CIO unions, that seemed to be most able to understand and accommodate racially or ethnically marginalized workers' vision of unionism as a vehicle for civil rights agitation and to recognize that working conditions for people of color were a result of their less-than-full citizenship status—one could not be ameliorated fully without progressive change in the other.[98] Leftists hoped to connect unionism to a larger movement for social justice. Black and brown union members, from cannery workers in California to sharecroppers in Alabama and Arkansas to pecan shellers in Texas to tobacco workers in North Carolina, shared this broader understanding and fused radical politics and union activism.[99] Thus, the suppression and expulsion of militant, leftist leadership that was committed in some way to social justice unionism significantly reduced the likelihood of effectively reaching and organizing workers of color.[100]

In surveying African Americans in the meat industry, industrial relations professor William Fogel and historians Roger Horowitz and Rick Halpern all trace the history of black people and unions in the industry. Fogel notes that the CIO-affiliated Packinghouse Workers' Organizing Committee (PWOC) and its successor, the United Packinghouse Workers of America (UPWA), were more successful than the AFL's AMBW in organizing black workers in the mid-twentieth century because of their "initial, racially equalitarian policies" and "plant-level activism for fair and equal treatment."[101] David Brody points out that "the Amalgamated was not among the discriminatory AFL organizations. . . . But the Amalgamated would not crusade on the race issue. This the PWOC did."[102] The "crusade" included extending "activism for fair and equal treatment" into the community.

This "social unionism," as Horowitz describes it, on the part of the PWOC/UPWA challenged African Americans' social and political as well as economic vulnerability. The UPWA made many overtures to black workers, from the filing of grievances contesting hiring discrimination and wage differentials to offering support outside the workplace, as reflected by donations to civil rights organizations such as the Southern Christian Leadership Conference.[103] It was not all activity by the PWOC/UPWA *on behalf* of African Americans. Horowitz and Halpern in particular analyze the way African Americans used the union as a platform from which to pursue their own political and economic struggles, indelibly shaping the character and the mission of the UPWA. Fogel argues that the AMBW was much less vigorous in its efforts to address issues that concerned black workers, a hesitancy rooted in part in AMBW locals' domination by and exclusionary practices of skilled white butchers. The result was that while black activism often thrived in UPWA locals, the AMBW initially "resisted most attempts to allow Negroes to be more than dues paying and almost nonparticipating members."[104] And it would be the AMBW, with its greater resources and more diverse (in terms of occupations) membership, that would take the lead in attempting to organize poultry workers, whose situation, by the 1960s, was increasingly black.

To be fair, the AMBW did publicly favor civil rights legislation and had operated on a national level under antidiscriminatory policies. David Brody suggests that as the union sought to organize industries such as seafood and poultry processing with significant black and brown workforces, "the union became more aggressive on race questions."[105] The organization established a Civil Rights Committee in 1960, for example, "to work . . . on all phases of civil rights" and later began to include a regular column on civil rights issues and concerns in its bimonthly newsletter.[106] Despite these overtures, unions such as the AMBW were unable fully to bridge the distance between organized labor and people of color generated by their unresolved "race issues" and conservatism. Labor's (often hesitant) collaboration with people of color on issues of civil rights in the 1950s and 1960s notwithstanding, more radical Americans viewed the unified

AFL-CIO, with its prowar stance, acceptance of exclusionary practices, and lack of people of color in high positions within its own ranks, as part of the establishment.[107]

A young Bill Clinton, whose own rise to power began in Arkansas, wondered if the mainstay of unions, collective bargaining, had become an "institutional arrangement against which man must assert himself."[108] A contemporary observer noted that "the trade unions have become institutionalized and respectable. They are scarcely participants in the momentous social change wracking contemporary American society. The civil rights revolution [and] the war against poverty . . . have found the labor unions dragging their feet and without inspired leadership."[109] Paul Buhle blames the "uninspired" leadership for suppressing militancy among workers. Even in unions such as the United Auto Workers, known for its progressive stance, officials often withdrew support or dispersed "radicals." Within the poultry industry, when a coalition of civil rights and labor organizations formed the Committee for Justice in Mississippi to fight for workers' rights, the International Chemical Workers' Union "pulled the rug out from under the coalition."[110] In poultry processing unions have not effectively reached out to or grasped the interrelated concerns of the people of color who overwhelmingly do the work.

In an industry characterized by its high percentage of women workers, unions have also not been well served by their legacy of deeply ingrained sexism. From the construction of women workers as a threat to men's jobs to the championing of a "family wage" for men, which dismissed the realities of women—often the primary or sole wage earners for their families or whose income was as necessary to family well-being as their husbands'—unions have, as historian Elizabeth Faue argues, "forged a web of symbols . . . that constructed work and the worker as male."[111] Of course, the pronounced gender bias has not stopped women from becoming dedicated, militant unionists, as historians have shown. Rather, a union culture that prioritized men and relied heavily on traditional definitions of gender roles marginalized women and their concerns and often subverted their attempts to improve their status.[112] Despite their successful efforts in the United Cannery, Agricultural, Packing and Allied Workers of America (UCAPAWA), Latinas were pushed out of union leadership.[113] The unionized waitresses of the Hotel Employees and Restaurant Employees (HERE) participated more and wielded more power in sex-segregated locals and resisted joining with men for fear of losing their autonomy.[114]

Mixed locals were typically dominated by men, and they could be exceedingly hostile to women's demands. Men of the UPWA Local 1 refused to cooperate when women entered jobs in meatpacking departments previously closed to them.[115] The men of Local 1 were interested in preserving sex-segregated work. The historical devaluation of work labeled "women's work"—in terms of status and remuneration—benefits those engaged in "men's work" psychologically and economically.[116]

The more conservative, top-down leadership that followed the suppression of leftists and the dismissal of women's issues meant that unions were unable to benefit fully from the grassroots organizing at which women historically have proven to be rather adroit. In the case of black women, racism has worked to keep African Americans impoverished and to deny them much of the meager assistance available to the poor. Yet working from values of collectivism, mutuality, and sharing, black women have proven themselves to be skilled organizers and institution builders in the face of racist opposition.[117] This is why, according to George Green, the strike at Eastex Company in Center, Texas, succeeded. Eastex Company's workforce was black, and they received much more community support and sustenance than did their white counterparts in Denison, a factor crucial to their ability to sustain the strike for eleven months.[118] The members of the Eastex employees' union interpreted the strike as a blow to the status quo.

Circumscribed by the location of the industry and hampered by their own shortcomings, the work of unions has further been hindered by the tactics employed by poultry processing companies. In terms of organizing, the characterization of poultry processing companies has changed little over the time. They are, for the most part, stridently antiunion. They posit reasons why their employees do not need unions, from the threat of the Communist menace in the early days to the more self-righteous declaration that they know how to treat their employees.[119] In the early years the myriad independent companies were already hard to organize, but consolidation and explosive growth have made the big processors of the twenty-first century extremely powerful and influential and perhaps even more able to rebuff organization. While the discourse supporting antiunionism and the organization of the industry have changed, the tactics have not. In 1944 the NLRB found an Iowa poultry processor guilty of firing and refusing to rehire striking workers.[120] Sixty years later Local 2008 accused Tyson of threatening employees with termination for engaging in union activities and signing union cards.[121]

In the 1950s Ray Clymer, owner of Denison Poultry in Center, Texas, exemplified the antiunion poultry processing boss. He never negotiated with the union, despite the fact that his company eventually went bankrupt. The AMBW ended the Denison strike after four years, counting it a loss.[122] In the half-century since Clymer made his stance, poultry processors have refined and built upon the model provided by Clymer's defiance. One consequence of the growth in the industry's size and power is that companies that refuse to bargain fairly or in good faith do not face the threat of bankruptcy that Clymer did. Tyson Foods is a prime example of Clymer's legacy, having adhered to it for the last fifty years. AMBW Local 425 tried to unionize Tyson's first processing plant, located in Springdale, Arkansas, in 1959, the same year that the plant opened. Tyson reacted by threatening and firing employees suspected of engaging in union activity before and after the NLRB elections. The effect, according to Robert Parker, president of the local, was that Local 425 lost the election by twelve votes. Parker lamented that so many union members had been fired, laid off, or forced to quit: "It would take a miracle for us to win if the NLRB sets the election aside."[123] Local 425 struck against Tyson, and the company admitted interfering in the organizational drive. The NLRB ordered Tyson to pay back pay and ordered a new election. Parker was less than enthusiastic about the results—Tyson continued firing and laying off employees and promising incentives, even after the NLRB's decision.[124]

These operations have become commonplace for poultry processing companies, part of what has developed into a strategy that Steve Striffler calls "harass, stall, and appeal" and Linda Cromer describes as "wait them out and wear them out."[125] The technique was showcased again in 1989, shortly after Tyson took over Holly Farms. After integrating the former Holly Farms long-haul truck drivers, who were unionized, with their own larger, nonunionized truckers, Tyson called for a new vote. The unionized truckers met this patent attempt to decertify the union with a strike. According to Striffler, despite the numerous rulings in favor of the workers and the union, Tyson kept stalling and appealing. Not until 1996 were the truckers able to return to work. Despite the legal defeat, Tyson benefited—many of the truckers had moved on, and the long battle had been hard on the employees and the union.[126]

Tyson's "harass, stall, and appeal" and Cargill's "wait them out and wear them out" are particularly effective for two reasons. The first is rooted in the nature and location of the poultry processing industry. Low pay and lack of job alternatives have meant that many employees simply cannot afford to unionize, either in the sense of the actual payment of dues or under the threat of being fired or laid off. In 1975 Richard Twedell, international vice president of the AMBW, noted that problems with Local 425 included the fact that it was composed mainly of poultry processing workers. "It is hard to maintain membership in these plants," he wrote Gorman, "because a $9.00–$10.00 deduction for dues has a major impact on income."[127] Given their economic situation, workers were swayed by incentives the company offered to keep the union out. In 1996 workers at a Tyson plant in Canton, Mississippi, worn down by their previous employer's version of "harass, stall, and appeal," decided to give the company a chance to make good on its promise of raises if they voted against unionization. They voted against the union, and wages rose almost immediately.[128] In Dardanelle, Arkansas, Tyson's promise of a raise and a cleaner, "easier" job persuaded one union member to begin a decertification petition and engage in a number of unfair labor practices to get signatures. The NLRB found that the woman acted as an agent of the company, in part because of evidence that management had measured the progress of her illegal attempts and refused to stop them.[129]

A second reason for the effectiveness of companies' tactics in dissuading workers from organizing is that these employers have been able to invoke them without fear of significant punishment. NLRB fines are low compared to corporate profits. Companies are well able to absorb the cost of fines, back pay to wrongfully fired workers, and court costs incurred in the fight against unions, counting such expenses as a cost of doing business.[130] This attitude is symbolic of another factor in labor's decline: the power of American business. Sociologists Rick Fantasia and Kim Voss argue that U.S. employers are truly exceptional when compared to business owners in other countries. They have created an "exceedingly hostile terrain for labor," an environment that prohibits labor from flourishing in the United States.[131] So powerful is American business that capital and its political allies have "hijacked" the labor law, according to David Brody, subverting it from its initial purpose of protecting workers and their right to organize until it is virtually meaningless.[132] Although the right to organize may exist on paper, it does not really exist when employers can violate the right with such weak threat of repercussions.

The workers in El Dorado were very much aware of unions' shortcomings. By the time the plant closed in 2009, many had become disillusioned with it. It did not begin that way, however. In 1975 Patrick Gorman, international secretary-treasurer of the AMBW, wrote that Local 425, headquartered in Arkansas, "is one of the strongest . . . of our unions in the Deep South."[133] Among the plants organized by AMBW Local 425 was J-M Poultry of El Dorado, Arkansas. El Dorado union members spoke highly of the local. Black employee Essie Mae Sheppard expressed excitement about the possibilities: "We got rid of a union . . . that did not know how to represent us and voted in . . . Local 425. They got us more in wages, benefits, seniority and security in seven days than this other union got us in seven years."[134] Sheppard shared the beliefs of thousands of black women union members that her membership in the union could better her status as a worker *and* as a black woman in the South.[135] "I was in court at El Dorado on a charge that originated from the color of my skin," she testified. "This union stood by me . . . and I was set free."[136] Other black women from J-M Poultry pinned their hopes on Local 425 too. An AMBW file photo shows a number of them, packed tightly onto pew-like benches, at a local meeting in 1965.[137] So impressed were the J-M employees with their union that they voted unanimously to urge workers at a Mississippi plant to select Local 425 as their union.[138]

Local 425 would undergo a number of changes in the last quarter of the twentieth century. The AMBW merged with the Retail Clerks International Association in 1979 to become the United Food and Commercial Workers (UFCW). Initially, the local remained number 425, but in 1992 it merged with Local 1583 to become Local 2008. The local continued to represent the employees of the El Dorado plant through its transitions. But more than the name had changed. Somewhere along the way, according to former employees of the El Dorado plant, UFCW Local 2008 lost the spirit of "true trade unionism" that Secretary-Treasurer Gorman had lauded and began to focus on the company instead of the worker. A number of plant employees filed complaints with the National Labor Relations Board, charging that the union had failed to fairly represent them.[139] Former union steward Janet Strong conveyed the feeling of disillusionment: "When I became the chief steward, I really wanted to make a difference. I wanted people to know they had rights. . . . [But] my union reps . . . they didn't want that. They wanted us to stay little people because they already had their hands in the company. . . . They were getting a paycheck, so it really didn't matter."[140] Poultry processing workers' disaffection with their labor union is not surprising. As one scholar notes, unions have become "more of an extension of management than a bargaining agent representing workers."[141]

The chief complaint against the union of El Dorado workers with whom I spoke was that after it merged, the union began to render the employees invisible and voiceless, taking up the cause of the company and losing touch with and interest in its members. This complaint began within a few short years after 1965. Several anonymous letters, scribbled or typed on a flyer denouncing the local, chastised the regional and international officers for remaining quiet about the growing rift between Local 425's officials and its members. "Are you going to do nothing and let the whole union drown?" one self-described longtime member asked Gorman in 1968.[142]

Rather than sharing decision making or formulating plans of action based on the individual nature of each workplace, Local 425 officials took a one-size-fits-all approach, rarely visiting the various plants it represented, according to union members. Essie Mae Sheppard had lauded the fact that "when we need a union man at our plant . . . there is always one there within hours." But as the limitations of the local's approach became apparent, more letters and several petitions poured into the offices of Gorman and international president Thomas Lloyd. "We are unable to get the officers of Local 425 to visit here," claimed some union members in Pine Bluff. They requested that Local 425 representatives begin making monthly visits or else "some one here should be given the authority to handle matters."[143] Another petition from Val-Mac employees in Waldron, Arkansas, reported similar circumstances: "We should have a right to be backed up when we have problems on the job. We don't even have an organized union staff. . . . No stewards and no union meetings have been set up for election of them."[144] Individual members tendered their withdrawals, accusing the local of ineffectual management and lack of interest.

El Dorado employees initially shared Sheppard's belief in the union. According to Vivian West, "It was good—it was helping you." Tavia Wright agreed: "When I started working, the union was for the people." Although Ruth James never had grievances of her own and therefore did not seek to enlist the support of union representatives directly, she remembered seeing "them help some people with the supervisors." Kenya Drayton recalled: "My mother was a member of the union and a strong advocate of the union because she felt it would fight for her rights. She even went to the meetings when they were getting ready to [negotiate] contracts. I can remember my mama always being there. She loves to go to church on

Sundays, but if their meetings were on Sunday, she would make a way to get up there." Yet after a while these women's optimism about the union waned. While some of their disappointment may be due to a tendency to believe circumstances had been better in the past or even to unrealistic expectations, given the uphill battles unions have fought with processors, these employees were convinced that Local 2008 acted in the best interest of the company.[145] Deena Shine and Margie Young both wondered if "the plant had bought the union."

When asked for examples of the betrayal, former workers readily shared them. In interactions over injuries, perceived wrongful terminations, and contract negotiations, many said that the union did not seem to be "for the people," in the words of Young. "When we changed from one management to another [from ConAgra to Pilgrim's Pride in 2003], the majority of the plant voted against the contract, but the union didn't even fight for us," Wright noted. One union member encouraged other members to hold out—for additional holidays and paid sick days and to refuse the point system. Instead of engaging her suggestions, which enjoyed popular support, Local 2008 sent out flyers denouncing the member as lacking adequate knowledge of negotiation proceedings and concerned solely for herself. The Local 2008 lauded the contract and promptly accepted it. After that Wright decided that "the union isn't worth anything."[146] The actions of union leadership revealed a number of long-standing processes that have troubled unions. They invoked old stereotypes of black women as ignorant and selfish, for example, giving the union's dismissal of the worker who spoke out a decidedly racist and sexist cast. And union leaders refused to take suggestions from the very workers who would be most affected by the new contract.

The history of Local 2008 reveals no significant activity on behalf of the employees at the El Dorado plant in the 1970s and 1980s. Rather than strikes or walkouts, then El Dorado employees seem to base their positive remembrances of what the union "used to be" on everyday actions and interventions by union representatives in dealings with supervisors and management. "One of the really good union stewards . . . she fought for us in that plant," Wright recalled. Young remembered her too, recalling that the union had seemed to want to get rid of her. Janet Strong said she joined because the head of the local "was truehearted and really wanted to make a difference." The union was good, claimed Vivian West, "when you had a floor steward who would stand up for you." By 2009, when the plant closed, those floor stewards were little more than a memory.

The efforts of poultry processing companies and management have fashioned and maintained a vulnerable, exploitable labor force, the kind most desired to do the grisly work of poultry processing. But even though workers are, realistically, constrained by economic need, geographic location, and deeply entrenched hierarchies, they do not submit quietly to their dehumanization.

CHAPTER 4

"THEY DON'T EXPECT THE HUMAN BODY TO BREAK DOWN!"

When this project was in its early stages, my mother sat down with me, at my urging, to watch the People for the Ethical Treatment of Animal's (PETA) short film, *Meet Your Meat* (2002). The film is a documentary that exposes some of the horrible (mis)treatment animals undergo at factory farms. In hindsight I acknowledge that extending that invitation to my mother was a move that reflected my own privilege—I would not be the one going back into a poultry processing plant, to a job upon which I depended for my livelihood, after seeing how many animals are cruelly treated. I would not have to deal with any guilt or second thoughts or the ultimate realization that I needed the job. Indeed, my mother was disturbed by the film; although it lasts fewer than thirteen minutes, she and I were not able to watch it all. Afterward I asked her what she thought. She noted that it was "a shame" the way the animals were treated. But she also made another observation; she wondered why people seemed to care so much about the animals but so little about her and her coworkers. "Neither one of them is right," she told me. "It's not right the way they treat the animals, but it's not right how they treat us."

Part of the reason poultry processing companies work so hard to dehumanize their workforce is that it facilitates the disregard for the consequences of the work on fragile human bodies. The effects of the work can also more easily be ignored when it happens to bodies that are devalued. By maintaining a gendered job division, plant management has set up a system in which those who have been constructed as most controllable and least valuable, poor women of color, work the worst jobs. A look at the actual physical arrangement of processes and people in a poultry processing plant sheds light on the nature of the work and its physical toll on line workers. And despite assertions to the contrary, the work has not become dramatically "safer" in recent decades. Why, then, do employees stay in these jobs, and how do they go about making the workplace more tolerable? Workers explained that it was a lack of skills, few work alternatives, attractive starting pay and benefits, and the presence of friends and family inside the plant that encourages workers to return each day to these slaughterhouses. In deciding to stay, they devise ways to combat, via the repeated assertion of their humanity and their value, as people and to the company, their reduction into machines.

"WHAT YOU FIND IN THERE"

Traveling the "back way," on Southfield Road Cutoff, as many Bernice workers did, or driving on Southwest Avenue through the city of El Dorado proper revealed one of the worst features about the poultry processing plant—you could smell it long before you saw it. "It's the first thing the new people notice," said longtime employee Ruth James. "They have to burn the feathers and mess. It *is* pretty bad." The sight of the plant was not much more welcoming. It was a collection of concrete and metal buildings, always smoking and contained by a chain link fence. At the front entrance stood a guard gate where someone checked identification badges and halted visitors' progress. Even so, according to James, "as bad as it looks on the outside, you still wouldn't expect what you find in there."[1]

Despite technological advances and enormous growth over the years, many of the features that workers "find in there" remained the same. Extreme temperatures, slippery work surfaces, and grueling labor have long existed at poultry processing plants. The push to increase the speed at which employees process birds also brought machinery into the plants to facilitate that goal. The result was a dangerous, debilitating environment in which many workers felt they were "never safe."[2]

The arrival of truckloads of chicken began the workday at the poultry processing plant in El Dorado. From the back docks where the birds arrived, employees next took the birds to live hang, where they suspended the chickens, upside down, from shackles and prepped them for slaughter. The heat was stifling, and lighting was dim, as poultry scientists have determined this helps calm the chickens.[3] Nevertheless, the birds would "scratch, peck, and defecate all over" the live hangers.[4] Anthropologist Steve Striffler describes the live hang stage: "The smell is indescribable, suffocating, and absolutely unforgettable. . . . Blood, shit, and feathers are flying everywhere."[5] During this early phase of processing, an electrically charged bath stuns the birds, and a machine slits their throats, removes their heads, and slices off their feet. A scalder, which produces the highest temperatures in the plant, removes most of the feathers, but "pinners" try to remove any left that are behind.[6]

The next stage of processing involved the chickens' passage through evisceration, what El Dorado employees called the "Big Line."[7] The temperature here was relatively high too—"ninety to ninety-five degrees" in Donna Bazemore's North Carolina plant—as machines eviscerated the chickens and line workers double-checked to make sure all entrails had been removed.[8] The repeated reaching into the birds' body cavities created incredible pressure on the hands and wrists. It also exposed employees to the hazards of bone splinters, rashes, and infections. "If one of the bones stabbed you," said Vivian West, "it would hurt so bad. Just swell up and be black and blue!"[9]

From the Big Line the conveyor took chicken through the chiller, a big metal vat that cooled the chickens to slightly above freezing. After the chiller the processing took place in much colder temperatures. The cold temperatures required in the plants' inner areas, as low as 26 degrees Fahrenheit, necessitate that workers dress warmly and in layers, even in Arkansas's sweltering summers. "No matter how many gloves you had on, it [is] just always cold in there," Kenya Drayton claimed. For her the cold was the most salient feature of the plant's physical environment: "When you came back from lunch, like you were just away for twenty minutes, it seemed even colder in there. That's just my impression of it. It's just that everything is always so cold. You would think some stuff would be hot being that they have to wash down the lines, but even that water was cold they washed down with! They would wash down your bin and wash down the place where you stood and the stool you stood on, and when you got back, even though you had rubber boots on, you could just feel the water seeping into your feet through the rubber boots. Your feet would get wet, and it would just be so cold. You'd be standing there with your feet wet and your hands cold and working the line."[10]

On the next two stops on the processing line at the El Dorado plant, workers were largely divided by gender. "The chickens go to vat holding," explained one longtime employee, "where men hang the birds, then women grade them."[11] Grading is the process in which workers label chicken blemish free, grade A, or slightly imperfect, undergrade.[12] Unless the plant had received a specific order for undergrade birds, the less-than-perfect pieces went back to be packed in ice for later processing.

Once the chicken was graded A, much of it was further processed, cut into pieces or processed by the deboning line. The boneless meat and the rest of the poultry all traveled through the pack-out line, or pre-pack, where employees arranged pieces on trays. A machine overwrapped them, and an employee put them on racks. Rack men loaded the racks onto dollies and pushed them into the "Blast," a temporary freezer. Chicken that would be transported that day then went to price and labeling and, finally, to shipping. The rest of it was stored in the "28 Degree Room" or in freezers upstairs. That is the typical fate of chickens that came through the doors of poultry processing plants. But what of the people?

"THE WOMEN, THEY HAD TO *WORK!*"

Along the way from live hang to price and labeling, the people who came into contact with the chickens and the fast-paced work were mostly women. In years past, for the jobs that required working "on the line," poultry processing employers hired predominantly women. Poultry processing workers in North Louisiana and South Arkansas witnessed the predominance of black women in line work. "It was just a line full of women. . . . The plant was made mostly of African American females," remembered Kenya Drayton. According to Trinity Mays, "Women ran that plant."[13] The Occupational Safety and Health Administration (OSHA) and the U.S. Department of Agriculture (USDA) ranks their jobs are some of the most dangerous in the country. The use of razor-sharp knives and scissors; the presence of heavy, moving machinery; the constantly wet and fat-slick floors; and the monotonous repetitive motions required for these jobs combine to increase line workers' risk of back and joint ailments, repetitive motion disorders, amputations, falls, and serious cuts and lacerations.[14]

Because of the nature of line work, women may be especially disadvantaged over the course of processing poultry and be victims of discrimination. A study funded by the United Food and Commercial Workers International (UFCW) suggests that the placement of women in the "most intricate" jobs involving sharp knives and scissors may be a form of sex discrimination, given the danger and intensity inherent in that type of work.[15] Another group of scholars argues that the "employment of large numbers of black and Hispanic women help producers keep costs low contributing to an environment that fosters disparities in working conditions and health."[16] The assignment of brown and black women to this particular work is rooted in the larger, structural problems of racism and sexism that sustain the employment of women of color in dangerous, dirty jobs for low pay.[17] Employers know that, quite often, women with few alternatives will not complain, and if they do, they are commonly ignored. The result for the companies has been lucrative, as illustrated by this quote from Marc Linder: "The location of poultry plants in small rural southern towns depressed by high unemployment and the hiring of large numbers of minority women, especially single mothers without other options, have fostered conditions under which 'poultry's Pashas' could profit from the gap between productivity and prices on the one hand and wages on the other. Whereas output per worker nearly tripled between 1960 and 1987, wages rose only half as quickly as chicken prices."[18]

Labeling the gendered division of work in poultry plants as an example of sex discrimination seems fitting when one explores the nature of women's work in these plants. Anthropologist Steve Striffler argues that the fact "that most on-line workers are women is [not] coincidence. . . . On-line jobs are the worst in the plant."[19] It is work, suggested Kenya Drayton, "that a lot of men would consider . . . degrading. No offense to men—they like the high-powered jobs, and the jobs on the line are not high-powered." Drayton located the reason for the dearth of men on line jobs in power dynamics, while other employees pointed to more concrete reasons. "[Women] get so dirty with the splashing and cutting. They get women to do the hands-on, dirty work," wrote Trinity Mays. When asked why she thought black women were assigned to line jobs, West's simple reply was "Because they were harder."[20] Thus, women line workers have perhaps been the most exploited of all groups in the poultry processing industry.

While they admitted pushing racks, dumping meat into tubs, and sweeping meat off the floor, as men once primarily did, was heavy work, other women suggested that employers hired women for line work because it was more difficult.[21] "To me the women did more work than the men. The men all had it made!" opined Margie Young. Sylvia Martin made a similar observation: "Lot of times, men would be standing around looking, and the women would be working." Drayton concurred: "Mostly, [men] got to walk around until there was something to push into the freezers. . . . You saw men standing around. But the women, they had to *work!*" When asked why she judged women's jobs as harder, Neysha Mallory explained: "Some of the men just using a broom sweeping up meat, pushing the meat, I sweep and mop at home, I feel like I could have done that, so yeah, I probably would have rather be[en] down there pushing a broom than holding that knife like I did all day."[22]

When the gendered division of labor did ease, it was more of a case of women beginning to do "men's" jobs, according to interviewees, than vice versa.[23] "Women did most of the work that was classified as men's jobs. . . . Everything that was in there," said Bella Dawes, "the women did." Vivian West noted, "When I first started, it was more that men were doing the floor jobs . . . but as time progressed, they started allowing the women [to do them]." Mallory agreed: "They would put a woman on the job to work the floor, to clean up the meat and wash down. You would look at it to be a man's job, but women done it as well."[24] Tavia Wright, who expressed the belief that there should be men's work and, to use her term, "ladies'" work, did not like the slight easing of the division. It was as if "sex means nothing. Some things they require of a lady, I think a man should do. Even though some of them want to be like men. But me? I don't want to be like a man."[25]

Because the plant's workforce was overwhelmingly black, black women poultry processing workers tended to look at their relegation to the least desirable jobs as solely a matter of gender discrimination. But the work they did in poultry processing plant fits into a larger pattern of the confinement of black women to "dirty" work based on their existence not only as women but as black and poor. Scholars have explored the ways in which work done by black women, particularly domestic and reproductive labor, is constructed as both dirty and appropriate for purportedly unfeminine black women to do.[26] In the case of domestic work the juxtaposition of white woman employer and black domestic worker has served the purpose of maintaining the status of white women as more feminine than and superior to black women. Evelyn Nakano Glenn contends that "many White women fulfilled White society's expectation of feminine domesticity only through the domestic labor of their servants, who were women of color." Similarly, Cheryl Gilkes argues that relegating black women to the task of white women's least desirable work "enhanced . . . protected, purified, and dignified" white women's status.[27]

In factory settings such as poultry plants, black women have traditionally been given work deemed "unfit for workers of a more 'sensitive' disposition," particularly white women.[28] The demands of poor black women's historic and modern work has required that they show physical strength, another trait deemed as unfeminine. Out of habit and necessity, black women commonly did the work required of them, only to have it become the basis of stereotypes about their extraordinary physical and mental strength.[29] While on the surface there is nothing wrong with being strong or resilient, the insistence that black women possess mythic strength obscures their exploitation, pain, and exhaustion. As Tamara Beauboeuf-Lafontant argues, "The cultural and societal expectation that black women will demonstrate strength and never break down physically or emotionally diminishes outrage about the status quo, as it assumes that black women have the reserves that allow them to face, bear, and perhaps surmount adversity."[30] Within the El Dorado plant complex the effects of the dichotomy that defines black women as stronger than and more suited for dirty work than delicate, clean white women were obvious. While there were white women who worked the line, there were never very many. The white women affiliated with the plant tended to work in the administrative offices, removed physically and culturally from the black women on the lines.[31] Trinity Mays both acknowledged and challenged this dichotomy: "Not too many white women are going to get dirty the way they expected us to. They act like [white women] wouldn't be able to stand it, but if they can't stand it, how can we? It tells you what they think about us."[32]

A SHOW OF HANDS

Because women do so much of the work that requires repetition of the same tasks at incredibly rapid speeds, they have a high incidence of musculoskeletal disorders (MSDs) such as carpal tunnel syndrome (CTS) and tendinitis.[33] These injuries have been partially the result, as Vivian West noted, of faster line speeds.[34] She suffers from CTS and dates the disorder back to her time on evisceration and then on the bag line and to the introduction of machines into the plant that elevated line speeds. Mechanization replaced some of the knife-wielding workers with cutting machines. Evisceration, once done by hand, was one of the most unpleasant jobs in the plant. Poultry processing workers' hands were chronically swollen and sore in those days. West admitted that not having to reach into the birds was an improvement, but, she said, "the machinery made the jobs harder because the machines stay [broken] a lot. Then, in the process of running the line so fast, trying to keep up with the machines, your joints and things would get tired and hurt."[35] A North Carolina poultry worker revealed a similar perception. "They started bringing in machines," said Rose Harrell, "and everything got faster."

These experiences—brought about by companies' willingness to sacrifice employee health in order to process more and more chicken—are familiar to many poultry workers. As West observed: "The first day they got the bag machine, all the ones that were working on the machine, when we came out of the plant, we just sat down because we were too tired to do anything else. We hurt all over. After a week or so, they were processing more and more birds on the bag line. I developed carpal tunnel syndrome, then I had to have surgery on my hands."[36] Line workers who cut and debone are especially vulnerable to developing MSDs, as they make "as many as 40,000 daily repetitions of a single defined movement."[37] Interviews with women who have worked the line in poultry processing plants revealed that over time many of them are simply unable to do the job anymore.[38] According to Neysha Mallory, who worked on the "cone" line deboning breasts, "People start being took off the line 'cause they can no longer use knives and scissors and stuff because that's just how [badly] their hands have been damaged from cutting and using scissors every day." The debilitating effects of MSDs, however, extend beyond the plant. If not treated, the diseases render those afflicted unable to do simple, everyday tasks such as use a brush or a fork, fasten their clothes or lock a door, or work in their gardens.[39]

Before the incredible line speeds, repetitive motion disorders were less pervasive among poultry workers. An Arkansas survey in 1976 labeled only 19 of 476 injuries and illnesses as being related to "inflammation of joints, etc."[40] In Virginia the state supreme court issued a 1986 ruling that repetitive motion diseases are "ordinary diseases of life," ineligible for workers' compensation.[41] Companies were historically unwilling to admit that the work being done for them caused any MSDs. Angela Strong said that the plant supervisors were careful to point out, "You can get carpal tunnel at home."[42] But as line speeds grew progressively faster, the incidence of MSDs also rose. Finally, in the late 1980s some state OSHAs began to monitor the disorders.[43] Increasingly, ergonomic studies identified the link between MSDs and rapid-paced, repetitive motion tasks in poultry processing. A 1994 survey of workers' compensation cases in the industry in Louisiana found a marked increase in MSDs, from 4 percent of compensable cases in 1987 to 20 percent in 1991. Similarly, in a survey of fifty-one plants, OSHA determined that MSDs were one of the most common afflictions in the industry. A 2007 study of black women in rural low-wage industries found that black women who work in poultry plants were 2.4 times more likely to suffer from upper extremity disorders such as CTS and tendinitis than their counterparts.[44] A February 2008 article in the *Charlotte Observer* quotes Dr. Pablo Forestier, who said of his patients who work at the Tyson plant: "Once I shake their hands, I know what they do."[45]

The observations of poultry processing workers also bear witness to the spike in MSDs. Of her time at Perdue, Bazemore says, "There are very, very few people that I know . . . that don't have a problem with their hands."[46] Steve Striffler, who worked at Tyson plants, remembered that those who had "worked anywhere on the line for six months definitely had a hand or wrist injury."[47] Even as studies revealed the connections between line speed and MSDs, many workers still hesitated to complain, both out of fear of losing their jobs and because they accepted the disorder as an unfortunate part of their work. That it is a natural result of their work is a view that poultry processing companies have encouraged. In the words of a Human Rights Watch report, "Meat and poultry industry employers set up the workplaces and practices that create these dangers, but they treat the resulting mayhem as a normal, natural part of the production process."[48] The company's insistence that these injuries are "normal" and "natural" is exemplified by the story of Natalie Davis, who battles CTS. She has prominent knots protruding from her outer wrists. She explained that they are "from doing the same thing over and over. [The company] won't admit it, but they'll pay for your care, you know? Like at first, they wouldn't say it was carpal tunnel, but they sent me to therapy where they worked on my hands."

The sometimes slow progression of MSDs encourages employees to work despite the disorders. CTS, for example, commonly begins with tingling and numbness. "You shake your hands and rub them," described Davis. "You think the feeling will come back. Especially in the kill plant, where people think it's just the cold."[49] At first some of the feeling does come back. Then the numbness becomes "like you can't feel at all. Can't use your hands."[50] Once workers experience permanent damage, employers have little use for them. Many employees reported being let go after they developed problems.[51] Again, they learned that they are disposable.

Of course, company executives do not agree with employees' observations. Bo Pilgrim described being devastated each time an employee is injured. According to Pilgrim, employees work, not so much *for* him as *with* him. They are called "partners," working with the company to improve product quality and, as Pilgrim said euphemistically, to feed the world.[52] "We seek to hire the best people [and] handle them with care," claimed Pilgrim.[53] That "company value" is not reflected in the reality of monotonous, repetitive work and what it does to people.

"LOST WORKDAY ILLNESSES AND INJURIES NOW STAND AT THE LOWEST LEVEL EVER RECORDED"

The poultry industry commonly rebuffs its critics by pointing to the fact that the injury and illness rate for the industry has declined dramatically. In 1994 the industry experienced 22.7 illnesses and injuries per 100 full-time workers. By 2009 the rate was 5.5 per 100 full-time workers, "the lowest level ever recorded."[54] Under the ownership of ConAgra, the El Dorado plant marked one million work hours without a lost-time accident in 1993. The Arkansas Department of Labor once commended the plant for having had three million work hours without a lost-time accident. Under Pilgrim's Pride that number climbed to over four million in 2005.[55] Clearly, some safety measures may have been implemented with success.[56] But scholars, government officials, and journalists who watch the industry posit more problematic reasons for the decline in injuries and illnesses: self-regulation and widespread underreporting. As the *Charlotte Observer* writers of the "The Cruelest Cuts" series explain, "Businesses are required to record most serious injuries and illnesses on [OSHA] logs. But it's an honor system and companies must give logs to regulators and employees only if asked."[57] The "Cruelest Cuts" journalists compared the OSHA logs from a number of plants with the testimony of community members who had been seriously injured while working in them. They found no mention in the company logs of most of the injuries. Once OSHA no longer mandated that poultry processors distinguish MSDs, some plants even claimed to go years without having a musculoskeletal injury reported, a claim that flies in the face of what is known about the work.[58]

There is an incentive for plant management to underreport injuries: fewer injuries result in fewer inspections. "The Cruelest Cuts" series includes an article that found inspections in the industry were at a "15-year low," largely a result of the plummeting reported injury and illness rate.[59] In 2005 the Government Accountability Office (GAO) admitted that given the "many hazards inherent in meat and poultry plants and the type of work performed, the dramatic decline in the industry's injury and illness rates [raises] a question about the validity of the data on which these rates are based."[60] Federal government inquiry continued in 2008, as the House Committee on Education and Labor held a hearing on the chronic underreporting of injuries and illnesses. Revelations from that hearing prompted the passage of a new law that required OSHA to institute a program to inspect the problems of underreporting and under-recording of injuries and illnesses.[61]

In addition to underreporting, management avoids the recording of lost-time accidents in other ways, according to plant employees.[62] After an injury "they'll tell you to come in for light duty, but you might not do anything except sit there all day," explained Tavia Wright. DeShaun Lowe agreed, saying, "They'll have you come in and sit in the break room, anywhere to keep from paying workman's compensation." The experience of LeeAnn Johnson supports Lowe's claim: "I had an injury. I was scrubbing my hopper while the machine was going. It caught my fingers. I broke my fingers and my fingernail came off. They had me working [the next day] in the break rooms cleaning the break rooms."[63]

Yet not all recommendations of light duty are heeded. Deena Shine suggested that the company sometimes put "people back to working before their injury was [healed]. The nurse would say, 'Well, they're able,' . . . and then if you refuse, that's like you don't want to do your job, and you get fired."[64] This was the experience of two of the employees who filed the 2003 suit against the El Dorado plant. Both men had had surgery for CTS, and their doctors had cleared them to return to the plant for light duty work. Supervisors ordered that they "perform work departing from the doctor's guidance." One of the men reinjured himself. The other protested the job he was assigned but told by his doctor not to do, and his supervisor responded by telling him, "I don't give a damn if your hands fall off, you are not going to sit around and do light duty work." The subsequent behavior of their supervisors, claimed both men, communicated management's desire that they quit.[65] Many employees just work through their pain.

Employees maintained that they could not look to the company's medical staff for help. Dawes described a typical response from company nurses as: "Oh, you okay, just sit here for a few minutes, then you go back to the line."[66] According to employees, the company nurse treated all manner of ailments with over-the-counter pain relievers and antibiotic ointment while encouraging employees to stay at work, thereby avoiding "lost time." Apparently, this is a common practice. Both "The Cruelest Cuts" and the *Southern Exposure* exposés describe nurses' and first aid attendants' habit of treating workers with over-the-counter medicines, creams, and bandages, no matter how intense workers claim their pain is. In Stuesse's study a participant named Alma explained, "It doesn't matter what problem you report. [The nurse] always does the same thing. She rubs you down with that Bengay ointment and she gives you a Tylenol."[67] In Striffler's Northwest Arkansas plant "there was hardly a sorer subject than the ineffective company nurse." He continues with the story of an employee named Maria: "Maria scoffed, 'When we go to the nurse, she just gives us Advil and tells us to go to back to work.' She lifts her arms. 'Look at my wrists. Do you think Advil is the answer?'"[68] This insistence on giving only basic first aid treatment might be because OSHA standards mandate that companies "must consider an injury or illness to meet the general recording criteria, and therefore to be recordable, if it results in . . . medical treatment beyond first aid."[69]

Poultry workers across the country share stories of nurses and doctors who deny the extent of their pain and the damage done and who try to attribute their MSDs to anything other than their paid work. Medical professionals often serve as an impediment to getting proper help. Nurses and doctors, many of women interviewed for this study said, seem more interested in the potential financial costs to the company than the physical costs to the employees. "In other words," said Deena Shine, "the doctor and the nurse . . . gonna side with the plant." But Bella Dawes and Lydia Martin took a more sympathetic view toward the in-plant nurses, suggesting that they work under the same fear and threat as other employees. Dawes recalled: "We had two nurses that would really see about those people. [But] if the nurses . . . would send those people home every time they got sick, [the nurses] wouldn't be there long—they'd find something to fire the nurses about." Termination had been the fate, according to Dawes, of the "two [nurses] who were nice to the people." Martin, who worked for a while as a nurse's assistant, interrupted her sister's complaint about the nurse to say: "Lot of the stuff the nurses did to the employees was by company's rules. . . . It's some of the stuff they telling her to do. [If she wants to keep her] job, she gon' do it."[70] Martin might be right—Tyson Foods once instructed its nurses to refer workers with symptoms of MSD to a doctor only after four weeks of in-house treatment.[71] Doctors may also be subjected to pressure by the company. According to the House committee investigating the underreporting of injuries among poultry workers, "employers may 'bargain' with or even threaten doctors to prevent the diagnosis of a recordable injury or illness."[72] The threat is an economically salient one, suggests Stuesse, who argues that the impartiality of doctors in rural areas, where much of their business is directed toward them from poultry company management, is "questionable."[73] Whether their sympathies lie with the company or the employees, the actions of many poultry plant nurses can be summed up in the words of a plant nurse in Mississippi: "We do everything we can to keep him here at the plant, and if he can't drive himself to work I will go to his house and pick him up. If he needs to sit and do nothing, that's fine too. But it's our goal to prevent a lost work time injury."[74]

In the last quarter-century labor and human rights organizations have devoted a great deal of time to exposing and condemning the conditions in which poultry processing workers labor. The most obvious solutions to the problem are slowing down line speeds and strengthening inspection guidelines. Poultry processors balk at the idea of a slowdown, however, because they claim they will lose profits. OSHA and the USDA seem too underfunded and understaffed to enact stricter inspections to protect workers and consumers. In fact, observers commonly state that the relaxed inspection guidelines of both agencies represents an abandonment of American workers to inhumane work and of American consumers to food often unfit for consumption. Achieving the goal of a safe workplace for poultry processing workers has thus been a long, difficult struggle, with the objective yet to be realized.

"BUT BLACK FEMALES, WE DIDN'T HAVE ANYWHERE TO GO"

Given the nature of work in poultry processing plants, employees constantly face the question "Why stay?" Many of them do not, as evidenced by the high turnover rates. Those who do stay report a number of reasons for doing so. One of the most important is the fact that poultry processing plants' locations in rural areas often mean they are the primary or sole source of employment for unskilled, marginalized workers. Drayton maintained that unskilled white women in the area had the possibility of obtaining clerical work, "but black females, we didn't have anywhere to go. You had to go to ConAgra unless you had a good education." Location could triumph over education, however, as she noted that there were "a lot of people that work at ConAgra that have degrees. Because they live in the area, they have to work at ConAgra."[75] The plants always seemed to be seeking new employees and many of them. The El Dorado plant, for example, was the largest employer in Union County for decades. The other area plant, thirty miles away in Farmerville, Louisiana, is the largest employer in Union Parish. When people are looking for a job along the central section of the Arkansas-Louisiana border, they often turn to the poultry industry.

The above–minimum wage starting pay is also an enticement. Poultry companies recognize that plant jobs are largely unappealing; therefore, they commonly offer wages and benefits above those of local competitors.[76] Even under bad conditions, poultry workers might "be satisfied 'cause it's more money than they've ever made."[77] Tavia Wright said that when she began work in El Dorado in 1986, the plant jobs were one of the "highest paying of the time."[78] Striffler surmised that because the cost of living in Arkansas was relatively inexpensive, poultry jobs that paid eight dollars an hour, offered insurance, and ensured a consistent forty-hour workweek provided "a tough way [for immigrants] to achieve upward mobility."[79] Local high school teacher Lillian Gafford worried that the next generation shares this perception: "This is the worst problem to me. A lot of students see their parents working many hours and getting a relatively decent check, so they set their goals on working in poultry instead of higher education. Some of them feel like, my parents didn't graduate, and they do okay. They tell me that, and, of course, I know it's not okay because my husband works there. So they put less effort into school, make jokes that they are going to ConAgra University. And some of them do drop out and go to the poultry [plants]."[80] Janae Earl and LeeAnn Johnson both noted that despite their short tenure in the industry, they were happy with their pay.[81]

Family and friend networks are another reason employees return to the plant each workday. Like many plants, while it was in operation, the El Dorado complex relied on kin and community recruitment to attract new employees.[82] When asked how they came to work in the industry, the majority of the women interviewed for this study named family members or friends who "got me on up there." In 1977 Janet Strong came to El Dorado looking for a job. Her sister already worked at the plant and referred her to personnel. "I went out there and immediately got hired," she recalled.[83] In Jackie Martin-Lowe's family, as she described in an interview, "it started out my mother worked there first, then it's seven of us kids, and all of us worked there at one time."[84] New employees often respected the fact that the family and friends who helped them secure jobs were stepping out on a limb. "When someone has talked for you, you don't want to mess it up," observed Natalie Davis. In 2002 she "talked for" her sister, who eventually left the plant, and her brother, who remains at the Farmerville plant. The practice of hiring family and friends provides employees with support and transportation networks and a sense of familiarity.[85] It may also empower them, argues David Griffith, "since firing one worker may lead to others' leaving."[86] Networking remained an important recruiting tactic until the plant's close.

Employees who stay also watch their work-related benefits increase. Most new hires are not eligible for vacation or insurance for up to a year. Long-term employees enjoy increased vacation time, health care coverage, seniority, and retirement benefits. Once employees begin receiving these benefits, they are more inclined to stay, according to Strong, who believes "you will find more people in the plant [who've] been there twenty years than you would been there a year."

Employees do reap some economic benefits from working in the industry. Bo Pilgrim claimed poultry companies have "a noble mission of saving rural North America," by bringing job opportunity and technology to these areas.[87] Industry historian Stephen Strausberg offered the rationale that despite the unsavory nature of the work, companies are doing workers and their communities a service by providing jobs and driving down unemployment in rural Arkansas. Union Parish resident Eleanor Holloway said that she "always respected the poultry industry because . . . when there was that interim there when there was no plant, the whole parish was about to go crazy, because the industry is needed. They're the largest employer in the parish, and when you lose that you've lost everything, you lose your tax base—where will these people work? Most of them are not highly skilled workers to go out into a professional job. Even in the professional world now, there are no jobs."[88]

For the women, who remain so heavily represented in the industry, the work enables them to take care of the children for whom many first took their jobs.[89] These women, argues Stuesse, are "often the sole bread winner[s] for their children[;] they have dreams of buying a home or helping to pay for their children's education."[90] Whenever I expressed concern over the conditions in which she and so many other black women worked, my own mother repeatedly reminded me that "ConAgra has paid for plenty of houses, cars, and educations."

Rural areas, however, pay a very high cost for these benefits. Huge amounts of chicken manure and plant wastes have polluted and contaminated wells and bodies of water throughout the South. In 1992 Arkansas poultry farmers dumped "urine/feces equal to the daily waste generated by a population of eight million people."[91] The neighboring state of Oklahoma has taken Arkansas to task for polluting its waters too.[92] State agencies have been slow to enforce environmental regulations because of the economic benefits of the industry.[93] The result is that Arkansas's waterways, fish, and wildlife have suffered immeasurably.[94]

Rural areas also bear another cost of poultry processing operations— the expense of caring for injured workers. Because plants do not offer insurance benefits from the first day of employment, some workers are hurt before they have health care coverage. Unable to pay for their medical care, such workers must rely on governmental assistance or the aid of local volunteer or religious associations. For workers who are injured after their medical insurance is effective, many find that their coverage is minimal or their deductible is too high.[95]

While poultry companies insist they provide good opportunities for unskilled rural workers, the increased use of machines to do some of the skilled cutting and sectioning may actually be a disservice to the workforce. Employees leave the plants with very few marketable skills, a result of "deskilling." Deskilling has made poultry processing workers' labor worth less, both in terms of remuneration and in their value to the company. Poultry companies have rendered a number of jobs within the plant, and thus a number of its workers, interchangeable.[96]

That "decent" starting wage turns out to be little more than a lure. On average, from 1972 (when the Bureau of Labor Statistics started compiling wage data for the industry) until 2002, poultry processing workers have only earned around 60 percent of the national average for manufacturing workers. The average income of poultry processing workers is not enough to bring them above or even equal to the poverty threshold. The UFCW reports that real wages for poultry workers in 2004 were the same as they had been in 1979. Although Wright was impressed by her starting pay of "around $6.00," after two decades, her pay only increased to $9.65 per hour.[97]

Furthermore, workers often do not receive their full wages. The Department of Labor (DOL) surveyed fifty-one plants in 2000 and found that all of them failed to pay workers for all their hours worked.[98] In El Dorado causes of this problem were numerous. Sometimes the time clock did not register when employees punched in. Other times supervisors "forgot" to pay workers for hours worked off the clock. In some plants, including the El Dorado one, workers were not paid for the time spent getting into and out of their work gear, a violation of the Fair Labor Standards Act.[99] El Dorado employees, like 65 percent of workers in the DOL survey, were often denied their overtime pay. According to Tavia Wright: "You think your check will be one thing, but it's another. And they never explain why it's short. They just tell you they'll put it in the next check."[100]

The process of kin recruitment can be a double-edged sword. While it helps employees bring a sense of community into the plant, it also gives employers a direct line to workers whose situation mirrors that of their family and community members. That is, they are often low-skilled workers with few options in a rural area. David Griffith also posits that network recruitment represents "the firm's increasing penetration of workers' lives and communities." Particularly in the experience of Latino workers, processors' efforts to recruit employees often include providing housing and transportation. Thus, workers find themselves beholden to the company, strengthening companies' labor control tactics.[101]

Finally, the promise of benefits is often little more than a promise.[102] Many workers simply do not stay long enough to reap benefits. Those who do stay often complain that the company tries "to get rid of" them, to avoid paying for more vacation time or retirement benefits. Other studies have shown that processing plants segment their labor force not only along lines of race/ethnicity and gender but between long-term "core" workers and short-term "marginal" workers.[103] The result is that companies privilege core workers at the expense of marginal ones. Marginal workers typically hold the lowest paying jobs in the plant; money "saved" from hiring these employees is redistributed as higher wages and bonuses for core workers.[104] Plant supervisors may also reward core employees with "preferred" tasks. These practices create a hierarchy among workers, allowing "established workers to feel superior . . . and empowered."[105]

"JUST LET ME KNOW YOU APPRECIATE MY WORK!"

Workers who "have to stay" report that they constantly resist an environment that devalues their work and their existence as people. Bazemore said she challenged the reduction of herself into a machine, telling her doctor: "I can't order parts from Sears. All these parts came with my body, and they're not replaceable."[106] Mallory described how she and her coworker demanded acknowledgment of a job well done: "Me and my friend, we started telling our supervisor . . . if we done done good, come back at the end of the day and say, 'Good job! Y'all did a good job!' Just let me know you appreciate my work. Don't just [act like] it didn't matter, long as y'all make y'all money, but show the people some appreciation, maybe they'll make people want care about this job more to come to work for y'all more. Do something, if we getting the job done!"[107]

In plants "where communication and self-expression among workers are muted . . . by the intensity of the work, the noise, and the supervision, knowing glances, practical jokes, cooperation and shared pain become ways that workers acknowledge . . . their shared experience," according to Steve Striffler.[108] Poultry workers shared their use of these techniques, particularly cooperation. Sylvia Martin described how "sometimes women had to come together and move [heavy things] they selves. 'Fore it was all over with, you had women moving 40 pound boxes and picking up boxes and tubs together in order to get things done 'fore you can go home."

Bella Dawes shared similar memories of this cooperative spirit among women in the plant. Dawes's story of pushing her coworker out of harm's way is also indicative of the endurance of human decency and bonds of affection. It is an endurance also noticed by Wright, who said of her co-workers, "There are some employees who consider 'This is one of my fellow employees. This is human. Those chickens wait. But human life cannot wait.' Most of the time, we stick together because we know the conditions we work under."[109] On at least one occasion that desire to help, to "stick together," proved fatal. A short notice in the *New York Times* in 1984 recounted the loss of two lives in the plant. Jewell Thompson had fallen into a vat, overcome by ammonia fumes. One of his coworkers, "Willie Earl White, called for help, then entered the vat to save Mr. Thompson." He also died, having made the supreme sacrifice for his coworker.[110]

Despite disillusionment with unions, poultry processing workers do not abandon collective action. Sometimes they jump-start the unions. More and more, they organize outside traditional unionism. Churches, for example, have developed a tradition of helping these workers.[111] In fact, clergy, through the Interfaith Worker Justice (IWJ), have been instrumental in founding Poultry Justice Alliances (PJA).[112] These alliances facilitate connections between workers and their communities and recognize the workers' plight in terms that the unions previously did not, as issues embedded within a broader system of social injustice:

> We know now that the grower who contracts with the companies, the chicken catchers who are sub-contracted out by the companies, and the process plant workers who work without a contract (if they are non-union) are all victimized by a vertically integrated system which is abusive and unjust to all parties concerned.
>
> We know also that the industry is polluting the streams, exposing workers and growers to hazardous chemicals and substances added to the feed, jeopardizing the health of the consumers by pumping the birds full of antibiotics, and ruthlessly manipulating and destroying the very animals being bred to feed us.
>
> We know that the poultry companies control the scales, the wages, the work atmosphere and the work conditions of all who work for them.[113]

The PJAs' core principles of self-determination, respect and dignity, and risk-taking influence the workers' lives inside and outside the plant; they hope to teach workers to be "effective agents of change." The executive director of the Georgia Poultry Justice Alliance believes that the PJA may have more success than a traditional union because "being in the South, the thought of a UNION is not welcomed with open arms. . . . the Alliance has a better chance to make a difference with the public and legislature. There is less resistance because we are not labeled as a union."[114]

Other organizations, such as the Center for Women's Economic Alternatives (CWEA), with which Donna Bazemore worked, have also tried to address the problems workers face in poultry processing. The CWEA, having "developed out of a number of struggles, primarily by women, over unfair and sexist treatment in low-income occupations," was particularly concerned with the structural issues that disadvantaged women in the industry.[115] The center hoped to "create a community of women, free of all oppressions." Although the industry presented the same kind of challenges to the CWEA that it did to unions, the CWEA distinguished itself from labor unions in its willingness to work *with* women and draw upon the invaluable resources they brought with them. The connections Bazemore spoke of wanting to create, for example, addressed an understanding of the interconnectedness of women's lives inside and outside the plants: "I really want to be able to do something for black women. To help them share their stories so they don't have to feel all alone, all pressed and stressed out. Let them see that there are other women out here who got beat up, who got put out of their house, who were abused at work. Let them know there's someone out here that cares, that will offer support."[116]

Bazemore's words give voice to the fact that women's economic vulnerability is often reflected in and shaped by marginalization in other aspects of their lives—in the case of the women in this study, primarily at the intersection of commonly their identities as black, poor, rural, and women. Their resultant social and economic vulnerability in the face of state violence, via structural racism and sexism that denies them equitable access to systems of government programs and provision and allows these systems to become tools to control their personal lives, are factors that have kept black women in dangerous, poorly remunerated work such as poultry processing.

In her work with the CWEA and her later affiliation with the New Life Women's Leadership Project, Bazemore (now Latimer) has made similar connections. The philosophy that guides her ongoing work with poor, rural women was described in a publication of the North Carolina Humanities Council: "The process entrapping people in poverty is not just lack of wealth, inadequate health care or gender discrimination, though these are important parts of the problem. It's also how these are linked to and reinforce systemic problems: racism; lack of affordable and adequate housing; limited skills with no education providing hope for better jobs at living wages; the state's economic development policies; no day care for the children of working parents; domestic abuse; and an unworkable welfare system that isn't adequate for human needs and that punishes public assistance recipients for trying to get out of poverty. A social system that creates and underpins these problems makes it impossible for work, alone, to be enough."[117] The narrow focus of traditional unions cannot adequately speak to and does not acknowledge the interrelatedness of these factors and the need to address them all.[118]

Poultry processing workers have also pursued legal justice. In the case of the El Dorado plant, at least two employees, John Johnican and George Williams, on different occasions, successfully sued ConAgra for subjecting them to a racially hostile environment. In 2002 a jury accepted Johnican's attorneys' arguments that ConAgra's treatment "was part of a pattern and practice of discrimination which had gone on for several years." Johnican was awarded $337,000. George Williams was fired in 2001, after an altercation with another supervisor, but maintained that his termination was racially motivated. Rather than address the racism in the plant, according to Williams, the plant fired him to silence him. DeShaun Lowe, who testified in Williams's case, said: "His lawyer was asking me were they racial. Did I see anything on the wall concerning racial slurs or the sort. Did the supervisor show favoritism more toward whites than blacks. . . . Yes, I seen them. I saw lots of things."[119] Williams's case was convincing; in 2003 a jury awarded him over fourteen million dollars in damages.[120]

The alliances and the legal system are no substitute for strong unions. The Georgia PJA maintains: "We believe that union organizing is the most effective long-term solution to workplace problems. A union contract can be workers' strongest tool to secure rights and benefits not provided for by the law."[121] How can unions set about organizing poultry processing more effectively? Some time ago, labor organizer Herbert Hill offered the suggestion that unions develop an approach to organizing black and Latino communities that discarded the old reliance on outside organizers.[122] By 2005 it seemed that unions were listening and trying to build up the grassroots momentum upon which social justice movements have historically thrived. The UFCW, having broken away from an AFL-CIO widely seen as out of touch and mired in traditions and corruption, sought to build coalitions of labor, faith-based, and human rights organizations. The UFCW joined the Change to Win (CtW) coalition, a group of unions with a primary focus of active organizing rather than using the passive techniques it associates with the AFL-CIO. The coalition emphasizes its bottom-up organizing, portraying itself as more responsive and attuned to the needs of low-wage laborers.

The CtW coalition's commitment to organizing immigrant workers is also significant to the poultry processing industry. As the industry moves toward a primarily immigrant, especially Latino, workforce, unions' abilities to reach these workers and understand their unique demands will be crucial to organization efforts. Latino immigrants have been historically left out of unions, though the Guatemalan poultry processing workers in Morganton, North Carolina, are an encouraging exception. While the AFL-CIO debated whether or not to organize immigrants, the PJA movement and the CtW coalition have reached out to them in the workplace and in their communities, defending their rights in the face of anti-immigrant sentiment.[123] How successful this new breed of unionism is "will be decisive in determining whether the labor movement will survive."[124]

CHAPTER 5

"THEY ARE ABOUT TO OUTNUMBER ALL THE DIFFERENT RACES"

May 11, 2006, marked graduation day at Bernice High School. The school observed its long-standing traditions—graduation was on a Thursday evening at seven thirty. But family and friends who packed the school's small gymnasium witnessed school history. For the first time two of the twenty graduates were Latino students born in Mexico. In a town accustomed to a black and white population, this was a significant achievement indeed.

For many years U.S. Highway 167 bisected Bernice, Louisiana, geographically and racially. Although both sides of the highway were once lined with homes and businesses owned by white citizens, one block west of the highway, beginning with Plum Street, lay the black section of town. Black residents built homes, churches, and businesses such as Rogers's Barbershop, Hull's Laundromat, and Sweet 'N Freeze—a combination shoe repair and ice cream shop. They frequented the grounds of the McDaniel Recreational Center and a troubled little nightclub aptly called "The Hole." Bernice's white residents lived east of the highway, close to the railroad tracks and storage warehouses reminiscent of the town's early sources of income. They also inhabited the "country" south and east of town, separated from the town proper by pine forests and rough dirt roads.

In the last decade of the twentieth century and the first decade of the twenty-first, the racial divisions along Highway 167 began to blur, with larger businesses established on both sides and black residents making their way east. The relaxation of geographical barriers marks only one change in the racial-ethnic composition of Bernice. The other is the arrival of a new group that challenges the binary nature of race in the town. For most of the twentieth century Bernice had been a largely biracial town. As late as 1990, the census recorded that 99.1 percent of town residents were black or white. The remaining 0.9 percent—14 residents—indicated they were of Latino origin. By 2000 the census listed 120 Latino residents, 6.6 percent of the population of 1,809. Six years later the Latino population of the small town was still growing; almost 20 percent of the children registered at the local K–12 school were of Latino origin. A 2007 estimate from the Folklife Program at Louisiana Tech in neighboring Lincoln Parish estimated that "40–45 (Mexican) families lived in Bernice—mostly from San Luis Potosi."[1] The 2010 census indicated that the percentage of the population that identified itself as Latino had almost exactly doubled in ten years, to 13.3 percent. Many of the newcomers were employed first by ConAgra and then by Pilgrim's Pride, as the local plants reached beyond their traditional labor pool.

Although there are numerous factors that have attracted Latino immigrants to the South, the existence of poultry processing has played a key role. Between 1990 and 2000 the Latino population of Arkansas, for example, grew 337 percent, due largely to the presence of the poultry industry. The town of Bernice, along the Arkansas-Louisiana border region, thus provides a meaningful context in which to examine how black, low-wage workers have perceived the effects of Latino immigration on their workplaces, community, and schools.[2] Like Helen Marrow, I "focus less on why immigrants have settled in new destinations and more on what has been happening . . . since their arrival."[3] Unlike Marrow, I examine this development through the lens of black residents' perceptions. Black residents and workers, afraid of job loss and community changes, have expressed wariness about their new neighbors. This competitive, conflict-ridden atmosphere has been promoted inside the plants by management and outside the plants by anti-immigrant rhetoric. Conflict and tension between African Americans and Latinos in areas such as Bernice are an extension of earlier patterns in U.S. history.[4] Here, however, the conflict is occurring outside the context of large cities, in areas with little experience in multiculturalism and with less fluid racial boundaries. The South has been inseparable from its complement of race.[5] The arrival of large numbers of Latinos reconfigures the pairing of "South and race" and "black and white," creating a very real need for southerners to negotiate how they will define themselves and their region and how both will be defined by others. For African Americans, who have long been associated with, if not defined by, low-wage, low-skilled southern labor, Latinos who threaten to alter that relationship are viewed with suspicion.[6]

Bernice is an interesting community in which to study these dynamics, positioned between the extremes of the explosive growth area of Arkansas and the slow-growth areas of the rest of Louisiana. Louisiana's Latino population grew only 16 percent in the 1990s, but the Latino population of Union Parish doubled, with the largest percentage settling in Bernice.[7] Bernice may be especially appealing to Latino immigrants they find the work available in its traditional forestry industry and the nearby poultry processing plants familiar. Residents observed the beginning of many changes, from the slow but steady entry of Latino children into the local school to the grocery and "dollar" stores' new practice of stocking items for Latino consumers. While they noted these subtle shifts, few seem to have realized the magnitude of change that could come.

THE *NUEVO* SOUTH

Poultry processing is altering the ethnic landscape of rural areas all over the South.[8] Historian Julie Weise cautions, however, that labeling this process as new (*nuevo*) is historically shortsighted, "products of the scholarly and popular imaginations rather than the historical record."[9] She documents the lives of Latinos in the South well before the twenty-first century and examines how their presence and their own attempts to situate themselves racially have affected the "racial ideologies" of the South.[10] In Bernice the life of Lisa Morales evidenced some of Weise's claims. Morales was born in Bernice in the 1980s to a black mother and Mexican immigrant father. Her father was one of a small number of Mexican men who had come to Bernice to work temporarily. They settled in black neighborhoods and nurtured friendships and intimate relationships with African Americans in the town. In time, however, legal troubles and lack of ongoing work opportunities forced her father to leave. Morales grew up grappling with racial and ethnic self-definition, viewing herself as "a black girl [who] lived with my black family" but also realizing that she "wasn't black like most of the black people in Bernice." As a teenager, she struggled to situate herself in the still largely black-white context of Bernice.[11]

Morales's father's settling in such a small southern town was not typical. In the United States Latinos are still predominantly located in urban areas, but between 1990 and 2000 the number of Latinos in nonmetropolitan areas swelled, with the rate of growth of the Latino population in these areas topping 70 percent.[12] One reason for this growth was the recruiting effort of industries with dangerous, low-skilled jobs such as poultry processing, which for a number of reasons needed new workers.[13] If, for example, better job opportunities arise, line workers prove willing, anecdotally, to leave the industry and its unpleasant work. A continued, strong domestic market combined with significant growth in global markets in the 1990s meant that processors vigorously sought new workers to staff their plants. Between 1993 and 1995 the value of U.S. poultry exports more than doubled. Poultry processing line work became one of the nation's fastest-growing occupations.[14]

Poultry processors began looking outward for labor, a practice with which they had some experience. Processors initially were able to staff their plants with local labor. Next, they recruited from neighboring towns and counties. Eventually, companies not only had to look to different geographic areas; they also had to look to different ethnic groups. The pull of "labor shortages . . . throughout the Midwest and South" coincided with the push of "anti-immigrant fever and a saturated job market in the West" to encourage Latin migration to the South.[15]

The poultry industry is not solely responsible for the amazing growth of the South's Latino population between 1990 and 2000, but many of the high-growth rural counties house or are near poultry producing companies. Further, that the growth rate of the Latino population in three of the largest poultry producing states topped 300 percent in a single decade supports the claim that there is a close connection between the industry and the expansion of the nonmetropolitan Latino population.[16]

Poultry processing companies and Latino workers both undertook the task of recruiting more Latinos to the plants. Their efforts proceeded as job opportunities in Latin American countries and in the "traditional migrant gateway cities" such as Chicago, Houston, and Los Angeles declined.[17] Companies advertised and sent recruiters to states with high Latino populations, promising incentives such as "transportation . . . and housing available. Good starting wages."[18] They worked with employment and government agencies such as the Job Training and Partnership Act offices to attract migrants to poultry producing areas.[19] Latino workers themselves used kin and fictive kin networks to recruit other migrants to the industry. By word of mouth, sharing recruitment posters, and making referrals to plant management, they helped expand Latino employment in the poultry processing industry. Latino networks, unlike those of black employees, have the added dimension of being international. Immigrants are able to spread or send word of work available in their home countries, attracting potential employees.[20] The Louisiana Tech Folklife Program study Catholic Mexicans in Bernice found that in this respect the town's Latino population was no different than similar populations across the South, as "many of the families that came to Bernice in the last decade came at the urging of siblings and extended family members who already had made Bernice their home."[21]

Recruitment is not the only factor that brought Latinos to poultry producing areas. The 1986 Immigration Reform and Control Act (IRCA) played a mixed role in that process. IRCA offered amnesty and the promise of future citizenship to almost three million undocumented immigrants. It also prohibited companies from knowingly hiring undocumented workers by establishing penalties and the practice of auditing employer I-9 forms.[22] IRCA increased the number of legalized Latino workers in poultry processing plants by giving them freedom to move to poultry processing areas and explore other options. And despite its intention to reduce hiring of undocumented workers, it also increased the pool of available undocumented workers by encouraging a lucrative market in illegal documents across the South.[23] As one congressman observed, two decades after IRCA's passage "the easy availability of counterfeit documents has made a mockery of IRCA. Fake documents are produced by the millions and can be obtained cheaply."[24]

The allegation of widespread use of black market documents was given some weight by the 2001 indictments of Tyson Foods executives on charges of racketeering and trafficking in undocumented immigrants. The Immigration and Naturalization Service (INS) accused Tyson of cultivating a culture "in which the hiring of illegal alien workers was condoned in order to meet production goals and cut costs to maximize profits." Similarly, the "Cruelest Cuts" journalists found that "five current and former House of Raeford supervisors and human resource administrators, including two who were involved in hiring, said some of the company's managers know they employ undocumented workers."[25] While the former House of Raeford employees claimed that they had simply refused to discern whether or not identification was valid, the indictment against Tyson alleged that Tyson actually aided and abetted these workers in obtaining fake documents.[26]

This document trade reached South Arkansas. According to Neysha Mallory, "In the end a lot of them had to go because they was either using somebody else's ID . . . just to be here. They ended up either having to quit or they had to leave 'cause they start sending the people in, or if they heard that immigration was coming." El Dorado plant employee DeShaun Lowe watched Latino employees quit or be terminated yet return in less than the normal rehire waiting period. Two employees who once worked under his supervision "came back under different names. I tried to talk to the lady, she wouldn't answer. But the man put his hand over his mouth, saying for me not to say nothing because he knew that I knew him. I don't know how it's possible . . . I think they're just going and changing social security numbers . . . just to become a citizen for a little while."[27] Lowe was sure that the personnel department knew these people had "worked there before, but they just pretend they don't know."[28]

Another attraction of the new settlement areas was the relatively small presence, first, of the INS and, later, of the Immigration and Customs Enforcement (ICE) agency. As the use of illegal documents grew, increased Border Patrol activity and ICE raids and investigations pushed undocumented immigrants out of states with historically large Latino populations (where ICE is most active) and pulled them toward areas with low Latino populations such as the South and Midwest.[29]

WORK THAT AMERICANS WON'T DO

Just as poultry processing took root in northwestern Arkansas long before it reached south-central Arkansas, Latino migrants arrived in the northwestern part of the state before they ventured south. Latinos entered northwestern Arkansas in the late 1980s. Fifteen years later they were the dominant ethnic group in poultry processing there.[30] Over time Latinos have moved beyond the four counties of northwestern Arkansas into other parts of the state, including the El Dorado area. Like many black workers, some Latino poultry processing workers settled across the border in Louisiana.

In Bernice this new population settled largely east of Highway 167, on Louisiana Avenue and Maple Street, near black residents. African Americans and Latinos are learning to share the public schools and social areas.[31] The McDaniel Recreational Center, for example, has long been the domain of black citizens. The center houses the local Head Start program, and the grounds have a basketball court and softball field dominated by black athletes. In recent years, however, the Head Start rolls have swelled with Latino preschoolers, and part of the grounds close to the softball field has been converted into a makeshift soccer field. These fledgling efforts toward peaceful coexistence are the first of many that will have to come.

The story in the workplace has been a little different. In north-central Louisiana and south-central Arkansas, poultry processing was constructed as black women's work both because it is grueling and monotonous and because black women were the vulnerable labor force most readily available to do it. In later years poultry processing, once a mainstay of low-wage black female employment, had moved from the category of black women's work to that of Latino men. There are a number of reasons for this shift, including the fact that while women are overrepresented in the nonimmigrant low-wage labor pool, for immigrants men dominate low-wage labor.[32] The status of immigrant poultry processing workers is much like that of black women when they first came into the industry. Immigrant workers, many of them ousted from agricultural labor, are typically poor, lack formal education, and are barred from many categories of social assistance.[33] They are often in desperate need of work. Many of the same stereotypical descriptions used to characterize black women workers in the middle of the twentieth century now rationalize the recruitment of immigrant men into poultry processing.[34] The growing number of Latino immigrant workers, primarily men, at first presented problems for black female workers, who dominated line work.[35] Black workers met the arrival of Latinos with caution and fear that they would lose an important category of jobs available to them.

In the case of poultry processing, plant management exacerbated black workers' fears by beginning, in the 1980s, to turn to Latinos as a preferred labor force.[36] Throughout the South personnel managers complained of black workers' laziness, absenteeism, and desire to "collect welfare payments and deal drugs."[37] Many poultry processing employees work in a cyclical pattern that may contribute to managers' complaints. They rotate "among different activities, multiple jobs, and periods of rest, relief and

work," a process essential to their ability to stay in the grueling industry.[38] In the industry surrounding El Dorado, black workers traditionally
rotated between periods of rest and working in one of the three plants in
the area.[39] Their ability to do so, however, was limited by the presence of
Latino workers, who could fill positions during workers' periods of rest.
Black workers, who have long "take[n] for granted the easy availability
of processing work," could no longer do so.[40]

In addition to their presence as "replacement" workers, Latinos' pur-
ported compliance is another source of contention for black workers.
In the discourse surrounding immigrant workers, one common refrain
is "there are hardly any complaints from [Latinos'] end."[41] Helen Marrow, for example, juxtaposes the "negative aspects" of working in poultry
processing with Latino workers' "positive depictions of their [poultry
processing] jobs."[42] A Tyson food representative said of Latino workers:
"They're loyal, they're on time. Our absenteeism has gone down. Turnover has gone down."[43] When asked about the growing number of Latino
workers in the El Dorado plant, Neysha Mallory said, "The Mexicans
come in here and they won't complain about how they was working the
mess out of them or whatever, and that's what made them start hiring
them!"[44] A plant manager for the House of Raeford lent this assessment
some validation. In a statement loaded with racism and dismissive of
the dangers of repetitive work, the manager noted: "Hispanics are very
good with their hands and working with a knife. We've gotten less complaints . . . . It's more like a natural movement for them."[45] According to
some scholars, this lack of complaint may be due in part to the fact that
"recent immigrants have a different reference point for wage levels and
working conditions, while undocumented workers have limited options."[46]
The Guatemalan Mayans in Morganton, North Carolina, for example,
came from an area in which the average daily wage was less than three
dollars.[47] Similarly, a poultry processing worker from Mexico recounted
making "like, $20 a week."[48] Thus, recent immigrants may be willing, even
eager, to work harder for less in terms of money and long-term benefits.

But the hard work and compliance are not all internally motivated.
Latino workers in Stuesse's study were cognizant of their position as
being easily exploitable, particularly those among them who were undocumented.[49] In the poultry industry at least one in five of all workers
is undocumented.[50] They labor under the threat of deportation, can be
fired for small complaints, and, even if they are fired unjustly, will not

necessarily be remunerated.[51] Aware of these dynamics, Tavia Wright observed that the plants are "hiring Hispanics because they can work them like they want."[52] A black Mississippian indicated that the plantation ideology has remained even if the exploited group has changed: "Some African Americans are concerned that the Hispanic community is driven by whites as slave labor, and some . . . pity Hispanics because they work 'em to death."[53] Mallory suggested that a similar sentiment was visible in El Dorado: "[Plant management] knowing these blacks gonna come in here [with the understanding that] I'm gonna work to make my money, but you not fixin' to work me like a dog and kill me."

Working in the same industries as new immigrants may pose problems for black workers in at least two other ways. First, the practice of network recruitment among Latinos, when used heavily by employers, is devastating to African Americans. Ethnic groups cluster or concentrate in certain industries or occupations, engendering "ethnic niches."[54] The creation of such niches in poultry processing might limit the opportunities of black workers who have long done the work because immigrants bring with them ethnic networks that may extend all the way back to their home countries. Once employers take advantage of the network, the workforce composition changes.[55] Traditional workers are effectively shut out of certain industries. Stuesse explains how this has worked at one Mississippi plant: "A former office assistant . . . claims that [the night manager] instructed her to throw African Americans' applications directly in the garbage. At other plants, dozens of Black applicants have complained to union representatives that they have been turned away while Hispanic workers continue to be hired. . . . Local Black workers report having a harder time getting hired for work in the chicken plants since Hispanic workers arrived."[56]

In El Dorado, DeShaun Lowe regarded the hiring of a Latino personnel manager as evidence that the company sought to recruit a primarily Latino workforce. Mallory agreed, but when she tried to express her concerns about possible displacement to her supervisor, she noticed that the fear was felt on a higher level as well: "He would just look at me because he know what I was saying was true, and at the same time he was kind of scared too 'bout trying to save his job. He was thinking they gonna get the Mexican supervisor to come in to take his job, so he just kind of just dealt with it." Deena Shine felt that the company had successfully begun to "weed us [black people] out."[57] Thus, network hiring, when used so extensively, can become a tool of discrimination. The exclusion of black workers from some industries has prompted some of them to file discrimination complaints with the U.S. Equal Employment Opportunity Commission.[58]

Second, since the late 1980s industries have used subcontracting to find workers. Companies pay individuals or smaller companies to find workers and/or assemble work crews. Initially, subcontracting allowed companies to circumvent the IRCA's prohibition against knowingly hiring immigrant workers. These workers were employees of the contractor and not the larger company. The introduction of a "middleman," or several layers of contractors, has meant a drop in worker pay in certain industries. Working for contractors can also leave workers without any pay at all and no clear idea of whom to address with grievances. Using contractors increases worker turnover rates and weakens collective bargaining: because employees are not directly hired by the company, they may be ineligible to join unions.[59] Subcontracting also helps industries such as poultry processing to hide workplace injuries: "When outside contractors [are] injured or killed, their injuries or deaths are not listed on the main employer's OSHA log, nor do they register in the primary employer's industrial classification."[60] This practice further obscures the danger of the work.

Companies have no interest in allaying workers' fears about each other. The ultimate beneficiaries in the conflict between black and Latino poultry processing workers are poultry processing companies. Employers often want to keep a distance between different ethnic groups to discourage their organization and protest. Favoring one group over another creates and sustains inter-group tensions. The widely expressed preference for Latino workers, for example, implies a critique of the black work ethic, rendering black workers as inferior to Latino workers.[61] At the same time, Latino workers in Mississippi reported feeling that blacks were the preferred employees and that plant management allowed black workers more privileges and more leniency to break workplace rules.[62] When management constructs the presence of each group as a threat to the other, it becomes a very real concern for poorly educated, low-skilled workers in rural areas. Juxtaposing the stereotypes of the "hard-working immigrant" with the "lazy African American" serves another purpose as well. Painting African Americans' reluctance to continue to do this type of work as a result of their inherent "laziness," rather than the poor working conditions and stagnant pay, helps the industry dodge criticism, as the stereotype is readily accessible and believable within American culture.

Those poor working conditions and stagnant pay are reasons that poultry processing work is readily available to new arrivals.[63] The industry is constantly in need of exploitable workers. Black workers indicate that they came to the industry typically because it was the only steady work they could find or because they received higher starting wages than they would elsewhere. Few in this study or others suggested that they actually liked the work or believed they were paid fairly. Thus, in response to concern over the growing Latino population in Arkansas, one newspaper editor succinctly told readers: "Pleasant work, this is not. A lot of people wouldn't do it, which is one reason why there are so many Hispanics around. They will do it."[64]

Indeed, claiming that there are jobs "Americans won't do" has been an integral part of the argument against restricting immigration and for offering amnesty programs. It is a phrase repeated by large businesses such as poultry processors but also by smaller ones such as landscaping companies and restaurants.[65] Some government officials have also adopted this platform. In 2006 President George W. Bush insisted that work Americans will not do is a "fact of life" and that the Senate, while considering an immigration reform bill, must acknowledge that fact.[66] The American people seem to have a mixed reaction to the sentiment: while many still accuse immigrants of taking jobs, a review of major surveys found that between 47 and 68 percent of those polled believe that immigrants took jobs other people did not want. In none of the surveys did a majority (or a plurality) of respondents indicate that immigrants took desired jobs away.[67]

Nevertheless, Americans should be wary of this argument. As law professors Jennifer Gordon and Robin Lenhardt point out, until recently Americans *did* do this work.[68] The problem may not be that Americans will not do the jobs but that "they cannot afford to do [them because] the wages have been depressed so much, it's not really worth it."[69] The labor shortage that immigrants fill is based not upon a lack of workers but on "the [poultry processing] industry's refusal to adjust working conditions and wages."[70] When Latino immigrants left their jobs in the wake of an immigration raid, the company aggressively recruited black workers and raised hourly wages by more than a dollar.[71] And one economist found that, contrary to popular belief, it is black workers who "appear to take jobs that otherwise similar native whites and Hispanics *and immigrants too,* are unwilling to take."[72] Additionally, proclaiming that there is work Americans will not do demonstrates a very unsubtle form of ethnocentrism. It implies a judgment of work that is beneath Americans but desirable and/or suitable for people from other nations.

As poultry processing and other industries shift to an immigrant work-force, questions about the effect on nonimmigrant workers arises. Particularly prominent are the claims that immigrant workers displace native-born workers and drive down wages. Government data and company representatives alike deny that immigrant workers are displacing native-born workers. In poultry producing areas, for example, unemployment still tends to be low, despite population growth.[73] According to Hudson Foods, before the rise in immigration, the company was unable to fully staff one of its major plants in Noel, Missouri, with local labor. Hundreds of miles away, in Laurel, Mississippi, plant managers reported the same problem. Stuesse argues that we should be wary of the invocation of "labor shortages" as justification for immigrant recruitment, however, because "it is [a term] often employed to justify racialized strategies of labor control." According to poultry processing companies, labor shortages are created by black workers' unwillingness to work hard, thereby warranting companies' recruitment of immigrants. This recruitment occurs because of immigrants' work ethic, explains company management. Never do they mention immigrants' vulnerability and lack of alternatives, which contribute to their status as a controllable workforce.[74]

The increase in the South's Latino population has actually created more jobs, especially in service and social service fields, many of which are only open to more skilled workers. In the context of a growing economy, native-born workers with more education are able to move up and out of poultry processing plants.[75] Newer Latino workers who come from a pool of migrants in which most lack legal status, have no high school diploma, and speak little English or none at all become the ones trapped in an industry that teaches few skills of value anywhere else.[76]

The data on whether or not immigrant workers drive down wages of native-born workers is mixed. As a whole, U.S. native-born workers benefit from immigration.[77] Studies that have found that immigration has an adverse impact on nonimmigrant wages typically find the impact is slight.[78] The problem with extrapolating from such large studies, according to sociologist Stephen Steinberg, is that they are based on large aggregates. They obscure the fact that "immigration may have negative effects on low-wage workers and positive effects on high-wage workers, thus cancelling each other out."[79] Similarly, Gordon and Lenhardt argue that "while the majority of studies conclude that the aggregate economic impact of immigration on the wages and job prospects of native born workers is either insignificant or positive, many—but not all—scholars concur that immigration *does* have a measurable negative impact on the wages of less-skilled native-born workers [a group in which African Americans are disproportionately represented]."[80]

Some studies that focus specifically on low-wage workers may not include occupations such as poultry processing, in which some African Americans have undoubtedly been displaced by Latinos.[81] In fact, when scholars look at smaller units (certain workers or certain industries), many find that immigration does in fact have negative effects on black workers. Economist George Borjas finds, for example, that "even though immigration raises the per capita income of U.S. natives, it has an adverse impact on the per capita income of black natives."[82] Labor economist Vernon Briggs contends that immigration lowers wages for less-skilled blacks and drives many out of the job market.[83]

Government and industry data have not been enough to change the perceptions of Bernice residents, who lean toward Borjas's and Briggs's theories. Many of them believe the contention that undocumented immigrants take jobs from U.S. citizens, particularly those who work in low-wage industries. One banker observed, for example, "Most of those employed from Bernice have to travel out of town for jobs when Hispanics are working here in town without citizenship."[84] The expansion of immigration to the South and the fact that Latinos are the predominant group in many southern plants have meant that many black poultry processing workers have developed this perception.[85] Thus, native-born poultry processing workers, especially black workers, have regarded the arrival of Latinos with suspicion. Vivian West noted that when she left the El Dorado plant in 1991, "they had started to hire Hispanic people, but not very many."[86] Years later Tavia Wright believed the situation had changed dramatically: "The Hispanics are about to outnumber all the different races." Deena Shine agreed, noting: "Before I left that plant, probably the majority was ran by Hispanics. . . . They basically was bringing them from other places, putting them in our jobs."[87]

Black residents also believed that immigrant workers drove wages down. "They will work cheap," noted many of those surveyed for this study, "for any pay" or, most tellingly, "for less than Americans."[88] Mallory was convinced that her company "takes some Mexicans and work them and maybe pay them just a little bit cheaper than they pay the blacks. They know you gonna [have to] pay [African Americans] minimum wage or more, as to where they might take this Mexican they know [is] not legal and say, well, here, I'm gonna pay you this and I'm gonna give you cash money." The result, according to one resident, is that "wages are being cut because of Hispanics and we are left without jobs."[89]

It is unclear whether immigrants displace native-born workers; scholars, for example, come down on both sides of the issue. In the poultry processing industry, however, it is fair to say that Latino immigrants are replacing black workers. The largest proportion of workers in the meat and poultry industry are young Latinos.[90] This replacement does not always occur in a negative context for black women. Some women interviewed for this study followed the path up and out of the plants—Kenya Drayton is now a schoolteacher, Trinity Mays works in financial operations, and Jackie Martin-Lowe is a nurse. Within the plants LaDonna Island and Natalie Davis worked their way up to salaried positions before both left, Island for a professional job and Davis to return to college. Nevertheless, as the belief that poultry processing work would always be available began to wane, many more of these women searched the meager pool of low-wage jobs for employment or turned to various social services programs.

Workplace conflicts are not solely constrained to issues of potential job loss. Black poultry processing workers, acclimated to overwhelmingly black, English-speaking workplaces, must adapt to the environmental changes in their workplace. Latinos did not change the work environment at her Farmerville, Louisiana, plant much, according to Davis. "We only have a few on the lines," she noted, "and they started when I started." Her Pilgrim's Pride plant may have been unusual on that count, as the number of Latino workers who process poultry continues to grow. Because poultry processing workers often sing and talk to each other while on the line, verbal communication is vital to their work environment. The introduction of workers who do not speak the same language is problematic for established workers when the new group becomes more substantial, decreasing the sense of community that workers have on the line. The resultant change in the language and culture of the "shop floor" creates a sense of isolation and may push traditional workers out of the plant. Even in Farmerville, where the number of Latino workers was small, the language differences presented challenges. LaDonna Island described the difficulties when she still worked at the plant: "A lot of times we have to have some of the English-speaking employees translate for us because some of the newer ones just don't understand what we're asking them to do. Sometimes we're able to do some sort of sign language . . . to indicate what we want them to do, and they'll understand, and they can go from there. If no one is around, we actually have to stop and show it to them so they can get it."[91]

Forty miles away, in El Dorado, the effect of the growth in the number of Latino workers was much more keenly felt than what Davis reported for the old Pilgrim's Pride plant. This effect was demonstrated by the plant's reliance on Latino labor, a fact that DeShaun Lowe and Neysha Mallory did not fully appreciate until the plant tried to operate without many of its Latino employees. In the spring of 2006 many Latino workers fled the plant or did not report to work, fearing a rumored ICE raid. According to Lowe: "The evening shift had to start up and they couldn't because they didn't have enough people on a certain line. There's more than sixty people on that line and didn't but fifteen show up. That line is only Hispanics right now."[92] Mallory described a similar experience: "One day we might have been short maybe three lines because at lunchtime they heard immigration was coming. Nearly all the Mexicans [did not come to work]. We found out who was legal and who wasn't. And evening shift that day they actually made us work over two hours because the evening shift consisted of mainly just Mexicans on the cone line, so we had to stay because they weren't coming in because . . . they thought immigration had come in."[93]

The realization that Latinos have become central to the production process has been problematic for black workers, who are accustomed to having some small measure of power, derived from the knowledge that the plant could not operate without black labor. That power must now be shared with, and perhaps will ultimately be usurped by, Latino workers. This shift changes the workplace environment in a nonphysical sense, by altering the position of power of black workers relative to white management.

SHARING PLACES WITH NEW FACES

More than workplace changes, the transformations within their local communities and schools resulting from the growing Latino population has elicited strong reactions among longtime Bernice residents. The black-white paradigm so symbolic of the South is largely a construct of the past. In response to the wave of immigration, many native-born southerners, black and white, express concern that Latinos are "taking over."[94] They worry that they are losing "ownership" of their towns and villages and that their children will one day be the outsiders. "I worry," described one Arkansas resident, "that I'm being swallowed up in a culture that isn't mine."[95]

In Bernice changes are occurring on a much smaller scale. A local hairstylist observed that businesses have begun "catering to [the immigrant community] by having Hispanic products available for sale."[96] Some residents are wary of what is to come: "Bernice is a small community that doesn't like change, but we're starting to see some. . . . The stores have more products for Hispanics. Just from being in town, you can hear Spanish being spoken and hear the music [Latinos] like . . . as more Hispanic people come, we're going to see more changes. I'm not sure how the older people will feel, but I'll bet it won't be good."[97]

That Americans feel threatened by the growth of ethnically different immigrants is nothing new given the country's national emphasis on assimilation (via the melting pot) and its history of exclusionary movements and narrowly defined citizenship. What is new is that the issues of community ownership have spread to previously insulated areas. Nonimmigrants worry that newcomers will not appreciate local systems of reciprocity and contribution. Related to the issues surrounding immigrant use of social services is the belief that immigrants do not give back to their new communities. Several survey respondents insisted that immigrants come to Bernice because "they don't pay any [income] taxes."

For some native-born residents, immigrants' practice of sending remittances to their home country serves as evidence that they are unconcerned with the well-being of host communities. "Most are here only a short time and all money is sent back home for the extended family," according to one Bernice resident.[98] Mallory echoed this idea, opining that "they just trying to make their pile of money to send their families in Mexico." Forty-two percent of adult, foreign-born Latinos indeed regularly send home remittances. Remittances to the Dominican Republic, El Salvador, Guatemala, and Mexico hovered around eight billion dollars in 2000.[99] "They don't make much," declared one survey respondent. "What is left for them to put into [Bernice]?"[100]

The arrival of a new group of racially or ethnically marginalized people revives old claims that they will bring down property values and makes clear that practices of residential segregation are still strong. Older residents point to dramatic examples to justify their fears: citizens in one Arkansas town reported being appalled by Latino residents' keeping and slaughtering of chickens and goats in their yards.[101] A Bernice homeowner lamented that "[people] communicate back home and the next thing you know, four families would be living in one house, [doing] no upkeep around their homes."[102] The practice of subdividing once single-family units into apartments accelerates wear and tear on what are often already older homes, rendering them increasingly less appealing. Combined with the increase in the number of low-value mobile homes and the demand for low-cost, rental housing, these factors lead native residents to worry that their new neighbors will transform local neighborhoods into unattractive, dangerous spaces. Such concerns have preoccupied Americans for much of this country's history. American citizens tend to impose their own standards of housekeeping on immigrants and judge them deficient and dirty.[103]

Rarely do Americans acknowledge the underlying issues that point to long-term residents' responsibility in confining new immigrants to poor housing. Mallory said, for example, "Look how many of them will stay in one household. As to where we not gonna pile up no ten or fifteen in one house, that's how they get to do it." Her observation does not mention the fact that unscrupulous local landlords have quickly learned to take advantage of migrants' need for shelter. In Laurel, Mississippi, rental home owners charged exorbitant rates for poor-quality housing.[104] Another practice is to subdivide houses, then charge male coworkers who live together as individuals rather than as one family unit. By such practices landlords greatly improve their earnings: "With four men to a house, [the owner] collected $800 monthly for a residence that had a fair market rental value of $300."[105]

In the poultry processing industry substandard housing is commonly provided by the company in its haste to bring in new workers. When companies began their recruiting efforts in the 1980s, they gave little thought to where workers and their families would reside. Small communities were poorly equipped to house large numbers of newcomers. Many migrants found themselves staying in hotels and substandard housing. In the mid-1990s, for example, the Hudson Foods plant in Noel, Missouri (near the Arkansas border), contracted with a local hotel to house incoming workers. A reporter who posed as one of these workers described the hotel as a "squalid migrant camp."[106]

Some companies did venture into providing housing for migrant employees. The facilities were inadequate, however, prompting one Hudson official to note, "We're in the chicken business, not the real estate business."[107] On the Delmarva Peninsula the executive director of the Delmarva Poultry Industries pronounced such programs a disaster and justified his company's abandonment of them: "The units were not maintained by the tenants and it was just a bad situation."[108] Again, the newcomers are blamed for this manifestation of their exploitation.

Real estate agents, bowing to pressure from residents who do not want new faces in their neighborhoods, often discourage immigrants from buying in certain areas or simply hide the availability of homes in those areas. In the same vein immigrants might find it difficult to secure financing for buying homes from local banks.[109]

It is not just individual homes or neighborhoods about which native-born residents express negative judgments. The Latino population has grown so phenomenally in terms of speed and numbers that rather than being absorbed into rural areas, they have been able to establish their own places within social spaces. The result is that the South's countryside is now dotted with "Little" Mexicos and Guatemalas and increasing numbers of Latino-owned or Latino-centered shops, stores, and restaurants.[110] These changes are particularly jarring because native-born southerners have largely defined Latino newcomers as workers. Thus, their expressions of identities as residents, neighbors, and consumers change not only the physical landscape but also the racial-ethnic one. To some established residents, this process of "Hispanization" seems to be proceeding more rapidly than that of Americanization.

No other factor is taken as a sign of Hispanization more than the retention of the Spanish language. Many natives contend that Latino immigrants simply will not learn English. The literal inability to communicate with neighbors and coworkers creates conflict between nonimmigrants and newcomers. It also creates new demands on native-born residents who come into contact with immigrants within a professional setting.[111] Some of the teachers and bankers as well as the sole social service analyst surveyed indicated that they expected learning Spanish might become a new job responsibility as immigration continues. It is "necessary that we learn the language . . . we work with them, teach them, live with them."[112]

The acts of speaking and preserving native language are intensely politicized, a space for debate about what it means to be American. This debate has a long history, extending back at least as far as 1753, when Benjamin Franklin criticized German Pennsylvanians for their efforts to retain their language and culture. In a country where learning and knowing "the" language—English—indicates a willingness to assimilate, a perceived refusal to do so is seen as a snub to the American national identity. After all, as the writer and theorist Frantz Fanon noted decades ago, "to speak [a language] . . . means above all to assume a culture, to support the weight of a civilization."[113] Speaking Spanish, especially, has moved from being seen as a link to a long cultural heritage to being problematic, fragmentary, and anti-American. As such, it has been under attack since the 1980s, most notably by English-only movements and the enactment of English-as-the-official-language legislation across the nation.[114]

It is unfair to assume that Spanish language retention always equals an unwillingness to become "American." Such a claim is based in part on a romanticized notion that previous immigrants easily abandoned their cultures and languages in order to assimilate. This is not the case, according to historian Gary Gerstle, who points to a historiographical trend that emphasizes that Americanization was coercive and that immigrants were not always eager to cast aside their old-world cultures.[115]

The implication that speaking Spanish is problematic also relies on a definition of American that is rooted in being "English-speaking." It assumes that ethnic and national identities cannot peacefully coexist. It upholds the notion that immigrants "refuse" to learn English, a claim not borne out by surveys—in which 96 percent of foreign-born and 88 percent of native-born Latinos say they feel that teaching English to immigrant children is very important—or long-term studies that show that Latinos tend to be English-language dominant by the second generation.[116] Finally, such a claim ignores the fact that there are other reasons besides "unwillingness" that prohibit immigrants from learning English. When immigrants live in neighborhoods with people who speak their first language, they acquire English more slowly. For Spanish speakers "the proximity of the country of origin with the increased possibility of multiple migrations needs also to be considered a factor."[117] In Bernice, observed the Louisiana Tech folklorists:

> Mexican adults . . . have a much more difficult time learning English than
> their children do. They work long hours, usually surrounded by other Span-
> ish speaking laborers. In the evenings or on the weekend, there are no

English classes available to them. Another factor that makes it difficult for Mexican adults to learn English is that many are illiterate in Spanish; the majority of Mexican children who grow up in rural villages, such as the ones in San Luis Potosi, leave school to work after the 2nd grade. While Mexican adults are exposed to English on radio and TV and grew to understand much of what they hear, even longtime Mexican adult residents of Bernice have little opportunity to practice speaking English. This is particularly true since adults grow to depend on the bi-lingual language skills of their children.[118]

Many times these children have encountered their own struggles in learning English. In Union Parish the difficulty immigrant students face learning English is a product of problems in their sending and receiving communities. Ana Smith, English as a Second Language coordinator for the parish school board, described an optimal case: "A student comes from Mexico to study in the United States and is placed in 6th grade without speaking a word of English, his chances of learning the language are going to be high if he knows how to read, write, speak, and understand Spanish at the same level of his classmates. He will make connections of the knowledge in the first language and use it to learn the second." That was not often the case in Union Parish, where "our English Language Learners [ELLs] . . . come from rural areas from the state of San Luis Potosi, many of them have not receive[d] a formal education. Their parents have just a few years of education, and some others are illiterate. Some of my families are illegal immigrants, making the situation more risky."

Local teachers have been ill equipped to deal with these conditions. Smith explained the parish's particular circumstances: "[It] is a rural area where [bilingual] education is not comparable to other places in this country. ELLs need good programs where they learn content area skills while learning English. Many teachers do not know how to make accommodations to promote English language acquisition."[119]

Increases in numbers of students with "Limited English Proficiency" have produced an immediate and unfamiliar need for bilingual education. In 1994 Greenwood, South Carolina, became a multiracial town virtually overnight. According to the principal of one elementary school, "A man . . . told her that he had 23 Latino children to enroll in school. Prior to that day, the school had never had a Latino student and . . . had no experience in providing instruction to Latino children, many of whom only spoke Spanish."[120] In six southern states—Alabama, Arkansas, Georgia, North

Carolina, South Carolina, and Tennessee—the Latino school age population (ages five through seventeen) grew by 322 percent between 1990 and 2000.[121]

Because most of the Latino migrants to the South are foreign-born, their children are more likely than Latino children in many other regions to speak limited or no English. Lillian Gafford, a local teacher in Bernice, where the parish school board still has not implemented programs to address the language issue effectively, gave the following synopsis:

> I have taught Latino children for the last five years. Our school is K–12, and we have an average 80–85 Latinos [in a school population of 425] in these grades. The sad situation is that in the last five years only three Latino students have managed to graduate. School is very difficult for them. Language is a terrible barrier. Some of the Latino students can speak some English, maybe write some, but not enough to pass [the] tests required to pass grades. There isn't a single teacher at Bernice High School right now who is able to speak Spanish. The Union Parish School Board employs one woman, Ana Smith, to service the entire parish and work with the Latino students. She comes to each school once a week, and God knows she does the best she can, but it is not enough. The school board is not doing its part to ensure these students receive an appropriate education. Many quit because it is such a struggle trying to learn without knowledge of the language in which they are being taught. They quit school rather [than] keep struggling in a system that is ill equipped to teach them. I often feel sorry for these students, and although I try to ensure they understand what is going on in my classroom, I also am at fault, because I know I could do better in trying to learn Spanish so that I can assist them in learning English.[122]

Smith was more succinct: "I am the only one for the parish, and I have my hands full." When she was hired in the late 1990s, Smith worked with one child. By 2004 she worked with 145. And the number "continuously grows. Not in small amounts, in larger amounts." As the 2006–7 school year approached, Smith expressed some hope because the parish school board had hired two teachers from Mexico. Even so, Smith wanted the district to "do more."[123]

These attempts, fledgling as they may be, are met with a wary eye by some parents, mostly black, in Bernice. In a parish that has already lost millions of dollars of funding in the last two decades—mostly because of white flight to Christian, private, and charter schools and schools in

neighboring parishes—any nontraditional expenditures are viewed criti-
cally.[124] Parents worry that rural schools, often poor already, will have to
spend disproportionate amounts of funding on bilingual education. The
fact that well into the 1990s, the number of migrant students increased
while federal funding remained the same in Arkansas partially validated
this concern.[125] Nationally, the federal government has not adequately met
the additional cost of teaching immigrant children.[126]

Native-born residents have voiced concerns that their children would
suffer because of the demands made on school personnel by the migrant
population. In Bernice one survey respondent argued that "more attention is focused on non-English-speaking students instead of American
students that may require additional attention."[127] Janae Earl felt the
Union Parish School District was more sympathetic and willing to render assistance to Latino children than to black and white children: "The
school had to step in and help out. I think Union Parish has done . . . they
try hard to help with the families. At the same time, some of the African
American or Caucasian kids don't have this either, and then sometimes
we find ourselves trying to give them too much and not give to our own
races. It's okay to help, but I feel like sometimes we do a little too much
and not think about our own race. If a kid would come to school and they
don't have a uniform or clothes or something or they don't have money
to go on a field trip or they don't have money to participate in something,
we try to help them out more than we would help our own, and I don't
see that as being fair." Her interpretation reveals a clear "us versus them"
orientation that characterizes many native-born residents' responses to
increased immigration.

Earl's observations also point to a fear of being "crowded out."[128] The
issue of crowding out is part of a larger problem in which parents fear they
will lose control over "their" schools to another group.[129] Parents identify
control of the schools as a significant issue because it offers them the
chance to influence who teaches their children and what their children
are taught. A loss of control to another group means that the school might
no longer be welcoming to their children.

School personnel surveyed posited another reason for the district's
struggle to educate Latino children: "The culture of the Hispanic population is one in which jobs for the older males are more important than education." One assistant principal concurred, writing, "When the Hispanic

students get high school age, they quit! Education is not promoted in the home."[130] The assumption that "culture and home are solely attributable for these rates" are unfair and ignore structural factors that limit educational access. Latinos are in fact the most educationally disadvantaged group in the country. They have lower high school graduation and college enrollment rates than African Americans or whites.[131] A number of studies suggest that Latino parents have high educational goals for their children and set strict standards to help their children meet those goals.[132] Inadequate school funding, language differences, and negative interaction between Latino students and students and teachers of other races contributes to Latino underperformance. These environmental factors have been at play in Bernice. Smith posited that many teachers see ELLs as a barrier. Lacking material and human resources to reach out to Latino parents and students, Bernice school officials watched Latino students drop out at disheartening rates.[133]

Given these circumstances, it is no wonder why, on May 11, 2006, Gafford was elated to see the two Latino students graduate. She was particularly proud of one of them, a young man named Luis Perez. Luis's life was busy; he had a job and often had to act as an interpreter for people in his community. Even with the many demands he faced, Luis was an honor graduate and promised Gafford that he would head to college in the fall. Luis was her proof that "despite the obstacles, Bernice High can educate and graduate Latino students."[134] But Union Parish has yet to learn how to do that consistently.

NOT SOLELY A MATTER OF BLACK AND BROWN

The focus here on black residents' and workers' perceptions of their new Latino neighbors is not meant to obscure the ways in which white society, and whiteness itself, affects immigrants' lives and their relationships with black Americans. After all, in the larger context the wariness and conflict are occurring within a white supremacist structure in which black and brown people must fight over low-wage, arduous jobs and accept the zero-sum philosophy that benefit to either marginalized group will come at the expense of the other.[135] Thus, black people in Bernice often juxtaposed their own vulnerable position with what they saw as Latinos' less vulnerable one. Based on an informal survey of her classroom, Gafford wrote,

"I find it amazing that African Americans who live in Bernice all of their lives never realize the American dream of home ownership, yet Hispanic families move here and within two to three years, they [are buying] their own homes."[136] Similarly, Delores Biles remarked, "You see more of them [have] the nicer homes, the vehicles . . . material things than what we do."

Scholars such as Claudine Gay have shown that the perception that Latinos are economically advantaged when compared to African Americans fosters and sustains anti-Latino hostility among African Americans.[137] Angela Stuesse also observes this phenomenon, citing the impressions of Keisha Brown, a former poultry processing worker: "You do have some [black] people that feel intimidated because Hispanics is getting new places and new cars, because when you first see some, they do automatically be able to come and get a brand new home, or a brand new trailer, or a brand new car. And, I mean, you have some people that's done *been here for years,* but [white folk] won't even work with you to give you nothing. . . . I'm gonna be honest. When I first started seeing how they was coming over here, you know, and I was looking, I was like, 'Man, they just heading over here. They got a brand new house, car. I done been here for ten years, and I can't even get a house,' you know?" In these cases black workers have internalized messages about who deserves material wealth in American society. While they questioned and were sometimes angered by the economic success of Latinos, particularly because they felt it came at their expense, they did not express the same feeling about the white people in their communities who were more prosperous than they were.

LaDonna Island made a similar observation about home ownership, attributing it to the fact that whites are "more accepting" of Latinos and thus Latinos "can do more things than blacks."[138] Her opinion hints at another worry that African Americans have—namely, that the presence of Latinos further distances them not from white people per se but from the power that whiteness confers. African Americans may fear that Latinos will do as other ethnic groups have done, distancing themselves from blacks while trying to align themselves with whites and gain the privileges of whiteness.[139] This is the "lesson of racial estrangement" that Nicolas Vaca has illuminated.[140] Yet it is not a new lesson, and black people have historical cause to worry. bell hooks maintains that "white immigrants to the United States . . . establish their right to citizenship within a white supremacist society by asserting it . . . through acts of discrimination and assault [against] black people and darker-skinned immigrants."[141]

And Toni Morrison concludes: "It doesn't matter anymore what shade the newcomer's skin is. A hostile posture toward resident blacks must be struck at the Americanizing door before it will open."[142]

Some African Americans assert that Latinos have already taken this path. "It's because of the color," explained one black woman. "Hispanics can assimilate more than a black person because there is no way a black person can hide his or her color." Another insisted that "Hispanics believe they are better than African Americans and they look down on African Americans."[143] Stuesse observes some of those sentiments in her study as well as evidence of racial distancing: "Latin American migrants' possessive investment in whiteness and neoliberal thought is also evidenced by their overwhelming belief that hard work begets success and that by pulling themselves up by their 'bootstraps' they can grasp a bit of the 'American Dream.' While it has begun to become a reality for some lighter-skinned Hispanics, for most others it remains a dream. Nevertheless, the dream functions not only to keep them giving 110% to benefit corporate profit in the chicken plants, but also to define new immigrants of myriad backgrounds in opposition to Blackness and Black Mississippians."[144] Some Latino immigrants may come to the United States with negative perceptions of black people firmly in place and are thus able to adapt those perceptions easily, according to Stuesse, to the racialized categories present in the United States that label African Americans as criminal and lazy.[145]

Black and brown workers have also internalized messages that portray them as burdens to society in contrast to the "hardworking taxpayers" commonly constructed as white. They use these messages effectively against each other. For my study, which centers on the perspectives of African Americans, I commonly found black people critical of Latinas' fertility and convinced that Latinos exploit the social services system. A number of those surveyed or interviewed included observations about Latinas' "repeated" pregnancies, "too many kids," or "having more children than we are." They expressed their fear of Latinas' fertility in another way—by commonly using the language of "taking over" and "outnumbering" and expressing the opinion that there was a Latino majority. At just over 13 percent Latino in 2010, Bernice had nowhere near a Latino majority. When the El Dorado plant closed a year earlier, it still had a black majority. These facts, however, had little effect on perceptions.

The preoccupation with Latinas' reproductive choices has developed from the assertion that Latinos abuse social service provisions. Much of the negative commentary about social services use is rooted in the larger historical stigmatization of welfare and the debates surrounding the issue of immigrants' reliance on government-sponsored social services that arose in the 1990s. As the immigrant Latino population increased after 1986, issues surrounding the impoverished status of many of the lowest-paid workers gained national prominence. Yet instead of working to redress poverty, many Americans worked to exclude immigrants from the system of social provision. Measures such as California's 1994 Proposition 187 built on the notion that Latino immigrants come "to sit back and be a burden on those who were already here."[146] Thus, as the immigrant Latino population and rates of poverty grew over the 1990s, their eligibility for social services was severely curtailed. Encouraged by citizen movements such as the one that backed Prop 187 and literature such as that by Peter Brimelow, which warned that Mexicans crossing the border would turn the United States into a poor "Alien Nation," the federal government took steps to discourage the migration of people who supposedly came to this country to benefit from its social services.[147]

Although welfare programs had long been under attack, in 1996 Congress ended "welfare as we knew it" with the Personal Responsibility and Work Opportunity Reconciliation Act (PRWORA). The act contained specific provisions for immigrants. It reiterated the exclusion of undocumented immigrants from programs such as Aid to Families with Dependent Children (which became Temporary Assistance to Needy Families) and food stamps but went further, barring them from housing assistance and their children from free immunizations and school lunches.[148] The PRWORA also prohibited legal immigrants from obtaining food stamps and Supplemental Security Income. These provisions were an outcome of theories that U.S. welfare was a magnet "influencing immigrants' migration decisions" and led to a "decline in the quality of new immigrants."[149]

But in accepting these theories, lawmakers and residents of new settlement areas ignored other important factors. First, Proposition 187 and the PRWORA came during a time of increased anti-immigrant sentiment, possibly as Americans first noticed the effects of the Immigration Reform and Control Act and the North American Free Trade Agreement.[150] Second, these theories were contested even in the 1990s, as researchers pointed out immigrants' use of social services was not disproportionately high and that immigrants, especially Latino immigrants, typically came to the United States to work. Indeed, the immigrants most likely to use social services are refugees and the elderly, not the "able-bodied" young.[151] Third, new immigrants from predominantly Catholic nations quite often turn to the Church before they apply to government programs, especially if they are undocumented.[152] Finally, Latino immigrants have a long history of providing community and social services to themselves. For generations they brought with them standards of altruism, reciprocity, and obligations expressed in earlier parts of the twentieth century through *mutualistas* (mutual aid societies) and kin networks such as *compadrazgos* and *commadrazgos* (forms of coparenthood/godparenthood).[153] As one scholar has argued, "While aspects of mutual aid underlie any society, the importance of reciprocity was more powerful among immigrants."[154]

In Bernice data indicating that immigrants do not disproportionately receive social assistance has not had as much effect on residents' opinions as accusations that they do. Longtime citizens complain that "[Latinos] come to live for free" and that "they get everything!"[155] A social service analyst employed by the local Office of Family support noted that immigrants can circumvent some of PRWORA's prohibitions: "If their children are born here, they can receive the same public assistance [for the children] as any other citizen of the U.S., e.g., medical, food stamps, etc."[156] Black people's critiques of Latinos on issues from housing to childbearing, in which Latinos are unfavorably compared to themselves, may be an indication that they are attempting to do some racial distancing of their own.

"WE LAUGH AND TALK TO EACH OTHER"

The relationship between African Americans and Latinos is not all focused on difference and conflict. Some African Americans recognize that Latinos are in a position much like their own and that the plantation mentality has not died. After all, if one looks at the plant as the center of this metaphorical plantation, it is easy to see some elements that are in keeping with historical plantation organization. The company provides housing and arranges it around the plant, often isolating workers from others within the larger community. Pay for this housing and other expenses workers incur are commonly deducted from workers' paychecks without their approval. Latino workers labor under the same abusive supervision by white or white-identified (in terms of loyalty) people of color, with little regard for their health or well-being. The economic and educational status of immigrant poultry processing workers is much like that of African Americans when they poured into the industry in the 1960s. Immigrant workers are the new pool of cheap, docile labor.[157] In 2004 civil rights activist Rev. James Orange recognized the similarity in the stories of poor black and brown people: "Here we are, 40 years later and we're still fighting the same battles we thought we had already won in the Civil Rights struggle. But now we're fighting for the rights of our immigrant brothers and sisters. Some of these laws being proposed [against immigrants in] Mississippi are just as oppressive as the old Jim Crow laws."[158] Other African Americans have also seen these parallels and work with their "immigrant brothers and sisters" to organize and build relationships "across difference."[159]

There are no organizations in Bernice that specifically foster intergroup solidarity, communication, or problem solving. If relationships between African Americans and Latinos in the town are progressing, it is because of everyday connections. A young survey respondent in Bernice indicated he had had positive relationships with his Latino neighbors, remarking, "They're 'all good' with me." Another native-born resident noted that her children's friendly interactions with Latino children have resulted in their desire to learn Spanish. Poultry processing employee Tavia Wright believed that Latino plant workers had begun to understand the concerns of their black coworkers: "After so long, anyone wises up, and now they're wising up. They used to be glad for overtime, but now they've caught on to it, like us. They figured out they were being worked more for less pay."[160] Another poultry processing worker described her experience with black-Latino relationships: "I work on a line with African Americans and Hispanics. We all get along well. [Hispanics] do not keep to themselves. We laugh and talk to each other."[161] And when Luis Perez walked across the stage to receive his diploma, he received a standing ovation from the mostly black audience. Perhaps they were glad because they realized, as one survey respondent argued, "it won't do no good—we can't get it no better for us unless we get it better for them too."

CONCLUSION

In January 2007 Pilgrim's Pride finished its acquisition of Gold Kist, beating out Tyson Foods for the title of largest poultry producer in the country. Of this transition Bo Pilgrim remarked, "We begin 2007 as the preeminent player in the chicken industry, positioned for long-term growth, leadership and value creation for our customers and stockholders."[1] Two months later Pilgrim's Pride appeared on *Fortune Magazine*'s list of America's Most Admired Companies, ranked number two in the food production industry. O. B. Goolsby Jr., president and chief executive officer of Pilgrim's Pride, linked this honor directly to Bo Pilgrim's promise. Pilgrim's Pride's position on the list was a reward for "focus[ing] on delivering outstanding service, quality and value to our customers every day."[2]

But what of the "partners" who work daily making the company the "preeminent" force in the chicken industry? When Pilgrim's Pride acquired Gold Kist, Goolsby mentioned the company's "long-standing reputation" for delivering value to the employees too. On its website Pilgrim's Pride counts as one of its most important goals "creat[ing] an empowering environment where all Partners can excel."[3] Yet the company has not lived up to the imagined reputation or the lofty goal. Instead, it has fostered an atmosphere in which plant workers and poultry farmers feel they do not matter.

The treatment of each partner as less than a person is undoubtedly an outgrowth of the historic selling of southern laborers as a prized commodity. Southern boosterism did not initiate in the post–World War II era, but it accelerated with a vengeance then. Southern businessmen focused on quantity of jobs over their quality in the industrial recruitment drive that changed the region into a euphemistically titled "Sunbelt."[4] "The term Sunbelt," writes Karl Raitz, "implies that the climate is mild and sunshine copious,"[5] and to attract industry to the region, boosters promised that those adjectives also described the unskilled workforce. In El Dorado laborers are still for sale. Boosters, in the guise of the chamber of commerce, entice industries to locate in the small city, where the affordability of labor is still a major selling point.

The status of black women, and especially single mothers, in Bernice is still tenuous. Long after the 1960 crisis, Louisiana, especially through Senator Russell Long, stayed at the forefront of efforts to "reform" welfare and vilify single motherhood.[6] The result is that the problems of the 1960s, especially the lack of job alternatives and the absence of an adequate social safety net, are still present. The 2000 census recorded that black women headed 85 percent of female-headed households with related children in Bernice. More than half of female-headed households lived below the poverty level.[7] Of these impoverished families, less than 28 percent received supplemental security income or another form of public assistance.

In the aftermath of the 1996 Personal Responsibility and Work Opportunity Reconciliation Act, the state legislature finished what its 1960 predecessor began. With the entitlement to welfare gone, the state legislature crafted the Personal Responsibility and Universal Engagement Act based on the premise that "all families should be actively and universally engaged in work activities." Work inside the home and within the community was dismissed and further constrained by the Strategies to Empower People (STEP) program.[8] Further, as one study suggests, Louisiana legislators place a greater premium on removing poor mothers and children from welfare than on funding job training or ensuring the availability of jobs with wages sufficient enough to care for families.[9] In seeking to minimize "dependency," the legislature forced poor mothers to become dependent on men or low-wage work.[10]

Despite the hopes of most of the Bernice residents interviewed for this study, the educational system in Bernice, in its present state, will not equip their children to escape low-wage work. For the 2005–6 school year, the Louisiana Department of Education gave Bernice High School one star (out of five) in its district performance accountability system. The kindergarten through twelfth grade school was classified as "in decline."[11] Inadequate funding meant that there were no ancillary or after-school educational programs, no college prep classes, not even an official guidance counselor. But in 2007 parish residents, who were determined to hold onto their neighborhood schools rather than consolidate, voted down a tax that would have benefited the schools.[12] In the end parents lost the fight to hold onto the school. The parish cut the school to kindergarten through eighth grade in 2009, then kindergarten through fifth grade a year later. Even with these "cost-saving" measures, the plight of Bernice's one school is perhaps best symbolized by the fact that it lacks even a library.[13]

And what of poultry processing work? The industry in El Dorado, for now, is at a standstill. This time the concern that had first prompted the chamber of commerce to seek out the poultry industry—that El Dorado would suffer an unbalanced economy by becoming overly dependent on one industry—proved valid, particularly in the case of low-skilled and unskilled workers. Journalist Susan Thomson asserts, "As chicken processing evolved into a big business, the plan grew accordingly—into a linchpin of the local economy."[14] In the summer of 2008 Pilgrim's Pride management informed employees that their jobs were in danger because of poor productivity and low return on the company's investment.[15] The company was struggling through financial difficulties, and management warned that the plant might close unless employees improved immediately and agreed to accept concessions. The company temporarily cut an hour of the workday. This move, combined with the reality of earlier closures, heightened fears of an imminent shutdown.

On Friday, February 27, 2009, these fears were realized. Pilgrim's Pride further stunned poultry processing workers and El Dorado industrial leaders by announcing that the plant would close.[16] El Dorado's mayor referred to the day as "Black Friday" and predicted, "This will be felt on all levels of our society."[17] A group of local investors tried to buy the plant, but Pilgrim's Pride rejected the bid. The remaining eight hundred workers were left jobless.

El Dorado's plight was exacerbated by the fact that other businesses had been laying off employees and closing as well. Thomson offers two examples: "The town's once bedrock manufacturing industry was eroding and taking its toll. In 2003, lighting manufacturer Prescolite Inc. pulled out of El Dorado, moving the work of its 270 employees to Mexico. Two years later, Cooper-Standard Automotive closed its local vehicle-parts plant and consolidated production in Auburn, Ind., eliminating another 400 jobs."[18] Thus, the city was left with unemployed industrial workers of various skill levels at a time when industrial employment is disappearing not only from Arkansas but from the nation as a whole. The chamber of commerce's claim that "the city's unique strengths in the oil and timber industries continue to help our economy grow and diversify" is true—Murphy Oil Corporation endowed a program called "The El Dorado Promise" that helps finance college educations for graduates of El Dorado High, and the timber and chemical industries still have a presence.[19] But for the hundreds of plant workers and chicken growers whose fortunes were tied so closely to Pilgrim's Pride, the chamber of commerce's claim proves little comfort. Still, El Dorado boosters know that the city has remade itself numerous times during its history, from timber town to boomtown to poultry center. They are counting on that legacy of experimentation and adaption to carry "Arkansas's Original Boomtown" into the future.

The story of poultry processing where plants still operate has not changed. It is still poorly paid work. Under the last contract negotiated for the El Dorado plant, between Pilgrim's Pride and United Food and Commercial Workers Union Local 2008, the base "top pay" for employees was still below ten dollars an hour.[20] Arkansas's poultry processing workers are some of the lowest paid people in all of meat, fish, and poultry cutting and trimming. Despite its reputation for being physically and economically crippling, the work has changed little. It is still too fast for human hands, but poultry processors stand behind the defense offered by Stephen Strausberg: "The narrow profit margin and sharp competition preclude slowing down the pace of operations."[21] In this matter workers receive no help from the agencies that should protect them. As Lance Compa of Human Rights Watch said: "The U.S. Department of Agriculture (USDA) assesses permissible line speeds, but solely in terms of food safety considerations, not worker safety. OSHA [Occupational Safety and Health Administration] is responsible for worker safety, but OSHA has not set standards for line speed to protect workers."[22] Indeed, Compa contended that the USDA is implicit in the steady speedup of the lines.[23]

The abandonment of poultry processing workers by government agencies is a long-standing and ongoing problem. The poultry inspection system that Shirley Barker and the Amalgamated Meatcutters and Butcher Workmen officials thought would help ameliorate the plight of poultry processing workers is still woefully inadequate. Deregulation in the Reagan era gutted programs such as OSHA and the Food Safety Inspection Service (FSIS) and erased the incremental gains such agencies made.[24] Although the 1990s brought demands for reinstatement of regulatory policies, the spirit of the Reagan years, aided by anti-regulation arguments such as those presented by Philip Howard in *The Death of Common Sense,* triumphed.[25] Inside some plants employees labor amid "mixtures of excrement, blood, oil, grease, rust, paint, insecticides, and rodent droppings. . . . Maggots . . . breed in . . . processing equipment and packaging and they drop onto the conveyor belt from infested meat splattered on the ceiling."[26]

The El Dorado plant was closed in 2001 for failing to clean the plant between shifts, a problem Con Agra "repeatedly failed to address," despite warnings from the FSIS.[27] Deregulation also keeps consumers at risk. After USDA policies that let companies take the lead on inspection and safety matters went into effect, the nation saw an increase in foodborne illness outbreaks.[28] Even when inspectors are present, they cannot adequately inspect the meat because it flies by them so quickly and because they are pressured by companies to let the lines keep running.[29]

Local 2008 did not find a way to generate and sustain active unionization among the people of color who worked in El Dorado. Employees held out little hope that the union would help them. Despite the fact that nationally the UFCW claimed to recognize the need for more rank-and-file participation and organization that focuses on the need of the workers, Local 2008 officials held onto the model of business unionism. In 2005 Tavia Wright observed: "Just like now, we're supposed to be in negotiations for the contract. When they go to negotiations, they don't tell us anything. They'll do like last time; they'll just throw the contract on us." Janet Strong echoed her sentiment, observing, "We have [union] leaders who don't care about us." Local 2008 stewards, chosen by union officials, are not motivated to care for members' interests in the plants, according to Strong: "Normally when a person is picked by somebody, that's who they work for. But if you are elected, you work for the people."[30]

Local 2008 has seemed just as out of touch with its growing Latino constituency. Well into the first decade of the twenty-first century, one union representative served "all Spanish speaking areas." Given the shift to a largely Latino workforce in the northern part of the state and the similar changes occurring in the southern portion, the local could not effectively organize without better outreach to Latino workers. A study of immigrant poultry processing workers in Morton, Mississippi, reveals that despite concerted efforts to organize the local plant, UFCW Local 1529 was troubled by the familiar problems of ideological opposition, tenuous membership, economically vulnerable workers, and desperate strikebreakers.[31] Again, labor unions are stymied by their own internal politics: until recently, unions have been at best lukewarm to Latino immigrants and at worst openly hostile, viewing immigrants as a threat to "American" jobs and wages. Even recognizing the significant role immigrant, particularly Latino immigrant, workers will play in the future of the unionization, they remain unequipped to garner the support of large numbers of these workers.[32]

So, what can be done, within the industry and within specific plants, to make poultry processing a "better" job? Processing poultry is never going to be pleasant or easy. There is, by the nature of it, blood and gore, smells and sounds, that most people find disagreeable. Cold temperatures are necessary for preserving the meat, and repetitive motions are necessary.

Nevertheless, companies can improve the physical plight of poultry processing workers. Slowing down the line is the most obvious solution, yet there are smaller steps. Ensuring that knives and scissors are razor-sharp and allowing employees to rotate jobs can decrease the incidence of musculoskeletal injuries. Processors can allow employees to take brief rests and provide stools and footrests for comfort. Across the industry poultry processors need to engage in fair practices that demonstrate that employees really are partners. The routine denial of employees' wages—especially overtime and preparation time pay—and of their right to organize are but two techniques processors use to exploit low-wage laborers. Pilgrim's Pride claims to aspire to creating a company in which all partners can be empowered and be creative. But industry practices emphasize how very vulnerable employees are. If Pilgrim's Pride and other poultry companies want to see all of their employees empowered, they must commit to making some changes.

The fate of black women workers from Bernice, Louisiana, is of course not yet fully known. Many of the former poultry workers proudly told me about returning to school or working "cleaner" jobs or taking time to engage in full-time family work. Others fell back on the paid jobs historically assigned to them, becoming cooks and nurses' aides and care providers or positions in other low-wage occupations. Their concerns are numerous: they worry, as mothers, about the failing school system and, as providers, about dwindling economic opportunities. Many told me that they turn their worries over to God, and I see them as they pack the pews of the local Baptist churches, sustaining a rich, spiritual heritage. I am so honored to have talked to them and known them and to have witnessed the resilience of their spirits.

But so much of this project has been about what I have derived and what I have learned. Beside my door I keep two posters. One displays a quotation by Gloria Anzaldúa that reads: "I write to record what others erase when I speak, to rewrite the stories others have miswritten about me, about you. To become more intimate with myself and you. . . . And I will write about the unmentionables."[33] The other bears Audre Lorde's admonishment, "We can sit in our corners mute forever while our sisters and our selves are wasted, while our children are distorted and destroyed, while our earth is poisoned; we can sit in our safe corners mute as bottles, and we will still be no less afraid."[34] These words have been ongoing motivations for me as a working-class black woman in the academy trying to tell a story that I found both crucial and neglected. But, again, telling that story was about my needs and my path as a writer. I was worried, when I reflected upon it, about whether or not I offered *anything* to the women who so graciously agreed to participate in this study.

Then I thought of the ongoing tradition of and dedication to celebrating women's stories, the *testimonios* and autobiographies and oral traditions in the literature of "third-world" women. Oppressed women engage in verbal and physical storytelling every day that writes them back into the historical record in their own terms. As Lorde suggested, if we do not undertake acts of self-definition, we stand to "be crunched into other people's fantasies . . . and eaten alive."[35] Clearly, these women were tired of being crunched into the fantasies of poultry processors. And as I thought of their motivations for participating in this study, in the margins of my manuscript I scribbled, "Maybe they challenge the structures of violence they encounter by telling the narratives themselves." A few weeks later my dear friend Nadia Abou-Karr, a Palestinian American artist-activist, told me about a former student who wrote, "We overcome by our testimony." It is the sentiment of what I scribbled, said much more eloquently and concisely. I remembered Janet Strong's admonishment to me: "Somebody should write about this. Should help us. Should tell somebody what they do to us." If this work can do that, if it can, in any small way, serve as an outlet for poor black women's testimony, for their audacious act of telling the story themselves, for their recognition of the ways in which they are marginalized and the ways in which they challenge such efforts, then maybe I can give these women just a small bit of what they gave to me.

BIOGRAPHIES

A brief biographical sketch of those whose remembrances and experiences are currently used in this work. All names are pseudonymous, unless otherwise noted, and all information is current as of October 2013. This list does not include nine participants with whom I conducted interviews but whose interviews have not yet been transcribed and used.

DeLores Biles grew up in Summerfield, La., before moving to Bernice. She worked at the El Dorado poultry processing plant for thirteen years.

Sherry Carter grew up in Bernice in the 1950s and 1960s. She worked briefly at the El Dorado processing plant in the 1970s.

Timothy Carter walked into the El Dorado plant in the summer of 1977 on the same day that his wife walked out for the final time. He started work as a floor person (cleaning meat off the plant's floors) the next day. Within two years he was an Area Manager. He went on to work in the industry in Georgia and in Arcadia, La., before retiring in 2002.

Natalie Davis, a lifelong resident of Bernice, worked briefly at ConAgra Poultry in El Dorado in the late 1990s. On June 5, 2000, she began working at the ConAgra plant in Farmerville, La. She worked there until 2009.

Bella Dawes has, in her own words, been "nowhere but Bernice, Louisiana." She worked in the El Dorado plant from 1978 until 2009.

Kenya Drayton is a native of Bernice. She worked at ConAgra Poultry in El Dorado in 1997 to pay for college expenses. She is currently a classroom teacher.

Janae Earl is a mother of three and a lifelong resident of Bernice. She went to work at the Farmerville, La., processing plant in 2007 to supplement her pay from her primary job and her husband's income.

Rosalynn Evans-Greshom (not a pseudonym) has worked with the Georgia Poultry Justice Alliance (GPJA) since she was in the eleventh grade. In 2003, shortly after receiving her bachelor's degree, she began her current job as executive director of the GPJA.

Ella Foster is a native of Spearsville, La., but has lived all over the parish, including in Bernice. She worked at the El Dorado plant from 1965 until 1998, becoming one of the few black women to make it to the rank of supervisor.

Lillian Gafford was a high school teacher for the Union Parish School Board in Louisiana who worked briefly in the El Dorado plant. She is a native of Bernice and the wife of a poultry processing worker.

Eleanor Holloway lives in Union Parish, La., and worked for the school district as classroom teacher and principal.

LaDonna Island was born and has lived most of her life in Bernice. She holds a bachelor's degree in sociology but found no satisfactory, degree-related employment in the Bernice area. She began work at the Farmerville, La., poultry processing plant in January 2003 and worked there until June 2008.

Ruth James worked at ConAgra Poultry in El Dorado from 1982 until 1992, when she left to care for her disabled husband. She has lived her whole life in Bernice and currently works in the mental health care field.

LeeAnn Johnson, a Bernice native and resident, followed her mother, father, grandmother, and aunts into the poultry processing industry. Except for a brief break, she has worked in the industry since 2008.

Aarica Jones has lived most of her life between Bernice and Spearsville in Union Parish, La. She went to J-M Poultry in the mid-1960s and stayed there until illness rendered her incapable of doing the demanding work.

DeShaun Lowe worked at the El Dorado poultry processing plant from 1989 until the plant closed in 2009. Two years later he began working in the Farmerville, La., plant. He was born and still lives in Bernice.

Neysha Mallory is a Bernice native who worked for ConAgra, then Pilgrim's Pride, in El Dorado, from 1997 until 2009.

Lydia Martin was born in Claiborne Parish, La., and lived in Bernice until 2012. She worked for twenty-five years at the El Dorado poultry plant under the management of Country Pride and Con Agra.

Sylvia Martin was born in Claiborne Parish, La., and lives in Bernice. She worked for twenty-four years at the poultry plant in El Dorado until it closed in 2009.

Jackie Martin-Lowe was born in Claiborne Parish, La., but has lived in Bernice since the early 1990s. She worked at ConAgra Poultry in El Dorado from 1992 to 1994.

Trinity Mays is a Bernice native who worked for ConAgra Poultry in Farmerville, La., from 2002 until 2003.

Faith Monroe was born in Union Parish, La. She worked at the El Dorado plant for almost twenty-six years, beginning in 1965.

Deena Shine has spent most of her life in Bernice. She worked at the El Dorado poultry plant for thirty years.

Ana Smith, the former English as a Second Language Coordinator for the Union Parish School Board, is from Mexico City. She has lived in the United States for over thirty years.

Janet Strong lives in El Dorado. She worked at the poultry processing plant there from1977 until 2009.

Lizzie Thomas has lived her whole life in Spearsville, La. She started at J-M Poultry in May 1965 and worked at the processing plant until 1979.

Geeta Tyler was a single mother who left the garment manufacturing industry in the early 1970s to work in the El Dorado plant. She worked there for over thirty years, until she left permanently to treat her cancer. She has lived her whole life in Bernice.

Vivian West was born in Spearsville, La., but moved the few miles to Bernice in 1974. She worked at the El Dorado poultry processing plant from 1969 until 1990.

Tavia Wright is a native of Bernice and worked at the El Dorado plant from 1986 until 2009.

Margie Young, of Bernice, worked thirty-one years—"from 1978 until close," in her words—at the El Dorado plant.

INTERVIEW QUESTIONS

What follows is the script for questions asked of interviewees. Their revelations sometimes prompted unscripted follow-up questions. (The questions were adjusted for interviews that took place after the closing of the El Dorado plant in 2009; here they appear in the present tense.)

1. Could you begin by telling me about your background? That could include where you're from, details about your family and education, or anything else you want to tell me about yourself.

2. When and how did you come to work in the poultry industry?

3. Describe the different jobs you do in the plant.

4. Tell me about your typical workday.

5. How do you feel about your work?

6. Do you see a difference in the jobs men and women perform inside the plant?

   If YES: Describe the types of jobs women do.
   Describe the types of jobs men do.
   Why do you think jobs are divided this way?
   How do you feel about the way jobs are divided?

7. Do you see a difference in the jobs black and white people perform inside the plant?

    If YES: Describe the types of jobs black people do.
              Describe the types of jobs white people do.
              Why do you think jobs are divided this way?
              How do you feel about the way jobs are divided?

8. If you did not work at the plant, what type of work might you be doing in this area?

9. How do you balance your family responsibilities, particularly parenting, with your work responsibilities?

10. Are they hard to balance?

    If YES: Why? Do you feel you have had to make sacrifices?

11. If you had to use *difficult* or *easy* to describe your job, which would you choose? Why?

12. What kind of illnesses or injuries do you see people experience?

13. If someone is injured or falls ill on the job,

    a. How do the supervisors react?
    b. How do your coworkers react?
    c. How does the nurse react?

14. Describe how the supervisors and line leaders interact with the line workers.

    a. Do they interact differently with men than they do with women?
    b. Do they interact differently with black people than they do with white people?

15. Do you believe you were paid what your work was worth?

16. Do you belong to the union? Why (or why not)?

    If YES: Describe your experiences with the union as a union member.

17. Do you think the union is effective? Why (or why not)?

18. Do you think the union reaches out to the employees?

19. Can you describe any events in which you felt the union strongly supported the employees?

20. Can you describe any events in which it seems the union supported the company?

21. Could the union be better?
    If YES: How?

22. Aside from going to the union, if the employees are unhappy with the company, how do they express their unhappiness?

23. The number of Latino employees working in the El Dorado plant has grown noticeably in recent years. In your opinion, why has that happened?

24. Do you think it has had any affect on the black employees that usually do these jobs? Do you feel that there is a preference for employees of a certain racial background?
    If YES: What makes you feel that way?
    What might account for the preference?

25. Have you seen changes in the plant that you feel are the result of the growing number of Latino employees?
    If YES: Describe these changes.
    How do they make you feel?

26. Have you seen changes in your community as Latino families settle in?
    If YES: Describe these changes.
    How do they make you feel?

27. Do you feel that you have been required to make any changes, at work or at home, as the result of the growing number of Latino workers and their families?
    If YES: Describe these changes.
    How do they make you feel?

28. How do you think the plant could be better?

29. What do you think are the effects of the industry dramatically reducing its presence in North Louisiana and South Arkansas?

30. Is there anything you would like to add?

NOTES

INTRODUCTION

1. "Simmons Celebrates 50 Years," *Partners,* a publication of the University of Arkansas, Division of Agriculture, Center of Excellence for Poultry Science, 7, no. 2 (1999): 6.

2. Marc Linder, "I Gave My Employer a Chicken That Had No Bone: Joint Firm-State Responsibility for Line-Speed-Related Occupational Injuries," *Case Western Reserve Law Review* 46, no. 1 (1995): 33.

3. David Harvey, *Justice, Nature, and the Geography of Difference* (Malden, Mass.: Blackwell Publishers, 1997), discussed throughout chapter 2.

4. All names used in this study are pseudonymous, except that of Rosalynn Evans-Greshom.

5. Employees at this plant come from a number of neighboring towns and counties/parishes.

6. See, e.g., Timothy Minchin's *Fighting against the Odds: A History of Southern Labor since World War II* (Gainesville: University Press of Florida, 2005); Alan Draper, *Conflict of Interests: Organized Labor and the Civil Rights Movement in the South, 1954–1968* (Ithaca, N.Y.: ILR Press, 1994); Barbara Griffith, *The Crisis of American Labor: Operation Dixie and the Defeat of the CIO* (Philadelphia: Temple University Press, 1988). James Cobb asserts that government and community partnership with industry "confirmed the established pattern of low wages for southern workers," in *The Selling of the South: The Southern Crusade for Industrial Development, 1936–1980,* 2nd ed. (Urbana: University of Illinois Press, 1993), 96.

7. Gwendolyn Mink, *Welfare's End* (Ithaca, N.Y.: Cornell University Press, 1998); Ruth Sidel, *Keeping Women and Children Last: America's War on the Poor* (New York: Penguin Books, 1998).

8. Jacqueline Jones, *Labor of Love, Labor of Sorrow: Black Women, Work, and the Family from Slavery to the Present* (New York: Vintage Books, 1985). Even in the immediate aftermath

of emancipation, black women were determined to negotiate the terms of domestic service to distance it as much as possible from the terms in which they had done similar labor as slaves (Tera Hunter, *To 'Joy My Freedom: Southern Black Women's Lives and Labors after the Civil War* [Cambridge: Harvard University Press, 1997]).

9. Phyllis Palmer, *Domesticity and Dirt: Housewives and Domestic Servants in the United States, 1920–1945* (Philadelphia: Temple University Press, 1989). While paltry pay and low status were real concerns for black women as domestic workers, they also disliked domestic service because white employers and the work itself denied their womanhood—their roles as mothers, wives, and community workers. It was these roles that constituted their "labor[s] of love," according to Jones. This issue is also discussed by Sharon Harley in "For the Good of Family and Race: Gender, Work, and Domestic Roles in the Black Community, 1880–1930," *Signs* 15, no. 2 (1990): 336–49; and Evelyn Nakano Glenn in "From Servitude to Service Work: Historical Continuities in the Racial Division of Paid Reproductive Labor," *Signs* 18, no. 1 (1992): 1–43. Black women contested the perceptions of white employers who viewed black women's work as the most important part of their identities (see Jones, *Labor of Love, Labor of Sorrow;* and Sharon Harley, "When Your Work Is Not Who You Are: The Development of a Working Class Consciousness among Afro-American Women," in *Gender, Class, Race and Reform in the Progressive Era,* ed. Noralee Frankel and Nancy Dye [Lexington: University Press of Kentucky, 1991]).

10. Dolores Janiewski, *Sisterhood Denied: Race, Gender, and Class in a New South Community* (Philadelphia: Temple University Press, 1985). This location of black women at the nexus of an interlocking system of oppressions is a theme present in much literature on black women and shows the unique place that they occupy, a space not shared by black men or white women.

11. Robin Kelley, *Hammer and Hoe: Alabama Communists during the Great Depression* (Chapel Hill: University of North Carolina Press, 1990); and Janiewski, *Sisterhood Denied,* provide more illustrative examples of the backbreaking labor typical of a farmwoman's day.

12. James Green, *World of the Worker* (New York: Hill & Wang, 1980).

13. Karen Tucker Anderson, "Last Hired, First Fired: Black Women Workers during World War II," *Journal of American History* 69, no. 1 (1982): 82–97.

14. Jacqueline Jones and Karen Anderson both discuss the role of the Women's Bureau, which was largely unresponsive to black women during the war, in encouraging black women to return to household labor. Other federal entities also worked to return women to the "status quo antebellum"; the United States Employment Service, e.g., denied unemployment benefits to women who turned down acceptable employment. For black women that acceptable employment was usually domestic work. Black women's postwar plight was further exacerbated by their inability to gain strong footholds during the war in two of the largest fields that employed women: textiles and clerical work.

15. Greta de Jong discusses how devastating AAA policies were for black sharecroppers in *A Different Day: African American Struggles for Justice in Rural Louisiana, 1900–1970* (Chapel Hill: University of North Carolina Press, 2002).

16. Jill Quadagno notes that union's exclusionary practices were aided by the discriminatory practices of the United States Employment Service, which offered African Americans (when it offered at all) menial, difficult work (*The Color of Welfare: How Racism Undermined the War on Poverty* [New York: Oxford University Press, 1994]).

17. Jones, *Labor of Love;* Green, *World of the Worker;* and Kelley, *Hammer and Hoe* all discuss the failure of federal relief to reach black families. Jones, in particular, outlined the discriminatory policies of the Works Projects Administration (WPA), including channeling black women and men, regardless of educational levels, into the most tedious work. Stephanie Shaw provided a similar evaluation in *What a Woman Ought to Be and Do: Black Professional Women Workers during the Jim Crow Era* (Chicago: University of Chicago Press, 1996).

18. In *The Politics of Whiteness: Race, Workers, and Culture in the Modern South* (Princeton: Princeton University Press, 2001) Michelle Brattain argues that the Fair Employment Practices Commission (FEPC) was especially ineffective in the South, where employers and other whites used any means necessary to circumvent antidiscrimination policy. Brattain and Anderson note that employers often hid behind the claim that their white employees would not stand for integration of African Americans into the workforce.

19. Perhaps the most positive evaluation of the FEPC comes from historians who assert that the committee's accomplishments lay not completely in its tangible gains but partially in the spirit it invoked in black workers. The FEPC vigorously publicized and challenged racist conditions and sparked black worker activism. FEPC activity and black worker militancy reinforced each other. Despite the committee's lack of power, the FEPC was a useful and significant agency for black workers (Robert Korstad and Nelson Lichtenstein, "Opportunities Found and Lost: Labor, Radicals, and the Early Civil Rights Movement," *Journal of American History* 75, no. 3 [1988]: 786–811; William H. Harris, "Federal Intervention in Union Discrimination: FEPC and West Coast Shipyards during World War II," *Labor History* 22, no. 3 [1981]: 325–47).

20. Cobb, *Selling of the South,* 267.

21. Rick Halpern and Roger Horowitz, *Meatpackers: An Oral History of Black Packinghouse Workers and Their Struggle for Racial and Economic Equality* (New York: Twayne Publishers, 1996); Rick Halpern, *Down on the Killing Floor: Black and White Workers in Chicago's Packinghouses, 1904–1954* (Urbana: University of Illinois Press, 1997); Roger Horowitz, *"Negro and White, Unite and Fight!" A Social History of Industrial Unionism in Meatpacking, 1900–1930* (Urbana: University of Illinois Press, 1997).

22. Bruce Fehn, "Chickens Come Home to Roost: Industrial Reorganization, Seniority, and Gender Conflict in the United Packinghouse Workers of America, 1956–1966," *Labor History* 34, nos. 2–3 (1993): 324–41. The women Fehn studies decried union men's sexist behavior and the men's attempts to silence them in union activities ("African-American Women and the Struggle for Equality in the Meatpacking Industry, 1940–1960," *Journal of Women's History* 10, no. 1 [1998]: 45–69).

23. Robert Bussel, "Taking On 'Big Chicken': The Delmarva Poultry Justice Alliance," *Labor Studies Journal* 28, no. 2 (2003): 1–24.

24. Various authors, "Ruling the Roost: A Special Report on the Poultry Industry," *Southern Exposure* 17, no. 2 (1989). The issue won the National Magazine Award in 1990.

25. U.S. Department of Homeland Security, Federal Emergency Management Agency, U.S. Fire Administration, *Chicken Processing Plant Fires: Hamlet, North Carolina and North Little Rock, Arkansas,* report no. 57 of the Major Fires Investigation Project, www.usfa.dhs.gov/downloads/pdf/publications/tr-057.pdf (last accessed October 18, 2011).

26. Harvey, *Justice, Nature, and the Geography of Difference,* 337–41, quote from 341.

27. Eric Schlosser, *Fast Food Nation: The Dark Side of the All-American Meal* (Boston:

Houghton Mifflin, 2001), 139. In 1997 the report from the National Commission on Small Farms noted that contract growers described having a "general feeling of servitude" (U.S. Department of Agriculture, National Commission on Small Farms, *A Time to Act: A Report of the USDA National Commission on Small Farms,* January 1998, www.csrees.usda.gov/nea/ ag_systems/pdfs/time_to_act_1998.pdf [last accessed October 18, 2011]). A good, fictionalized account of the plight of poultry growers is Sylvia Tomlinson, *Plucked and Burned* (Victoria, Tex.: Redbud Publishing, 2003).

28. Human Rights Watch, "Blood, Sweat, and Fear: Workers' Rights in U.S. Meat and Poultry Plants," January 2005, www.hrw.org/reports/2005/usa0105/usa0105.pdf (last accessed October 18, 2011).

29. Ames Alexander, Franco Ordoñez, Kerry Hall, and Peter St. Onge, "The Cruelest Cuts: The Human Cost of Bringing Poultry to Your Table," *Charlotte Observer,* February 10–15, 2008.

30. David Griffith, *Jones's Minimal: Low-Wage Labor in the United States* (Albany: State University of New York Press, 1993). Griffith has written a number of articles, several of which were consulted for this study.

31. Angela Stuesse, "Globalization 'Southern Style': Transnational Migration, the Poultry Industry, and Implications for Organizing Workers across Difference" (Ph.D. diss., University of Texas, 2008).

32. Helen B. Marrow, *New Destination Dreaming: Immigration, Race, and Legal Status in the American South* (Stanford, Calif.: Stanford University Press, 2011).

33. Steve Striffler, *Chicken: The Dangerous Transformation of America's Favorite Food* (New Haven: Yale University Press, 2005).

34. David Brody, *The Butcher Workmen: A Study of Unionization* (Cambridge: Harvard University Press, 1964).

35. Monica Gisolfi, "From Cotton Farmers to Poultry Growers: The Rise of Industrial Agriculture in Upcountry Georgia, 1914–1960" (Ph.D. diss., Columbia University, 2007); and "From Crop Lien to Contract Farming: The Roots of Agribusiness in the American South, 1929–1939," *Agricultural History* 80, no. 2 (Spring 2006): 167–89.

36. Gisolfi, "From Crop Lien to Contract Farming," 168.

37. Brent Riffel, "The Feathered Kingdom: Tyson Foods and the Transformation of American Land, Labor, and Law, 1930–2005" (Ph.D. diss., University of Arkansas, 2008).

38. Griffith writes about black workers but as one subset of marginalized workers and in the context of the industry's shift from black to Latino workers.

39. Ken Lawrence and Anne Braden, "The Long Struggle," *Southern Exposure* 11, no. 6 (1983): 85–89. Vanessa Tait mentions the MPWU briefly in *Poor Worker's Unions: Rebuilding Labor from Below* (Cambridge, Mass.: South End Press, 2005). The Sanderson Farms strike was profiled earlier by David Moberg, "Puttin' Down Ol' Massa: Laurel, Mississippi, 1979," in *Working Lives: The* Southern Exposure *History of Labor in the South,* ed. Marc S. Miller (New York: Pantheon Books, 1980).

40. Linda Cromer, "Plucking Cargill: The RWDSU in Georgia," *Labor Research Review* 9, no. 2 (1990): 15–23.

41. Yvonne Yen Liu and Dominique Apollon outline four stages in the food system: Production, Processing, Distribution, and Retail and Service. Within the United States people of color constitute just under 35 percent of the general population but 45 percent of food processing workers. The average wage paid to white people in food processing is $18.12. For people of

color that wage drops to $12.08. Within the food system women are more poorly remunerated than men. For every dollar a white man who works in the food system makes, black women make just 53 cents. Liu and Apollon, "The Color of Food," prepared for the Applied Research Center, February 2011, http://arc.org/downloads/food_justice_021611_F.pdf (last accessed November 19, 2012).

42. Chapter 5 looks at the changing face of poultry processing workers and the South. The rapid increase in Latino immigration to the South and the entry of Latino workers into the poultry industry elicit mixed reactions from black workers. Fear over the loss of jobs, social services, and residential spaces, along with a heated debate over immigration, foster animosity between marginalized groups.

43. In chapter 1 I will more fully explore the ways in which the industry was touted as the salvation of some rural areas.

44. Lauren Etter, "At Chicken Plant, a Recession Battle," *Wall Street Journal,* June 30, 2009, http://online.wsj.com/article/SB124631125369670273.html (last accessed November 28, 2012); Robert Travis Scott, "Foster Farms Chicken Production Expansion in Farmerville Put on Hold Due to Rising Corn Prices," *New Orleans Times-Picayune,* October 20, 2010, www.nola.com/politics/index.ssf/2010/10/foster_farms_chicken_productio.html (last accessed November 28, 2012).

45. "Governor Jindal Says Pilgrim's Pride Agreement to Sell to Foster Farms Major Victory for LA," State of Louisiana, Office of the Governor, press release, March 20, 2009, www.gov.state.la.us/index.cfm?md=newsroom&tmp=detail&catID=2&articleID=1081&navID=3 (last accessed November 28, 2012). Losing the plant *would* have been devastating for Union Parish; indeed, Jindal estimated that in addition to the eleven hundred plant jobs, hundreds of chicken growers would be out of work, and local and state government would lose "over $100 million in tax revenues over the next ten years" ("Governor Bobby Jindal Announces Foster Farms Deal Final," State of Louisiana, Office of the Governor, press release, May 21, 2009, www.gov.state.la.us/index.cfm?md=newsroom&tmp=detail&catID=2&articleID=1251 &navID=12 [last accessed November 28, 2012]; and "Governor Bobby Jindal and Ron Foster Mark Opening of New Foster Farms Facility in Farmerville," State of Louisiana, Office of the Governor, press release, July 11, 2009, www.gov.state.la.us/index.cfm?md=newsroom&tmp =detail&articleID=1422 [last accessed November 28, 2012]). Immediately after the plant was closed, Louisiana's unemployment claims rose by 30 percent ("Jobless Claims Jump with Pilgrim's Pride Closure," *The Street,* May 15, 2009, www.thestreet.com/story/10501924/1/ jobless-claims-jump-with-pilgrims-pride-closure.html [last accessed November 28, 2012]).

46. Mary Nash-Wood, "'Resurrected': Foster Farms Officially Takes Over Farmerville Poultry Plant," *Farmerville Gazette,* July 15, 2009, www.fgazette.com/news.php?id=998 (last accessed November 28, 2012).

47. "Foster Farms Earns Trade and Industry Development Magazine's CiCi Community Impact Award," Foster Farms press release, March 12, 2010, www.fosterfarms.com/about/ press/press_release.asp?press_release_id=111 (last accessed November 28, 2012).

48. Kimberly Nance, *Can Literature Promote Justice: Trauma Narrative in Latin American Testimonio* (Nashville, Tenn.: Vanderbilt University Press, 2006), 7. See also the works collected in George Guggleberger, ed., *The Real Thing: Testimonial Discourse and Latin America* (Durham, N.C.: Duke University Press, 1996); Anne Valk and Leslie Brown, eds., *Living with Jim Crow: African American Women and Memories of the Segregated South* (New York: Palgrave

Macmillan, 2010); Danielle L. McGuire, *At the Dark End of the Street: Black Women, Rape, and Resistance—A New History of the Civil Rights Movement from Rosa Parks to the Rise of Black Power* (New York: Knopf, 2010).

49. McGuire, *At the Dark End of the Street,* xviii–xix.

1. "ARKANSAS'S FIRST BOOMTOWN"

1. "Local Poultry Plant Leased to Two Chicago Businessmen," *Town Talk,* October 23, 1954.

2. Jess Merkle, interview by the University of Arkansas–Fayetteville Center of Excellence for Poultry Science, May 1987, 322, Shiloh Oral History Collection, Shiloh Museum, Springdale, Ark.

3. El Dorado League of Women Voters, *El Dorado: Where Oil Flows and Soft Pine Grows,* 1958, 3.

4. Merkle, interview, 323.

5. These statistics were noted in the July 29, 1956, issue of the *El Dorado Daily News,* with the initial number of employees given as eighty-five. But an undated draft of a speech (from box 1, folder 18, of the O. C. and Marjorie Bailey Collection of the Special Collections at Riley-Hickingbotham Library, Ouachita Baptist University) gives the number of employees as fifty, processing two thousand chickens per day. Bailey was elected chair of the executive committee of the GEC in 1957.

6. Don Wales, "History of Pilgrim's Pride–El Dorado Complex" (speech presented to the El Dorado Chamber of Commerce, El Dorado, Ark., April 2005).

7. Poultry never entirely displaced the city's petrochemical industry, which has a strong economic and cultural presence even today.

8. David Griffith and David Runsten, "The Impact of the 1986 Immigration Reform and Control Act on the U.S. Poultry Industry: A Comparative Analysis," *Policy Studies Review* 11, no. 2 (1992): 118–30.

9. Dallas T. Herndon, *Centennial History of Arkansas* (Chicago: S. J. Clarke, 1922), 2:8–9. The full text of this volume is also available at www.archive.org/stream/centennialhistor00hern/ centennialhistor00hern_djvu.txt (last accessed October 20, 2011).

10. Riffel, "Feathered Kingdom," 42–43.

11. Riffel, "Feathered Kingdom," 43. Riffel quotes Allen Gilbert, *A Fullbright Chronicle* (Fayetteville: Fullbright Investment Co., 1980), 23.

12. Broilers are young, "tender" chickens, the majority of birds currently processed. Stephen Strausberg, *From Hills and Hollers: Rise of the Poultry Industry in Arkansas,* Arkansas Agricultural Experiment Station, Special Report 170 (Fayetteville: University of Arkansas, 1995), 14; Clifton Hull, "Apple Orchard Disease Gave Birth to Broiler Industry," *Arkansas Democrat-Gazette,* March 29, 1970, from Special Collections, University of Arkansas Libraries, Fayetteville; University of Arkansas Industrial Research and Extension Center, *Potential Broiler Production in Southwest Arkansas* (Fayetteville: University of Arkansas, 1957), 1.

13. Riffel, "Feathered Kingdom," 43.

14. Strausberg discusses the Arkansas efforts throughout *From Hills and Hollers.* Melissa Walker describes such initiatives as part of the "golden age of agriculture," when "reformers

and governmental officials began to attend to the problems of southern agriculture" in hopes of "convincing farmers to adopt scientific agricultural practices" ("The Changing Character of Farm Life: Rural Southern Women," in *Southern Women at the Millennium: A Historical Perspective,* ed. Melissa Walker, Jeanette R. Dunn, and Joe P. Dunn [Columbia: University of Missouri Press, 2003], 155).

15. Strausberg, *From Hills and Hollers,* 19. Riffel also comments upon these obstacles in "Feathered Kingdom," 43–44.

16. Lu Ann Jones, *Mama Learned Us to Work: Farm Women in the New South* (Chapel Hill: University of North Carolina Press, 2002), 95.

17. Stephen Strausberg notes the efforts of the Station's scientists to improve chicken breeds and the quality of chicken meat, in *A Century of Research: Centennial History of the Arkansas Agricultural Experiment Station* (Fayetteville: Arkansas Agricultural Experiment Station, 1989).

18. Michael Ollinger, James MacDonald, and Milton Madison, *Structural Change in U.S. Chicken and Turkey Slaughter,* Economic Research Service, U.S. Department of Agriculture, Agricultural Economic Report No. 787, September 2000, 3.

19. Strausberg, *From Hills and Hollers,* 11.

20. William Boyd and Michael Watts, "Agro-Industrial Just-in-Time: The Chicken Industry and Postwar American Capitalism," in *Globalising Food: Agrarian Questions and Global Restructuring,* ed. David Goodman and Michael Watts (New York: Routledge, 1997), 195; Roger Horowitz and Mark Miller, *Immigrants in the Delmarva Poultry Processing Industry: The Changing Face of Georgetown, Delaware and Environs,* Occasional Paper No. 37, Latino Studies Series, Julian Samora Research Institute, January 1999, 2; Roger Horowitz, *Putting Meat on the American Table: Taste, Technology, Transformation* (Baltimore: Johns Hopkins University Press, 2006), 103; Chul-Kyoo Kim and James Curry, "Fordism, Flexible Specialization, and Agri-industrial Restructuring: The Case of the U.S. Broiler Industry," *Sociologia Ruralis* 33, no. 1 (1993): 66–67.

21. Milton D. Rafferty, *The Ozarks: Land and Life* (Fayetteville: University of Arkansas Press, 2001), 168.

22. Melissa Walker, *All We Knew Was to Farm: Rural Women in the Upcountry South, 1919–1941,* "Revisiting Rural America" Series (Baltimore: Johns Hopkins University Press, 2000), 73.

23. Carolyn Sachs, *Gendered Fields: Rural Women, Agriculture, and Environment* (Boulder, Colo.: Westview Press, 1996), 106. Similarly, in Arkansas "poultry and eggs had long provided a small source of cash income to farm families" but "was generally considered women's work and thus little more than . . . supplementation" (Brook Blevins, *Hill Folks: A History of Arkansas Ozarkers and Their Image* [Chapel Hill: University of North Carolina Press, 2002], 162).

24. Jones, *Mama Learned Us to Work,* 85; Gilbert Fite, *Cotton Fields No More: Southern Agriculture, 1865–1980* (Lexington: University Press of Kentucky, 1984), 199–200. Gisolfi also comments on this in "From Crop Lien to Contract Farming: The Roots of Agribusiness in the American South, 1929–1939," *Agricultural History* 80, no. 2 (Spring 2006): 177–78.

25. Ila J. Blue (b. 1914), interview in *Living with Jim Crow: African American Women and Memories of the Segregated South,* ed. Anne Valk and Leslie Brown (New York: Palgrave Macmillan, 2010), 25.

26. Vermelle Ely (b. 1933), interview in Valk and Brown, *Living with Jim Crow*. Sachs argues that "during hard economic times . . . women's egg money saved many farms" (*Gendered Fields,* 107). Throughout "Changing Character of Farm Life" and *All We Knew Was to Farm,* Melissa Walker describes chicken and egg farming as one of the many activities in which farm women engaged that often kept their families fed and able to survive.

27. Mrs. O. H. Cooper, quoted in Gisolfi, "From Crop Lien to Contract Farming," 178.

28. Psyche A. Williams-Forson, *Building Houses Out of Chicken Legs: Black Women, Food, and Power* (Chapel Hill: University of North Carolina Press, 2006), 1, 13–37. Jacqueline Jones also comments on black women who "relied on their . . . poultry-raising skills in an effort to make money" (56).

29. Walker, *All We Knew Was to Farm,* 77.

30. Marilyn Irvin Holt, *Linoleum, Better Babies and the Modern Farm Woman, 1890–1930* (Albuquerque: University of New Mexico Press, 1995), 27.

31. Rebecca Sharpless also discusses women's roles in raising, dressing, and preparing chickens and helping make them standard fare on southern plates (*Cooking in Other Women's Kitchens: Domestic Workers in the South 1865–1960* [Chapel Hill: University of North Carolina Press, 2010], 50–53).

32. Walker, *All We Knew Was to Farm,* 77–78, quotes from 78.

33. Gordon Sawyer, *The Agribusiness Poultry Industry: A History of Its Development* (Jericho, N.Y.: Exposition Press, 1971), 37; definition of Delmarva from Bussel, "Taking On 'Big Chicken,'" 3; Roger Horowitz, *Putting Meat on the American Table,* 108.

34. "Hatchery Is Going Concern," *Arkansas Democrat,* January 14, 1940, from the collection entitled "Poultry," eighth drawer of the vertical files, Archives at Torreyson Library, University of Central Arkansas (UCA), Conway.

35. Sachs, *Gendered Fields,* 107.

36. Such terms were commonly used, as many believed that the "nurturing" skills displayed by female farmers "were extensions of women's mothering role" (Walker, *All We Knew Was to Farm,* 73).

37. Gisolfi, "From Crop Lien to Contract Farming," 179–80. Similarly, Roger Horowitz commented that "while husbands and children may have become involved in this business, women remained central to raising the broilers for market" (*Putting Meat on the American Table,* 109).

38. On the suffering of Arkansas farmers in the 1920s and 1930s, see Nan Elizabeth Woodruff, "The Failure of Relief during the Arkansas Drought of 1930–1931," *Arkansas Historical Quarterly* 39, no. 4 (1980): 301–13; Jeannie Whayne, *A New Plantation South: Land, Labor, and Federal Favor in Twentieth Century Arkansas* (Charlottesville: University Press of Virginia, 1996), esp. chap. 6. On the overcrowding of farmland, see Donald Holley, "The Second Great Emancipation: The Rust Cotton Picker and How It Changed Arkansas," *Arkansas Historical Quarterly* 52, no. 1 (1993): 44–77; and S. Charles Bolton, "Turning Point: World War II and the Economic Development of Arkansas," *Arkansas Historical Quarterly* 61, no. 2 (2002): 123–51. On the overreliance on cotton, see Fite, *Cotton Fields No More,* chap. 4; Holley, "Second Great Emancipation"; Carl Moneyhon, *Arkansas and the New South: 1874–1929* (Fayetteville: University of Arkansas Press, 1997), 96–97, 135. On the Great Flood of 1927, which left well over a million acres of Arkansas farmland under water, see Whayne, *New Plantation South,* 146–47;

and for a broader view (with good detail on Arkansas), see John Barry, *Rising Tide: The Great Mississippi Flood of 1927 and How It Changed America* (New York: Simon & Schuster, 1997). The flood also destroyed much of eastern Arkansas's efforts in poultry growing, decimating poultry houses and equipment (Strausberg, *From Hills and Hollers,* 42; John Barry, "After the Deluge," *Smithsonian* 36, no. 8 [2005]: 114–21; Ben Johnson, *Arkansas in Modern America, 1930–1999* [Fayetteville: University of Arkansas Press, 2000], 9). For the drought of 1931, see Nan Elizabeth Woodruff, *As Rare as Rain: Federal Relief in the Great Southern Drought of 1930–1931.* In northwestern Arkansas apple farms were also decimated by a freeze and the failure of two crops, as noted by Strausberg in *From Hills and Hollers;* and Fite, *Cotton Fields No More,* 200.

39. Woodruff, "Failure of Relief during the Arkansas Drought of 1930–1931," 302.

40. Pete Daniel, *Breaking the Land: The Transformation of Cotton, Tobacco, and Rice Cultures since 1880* (Urbana: University of Illinois Press, 1985), 72.

41. Whayne, *New Plantation South,* 152–56; Johnson, *Arkansas in Modern America,* 10; Woodruff, *As Rare as Rain,* 45–48, 85; Daniel, *Breaking the Land,* 71–72.

42. Whayne, *New Plantation South,*142; Strausberg, *Century of Research,* 67.

43. Moneyhon, *Arkansas and the New South,* 134. Stephen Strausberg also notes that "the Depression and drought years had nearly wiped out the apple industry" (*Century of Research,* 79). C. Curtis Cable notes the hardships of apple farmers and the dramatic drop in the number of apple trees in the two main apple producing counties in the first half of the twentieth century from four and a half million in 1910 to about 500,000 in 1945 (*Growth of the Arkansas Broiler Industry,* Arkansas Agricultural Experiment Station, Bulletin no. 520 [Fayetteville: University of Arkansas, April 1952], 9–10).

44. Moneyhon, *Arkansas and the New South,* 135–36.

45. Cable, *Growth of the Arkansas Broiler Industry,* 8–10. Cable specifically links the spread of poultry growing among northwestern Arkansas farmers to "the failure of the apple industry to supply the farm population with adequate cash income" (Strausberg, *From Hills and Hollers,* 15; Jack Kirby, *Rural Worlds Lost: The American South, 1920–1960* [Baton Rouge: Louisiana State University Press, 1987], 356–57; Horowitz, *Putting Meat on the American Table,* 111).

46. Strausberg, *From Hills and Hollers,* 11–20, 30; Kirby, *Rural Worlds Lost,* 356–57; University of Arkansas Industrial Research and Extension Center, *Potential Broiler Production in Southwest Arkansas.*

47. Strausberg, *Century of Research,* 79; Fite, *Cotton Fields No More,* 200.

48. Strausberg, *From Hills and Hollers,* 21.

49. Strausberg, *From Hills and Hollers,* 40; Sawyer, *Agribusiness Poultry Industry,* chap. 4, esp. 54–65; Kirby, *Rural Worlds Lost,* 356; Bussel, "Taking On 'Big Chicken,'" 3. The industry based on the peninsula produced the majority of broilers consumed in the United States in the 1930s.

50. Martin Schwartz, *Tyson: From Farm to Market* (Fayetteville: University of Arkansas Press, 1991); Johnson, *Arkansas in Modern America,* 77.

51. "Poultry Raising Industry Takes High Rank," *Springdale News,* April 29, 1937, from Special Collections, University of Arkansas Libraries, Fayetteville.

52. Johnson, *Arkansas in Modern America,* 76.

53. These events are described in detail by Whayne in *New Plantation South;* Keith J. Volanto, "The AAA Cotton Plow-Up Campaign in Arkansas," *Arkansas Historical Quarterly* 59, no. 4 (2000): 388–406; Daniel, esp. in chaps. 5 and 8 of *Breaking the Land* and in bk. 1 of *Lost Revolutions: The South in the 1950s* (Chapel Hill: University of North Carolina Press, 2000); Donald Holley, *The Second Great Emancipation: The Mechanical Cotton Picker, Black Migration, and How They Shaped the Modern South* (Fayetteville: University of Arkansas Press, 2000); Bruce Schulman, *From Cotton Belt to Sunbelt: Federal Policy, Economic Development, and the Transformation of the South, 1938–1980* (New York: Oxford University Press, 1991), 15–20; Fite, *Cotton Fields No More,* esp. chaps. 6–9.

54. On the lure of industrial work, see Nan Elizabeth Woodruff, "Pick or Fight: The Emergency Farm Labor Program in the Arkansas and Mississippi Deltas during World War II," *Agricultural History* 64, no. 2 (1990): 74–85; and Charles Chamberlain, *Victory at Home: Manpower and Race in the American South during World War II* (Athens: University of Georgia Press, 2003), esp. chap. 3, "'On the Train': Worker Mobility in the Cotton Belt, 1941–1945."

55. Strausberg, *From Hills and Hollers,* 32.

56. The entire production of an egg drying plant in Harrison, Ark., e.g., went to the Agriculture Market Administration to feed the U.S. military (Tom Shiras, "Arkansas Eggs by the Barrel," *Arkansas Democrat-Gazette,* August 9, 1942, from the UCA Archives, eighth drawer). The expansion of the poultry processing industry in the South during World War II was, of course, part of a much broader southern industrialization trend. Schulman, *From Cotton Belt to Sunbelt,* chap. 4; Daniel, *Lost Revolutions,* 8–21; Bolton, "Turning Point."

57. Strausberg, *From Hills and Hollers,* 46–48; Ben Johnson, *Arkansas in Modern America,* 77.

58. Sawyer, *Agribusiness Poultry Industry,* 82–83; Kirby, *Rural Worlds Lost,* 356: Boyd and Watts, "Agro-Industrial Just-in-Time," 198.

59. University of Arkansas Industrial Research and Extension Center, *Potential Broiler Production in Southwest Arkansas,* 2; Strausberg, *From Hills and Hollers,* 47.

60. Johnson, *Arkansas in Modern America,* 77.

61. Kirby, *Rural Worlds Lost,* 356; Strausberg, *From Hills and Hollers,* 61; Justin R. Anderson, "What the Big Contest's All About: Development of All-Purpose Chicken," *Arkansas Democrat,* August 4, 1951, from UCA Archives, eighth drawer.

62. Sawyer, *Agribusiness Poultry Industry,* 142–43.

63. George Church to Lewis W. Jones, August 2, 1951, Chicken-of-Tomorrow Contest Papers (MC 580), box 1, folder 1, Special Collections, University of Arkansas Libraries, Fayetteville. The resolution was attached to this letter.

64. Lewis W. Jones to George Church, August 6, 1951, Chicken-of-Tomorrow Contest Papers (MC 580), box 1, folder 1, Special Collections, University of Arkansas Libraries, Fayetteville.

65. Kirby, *Rural Lost Worlds,* 356; Strausberg *From Hills and Hollers,* 70–71; Deane Allen, "Poultry Show Ends as UA Gets Houses," *Arkansas Democrat,* June 16, 1951; and Mort Stern, "Federal Poultry Chief Declares U of A Setting Pace in Research," *Arkansas Gazette,* June 17, 1951, from UCA Archives, eighth drawer.

66. "Broilers in State Worth $37 Million," *Arkansas Democrat,* June 17, 1951; and "State among Top Broiler Producers," *Arkansas Democrat,* June 24, 1951, from UCA Archives, eighth drawer.

67. Schwartz, *Tyson,* 11; and Riffel, "Feathered Kingdom," 19–20.

68. George Arnold and Shea Hutchens Wilson, *Then and Now: A Guide to Historic Union County* (El Dorado, Ark.: News-Times Publishing Co., 1994), 94.

69. Ben Johnson, "History of El Dorado, Arkansas," GoElDorado.com (official website of El Dorado), http://goeldorado.com/CatSubCat/CatSubCatDisplay.asp?p1=210&p2=Y&p7=0&p8=1844&p9=CSC4 (last accessed November 23, 2012).

70. James S. Parker, *A Deeper History: The Oil Boom of the 1920s in Union County Arkansas* (Fayetteville: University of Arkansas Press, 2000); Juanita Whitaker-Green, *The History of Union County, Arkansas* (1954): 34–62.

71. Whitaker-Green, *History of Union County,* 48.

72. Whitaker-Green, *History of Union County,* 51–52.

73. Anna Harmon Cordell, "El Dorado: Place of Riches," *Arkansas State Magazine* (Spring 1967): 32.

74. A. R. Buckalew and R. B. Buckalew, "The Discovery of Oil in South Arkansas: 1920–1924," *Arkansas Historical Quarterly* 33, no. 3 (1974): 207–8; Cordell, "El Dorado," 36.

75. Buckalew and Buckalew, "Discovery of Oil in South Arkansas," 204.

76. Anna Harmon Cordell, *Dates and Data of Union County Arkansas, 1541–1948* (Monroe, La.: Century Printing and Publishing, 1984), 79.

77. John G. Ragsdale, *As We Were in South Arkansas* (Little Rock, Ark.: August House Publishers, 1995), 90.

78. Cordell, "El Dorado," 36.

79. Arnold and Wilson, *Then and Now,* 10. See also J. Scott Parker, "A Changing Landscape: Environmental Conditions and Consequences of the 1920s Union County Oil Booms," *Arkansas Historical Quarterly* 60, no. 1 (2001): 31–32.

80. Parker, "Changing Landscape," 32.

81. Moneyhon, *Arkansas and the New South,* 137; Bill Craig, *The Tall Pines of Union County: Twenty-Two Unique Lives* (self-published, 2007), 37–39; in a section on T. H. Barton, president of El Dorado's Lion Oil Company, Craig recounts the financial difficulties visited upon the company by the banking crisis and the depletion of its oil reserves. The careless use and abuse of oil reserves is discussed in detail by Parker in "Changing Landscape." A smaller boom occurred in 1937, but the glorious days of the 1920s were long gone.

82. Cordell, "El Dorado," 36.

83. James C. Cobb, *The Selling of the South: The Southern Crusade for Industrial Development, 1936–1980,* 2nd ed. (Urbana: University of Illinois Press, 1993), quote from 57.

84. Johnson, *Arkansas in Modern America,* 72–75.

85. Jim Lester, *A Man for Arkansas: Sid McMath and the Southern Reform Tradition* (Little Rock, Ark.: Rose Publishing Co., 1976), 128.

86. Johnson, *Arkansas in Modern America,* 75.

87. "General Assembly Responds to Governor's Challenge for New Jobs in Both Agriculture and Industry," undated document found in the papers of the Arkansas Division of Agriculture and Industry, Resources and Development Commission, July 1955–January 1963, archived at the Arkansas History Commission, Little Rock. Historian Donald Holley also contends that the AIDC was created to address a job shortage that contributed to the out-migration of the state's "ambitious," educated young people ("Leaving the Land of Opportunity: Arkansas and the Great Migration," *Arkansas Historical Quarterly* 64, no. 3 [2005]: 248). On Arkansas's

loss of population, see Bolton, "Turning Point," in which the author notes that the population of Arkansas fell "drastically" between 1929, when Arkansas's population was 1.52 percent of the U.S. population, and 1960, "when it stabilized at around 1 percent of the American population." Holley observes that "by the 1940s, when the national economy shifted to war production, the migration stream that had previously been a steady leak turned into a torrential flood" ("Leaving the Land of Opportunity," 246–47).

88. "General Assembly Responds to Governor's Challenge for New Jobs in Both Agriculture and Industry."

89. "Arkansas Seeks Skilled Workers," *New York Times,* October 8, 1961; Herbert Hill, "Recent Effects of Racial Conflict on Southern Industrial Development," *Phylon Quarterly* 20, no. 4 (1959): 319–26; John Peterson, "News and Notes: University of Arkansas Industrial Research and Extension Center," *Industrial and Labor Relations Review* 12, no. 2 (1959): 325; Foy Lisenby, "Winthrop Rockefeller and the Arkansas Image," *Arkansas Historical Quarterly* 43, no. 2 (1984): 143–52.

90. Rockefeller's success was noted in contemporary sources—Orval Faubus, e.g., lauded the AIDC in a number of pieces of correspondence—as well as appraisals that came later. Positive evaluations of the AIDC's achievements can be found in newspapers from throughout the state. The Resources and Development Commission noted that as "industry began filtering into Arkansas" after 1955, "the upturn in population has been continuous" ("523 New Plants since 1955 Have Located across the Entire State," papers of the Arkansas Division of Agriculture and Industry, Resources and Development Commission, July 1955–January 1963, archived at the Arkansas History Commission, Little Rock). Charles S. Bolton observes in "Turning Point" that under Rockefeller's "energetic leadership of the newly created Arkansas Industrial Development Commission . . . 600 new manufacturing plants opened in Arkansas, providing jobs for 90,000 people" (147). His work echoes similar observations made by Billy B. Hathorn in "Friendly Rivalry: Winthrop Rockefeller Challenges Orval Faubus in 1964," *Arkansas Historical Quarterly* 53, no. 4 (Winter 1994): 446–73. In "Winthrop Rockefeller and the Arkansas Image" Foy Lisenby contends that Rockefeller recognized that to change Arkansas from *within,* by attracting industry and improving economic opportunity, the state's image from *without* had to be improved and that he worked diligently toward that goal.

91. From a document dated July 18, 1961, authored by the Greater El Dorado Committee (GEC). The document is in the files of the El Dorado Chamber of Commerce. In an application for exemption from federal income tax dated March 18, 1955, the chair of the GEC noted the committee was initially created "April 15, 1954, [but] is just now getting well organized."

92. Thomas L. Reynolds to Orval E. Faubus, June 17, 1955, Orval Faubus Papers (MC F27 301), box 243, file 8, Special Collections, University of Arkansas Libraries, Fayetteville.

93. Merkle, interview, 324.

94. From a document dated July 18, 1961, authored by the GEC. The document is in the files of the El Dorado Chamber of Commerce.

95. Annual Report of the Greater El Dorado Committee, June 1, 1956, Orval Faubus Papers (MC F27 301), box 244, file 3.

96. Merkle, interview, 324.

97. Johnson, *Arkansas in Modern America,* 112. Also noted in the Merkle interview; and in "Ruston Misses Poultry Plant Which Would Have Hired 75; Paid Growers $2¼ Million," *Ruston Daily Leader,* March 1, 1956.

98. Letter dated February 18, 1956, from the GEC to J-M Poultry Packing Company, Inc., in the files of the El Dorado Chamber of Commerce. Also noted in an undated draft of a speech from box 1, folder 18, of the O. C. and Marjorie Bailey Collection.

99. Undated draft of a speech from box 1, folder 18, of the O. C. and Marjorie Bailey Collection.

100. Letter dated February 18, 1956 from the GEC to J-M Poultry Packing Company. From an undated resolution written by the EIDC resolving to transfer to J-M Poultry "property above described and identified in [the] Lease Purchase Agreement." The resolution is probably from 1961; a letter stored with it from June 14, 1961, from Jess Merkle's attorney advises that "our client would like to generally complete the purchase of the two properties involved in this matter."

101. University of Arkansas Industrial Research and Extension Center, *Potential Broiler Production in Southwest Arkansas*, 3.

102. By 1964 the plant added a second shift, increasing its daily output of birds by more than 150 percent and making J-M the home of "one of the largest numbers of employees in any one industry in this area" ("Firm Opens New Office," *El Dorado Times*, June 12, 1964).

103. "During the period from 1953 to 1957, production in Southwest Arkansas increased almost 200 percent while production in the Northwest increased 380 percent," according to University of Arkansas Industrial Research and Extension Center, *Potential Broiler Production in Southwest Arkansas*, 2–3.

104. "The Poultry Festival," *El Dorado Daily News*, May 8, 1962.

105. The ad is located on p. 10 of the July 2, 1956, edition of the *El Dorado Daily News*.

106. From an undated document describing the industrial development of El Dorado in the 1950s and 1960s; the document is in the files of the El Dorado Chamber of Commerce. "Poultry Industry on Display: Bright Future Is Predicted," *El Dorado Evening Times*, July 31, 1959; undated draft of a speech from box 1, folder 18, of the O. C. and Marjorie Bailey Collection. Another document in that file named the veneer plant as "Reynolds Draper Box Mill."

107. "Poultry Plant Process Told in Pictures," *El Dorado Daily News*, July 15, 1956, no. 36.

108. "Poultry Industry on Display."

109. Cordell, "El Dorado," 36.

110. Strausberg, *From Hills and Hollers*, 76–77. The state legislature adopted a number of industrial financing laws, including one that allowed the government to issue tax-free revenue bonds to build new plants (see "Arkansas Seeks Skilled Workers"). Lourdes Gouveia provides a description of state-sponsored tax breaks, grants, and funds from which meatpacking companies have benefited ("Global Strategies and Local Linkages: The Case of the U.S. Meatpacking Industry," in *From Columbus to ConAgra: The Globalization of Agriculture and Food*, ed. Alessandro Bonanno et al. [Lawrence: University Press of Kansas, 1994], 137–39). Cobb also discusses these initiatives, in *Selling of the South*.

111. D. Gordon Bennett, "Population Change and Mobility: A Case Study of an Arkansas State Economic Area," *Land Economics* 46, no. 2 (1970): 206; Holley, "Leaving the Land of Opportunity," 245–61.

112. The description "Ideal Geographic Location, Sufficient Production Laborers" comes from Wade Barron, Marketing Director of the Arkansas Livestock Commission, to Howard A. Stamper, March 29, 1966, Orval Faubus Papers (MC F27 301), box 256, file 12.

113. Fite, *Cotton Fields No More*, 202.

114. Floyd A. Lasley, *The U.S. Poultry Industry: Changing Economics and Structure,* U.S. Department of Agriculture, Economic Research Service, Agricultural Economic Report No. 502 (Washington, D.C.: GPO, 1983), 2; Boyd and Watts, "Agro-Industrial Just-in-Time," 192–93; Horowitz and Miller, *Immigrants in the Delmarva Poultry Processing Industry,* 13. Broilers account for over 96 percent of chickens consumed.

115. Ollinger et al., Report No. 787, 3; Z. Z. Ahmed and Mark Sieling, "Two Decades of Productivity Growth in Poultry Dressing and Processing," *Monthly Labor Review* (April 1987): 35.

116. Resources and Development Commission, "General Assembly Responds to Governor's Challenge"; and Floyd A. Lasley, Harold Jones, Edward Easterling, and Lee Christensen, *The U.S. Broiler Industry,* U.S. Department of Agriculture, Economic Research Service, Agricultural Economic Report No. 591 (Washington, D.C.: GPO, 1988), 12.

117. Ahmed and Sieling, "Two Decades of Productivity Growth," 34, Riffel, "Feathered Kingdom," 80–85. Gordon Sawyer offers a slightly earlier date for Georgia, noting the integration efforts of Jesse Jewell (*Agribusiness Poultry Industry,* 89–92).

118. Johnson, *Arkansas in Modern America,* 77.

119. Early vertical integration is described in Cable, *Growth of the Arkansas Broiler Industry.*

120. Merkle, interview, 326.

121. Griffith, *Jones's Minimal,* 85.

122. C. H. Hamilton, "The Sociology of a Changing Agriculture," *Social Forces* 37, no. 1 (1958): 5. The significant role of vertical integration in strengthening and expanding the poultry industry is well documented.

123. From a fact sheet on the history of the El Dorado poultry processing complex distributed by plant management.

124. Paul Aho and Allan Rahn, "Broilers in the Midwest?" *Broiler Industry* (January 1989): 75.

125. William D. Heffernan and Douglas H. Constance, "Transnational Corporations and the Globalization of the Food System," in *From Columbus to ConAgra: The Globalization of Agriculture and Food,* ed. Alessandro Bonanno et al. (Lawrence: University Press of Kansas, 1994), 33.

126. Aho and Rahn, "Broilers in the Midwest," 74.

127. National Planning Association (NPA), *New Industry Comes to the South,* NPA Committee of the South Reports, Report No. 1 (Washington, D.C.: National Publishing Company, 1949), v.

128. NPA, *New Industry Comes to the South,* 17–18.

129. NPA, *New Industry Comes to the South,* 18–19.

130. NPA, *New Industry Comes to the South.*

131. Aho and Rahn, "Broilers in the Midwest," 83.

132. Kim and Curry, "Fordism," 76.

133. Undated document entitled "Problem Areas" and manually labeled "Endustrial [*sic*] Development Matters," clipped with a number of documents about Act 404 and the establishment of the AIDC (Orval Faubus Papers [MC 301 F27], box 243, file 11).

134. Jones, *Mama Learned Us to Work,* 104. Monica Gisolfi also discusses the "precarious position of poultry farmers" in "Leaving the Farm to Save the Farm: The Poultry Industry and the Problem of 'Public Work': 1950–1970," in *Migration and the Transformation of the Southern Workplace since 1945,* ed. Robert Cassanello and Colin Davis (Gainesville: University Press of Florida, 2009), 64–79. See also Steve Striffler, *Chicken: The Dangerous Transformation of*

America's Favorite Food (New Haven: Yale University Press, 2005), 79–89; and Barry Yeoman, "Don't Count Your Chickens," *Southern Exposure* 17, no. 2 (1989): 21–24.

135. Strausberg, *From Hills and Hollers,* 91. Jess Merkle also lauded the benefits of vertical integration (Merkle, interview, 325–27).

136. The comparison to tenancy refers to the fact that the companies own and provide the "crop" of chickens, while farmers and their families supply the labor to tend and grow them.

137. Although they could not opt out of the system, Arkansas farmers did express worry about the power imbalance, companies' unfair practices, and that their attempts to address their concerns with poultry companies would earn them the label "problem growers" (U.S. Department of Agriculture, Packers and Stockyards Administration, *The Broiler Industry: An Economic Study of Structure, Practices, and Problems* [Washington, D.C.: GPO, August 1967], esp. 26, where Arkansas farmers' fears over being labeled a "problem" are described, and 45–62). The report used interviews with farmers from Alabama, Arkansas, and Georgia.

138. Cable, *Growth of the Arkansas Broiler Industry,* 13

139. Fite, *Cotton Fields No More,* 200; Gisolfi, "From Crop Lien to Contract Farming," 168.

140. William D. Heffernan, "Constraints in the U.S. Poultry Industry," *Research in Rural Sociology and Development* 1 (1984): 238; Gisolfi, "From Crop Lien to Contract Farming," 182.

141. Gisolfi, "From Crop Lien to Contract Farming," 182; Heffernan, "Constraints in the U.S. Poultry Industry," 247–49.

142. Heffernan, "Constraints in the U.S. Poultry Industry," 247–49; Striffler, *Chicken,* 79–89; Yeoman, "Don't Count Your Chickens," 21–24. In 1999 the *Sun* ran stories culled from its thirteen-month investigation on the plight of poultry farmers. The series' authors concluded that "U.S. chicken farmers have become serfs in a feudal system ruled by the nation's largest poultry processors" (Dan Fesperman and Kate Shatzkin, "Taking a Stand, Losing the Farm," *Sun,* March 1, 1999). See also Monica Potts, "The Serfs of Arkansas," *American Prospect,* March 9, 2011, http://prospect.org/cs/articles?article=the_serfs_of_arkansas (last accessed September 26, 2011). A USDA report describes how vulnerable contract growers are to companies' whims, noting that companies engaged in many "unfair contract practices. These include early contract termination before the building loans were paid off, company requirements for building improvements at the grower's expense, underweighing of birds and feed, manipulation of quality and quantity of feed and birds, and retaliation against growers for attempting to organize grower associations." The report also mentions a 1995 Louisiana Tech study that found that contract growers make approximately $12,000 in profit *before* they pay themselves for their labor (U.S. Department of Agriculture, National Commission on Small Farms, *A Time to Act: A Report of the USDA National Commission on Small Farms* [January 1998], www.csrees.usda.gov/nea/ag_systems/pdfs/time_to_act_1998.pdf [last accessed November 28, 2011]).

143. Woodruff, *As Rare as Rain,* 101.

144. Woodruff, "Pick or Fight," 85. Socialist Party leader Norman Thomas accused the federal government of interfering "extensively . . . in the cotton economy of the South" (M. S. Venkataramani, "Norman Thomas, Arkansas Sharecroppers and the Roosevelt Agricultural Policies, 1933–1937," *Mississippi Valley Historical Review* 47, no. 2 [1960]: 236).

145. Numerous scholars comment on the benefit, at the expense of tenants and sharecroppers, of government policy to planters and the overwhelming efforts of the planter class to

maintain a raced and class hierarchy via the use of government agencies and political patronage. See, e.g., Fite, *Cotton Fields No More,* 134–36 and chap. 7; Whayne, *New Plantation South;* Schulman, *From Cotton Belt to Sunbelt;* Daniel, *Breaking the Land,* esp. 105–9; Cobb in *The Selling of the South;* Nan Woodruff, *As Rare as Rain;* Greta de Jong, *Different Day,* chap. 5; and Gisolfi, "From Crop Lien to Contract Farming," 174–75.

146. Whayne, *New Plantation South;* Woodruff, "Pick or Fight," 79; Jacob J. Kaufman, "Farm Labor during World War II," *Journal of Farm Economics* 31, no. 1 (1949): 131–42. In chapter 3 of *Victory at Home* Chamberlain discusses the policy of trying to "freeze" agricultural workers, particularly African Americans, in place during World War II, as does de Jong, *Different Day,* 132–36.

147. The possible effects of right-to-work laws are discussed more fully in chap. 4.

148. Johnson, *Arkansas in Modern America* 81.

149. David Goldfield, *Cotton Fields and Skyscrapers: Southern City and Region, 1607–1980* (Baton Rouge: Louisiana State University Press, 1982), 160.

150. Quote from Cobb, *Selling of the South,* 63; Brattain, *Politics of Whiteness,* chap. 1.

151. Brattain, *Politics of Whiteness,* chap. 1.

152. Cobb, *Selling of the South,* chap. 4.

153. Cobb, *Selling of the South,* 101.

154. Quotes from Griffith, *Jones's Minimal,* 86. On the reason for the poultry industry's location in the South, see U.S. Congressional Research Service, *Labor Practices in the Meatpacking and Poultry Industries: An Overview* (RL33002; July 20, 2005), by William G. Whitaker; Lawrence and Braden, "Long Struggle," 86; Fite, *Cotton Fields No More,* 200; Marc Linder, "I Gave My Employer a Chicken That Had No Bone: Joint Firm-State Responsibility for Line-Speed-Related Occupational Injuries," *Case Western Reserve Law Review* 46, no. 1 (1995): 45–46; and Heffernan, "Constraints in the U.S. Poultry Industry," 250. Cobb comments on the belief that southern boosterism "fostered runaway industry" in *Selling of the South,* 41.

155. Cobb, *Selling of the South,* 2.

156. On line workers, see Ahmed and Sieling, "Two Decades of Productivity Growth," 35–36; Striffler, *Chicken,* 114–15. Processors now aggressively recruit immigrant labor. As a result, some plants in northwestern Arkansas are currently staffed primarily by Latin Americans. In El Dorado, however, the workforce has remained largely black and, in terms of line work, female.

157. Johnson, *Arkansas in Modern America,* 113. Similarly, black Mississippian Fannie Bradford remembered that when black people applied at a new processing plant in her area, "white folks was calling [the plant, telling them] don't hire they cooks, don't hire they this and that" (quoted in Stuesse, "Globalization 'Southern Style,'" 112).

158. This is an important distinction to make for a city such as El Dorado in which some men, with higher skill levels and access to better-paying jobs, joined unions that actually helped lessen their vulnerability. The trend was not the same for black women.

159. Jacqueline Jones, *Labor of Love, Labor of Sorrow: Black Women, Work, and the Family from Slavery to the Present* (New York: Basic Books, 1983), 260.

160. See Jill Quadagno, *The Color of Welfare: How Racism Undermined the War on Poverty* (New York: Oxford University Press, 1994); and Linda Gordon, *Pitied but Not Entitled: Single Mothers and the History of Welfare* (Cambridge: Harvard University Press, 1994).

161. Tavia Wright, interview by author, Bernice, La., November 24, 2005.

162. Sachs, *Gendered Fields,* 108.

2. "I WAS A SINGLE PARENT"

1. Louisiana's "parishes" are the equivalent of "counties" in other states.

2. In local vernacular the poultry processing plant is routinely called "the poultry."

3. Anne Moody gives a vivid description of "reaching up and snatching out those boiling hot guts," in *Coming of Age in Mississippi* (New York: Dell, 1968), 165.

4. Lawrence and Braden, "The Long Struggle," *Southern Exposure* 11, no. 6 (1983): 85. Since the mechanization of evisceration, the process of live hanging, in which workers hang living, fighting chickens in shackles, has "earned" the title of worst job in the plant. See Stuesse, "Globalization 'Southern Style,'" 227–28; Russell Cobb, "The Chicken Hangers," *In the Fray,* February 1, 2004, www.inthefray.com/html/article.php?sid=208 (last accessed November 14, 2011); Steve Striffler, "Inside a Poultry Processing Plant: An Ethnographic Portrait," *Labor History* 43, no. 3 (2002): 306. Roger Horowitz notes that the industry's shift to the bloodier, more difficult process of eviscerating the bird (rather than selling chicken with the entrails still intact) led to the 1960s move away from hiring white women, "who had better job options," as line workers to the hiring of black women (*Putting Meat on the American Table: Taste, Technology, Transformation* [Baltimore: Johns Hopkins University Press, 2006], 115).

5. Vivian West, interview by author, Bernice, La., January 2, 2005.

6. Controlling black women's sexuality and fertility has preoccupied white Americans since the era of slavery. There have been a number of reasons, from wanting the economic asset and profit that enslaved children could bring to controlling the demographic "threat" that people of color represent in a majority white country to maintaining the status of white women via the reification of images of black women as hypersexual and out of control. See Deborah Gray-White, *Ar'n't I a Woman? Female Slaves in the Plantation South,* rev. ed. (New York: Norton, 1999); Patricia Hill Collins, *Black Feminist Thought: Knowledge, Consciousness, and the Politics of Empowerment,* 2nd ed. (New York: Routledge, 2000); Dorothy Roberts, *Killing the Black Body: Race, Reproduction, and the Meaning of Liberty* (New York: Pantheon Books, 1997); and Susan L. Thomas, "Race, Gender, and Welfare Reform: The Antinatalist Response," *Journal of Black Studies* 28, no. 4 (March 1998): 419–46.

7. In fact, the area that would become Bernice was once known as the Big Woods. J. T. Baldwin Jr., interview by R. B. Mabry, "'Three Apples for a Dime,' and Other Recollections of the Early Days of Bernice," *North Louisiana Historical Association Journal* 4, no. 2 (Winter 1973): 65–68; Cynthia V. Campbell, "Little Town in 'Big Woods' Offers Homespun Warmth," *Baton Rouge Advocate,* June 6, 1997, from the papers of the Bernice Historical Society, Collection No. M248 box 1, folder 7, Department of Special Collections, Manuscripts, and Archives, Prescott Memorial Library, Louisiana Tech University (LTU), Ruston; Edna Liggin, "Town Flourished in First 10 Years," *Bernice Banner,* September 23, 1976, from Collection No. M248, box 1, folder 6, LTU Special Collections; Sidney Lecky, "Union Parish, LA," MS from the Federal Writers' Project, Monroe (La.) Project, Blanche T. Oliver, supervisor, 1937, 2.

8. Morelle Elliott (b. 1920), interview in *I Remember Life in Union Parish, 1910–1960: A Collection of Personal Remembrances,* ed. Jean W. Jones (Farmerville, La.: Union Parish Council on Aging, 2004), 13. Other residents interviewed for the project testified to the centrality of cotton in Union Parish agriculture.

9. U.S. Federal Emergency Relief Administration (FERA), Division of Research, Statistics, and Finance, "The Western Cotton Growing Area: Union Parish, LA," *Rural Problem Areas Survey Report No. 65,* January 14, 1935, 4.

10. U.S. Department of Agriculture, Rural Electrification Administration, "Comprehensive Survey of Claiborne, Webster, and Union Parishes in Power, Fuel, Agricultural Products, Water, Skilled Labor, Etc." (Washington, D.C.: GPO, 1941), 38.

11. John McNeil and Felix Stanley, *Organizational Problems on Small Farms in North Louisiana Upland Cotton Area,* DAE Lithographed Circular No. 147 (Baton Rouge: Louisiana State University Press, 1953). The Union Parish Development Board created a much more extensive list and reported that potatoes were a major crop too (*Union Parish Resources and Facilities* [Baton Rouge: Department of Public Works, 1954], 21–36). *I Remember Life in Union Parish* contains many residents' remembrances of growing crops other than cotton.

12. The description of conditions faced by Union Parish farmers can be found in *Rural Problem Areas Survey Report No. 65.* The FERA labeled six agricultural regions as particularly problematic based on their high number of relief caseloads. Harrison Douglass also described the land as "hilly, dry, and lack[ing] fertility" ("Farm Practices in Animal Husbandry among Negro Farmers in Union Parish, Louisiana" [Master's thesis, Iowa State College, 1942], 7).

13. *Rural Problem Areas Survey Report No. 65,* 1. Douglass also commented on Union Parish farmers' reliance "on one phase of agriculture for their support and profit" ("Farm Practices in Animal Husbandry," 7).

14. This is one of the primary arguments of Douglass's thesis.

15. The length of the school year was noted by Truett West in "The Union Parish Conspiracy of 1933," *North Louisiana Historical Association Journal* 20, nos. 2–3 (1989): 79–94; and in Laval Franklin Taylor, "Development of Public Education in Union Parish" (Master's thesis, Louisiana State University, 1939). Black Bernice residents Hortince Bell Sutton and Rashia Lee Tatum, who were interviewed for the *I Remember Life in Union Parish* project, also commented upon it. Bell Sutton (b. 1925) and Tatum (b. 1917), interviews, both in *I Remember Life in Union Parish,* 36–37 and 105, respectively.

16. Pearl Adams Harris (b. 1918) and John Q. Watley (b. 1921), interviews, both in *I Remember Life in Union Parish,* 37 and 38–39, retrospectively.

17. Taylor, "Development of Public Education in Union Parish," chap. 5. A study conducted in Louisiana in the early 1940s found the state of black students' education and educational facilities in horrible conditions, circumstances fostered by white ambivalence and even hostility to educating black children: "Black schools in Louisiana suffered from extreme neglect and overcrowding. . . . [They were] often without lights, desks, blackboards, libraries, toilet facilities, adequate heating, bus transportation, or supervision" (Phillip J. Johnson, "Confronting the Dilemma: Charles S. Johnson's Study of Louisiana's Black Schools," *Louisiana History: The Journal of the Louisiana Historical Association* 38, no. 2 [Spring 1997]: 148).

18. West, "Union Parish Conspiracy of 1933," 83–84.

19. Sutton, interview, 36.

20. Sutton, interview, 36; Mary Gordon Meadors Adams (b. 1923), interview, in *I Remember Life in Union Parish,* 42.

21. Quoted in Hubert Humphreys, "In a Sense Experimental: The Civilian Conservation Corps in Louisiana," *Louisiana History* 5, no. 4 (1964): 356–57.

22. *Rural Problem Areas Survey Report No. 65,* 2.

23. Greta De Jong, *A Different Day: African American Struggles for Justice in Rural Louisiana, 1900–1970* (Chapel Hill: University of North Carolina Press, 2002), 93; Esther Douty, "FERA and the Rural Negro," *Survey* 70, no. 7 (1934): 215–16.

24. Douty, "FERA and the Rural Negro," 215–16; Mattie Lou Lester (b. 1909), interview, in *I Remember Life in Union Parish,* 17.

25. West writes that many of the white citizens of Union Parish just could not understand why some of the "best" African Americans were lured by the swindle, a question West himself echoed.

26. Undated anonymous letter referred to the Department of Justice, Straight Numerical Files, 1904–1937, found in box 1291, file 158260, December 20, 1933–January 10, 1934. A respected black preacher betrayed the plot, and eventually a coalition of Secret Service agents and Louisiana and Mississippi police arrested Walter Burnside. Houston Burnside was discovered months later. "'Judge Coty' Is Given a Five-Year Sentence," *Farmerville Gazette,* April 11, 1934; "Negro Killed by Officers When He Makes Resistance," *Farmerville Gazette,* November 22, 1933; "F'ville Negro Killed When Resist Arrest," *Ruston Daily Leader,* November 15, 1933; De Jong, *Different Day,* 92–93.

27. The venerable New Orleans NAACP attorney A. P. Tureaud was heavily involved in these cases. See the microfilmed Papers of the National Association for the Advancement of Colored People, pt. 3, Campaign for Educational Equality, Legal Department and Central Office Records, 1913–1950, "Orine Bright, et al. v. Union Parish School Board," reel 8, frames 1055–1069; and "Eric Cleveland et al., Appellants v. Union Parish School Board et al., Appellees," 406 F.2d 1331(U.S. Court of Appeals Fifth Circuit, 1969).

28. Adam Fairclough, *Race and Democracy: The Civil Rights Struggle in Louisiana, 1915–1972* (Athens: University of Georgia Press, 1995), 169–70.

29. U.S. Commission on Civil Rights, *Report of the United States Commission on Civil Rights, 1959* (Washington, D.C.: GPO, 1959), 569; John Fenton, "The Negro Voter in Louisiana," *Journal of Negro Education* 26, no. 3 (1957): 320.

30. The quote was the title of a pamphlet authored by the Citizens' Councils and distributed to registrars throughout the state. A facsimile of the pamphlet's cover is available in the *Report of the United States Commission on Civil Rights, 1959,* 102.

31. *Report of the United States Commission on Civil Rights, 1959,* 101–4; Fairclough, *Race and Democracy,* 195–99.

32. U.S. Congress, *Congressional Record,* 85th Cong., 1st sess., 1957, 103, pt. 7, 8607–9. Fairclough writes about the astounding power of the Citizens' Councils in Louisiana in chap. 8, "Counterattack." Louisiana registrars later admitted they strictly followed guidelines for administering literacy tests and opened their offices to council members during the councils' purge efforts (Claude Sitton, "Louisiana Registrar Fails Test She Gives to Poll Applicants," *New York Times,* May 6, 1961). Sitton had previously noted that this "extremist minority dominate[d] the fight" to maintain segregation ("Citizen's Council Fuels Louisiana Resistance," *New York Times,* November 27, 1960).

33. U.S. Congress, *Congressional Record,* 85th Cong., 1st sess., 1957, 103, pt. 10, 13334:5.

34. *Report of the United States Commission on Civil Rights, 1959,* 98.

35. Allan Lichtman, "The Federal Assault against Voting Discrimination in the Deep South 1957–1967," *Journal of Negro History* 54, no. 4 (1969): 346–67.

36. Fenton, "Negro Voter in Louisiana," 323.

37. *Report of the United States Commission on Civil Rights, 1959,* 569.

38. *Report of the United States Commission on Civil Rights, 1959,* 569.

39. U.S. Congress, *Congressional Record,* 86th Cong., 2nd sess., 1960, 106, pt. 4, 4134.

40. For more on the sense of "besiegement" felt by Louisiana segregationists in the face of civil rights victories, see Shannon Frystak, *Our Minds on Freedom: Women and the Struggle for Black Equality in Louisiana, 1924–1967* (Baton Rouge: Louisiana State University Press, 2009), chap. 4.

41. Janell Hobson, *Venus in the Dark: Blackness and Beauty in Popular Culture* (New York: Routledge, 2005), 24.

42. On the Jezebel/licentious image of black women, see Patricia Hill Collins, "Mammies, Matriarchs, and Other Controlling Images," *Black Feminist Thought,* 69–96; Gray-White, "Jezebel and Mammy: The Mythology of Female Slavery," *Ar'n't I a Woman,* 27–61; Paula Giddings, *When and Where I Enter: The Impact of Black Women on Race and Sex in America* (New York: Morrow, 1984), esp. chaps. 5–6.

43. Hill Collins, *Black Feminist Thought,* 45–68; Evelyn Nakano Glenn, "Cleaning Up / Kept Down: A Historical Perspective on Racial Inequality in 'Women's Work,'" *Stanford Law Review* 43, no. 6 (1999): 1342–43; Dorothy Roberts, "Welfare's Ban on Poor Motherhood," in *Whose Welfare?* ed. Gwendolyn Mink (Ithaca, N.Y.: Cornell University Press, 1999), 160; Roberts, *Killing the Black Body,* intro.

44. Dorothy Roberts, "Race, Gender and the Value of Mother's Work," *Social Politics* 2, no. 2 (1995): 196; and *Killing the Black Body,* 8–21; Julia Jordan-Zachery, *Black Women, Cultural Images, and Social Policy* (New York: Routledge, 2009), 80–81.

45. Michele Wallace, *Black Macho and the Myth of the Superwoman* (New York: Dial Press, 1979), 25–26.

46. Roberts, *Killing the Black Body,* 39. Roberts also discusses this issue in "Race, Gender and the Value of Mother's Work," 201.

47. Dorothy Roberts, *Shattered Bonds: The Color of Child Welfare* (New York: Basic Books, 2002), 7–10.

48. See, e.g., bell hooks, "The Integrity of Black Womanhood," *Killing Rage, Ending Racism* (New York: Holt, 1995), esp. 82–85; Roberts throughout *Shattered Bonds* and in the introduction to *Killing the Black Body;* and Gwendolyn Mink, "The Lady and the Tramp (II): Feminist Welfare Politics, Poor Single Mothers, and the Challenge of Welfare Justice," *Feminist Studies* 24, no. 1 (Spring 1998): 55–64.

49. U.S. Department of Labor, Office of Policy Planning and Research, "The Negro Family: The Case for National Action," March 1965, www.dol.gov/oasam/programs/history/webid-meynihan.htm (last accessed September 24, 2011). See also Roberts, "Race, Gender, and the Value of Mother's Work," Martha L. Fineman, "Images of Mothers in Poverty Discourses," *Duke Law Journal* 1991, no. 2 (April 1991): 274–95; Joya Misra, Stephanie Moller, and Marina Karides, "Envisioning Dependency: Changing Media Depictions of Welfare in the 20th

Century," *Social Problems* 50, no. 4 (November 2003): 482–504; and Thomas, "Race, Gender, and Welfare Reform."

50. Quote from Roberts, *Killing the Black Body*, 8. Mink briefly discusses 1960s-era politicians' vilification of poor single mothers in "Lady and the Tramp II," 59; as does Mimi Abramovitz in *Regulating the Lives of Women: Social Welfare Policy from Colonial Times to the Present*, rev. ed. (Boston: South End Press, 1996), chap. 10. Such discussions are woven throughout Jennifer Mittelstadt, *From Welfare to Workfare: The Unintended Consequence of Welfare Reform, 1945–1965* (Chapel Hill: University of North Carolina Press, 2005).

51. Melissa V. Harris-Perry, *Sister Citizen: Shame, Stereotypes, and Black Women in America* (New Haven: Yale University Press, 2011), 109.

52. See, e.g., Gwendolyn Mink, *The Wages of Motherhood: Inequality in the Welfare State, 1917–1942* (Ithaca, N.Y.: Cornell University Press, 1995); and Abramovitz, *Regulating the Lives of Women*.

53. Detailed analyses of the construction of the two-tier system of social provision are presented in Linda Gordon, *Pitied but Not Entitled: Single Mothers and the History of Welfare* (Cambridge: Harvard University Press, 1994); Jill Quadagno, *The Color of Welfare: How Racism Undermined the War on Poverty* (New York: Oxford University Press, 1994); Barbara Nelson, "The Origins of the Two-Channel Welfare State: Workman's Compensation and Mothers' Aid," in *Women, the State, and Welfare*, ed. L. Gordon (Madison: University of Wisconsin Press, 1990), 123–51; and Dorothy Roberts, *Killing the Black Body*.

54. In *Pitied but Not Entitled* Linda Gordon studies the vastly different welfare visions of black and white women and of white men. The triumph of white reformers' visions codified: (1) the myth of the family wage and the heteropatriarchal belief that women were best suited to the domestic sphere, thereby ignoring the realities of single working mothers' lives; and (2) racialized notions of which mothers were deserving of assistance.

55. See Quadagno, *Color of Welfare*. This was not the only time black women had been excluded purposefully from legislation. They were not covered under the protective legislation of the early twentieth century, and in 1938 agriculture and domestic work were left out of the Fair Labor Standards Act and maximum wages–minimum hours legislation. See, e.g., Phyllis Palmer, "Outside the Law: Agricultural and Domestic Workers under the Fair Labor Standards Act," *Journal of Policy History* 7, no. 4 (1995): 416–40. Labor laws in Louisiana mandated that "women may not be employed longer than 8 hours a day or 48 hours a week (*except in agricultural and domestic pursuits*)" ("Ecology of Ouachita Parish," 9, from box 225, folder 7, Charles Spurgeon Johnson Collection, Special Collections, John Hope and Aurelia E. Franklin Library, Fisk University, Nashville, Tenn.).

56. Ellen Reese, *Backlash against Welfare Mothers: Past and Present* (Berkeley: University of California Press, 2005), 51.

57. The effect of the exclusion of domestic and agricultural work on African Americans was immediately apparent. Albion Hartwell notes that these two categories encompassed 65 percent of African Americans' paid work before the Depression. Thus, the 50 percent of black workers who were unemployed in 1936 had "nothing to gain under this act. It disowns them and denies them any assistance whatsoever" (Hartwell, "The Need of Social and Unemployment Insurance for Negroes," *Journal of Negro Education* 5, no. 1 [1936]: 83).

58. Palmer, *Domesticity and Dirt*, 132.

59. L. M. Montgomery also explained the fact that African Americans were underserved in the foster care and adoption services of welfare departments for similar justifications: "Colored people usually find a way of their own for getting orphan children cared for" ("Ecology of Claiborne Parish," 11, from box 225, folder 5, Charles Spurgeon Johnson Collection, Special Collections, John Hope and Aurelia E. Franklin Library, Fisk University, Nashville, Tenn.). Johnson, chairman of the Department of Social Sciences at Fisk, led a study of Louisiana's black schools in various parishes beginning in late 1941. The ecologies of parishes studied, completed by his team, included descriptions not only of the schools but of other characteristics including population, the status of public welfare, government and political organization, and economic resources. The findings were summarized by Johnson in "The Negro Public Schools: A Social and Educational Survey," published in *The Louisiana Educational Survey* (Baton Rouge: Louisiana Educational Survey Commission, 1942). For a description of Johnson's work and findings, see Johnson, "Confronting the Dilemma," 133–55.

60. Quoted in Winifred Bell, *Aid to Dependent Children* (New York: Columbia University Press, 1965), 63.

61. Tavia Wright, interview by author, Bernice, La., November 24, 2005. The Old Shiloh Black School is discussed in a short article by Jack and Winnie Baldwin, "The Old Shiloh Black School: A One-Room Landmark," from Collection No. M248, box 1, folder 2, LTU Special Collections.

62. Wright, interview, November 24, 2005.

63. Aarica Jones, interview by author, Bernice, La., July 7, 2012.

64. James R. Bobo and Harris S. Segal, eds., "Table III-11 Public Assistance: Aid to Dependent Children, Recipients, Louisiana and the United States, 1947–1975," in *Statistical Abstract of Louisiana*, 6th ed. (New Orleans: University of New Orleans College of Business Administration, 1977), 109; Reese, *Backlash against Welfare Mothers*, 42–43.

65. In *Pitied but Not Entitled* Gordon argues that popular sentiment considered only white widows as "deserving" of assistance. American society regarded divorced, deserted, and never married white mothers and all mothers of color as suspicious. Thus, while many "pitied" the conditions of poor single mothers, Americans deemed only a few as being "entitled" to public aid. In the crusade for welfare, reformers used only widows to evoke sympathy, only widows as case studies, and only widows in their literature and statistics. As a result, when ADC was instituted, few non-widowed single mothers received assistance. Ellen Reese also discusses in detail the effects of the removal of "deserving" mothers from ADC on the public perception of the program in pt. 2 of *Backlash against Welfare Mothers*.

66. Reese, *Backlash against Welfare Mothers*, pt. 2, 38; Roberts, *Killing the Black Body*, 110. As sociologist K. Sue Jewell notes, "The social welfare system, which is perhaps the most stigmatized and despised of all government funded programs, is erroneously defined as a system for African American women and their charges" (*From Mammy to Miss America and Beyond: Cultural Images and the Shaping of U.S. Policy* [London: Routledge, 1993], 57).

67. Bell, in chap. 3 of *Aid to Dependent Children*, "Strides towards Democratic Administration," discusses the methods welfare workers used to exclude "nonwhite and illegitimate children" (40–56). See also Lisa Levenstein, "From Innocent Children to Unwanted Migrants and Unwed Moms: Two Chapters in Public Discourse on Welfare in the United States, 1960–1961," *Journal of Women's History* 11, no. 4 (2000): 10–33; and Taaryn Lindhorst and Leslie Leighninger, "'Ending Welfare as We Know It' in 1960: Louisiana's Suitable Home Law," *Social Service*

Review 77, no. 4 (2003): 566–69. Misra et al. discuss media portrayals of welfare recipients as "morally corrupt" and overly dependent, in "Envisioning Dependency."

68. This idea is addressed, e.g., by Leonard Gross in "Are We Paying an Illegitimacy Bonus?" *Saturday Evening Post,* January 30, 1960, 30. Susan L. Thomas also discusses this belief as it was manifested in the mid-twentieth century, in "Race, Gender, and Welfare Reform." Social workers tried to debunk the myth, to no avail. See, e.g., Margaret Thornhill, "Problems of Repeated Out-of-Wedlock Pregnancies," *Child Welfare* (June 1959): 1–4; and Mary Evelyn Parker, Commissioner, to Parish and Area Staffs, "News Release," State of Louisiana, Department of Public Welfare (Baton Rouge, February 1960), from Accession No. P 1995-17, Social Service Publications, 1941–1969, Records of the Louisiana Department of Welfare, State Archives of Louisiana, Baton Rouge.

69. Harris-Perry, *Sister Citizen,* 113.

70. Rickie Solinger, *Wake Up, Little Susie: Single Pregnancy and Race before Roe v. Wade* (New York: Routledge, 2000), 25.

71. Margaret Thornhill, "Problems of Repeated Out-of-Wedlock Pregnancies," *Child Welfare* (June 1959): 3–4.

72. Nancy Fraser and Linda Gordon, "Dependency Demystified: Inscriptions of Power in a Keyword of the Welfare State," *Social Politics* 1(1994): 13. Dorothy Roberts also discusses the systemic problem of humiliation and shame in the welfare system (*Killing the Black Body,* 226–29).

73. Solinger, *Wake Up, Little Susie,* 25.

74. Solinger, *Wake Up, Little Susie,* 193. This, of course, is still a popular technique. For examples, see the essays in Gwendolyn Mink, *Whose Welfare;* and Jordan-Zachery, *Black Women, Cultural Images, and Social Policy,* esp. chap. 4.

75. U.S. Social Security Administration, Department of Health, Education, and Welfare (HEW), Bureau of Public Assistance, "State Letter No. 452: Aid to Dependent Children—'Suitable Home' Requirements" January 17, 1961, from Accession No. P 1995-17, Social Service Publications, 1941–1969, Records of the Louisiana Department of Welfare, State Archives of Louisiana, Baton Rouge.

76. Jewell, *From Mammy to Miss America and Beyond,* 57–58.

77. Susan Thomas describes, e.g., how a number of politicians in the mid-twentieth century proposed eugenics sterilization laws for welfare recipients, out of fear of "undesirable" women's (including poor black "Negroes") immorality, "unregulated sexuality," and potential to "'swamp' society with their defective offspring" ("Race, Gender, and Welfare Reform," 423–25).

78. Donald Wollett writes that the acts were spurred by "impending integration . . . and a rash of . . . sit-in demonstrations" ("Race Relations," *Louisiana Law Review* 21 [1960–61]: 21, 85). A *New York Times* article records that state legislators "said openly that it was aimed at Negroes" ("Welfare Boards Act in Louisiana," September 18, 1960). Fairclough also links the acts to the Louisiana legislature's war on integration (*Race and Democracy,* 232–33).

79. For Acts 73 and 75, see West's *Louisiana Statutes Annotated, LSA-R.S.* 14:1.

80. For Act 251 and the similar Act 306, see West's *Louisiana Statutes Annotated, LSA-R.S. 45:1131 to 46:970.* For a discussion of the racial nature of many of the 1960 acts, see Wollett, "Race Relations," 85–93.

81. As evidence that Louisiana's suitable home laws were not truly about children's well-being, Bell recounts contemporary arguments that questioned why children were not removed

from "unsuitable homes" (*Aid to Dependent Children,* 145). She also notes (as do Lindhorst and Leighninger) that less than 1 percent of homes were found unsuitable based on "traditional evidences of neglect, abuse or exploitation" (139). Lindhorst and Leighninger, "'Ending Welfare as We Know It' in 1960," 571.

82. This is one of the central arguments of Lindhorst and Leighninger's article "'Ending Welfare as We Know It' in 1960." Jerome Schiele and Ellarwee Gadsden also discuss social welfare programs as a method of regulation or control of African Americans in "Racial Control and Resistance among African Americans in the Aftermath of the Welfare Reform Act of 1996," in *Social Welfare Policy: Regulation and Resistance among People of Color,* ed. Jerome H. Schiele (Thousand Oaks, Calif.: Sage Publications, 2011), 91–110. Quote from Anna Marie Smith, *Welfare Reform and Sexual Regulation* (New York: Cambridge University Press, 2007), 87.

83. Wright, interview, November 24, 2005.

84. Smith, *Welfare Reform and Sexual Regulation,* 87.

85. Mary Evelyn Parker, Commissioner, to State and Parish Staffs, "Tables on ADC Cases Closed because of Unsuitable Homes," State of Louisiana, Department of Public Welfare (Baton Rouge, August 25, 1960), from Accession No. P 1995-17, Social Service Publications, 1941–1969, Records of the Louisiana Department of Welfare, State Archives of Louisiana, Baton Rouge; Levenstein, "From Innocent Children to Unwanted Migrants and Unwed Moms," 13; Bell, *Aid to Dependent Children,* 137; Lindhorst and Leighninger, "'Ending Welfare as We Know It' in 1960," 564.

86. Explained in a form letter found in the Records of the State of Louisiana Department of Public Welfare, in which the right to appeal to the State Department of Public Welfare was clarified.

87. Parker, "Tables on ADC Cases Closed because of Unsuitable Homes"; Levenstein, "From Innocent Children to Unwanted Migrants and Unwed Moms," 13; Bell, *Aid to Dependent Children,* 137; Lindhorst and Leighninger, "'Ending Welfare as We Know It' in 1960," 564.

88. In *Welfare's End* Mink makes this argument about the 1996 Personal Responsibility and Work Opportunity Reconciliation Act that ended Aid to Families with Dependent Children. She discusses it in detail in "Lady and the Tramp (II)."

89. Jones, interview, July 7, 2012.

90. For black responses to the acts, see Levenstein, "From Innocent Children to Unwanted Migrants and Unwed Moms," 13; Bell, *Aid to Dependent Children,* 141; and Lindhorst and Leighninger, "'Ending Welfare as We Know It' in 1960," 572–75.

91. Parker's speeches were circulated with the following memo: Otis C. Edwards Jr., Deputy Commissioner of Public Welfare, to State and Parish Staffs, "Addresses by Mrs. Parker," State of Louisiana, Department of Public Welfare (Baton Rouge, March 31, 1960), State of Louisiana, Department of Public Welfare (Baton Rouge, February 1960), from Accession No. P 1995-17, Social Service Publications, 1941–1969, Records of the Louisiana Department of Welfare, State Archives of Louisiana, Baton Rouge; Parker, "News Release" (February 1960). Parker circulated the March 1960 issue of *Family Service Highlights,* which contained Norman M. Lobenz, "The Campaign against Helpless Children," and other defenses of ADC attached to the following memo: Mary Evelyn Parker, Commissioner, to State and Parish Staffs, "Reprint: 'The Campaign against Helpless Children,'" State of Louisiana, Department of Public Welfare (Baton

Rouge: May 5, 1960), from Accession No. P 1995-17, Social Service Publications, 1941–1969, Records of the Louisiana Department of Welfare, State Archives of Louisiana, Baton Rouge.

92. Parker, "News Release" (February 1960).

93. It is important to note that the work of the Department of Public Welfare to counter prominent stereotypes of black women was circumscribed by its social workers' own acceptance of these stereotypes and "worries" about unsuitable homes, as revealed in their interdepartmental correspondence.

94. Reese, *Backlash against Welfare Mothers,* 38. Mimi Abramovitz also discusses how changes in ADC and ADC recipients precipitated a (negative) change in the perception of and support for the program (*Regulating the Lives of Women,* chap. 10). Levenstein ("From Innocent Children to Unwanted Migrants and Unwed Moms") and Lindhorst and Leighninger ("'Ending Welfare as We Know It' in 1960") analyze these perceptions as well.

95. According to Levenstein, white journalists initially ignored the Louisiana crisis. Lindhorst and Leighninger record a similar reaction among mainstream social service agencies (e.g., the Red Cross and the precursor of the United Way). Winifred Bell observes that the parish boards, composed of ordinary citizens that could reinstate aid, proceeded unhurriedly. The fact that children were going without adequate food, shelter, and clothing seemed lost upon the white public. Their attention was directed toward punishing the mothers, at the expense of thousands of children. See also "Sins of the Father," *New York Times,* October 6, 1960.

96. "Governor Davis Comments," *New York Times,* September 23, 1960.

97. "Louisiana Refuses to Ease Its Rules on Child Aid," *New York Times,* November 9, 1960.

98. The state's response to HEW, including its defense of its suitable home policies and Governor Jimmie Davis's denouncement of HEW secretary Arthur Flemming's threat as illogical, can be found in a statement circulated by the chairman of the State Board of Public Welfare dated October 28, 1960, in the Records of the State of Louisiana Department of Public Welfare.

99. U.S. Social Security Administration, Department of HEW, Bureau of Public Assistance, "State Letter No. 452: Aid to Dependent Children—'Suitable Home' Requirements," January 17, 1961, and "State Letter No. 481: Aid to Dependent Children—'Suitable Home' Requirements—Amendments Made by New Federal Legislation," May 15, 1961 from Accession No. P 1995-17, Social Service Publications, 1941–1969, Records of the Louisiana Department of Welfare, State Archives of Louisiana, Baton Rouge. Louisiana politicians would stay at the forefront of the antiwelfare debate, as exemplified by Senator Russell Long, who notoriously called poor black and Latina mothers "brood mares" and insisted on the availability of these women for low-wage reproductive labor.

100. "Sovereignty Commission Lists Aims," *Farmerville Gazette,* September 1, 1960.

101. "Board Reaffirms Stand on Segregation," *Farmerville Gazette,* December 15, 1960.

102. "Local Citizens Back Governor in Segregation Fight," *Farmerville Gazette,* November 10, 1960.

103. The number of black farm operators in Louisiana dropped from 40,599 to 17,686 (U.S. Department of Commerce, Bureau of the Census, *U.S. Census of Agriculture: Final Report,* vol. 1: "Parishes," pt. 35: "Louisiana" [Washington, D.C.: GPO, 1961], 6–7).

104. Jones, *I Remember Life in Union Parish,* 23.

105. "Farm Workers," *Bernice News-Journal,* August 4, 1960; Lindsey Gin and Seed Co., "To Our Cotton Growing Friends," *Bernice News-Journal* September 15, 1960.

106. Parker, "Tables on ADC Cases Closed Because of Unsuitable Homes."

107. Parker, "Tables on ADC Cases Closed Because of Unsuitable Homes"; "Union Parish Welfare Cases Trimmed," *Bernice News-Journal,* July 28, 1960. In June 1960 there were 228 cases welfare cases in Union Parish. Data on poverty levels in Louisiana are from U.S. Office of Economic Opportunity Information Center, Community Profile: Union Parish Louisiana (1966), CP008–CP010. The profile also reported that poverty in Union Parish was "dramatically more severe than in the average United States county."

108. *Union Parish Resources and Facilities,* 55.

109. Dennis Evans, "A Study of Relative Quality of Life in Selected Louisiana Parishes" (Ed.D. diss., Louisiana State University, 1974), 74.

110. Nakano Glenn, "Cleaning Up / Kept Down," 1350–51.

111. *Union Parish Resources and Facilities,* 101.

112. Heffernan, "Constraints in the U.S. Poultry Industry," 246; LSUAgCenter.com, "Louisiana Poultry Industry Major Economic Factor," www.lsuagcenter.com/en/crops_livestock/livestock/poultry/Broiler+Production/Louisiana+Poultry+Industry+Major+Economic+Factor .htm (last accessed September 26, 2011).

113. Stuesse, "Globalization 'Southern Style,'" 134.

114. Bazemore is a former worker at a North Carolina Perdue Farms poultry processing plant. In 1989 and 1991 she gave testimony before Congress on the conditions faced by workers in plants and the hazards poultry processing techniques pose to consumers of chickens (U.S. Congress, Senate, Committee on Labor and Human Resources, *Poultry Safety: Consumers at Risk* 102nd Cong., 1st sess., June 28, 1991, 32).

115. See, e.g., Jones, *Labor of Love, Labor of Sorrow,* chap. 8; Bette Woody, *Black Women in the Workplace: Impacts of Structural Change in the Economy* (New York: Greenwood Press, 1992); Enobong Hannah Branch, *Opportunity Denied: Limiting Black Women to Devalued Work* (New Brunswick, N.J.: Rutgers University Press, 2011). By the late 1960s, frustrated by the lack of civil rights, legal redress, and economic opportunity, some African Americans in El Dorado were pushing back against circumstances they deemed unacceptable. Black leaders provided the mayor with a description of grievances, including "the lack of Negro policemen and firemen and poor job opportunities in industry and business here" (Robert Shaw, "El Dorado Mayor Blames Violence on Small Minority," *Camden News,* March 8, 1968). Former FBI agent Floyd Thomas remembered that in the late 1960s, in response to Ku Klux Klan violence, black people in south Arkansas decided they "wasn't gonna take this crap, so they started fighting back" (*Arkansas Memories: Interviews from the Pryor Center for Arkansas Oral and Visual History,* "Floyd Thomas Fights the Arkansas Ku Klux Klan," *Arkansas Historical Quarterly* 71, no. 1 [Spring 2012]: 74–78). In 1968, e.g., when a white youth charged with murdering a black teenager was acquitted, black El Dorado residents held a peaceful protest march. Later the same week, black youth took to the streets in a more violent demonstration against the verdict. See "Negros in March at El Dorado," *Camden News,* March 4, 1968; Shaw, "El Dorado Mayor Blames Violence on Small Minority"; "Leaders See Tensions as Serious; Peace Possible," *El Dorado Times,* March 8, 1968; and "Tear Gas Used," *El Dorado Times,* March 8, 1968.

116. Branch, *Opportunity Denied,* 1. In addition to Branch, on black women in "devalued" labor, see Jones, *Labor of Love, Labor of Sorrow;* Irene Browne, ed., *Latinas and African American Women at Work: Race Gender and Economic Inequality* (New York: Russell Sage Foundation, 1999); Nakano Glenn, "Cleaning Up / Kept Down" and "From Servitude to Service Work"; Sharon Harley, "'Working for Nothing but for a Living': Black Women in the Underground Economy," in *Sister Circle: Black Women and Work,* ed. Sharon Harley and the Black Women and Work Collective (New Brunswick, N.J.: Rutgers University Press, 2002), 48–66; Bonnie Thornton Dill and Tallese Johnson, "Between a Rock and a Hard Place: Mothering, Work, and Welfare in the Rural South," in Harley et al., *Sister Circle;* Ruth Sidel, *Keeping Women and Children Last: America's War on the Poor* (New York: Penguin Books, 1996).

117. Irene Brown and Ivy Kennelly, "Stereotypes and Realities: Images of Black Women in the Labor Market," in *Latinas and African American Women at Work: Race Gender and Economic Inequality,* ed. Irene Brown (New York: Russell Sage Foundation, 1999), 302. Indeed, the economic and employment gains made by black women had begun to erode by the 1980s.

118. Ella Foster, Faith Monroe, and Lizzie Thomas, interviews by author, August 31, 2012.

119. On the nature of cooking duties, see Sharpless, *Cooking in Other Women's Kitchens,* chap. 3; Palmer, *Domesticity and Dirt,* 79–81.

120. Gwendolyn Brooks, *Maud Martha, Blacks* (Chicago: Third World Press, 1993), 293–94, quoted in Williams-Forson, *Building Houses,* 110–11. Maud Martha's disgust over the "STUFF" that "splatted" in her eye is echoed by poultry processing workers such as and Kenya Drayton, Neysha Mallory, Sylvia Martin, and Tavia Wright, who commented on "stuff flying in your face."

121. Sharpless, *Cooking in Other Women's Kitchens,* 66.

122. I say in its most basic form because the relationship between domestic workers and their employers is a layered and complex one. See Sharpless, *Cooking in Other Women's Kitchens,* chap. 6; Judith Rollins, *Between Women: Domestics and Their Employers* (Philadelphia: Temple University Press, 1987), esp. chap. 5; Susan Tucker, "A Complex Bond: Southern Black Domestic Workers and Their White Employers," special issue on "Women in the American South," *Frontiers* 9, no. 3 (1987): 6–13; and *Telling Memories among Southern Women: Domestic Workers and Their Employers in the Segregated South,* pt. 1; Leon Litwack, *Trouble in Mind: Black Southerners in the Age of Jim Crow* (New York: Knopf, 1988), 167–74.

123. Rollins, *Between Women,* 156.

124. See Darlene Clark Hine, "Rape and the Inner Lives of Black Women: Thoughts on the Culture of Dissemblance," in *Hine Sight: Black Women and the Re-Construction of American History* (Brooklyn: Carlson Publishing, 1994), 37–47; and Charisse Jones and Kumea Shorter-Gooden, *Shifting: The Double Lives of Black Women in America* (New York: HarperCollins, 2003).

125. Nakano Glenn, "From Servitude to Service Work," 18; Tucker, "Complex Bond," 9;

126. Sharpless, *Cooking in Other Women's Kitchens,* 110.

127. Nakano Glenn, "Cleaning Up / Kept Down"; Nakano Glenn, "From Servitude to Service Work"; Mignon Duffy, "Doing the Dirty Work: Gender, Race, and Reproductive Labor in Historical Perspective," *Gender and Society* 21, no. 3 (2007): 313–36.

128. Striffler, *Chicken,* esp. chap. 1; Horowitz, *Putting Meat on the American Table,* esp. chap. 6; Schlosser, *Fast Food Nation;* Hannah Fairfield, "Factory Food," *New York Times,* April 3, 2010.

129. Liu and Apollon, "Color of Food."

130. Factory work may have paid more, but I add the caveat that with regards to the poultry industry in the 1960s, the AMBW repeatedly argued that workers labored for poverty wages. According to the AMBW, "The Poultry section of our Union is recognized by all of us as one of the most exploited sections of the industry" (*Butcher Workman* 55, no. 1 [January 1969]: 23). The hourly earnings of poultry processing workers were less than two-thirds the average of all production workers in the meat industry, and their weekly earnings were only about half that of meat packers. See, e.g., descriptions in the "Poultry, Egg, Fish, and Frozen Food Dept." section of *Butcher Workman* 54, no. 1 (January–February 1968): 31; *Butcher Workman* 55, no. 1 (January 1969): 23; *Butcher Workman* 55, no. 4 (April–May 1969): 25. On the comparison to production workers in other meat industry work, see Walter A. Fogel, *The Negro in the Meat Industry,* Report No. 12 of "The Racial Policies of American Industry," a series by the Industrial Research Unit, Department of Industry, Wharton School of Finance and Commerce, University of Pennsylvania (Philadelphia: University of Pennsylvania Press, 1970), 15 and 66.

131. Moberg, "Puttin' Down Ol' Massa," 293. For the preponderance of black women in poultry processing line work in the 1960s and the dearth of black foremen/supervisors and African Americans in managerial positions in the meat industry as a whole, see also Fogel, *Negro in the Meat Industry,* 14–15, 66, 86–95, 101–4. This is also noted in oral histories from former plant workers, the *Southern Exposure* exposé, Cromer in "Plucking Cargill," 15–23, and other works that focus on Latino workers but note that the workforce that preceded them was primarily black and female. While here I explore the attempted subordination of black women's family and community duties, in the next chapter I will explore the effects of this racial-gender hierarchy on other aspects of the work and workers' lives.

132. This issue is discussed in Nakano Glenn, "From Servitude to Service Work"; Jacqueline Jones, *Labor of Love, Labor of Sorrow: Black Women, Work, and the Family from Slavery to the Present* (New York: Basic Books, 1983); Sharon Harley, "When Your Work Is Not Who You Are: The Development of a Working Class Consciousness among Afro-American Women," in *Gender, Class, Race and Reform in the Progressive Era,* ed. Noralee Frankel and Nancy Dye (Lexington: University Press of Kentucky, 1991); Palmer, *Domesticity and Dirt,* chap. 4; and Sharpless, *Cooking in Other Women's Kitchens,* esp. chap. 5. Black women commonly contested this definition by others; as Nakano Glenn writes, "Domestics saw their responsibilities as mothers as the central core of their identity." See Sharon Harley, "For the Good of Family and Race: Gender, Work, and Domestic Roles in the Black Community, 1880–1930," *Signs* 15, no. 2 (1990): 336–49; and "When Your Work Is Not Who You Are"; Bonnie Thornton Dill, "'The Means to Put My Children Through': Child-Rearing Goals and Strategies among Black Female Domestic Servants," in *The Black Woman,* ed. LaFrances Rodgers-Rose (Beverly Hills, Calif.: Sage Publications, 1980), 107–23; and Tucker, "Complex Bond," 9–10.

133. Neysha Mallory, interview by author, August 3, 2011.

134. Mallory interview, August 3, 2011

135. Moberg, "Puttin' Down Ol' Massa," 292.

136. Lydia and Sylvia Martin, joint interview by author, August 7, 2011.

137. Lillian Gafford, interview by author, September 3, 2011.

138. West, interview, January 2, 2005.

139. When asked, some of the older mothers I interviewed expressed solidarity with young mothers but insisted the younger women did not "have it as bad." That judgment was not

based on paid work, however, but on social changes that allow younger women to share some domestic responsibilities with their partners and children and the availability of convenience foods. West also suggested that younger women "don't take the mess we had to."

140. Janae Earl, interview by author, August 4, 2011.

141. Lydia and Sylvia Martin, joint interview, August 7, 2011.

142. Earl, interview, August 4, 2011.

143. Gafford, electronic interview by author, September 4, 2006.

144. Eleanor Holloway, interview by author, August 3, 2011.

145. Leon Fink, *The Maya of Morganton: Work and Community in the Nuevo New South* (Chapel Hill: University of North Carolina Press, 2003), 180.

146. Tavia Wright, interview by author, Bernice, La., December 27, 2004. Faith Monroe, who worked at the plant from 1965 until 1990, remembered that when it came to taking time off to care for her children, her supervisors in the early years "was [*sic*] good about that" (Monroe, interview by Videssa Morris-Owens, August 31, 2012).

147. Mallory, interview, August 3, 2011. Barbara Goldoftas also discusses the point system and the policy of penalizing workers for "being late or missing part of the day *regardless of the reason*" ("Inside the Slaughterhouse," Ruling the Roost: A Special Report on the Poultry Industry, *Southern Exposure,* 17, no. 2 [1989]: 27, emphasis added).

148. Bella Dawes talked about the acknowledgment, on the part of ConAgra management, that women would be the ones prepping their children for the new school year: "Time for school, ConAgra would let them women off . . . they would always be prepared for that at school time." In the case of Pilgrim's Pride, however, "if you go, you pointed."

149. There are numerous works on black women's integral role in churches and church-led organizations and events. See Evelyn Higginbotham, *Righteous Discontent: The Women's Movement in the Black Baptist Church, 1880–1920* (Cambridge: Harvard University Press, 1993); Daphne Wiggins, *Righteous Content: Black Women's Perspectives of Church and Faith* (New York: New York University Press, 2005); and Aldon Morris, *The Origins of the Civil Rights Movement: Black Communities Organizing for Change* (New York: Free Press, 1984). Vivian West, e.g., is a minister's wife. Tavia Wright is a deaconess and choir member. Ruth James is the president of her church choir.

150. Wright, interview, December 27, 2004.

151. Kenya Drayton, interview by author, Houston, Tex., November 7, 2004.

152. Angela Davis, "Reflections on the Black Woman's Role in the Community of Slaves," *Black Scholar* 3, no. 4 (1971): 3–15. Similarly, Elsa Barkley Brown argues that her mother's "decision to be a wife and mother first in a world which defined Black women in so many other ways . . . was an act of resistance" (quoted in Hill Collins, *Black Feminist Thought,* 54–55).

153. While the economic circumstances of poor black women mandated that they work, middle-class black women, contend Sharon Harley and Deborah Gray-White, often had to defend their place in the workforce. Harley, "For the Good of Family and Race," 343–47; Gray-White, *Too Heavy a Load: Black Women in Defense of Themselves, 1894–1994* (New York: Norton, 1999).

154. See, e.g., bell hooks, "Rethinking the Nature of Work" in *Feminist Theory: From Margin to Center,* 2nd ed. (Cambridge, Mass.: South End Press, 2000), 96–107. Mink also discusses how white feminists' insistence that liberation is tied to work outside the home creates an ideological chasm between them and women of color ("The Lady and the Tramp [II]," esp. 59–61).

155. hooks, *Feminist Theory from Margin to Center*), 133–34.

156. Wright, interview, December 27, 2004; West, interview, January 2, 2005.

157. Donna Bazemore, interviewed by Bob Hall, in "I Feel What Women Feel," *Southern Exposure* 17, no. 2 (1989): 31.

158. Lydia and Sylvia Martin, joint interview, August 7, 2011.

159. Earl, interview, August 4, 2011.

160. Ruth Sidel posits that these pressures are aggravated by societal denigration of single mothers and their choices, leaving female-headed families in uniquely stressful situations (*Keeping Women and Children Last: America's War on the Poor* [New York: Penguin Books, 199], 33–57).

161. Ella Fields, quoted in Ernest Spaights and Ann Whitaker, "Black Women in the Workforce: A New Look at an Old Problem," *Journal of Black Studies* 25, no. 3 (1995): 283–96.

162. LaDonna Island, electronic interview by author, October 22, 2005.

163. Wright, interview, November 24, 2005.

164. Wright, interview, November 24, 2005..

165. Natalie Davis, interview by author, Bernice, La., January 15, 2005.

166. Sherry Carter, interview by Videssa Morris-Owens, November 24, 2012.

167. Trinity Mays, electronic interview by author, April 4, 2007.

168. Melody Hessing, "More than Clockwork: Women's Time Management in Their Combined Workloads," *Sociological Perspectives* 37, no. 4 (1994): 630.

169. Jones, interview, July 7, 2012; Davis, interview, January 15, 2005.

170. Hessing, "More than Clockwork."

171. Ruth James, interview by author, August 4, 2011.

172. Carter, interview, November 24, 2012; Wright, interview, December 27, 2004; West, interview, January 2, 2005.

173. Vivian West, interview by author, July 27, 2011.

174. Margie Young, interview by author, August 3, 2011. Delores Biles, interview by author, August 8, 2011.

175. Lydia and Sylvia Martin, joint interview, August 7, 2011.

176. Holloway, interview by author, August 3, 2011.

177. Drayton, interview, November 7, 2004.

3. "I LEARNED THIS—YOU AIN'T NOBODY!"

1. Carter, interview, November 24, 2012.

2. Drayton, interview, November 7, 2004.

3. The stories from interviewees are strikingly similar across time and across the South.

4. U.S. Government Accountability Office, *Safety in the Meat and Poultry Industry, While Improving, Could Be Further Strengthened,* GAO-05-96, January 2005, www.gao.gov/new .items/d0596.pdf (last accessed April 13, 2007). I will explore the physical environment and effects in the next chapter.

5. Bo Pilgrim, *One Pilgrim's Progress: How to Build a World-Class Company and Who to Credit* (Nashville: Thomas Nelson Publishers, 2005), 91.

6. Kerry Hall, Ames Alexander, and Franco Ordoñez, "The Cruelest Cuts," *Charlotte Observer,* February 10, 2008.

7. Bazemore, interview, 33. On the use of "scare tactics" in poultry plants, see Griffith, *Jones's Minimal,* 182–83.

8. Goldoftas, "Inside the Slaughterhouse," 26.

9. West, interview, January 2, 2005.

10. Moberg, "Puttin Down Ol' Massa," 293.

11. Bazemore, interview, 33.

12. Moberg, "Puttin Down Ol' Massa," 298.

13. Riffel, "Feathered Kingdom," 90–91.

14. Goldoftas, "Inside the Slaughterhouse," 25.

15. Gafford, interview, September 3, 2011.

16. Drayton, interview, November 7, 2004.

17. Stuesse, "Globalization 'Southern Style,'" 239. In 2008 Enrique Pagan, a former supervisor in a North Carolina plant, described his interactions with line workers to journalists: "He [Pagan] paced and often screamed. . . . He demanded they move faster and scolded them" (quoted in Franco Ordoñez, Kerry Hall, and Ames Alexander, "A Boss's View: Keep Them Working," *Charlotte Observer,* February 12, 2008).

18. Angela Goodwin et al. v. Con Agra Poultry Company and Pilgrim's Pride, Incorporated, Civil Action No. 03-1187 (U.S. District Court, Western District of Arkansas, El Dorado Division, 2003).

19. Pilgrim, *One Pilgrim's Progress,* 123.

20. Dawes, interview, August 4, 2011; Johnson, interview, October 1, 2011. This sense of betrayal by members of "our kind" is shared by Latino workers, who told North Carolina reporters that "what really hurt [was] the disparaging treatment by Latino supervisors who shared their background and understood the struggles of being an immigrant in the U.S." ("Boss's View").

21. Stuesse, "Globalization, 'Southern Style," 240.

22. Robert S. Starobin, "Privileged Bondsmen and the Process of Accommodation: The Role of Houseservants and Drivers as Seen in Their Own Letters," *Journal of Social History* 5, no. 1 (Fall 1971): 52. A former worker in Stuesse's study made a similar observation, comparing his former black supervisors to "'house slaves,' just one small step above the 'yard' and 'field' slaves doing the hard processing work" ("Globalization 'Southern Style,'" 109–10). It is important to note, however, another way that race might play a role in employees' perceptions of black supervisors: long accustomed to seeing white men in positions of authority, they might find it difficult, subconsciously, to accept the presence of a person of color in a position of relative power.

23. On the sexual exploitation of black women by white men, see Gray-White, *Ar'n't I a Woman,* esp. chap. 2; Sharpless, *Cooking in Other Women's Kitchens,* 138–41; Giddings, *When and Where I Enter,* 85–94; and Hine, "Rape and the Inner Lives of Black Women," 37–47.

24. Public Justice Center, *The Disposable Workforce: A Worker's Perspective: A Documentation Study Conducted of Working Conditions in Delmarva Poultry Processing Plants,* report, Baltimore, Md., n.d., 31, www.upc-online.org/workers/Poultrystudy.pdf (last accessed January 20, 2014).

25. Wright, interview, December 27, 2004.

26. LeeAnn Johnson, interview with author, August 4, 2011. Barbara Goldoftas writes that women in the industry recounted "supervisors pass[ing] by, pinching them or slapping their behinds" ("Inside the Slaughterhouse," 27).

27. Mays, electronic interview, April 4, 2007.

28. Goldoftas, "Inside the Slaughterhouse," 27.

29. Moberg, "Puttin Down Ol' Massa," 298.

30. Angela Goodwin et al. v. Con Agra Poultry Company and Pilgrim's Pride, Incorporated, Civil Action No. 03-1187 (U.S. District Court, Western District of Arkansas, El Dorado Division, 2003).

31. Wright, interview, December 27, 2004.

32. West, interview July 27, 2011; Dawes, interview, August 4, 2011; Bazemore, interview, 30; LaDonna Island, electronic interview by author, August 2011.

33. DeShaun Lowe, interview by author, March 21, 2005.

34. George Williams v. ConAgra Poultry Co., Civil Action No. 03-2976 (U.S. Court of Appeals, Eighth Circuit, Arkansas, 2004).

35. George Williams v. ConAgra Poultry Co., Civil Action No. 03-2976; Angela Goodwin et al. v. Con Agra Poultry Company and Pilgrim's Pride, Incorporated, Civil Action No. 03-1187.

36. Moberg, "Puttin Down Ol' Massa," 292.

37. Drayton, interview, November 7, 2004. Poultry processing workers interviewed by Stuesse reported similar threats. Supervisors would tell them: "If you don't want to be here, just leave. There are twenty, thirty people outside that want to work" ("Globalization 'Southern Style," 238).

38. Island, electronic interview, August 2011.

39. U.S. Congress, *Poultry Safety,* 54.

40. Bazemore, interview, 33.

41. Mallory, interview, August 3, 2011.

42. Drayton, interview, November 7, 2004.

43. Rick Thames, "Poultry Series Exposes an New, Silent Subclass," *Charlotte Observer,* February 10, 2008.

44. Drayton, interview, November 7, 2004. Drayton worked in the El Dorado plant in the first decade of the twenty-first century, when the presence of Latino workers began to grow.

45. Public Justice Center, *Disposable Workforce,* 15

46. Jim Lewis, "Grasshopper Power," in *Workers' Rights as Human Rights,* ed. James Gross (Ithaca, N.Y.: ILR Press, 2003), 543.

47. Quoted in Cromer, "Plucking Cargill," 20.

48. This is not uncommon in workplaces, of course, and scholars such as Leon Fink and Roger Horowitz have explored the process of building or the process of bringing (particularly in Fink's book) community into meat processing plants. See Fink, *Maya of Morganton;* and Horowitz, *Negro and White, Unite and Fight.*

49. Young, interview, August 3, 2011; Shine, interview, July 27, 2011; Mallory, interview, August 3, 2011.

50. Jones, *Labor of Love, Labor of Sorrow,* 140.

51. Tavia Wright, telephone interview by author, October 1, 2011.

52. Drayton, interview, November 7, 2004.

53. Wright, telephone interview, October 1, 2011.

54. Mallory, interview, August 3, 2011.

55. Wright, interview, December 27, 2004.

56. West, interview, January 2, 2005.

57. Lydia and Sylvia Martin, joint interview, August 7, 2011.

58. Dawes, interview, August 4, 2011

59. Wright, telephone interview, October 1, 2011; Mallory, interview, August 3, 2011; Lydia and Sylvia Martin, joint interview, August 7, 2011.

60. Biles, interview, August 8, 2011.

61. U.S. Congress, House, Committee on Education and Labor, Subcommittee on Labor-Management Relations, *Hearing on H.R. 3368, Whistleblower Protection Act* 101st Cong., 1st sess., November 16, 1989, 42.

62. Drayton, interview, November 7, 2004; West, interview, January 2, 2005; Eason, quoted in Goldoftas, "Inside the Slaughterhouse," 26; Dawes, interview, August 4, 2011; Wright, telephone interview, October 1, 2011.

63. Bob Hall, "Chicken Empires," *Southern Exposure* 17, no. 2 (1989): 15.

64. Stuesse describes "the repeated denial of bathroom breaks" as a "particularly chronic problem for poultry workers" ("Globalization 'Southern Style,'" 248). Donna Bazemore also comments upon the lack of adequate bathroom facilities and time in *Poultry Safety* (24). Sarah White, who worked in the catfish processing industry, where black women had similar grievances, and helped lead the largest strike by black workers in Mississippi's history, notes, "That strike was really about the bathrooms" (quoted in Kristal Brent Zook, "Dreaming in the Delta: A Memoir Essay," *Meridians* 3, no. 2 [2003]: 284).

65. Moberg, "Puttin Down Ol' Massa," 279.

66. Goldoftas, "Inside the Slaughterhouse," 27.

67. Public Justice Center, *Disposable Workforce,* 38; Fink, *Maya of Morgantown,* 27–28. Bazemore also reported this as a common occurrence (*Hearing on H.R. 3368, Whistleblower Protection Act,* 42).

68. Drayton, interview, November 7, 2004.

69. Mallory, interview, August 3, 2011.

70. West, interview, January 2, 2005. David Griffith reports that employees in a North Carolina plant routinely spend their entire break in line (*Jones's Minimal,* 177).

71. West, interview, January 2, 2005.

72. *Jones's Minimal,* 178; Horowitz and Miller, *Immigrants in the Delmarva Poultry Processing Industry,* 3.

73. Quoted in Stuesse, "Globalization 'Southern Style,'" 250.

74. Brody, *Butcher Workmen,* 247. In El Dorado, e.g., Klansman had forced an attorney for IWW members out of town (Charles C. Alexander, *The Ku Klux Klan in the Southwest* [Norman: University of Oklahoma Press, 1995], 52).

75. Michael Honey, "Industrial Unionism and Racial Justice in Memphis," in *Organized Labor in the Twentieth Century South,* ed. Robert H. Zieger (Knoxville: University of Tennessee Press, 1991), 153.

76. The South is *not* exceptional purely because of antiunion sentiment. U.S. history is, of course, replete with stories, across regions, of antiunion fervor. What seems to be noteworthy about the South is the exceptional level of its hostility toward unions and the inability of unions to gain significant ground there.

77. Draper, *Conflict of Interests;* Griffith, *Crisis of American Labor.* Nelson Lichtenstein also recounts southern white elites' machinations to maintain power and keep southern workers disfranchised and impoverished (*State of the Union: A Century of American Labor* [Princeton: Princeton University Press, 2002]: 110–14). Jonathan Gentry, "'Christ Is Out, Communism Is On': Opposition to the Congress of Industrial Organizations' 'Operation Dixie' in South Carolina, 1946–1951," *Proceedings of the South Carolina Historical Association* (2003): 15–24. On the specific struggle in poultry processing, see Moberg, "Puttin' Down Ol' Massa"; Lawrence and Braden, "Long Struggle"; and Cromer, "Plucking Cargill."

78. Barbara Griffith, *Crisis of American Labor;* Gentry, "'Christ Is Out, Communism Is On,'" 16.

79. Gentry, "'Christ Is Out, Communism Is On,'" 20.

80. Robert H. Zieger, *American Workers, American Unions,* 2nd ed. (Baltimore: Johns Hopkins University Press, 1994), 108–14.

81. Stephen Norwood, *Strikebreaking and Intimidation: Mercenaries and Masculinity in Twentieth Century* (Chapel Hill: University of North Carolina Press, 2002): 231; Lichtenstein, *State of the Union,* 118.

82. Within a few years Louisiana was the only southern state without right-to-work laws.

83. In "The Effects of Right-to-Work Laws: A Review of the Literature," *Industrial and Labor Relations Review* 38, no. 4 (1985): 571–85, e.g., William J. Moore and Robert J. Newman posit that the effects of right-to-work laws are more symbolic than substantive. David Ellwood and Glenn Fine, "The Impact of Right-to-Work Laws on Union Organizing," *Journal of Political Economy* 95, no. 2 (1987): 250–73. Ellwood and Fine find that union organizing was reduced by almost 50 percent in the first five years following the passage of a right-to-work law (271). Thomas Carroll maintains that right-to-work laws have observable economic side effects because unions are rendered weaker in collective bargaining, resulting in lower average earnings ("Right-to-Work Laws Do Matter," *Southern Economic Journal* 50, no. 2 [1983]: 508).

84. Ellwood and Fine, "Impact of Right-to-Work Laws," 271.

85. Moberg, "Puttin' Down Ol' Massa," 300.

86. Moore and Newman, "Effects of Right-to-Work Laws," 581.

87. Cobb, *Selling of the South,* esp. chap. 4.

88. Evelyn Nakano Glenn uses the term *racial-ethnic* "to refer collectively to groups that have been socially constructed and constituted as racially as well as culturally distinct from European Americans and placed in separate legal statuses from free whites" ("From Servitude to Service Work," 2). It accurately describes the various groups of people who, at one time or another, have been excluded from unionism.

89. Fogel traces the often contentious relationship between unions and black workers in the meat processing industry (*Negro in the Meat Industry,* 30–43), arguing that, among other factors, black workers did not support or trust unions because they realized "trade unions generally had not been hospitable to members of their race," and they recognized the "prejudice" of white union members toward them not only within the industry but "in a variety of interpersonal and community relations" (36–37).

90. Brody, *Butcher Workmen,* 247–51.

91. The Poultry Department, Amalgamated Meat Cutters and Butcher Workmen of North America (AMBW), "Suggested Press Release," March 27, 1957, from the papers of Samuel Twedell, AR44-31-2.

92. Letter dated March 1, 1957, from Shirley W. Barker to Secretaries of Local Unions Having Swift and Co. Agreements from the papers of Samuel Twedell, AR44-31-2.

93. Lawrence and Braden, "Long Struggle," 86.

94. Lawrence and Braden, "Long Struggle," 17–19.

95. Fink, *Maya of Morganton,* esp. chaps. 3–5.

96. On the rise of a more conservative "business unionism," see Kim Moody, *An Injury to All: The Decline of American Trade Unionism* (London: Verso, 1988); Mike Davis, *Prisoners of the American Dream: Politics and Economy in the History of the U.S. Working Class* (London: Verso, 1986); Victoria Hattam, *Labor Visions and State Power: The Origins of Business Union-ism in the United States* (Princeton: Princeton University Press, 1993); Judith Stepan-Norris and Maurice Zeitlin, *Left Out: Reds and America's Industrial Unions* (Cambridge: Cambridge University Press, 2003); and Fantasia and Voss, *Hard Work,* chap. 2.

97. Reflecting the atmosphere of the Cold War, Taft-Hartley required union organizers to declare that they were not Communists, leading to the expulsion of Communists, which further distanced unions from a leftist orientation that was sympathetic to the struggles of people of color. On CIO infighting, see Zieger, *American Workers, American Unions,* 2nd ed., 123–34. Michael Honey chronicles the hope that black workers invested in the CIO, the Cold War struggles that sparked CIO infighting and outside attacks, and the effects that the CIO's choice to take a less radical path had on the organization and the black workers it represented (*Southern Labor and Black Civil Rights: Organizing Memphis Workers* [Urbana-Champaign: University of Illinois Press, 1993]).

98. See, e.g., Michael Goldfield, "Race and the CIO: The Possibilities for Racial Egalitarian-ism during the 1930s and1940s," *International Labor and Working-Class History* no. 44 (1993): 1–32; Honey, *Southern Labor and Black Civil Rights;* Kelley, *Hammer and Hoe;* and Halpern and Horowitz, *Negro and White, Unite and Fight.* The CIO was no uniformly safe haven for workers of color, however, and was troubled by its own inability to overcome racism in its locals and its leadership. Barbara Griffith suggests that the CIO suffered from its own lack of a firm stance on race issues. William Jones posits that Operation Dixie ultimately failed because of the CIO's move away from the Left and away from a racially principled program ("Black Workers and the CIO's Turn toward Racial Liberalism: Operation Dixie and the North Carolina Lumber Industry, 1946–1953," *Labor History* 41, no. 3 [2001]: 279–306). A closer look at CIO policy led historians such as Herbert Hill and Robert Norrell to dispute the federation's supposedly enlightened stance on racial issues. See Hill, "Problem of Race"; and Norrell, "Caste in Steel: Jim Crow Careers in Birmingham, Alabama," *Journal of American History* 73, no. 3 (1986): 669–94. Bruce Nelson argues that there was a disconnect between the CIO's rhetoric, which invoked "a more inclusive vision that promised to bestow equal rights on white and black alike," and its practice, which "privileged the interests of the white majority" ("'CIO Meant One Thing for the Whites and Another Thing for Us': Steelworkers and Civil Rights, 1936–1974," in *Southern Labor in Transition, 1940–1995,* ed. Robert H. Zieger [Knoxville: University of Tennessee Press, 1997], 114). The Communist Party sometimes impeded civil rights agitation. See Steve Rosswurm, ed., *The CIO's Left-Led Unions* (New Brunswick: Rutgers University Press, 1992), 9–12; and Eric Arnesen, "A. Philip Randolph, Black Anticommunism, and the Race Question," in *Rethink-ing U.S. Labor History: Essays on the Working-Class Experience, 1756–2009,* ed. Donna T. Haverty-Stacke and Daniel J. Walkowitz (New York: Continuum, 2010), 137–67.

99. Ruiz, *Cannery Women;* Kelley, *Hammer and Hoe;* Grubbs, *Cry from the Cotton;* Zaragosa Vargas, "Tejana Radical: Emma Tenayuca and the San Antonio Labor Movement during the Great Depression," *Pacific Historical Review* 66, no. 4 (1997): 553–80. Korstad links black workers' activism in the union to the reinvigoration of the local branch of the National Association for the Advancement of Colored People (NAACP), voter registration drives, and political rallies. The labor movement, Korstad suggests, was the birthplace of more militant black activists. Rick Halpern and Roger Horowitz describe the vision of black meatpackers such as L. C. Williams who "wanted to use their union to end segregation and discriminatory treatment" (*Meatpackers,* 108). Dorothy Sue Cobble observes that most of the "labor feminists' she studied were concentrated in "left-liberal," though anticommunist, CIO unions. They, too, favored a unionism that would improve their status as workers *and* as family and community members (*The Other Women's Movement: Workplace Justice and Social Rights in Modern America* [Princeton: Princeton University Press, 2004]).

100. Judith Stepan-Norris and Maurice Zeitlin, *Left Out: Reds and America's Industrial Unions* (Cambridge: Cambridge University Press, 2003), 264–65, 327. The suppression of leftism, particularly via anticommunism and McCarthyism, circumscribed the attempts by African Americans to gain social and economic justice, struggles that were intertwined. See the essays in Robbie Lieberman and Clarence Lang, eds., *Anticommunism and the African American Freedom Movement: Another Side of the Story* (New York: Macmillan, 2009).

101. Fogel, *Negro in the Meat Industry,* 68–69. The PWOC's/UPWA's militancy made it an attractive alternative to black and white workers in the meat industry, who were "stymied by the conservatism of the AFL," according to Horowitz, *Negro and White,* 31.

102. Brody, *Butcher Workmen,* 176.

103. See Fogel, *Negro in the Meat Industry,* 69–70; and Horowitz, *Negro and White,* esp. chap. 9. David Brody also comments on the PWOC's "communal activities" (*Butcher Workmen,* 177). Stories of union members leading the charge against discrimination in their communities are woven throughout Halpern and Horowitz, *Meatpackers.*

104. Horace R. Cayton and George S. Mitchell, *Black Workers and the New Unions* (Chapel Hill: University of North Carolina Press, 1939), 272, quoted in Fogel, *Negro in the Meat Industry,* 69.

105. Brody, *Butcher Workmen,* 251.

106. The AMBW's national policies are noted by Fogel (*Negro in the Meat Industry,* 67–73) and by AMBW officials in various issues of the AMBW's newsletter (*Butcher Workman*). In 1942 the AMBW began including in its negotiated contracts a clause that required "employers not to discriminate against employees—or applicants—for reasons of color, creed, sex, nationality or political belief" (quoted in the "On the Civil Rights Front" column in the *Butcher Workman* 55, no. 5 [June–July 1969]: 30). Fogel argues that while this may have been their rhetoric, the union did not push locals to follow it.

107. On labor's hesitance to join broader social justice struggles and its own internal struggles with racism in the mid-twentieth century, see, e.g., Jill Quadagno, "Social Movements and State Transformation: Labor Unions and Racial Conflict in the War on Poverty," *American Sociological Review* 57 (1992): 616–34; Zieger, *American Workers, American Unions,* 168–92.

108. Lichtenstein, *State of the Union,* 168. This is not to imply that Clinton should be perceived as radical.

109. Jerome Wolf, *Ferment in Labor* (Beverly Hills, Calif.: Glencoe Press, 1968), 136–37.

110. Quote from Lawrence and Braden, "Long Struggle," 89; Buhle, *Taking Care of Business: Samuel Gompers, George Meany, Lane Kirkland, and the Tragedy of American Labor* (New York: Monthly Review Press, 1999); Korstad and Lichtenstein, "Opportunities Found and Lost," 786–811. Marion Crain and Ken Matheny maintain that unions marginalized themselves by helping shape labor law in a way that "social justice issues were severed from class issues" ("Labor's Identity Crisis," *California Law Review* 89, no. 6 [2001]: 1767–1846).

111. Martha May, "Bread before Roses: American Workingmen, Labor Unions and the Family Wage," in *Women, Work and Protest: A Century of U.S. Women's Labor History,* ed. Ruth Milkman (Boston: Routledge & Kegan Paul, 1985), 8–14. Deborah Gray-White in *Too Heavy a Load,* Jacqueline Jones in *Labor of Love, Labor of Sorrow,* and Tera Hunter in *To 'Joy My Freedom,* all discuss the necessity of black women's income to their families. Stepan-Norris and Zeitlin note the belief among unionists that women worked not for a living but for "pin money" (189). Quote from Elizabeth Faue, *Community of Suffering and Struggle: Women, Men and the Labor Movement in Minneapolis, 1915–1945* (Chapel Hill: University of North Carolina Press, 1991), 71.

112. Norwood notes, in *Strikebreaking and Intimidation,* e.g., that A. Philip Randolph encouraged black men to join unions "to stand fully erect as men" (112).

113. Vicki Ruiz, *Cannery Women, Cannery Lives: Mexican Women, Unionization, and the California Food Processing Industry, 1930–1950* (Albuquerque: University of New Mexico Press, 1987).

114. Dorothy Sue Cobble, "Rethinking Troubled Relations between Women and Unions: Craft Unions and Female Activism," *Feminist Studies* 16, no. 3 (1990): 519–48.

115. Fehn, "Chickens Come Home to Roost," 338.

116. Anne Munro explores unions' policies of upholding sex-segregated work in *Women, Work, and Trade Unions* (New York: Mansell, 2000). Scholars such as Munro argue that unions fail to reach women because they do not challenge long-standing problems such as why some work is defined as women's work and how the demands of the double day circumscribe women's union activism. See also Alice Cook, with Val R. Lorwin and Arlene Kaplan Daniels, *The Most Difficult Revolution: Women and Trade Unions* (Ithaca, N.Y.: ILR Press, 1992). E. J. Graff and Evelyn Murphy offer a brief look into how men in heavily unionized occupations, such as firefighters and police officers, still work to keep or force women out of these jobs ("The Skinny Pink Paycheck Syndrome," *Los Angeles Times,* February 12, 2006).

117. Elsa Barkley Brown posits the importance of community building in black women's lives ("Womanist Consciousness: Maggie Lena Walker and the Independent Order of St. Luke," *Signs* 14, no. 3 [1989]: 610–33). See also Glenda Gilmore, *Gender and Jim Crow: Women and the Politics of White Supremacy in North Carolina, 1896–1920* (Chapel Hill: University of North Carolina Press, 1996); and Gray-White, *Too Heavy a Load.*

118. George Green, "The Texas 'Sick Chicken' Strike, 1950s," *East Texas Historical Association* 26 (1988): 14–30. The role of black women in founding and sustaining struggles for rights is impressive. Charles Payne identifies them as organizers whose true goal has been to empower and enlighten community members to lead themselves to freedom (*I've Got the Light of Freedom: The Organizing Tradition and the Mississippi Freedom Struggle* [Berkeley: University of California Press, 1995]).

119. Smothers, "Unions Try to Push Past Workers' Fear"; Striffler, *Chicken,* 72.

120. U.S. National Labor Relations Board (NLRB), "Decision and Order in the Matter of Fairmont Creamery Company and Amalgamated Meat Cutters and Butcher Workmen of North America, Local No. 142 A. F. of L.," Case No. 18-C-1085, November 15, 1945, from the Amalgamated Meat Cutters and Butcher Workmen of North America, Records, 1903–1980, frames 452–61, Wisconsin Historical Society (WHS).

121. "Complaint and Notice of Hearing," USA before the NLRB, Region 26, Tyson Foods, Inc. and United Food and Commercial Workers Union, Local 2008, Case 26-CA22270, February 17, 2006, received from the U.S. NLRB in response to FOIA Requests 6350 and 6351.

122. "Complaint and Notice of Hearing," 26. Eastex owners negotiated after eleven months, for reasons that will be explored later in the chapter. Despite the loss at Denison, the Center strikes did lead to another victory for the AMBW: the institution of mandatory, government-enforced inspection of poultry. Beginning January 1, 1959, the USDA would conduct inspections. Compulsory inspections had been a goal of the poultry department—Barker recounted that the union had been pushing for inspections since 1946. The AMBW had used the Center strikes as an opportunity to publicize how unscrupulous processors sold "sick chickens" to the public. Although inspections were of obvious benefit to the consumer, the AMBW championed them as a victory for poultry processing workers because they would minimize the health dangers that resulted from processing diseased poultry (Statement by Shirley W. Barker, Director of the Poultry Department Amalgamated Meat Cutters and Butcher Workmen of North America, AFL-CIO, on Mandatory Poultry Inspection Legislation before the Senate, Committee on Agriculture and Forestry, February 28, 1957, from the papers of Samuel Twedell, AR44-33-12).

123. Letter dated April 21, 1959, from Robert Parker to an unnamed AMBW official, from the papers of Samuel A. Twedell, AR44-39-2.

124. Letter dated August 29, 1959, from Robert Parker to an unnamed AMBW official, from the papers of Samuel A. Twedell, AR44-39-2. The situation between Tyson and Local 425 was virtually unending. Although the NLRB certified the union, Tyson still refused to negotiate fairly, prompting an employee walkout in August 1965. Again, the union boycotted and struck. The NLRB issued a refusal to bargain complaint against Tyson. In 1971 the NLRB voided an election held at a Tyson plant and again ordered the company to bargain in good faith, a possibility Local 425 secretary-treasurer Jess Riley believed unlikely. In the 1980s Tyson management "busted" the union at a plant in Waldron, and the NLRB found that the company had illegally support a decertification drive in Dardanelle in the early 1990s. In 2005 Local 2008 had cause to charge Tyson, once again, with unfair labor practices.

125. Striffler, *Chicken*; Cromer, "Plucking Cargill."

126. Striffler, *Chicken,* 78.

127. Letter dated August 29, 1959 from Robert Parker to an unnamed AMBW official.

128. Smothers, "Unions Try to Push Past Workers' Fears."

129. U.S. NLRB, "Decision and Order in the Matter of Tyson Foods, Inc. and United Food and Commercial Workers, Local 425, AFL-CIO," Cases 26-CA-14731 and 26-CA-14821, May 28, 1993.

130. Striffler, *Chicken,* 76–78; Norwood, *Strikebreaking and Intimidation,* 247; John Schmitt and Ben Zipperer, "Dropping the Ax: Illegal Firings during Union Election Campaigns," Center for Economic and Policy Research, January 2007, www.cepr.net/documents/publications/unions_2007_01.pdf (last accessed March 25, 2007).

131. Rick Fantasia and Kim Voss, *Hard Work: Remaking the American Labor Movement* (Berkeley: University of California Press, 2004), 33–36. Frank Perdue, CEO of Perdue Farms, notoriously consulted with mafioso Paul Castellano, hoping Castellano would help him "bust" unions.

132. Brody, *Labor Embattled*. Similarly, Stephen Norwood quotes an AFL-CIO official's statement that the right to organize is a "legal fiction" (*Strikebreaking and Intimidation*, 247).

133. Letter dated March 27, 1975 from Patrick Gorman to Richard Twedell, International Vice President, Amalgamated Meat Cutters and Butcher Workmen of North America, from the papers of Richard Twedell, AR264-11-8, Special Collections, Central Library, University of Texas at Arlington (UTA), Arlington.

134. AMBW Records, 1903–1980, reel 138, frame 74, WHS, Madison (*http://digicoll .library.wisc.edu/cgi/f/findaid/findaid-idx?c=wiarchives;view=reslist;subview=standard;di dno=uw-whs-micr0935* [last accessed January 20, 2014]). The J-M employees seem to have been eager for union representation. A copy of the case record card shows that more than 85 percent of the 258 eligible employees voted for the union.

135. In this sense Sheppard resembled labor feminists, who believed the labor movement was a vehicle through which the lives of most women could be bettered (Cobble, *Other Women's Movement*, 3).

136. AMBW Records, 1903–1980, reel 138, frame 74.

137. AMBW Records, 1903–1980, reel 138, frame 75.

138. AMBW Records, 1903–1980, reel 138, frame 75.

139. Strong, interview, August 8, 2005. The NLRB has records of thirteen cases filed against Local 2008, one of which was still pending in January 2007. Of the twelve cases available, eight involve workers who charged that the union failed to represent them or their grievances.

140. Strong, interview, August 8, 2005.

141. Hackenberg, "Joe Hill Died for Your Sins," 234.

142. AMBW, 1903–1980, reel 478, frame 552.

143. AMBW, 1903–1980, reel 478, frame 308.

144. AMBW, 1903–1980, reel 478, frame 160.

145. West, interview, January 2, 2005; Wright, interview, December 27, 2004, James, interview by author, November 19, 2005; Drayton, interview, November 7, 2004.

146. Wright, interview, December 27, 2004; Deshaun Lowe and Jackie Martin-Lowe, interview by author, March 21, 2005.

4. "THEY DON'T EXPECT THE HUMAN BODY TO BREAK DOWN!"

1. James, interview, November 19, 2005.

2. Janet Strong, interview by author, August 8, 2005.

3. On temperature and lighting, see Striffler, "Inside a Poultry Processing Plant," 306; and U.S. Department of Labor, Occupational Safety and Health Administration (OSHA), "Poultry Processing Industry E-Tool, Receiving and Killing, Task 3: Live Hang, Poor Lighting," www.osha.gov/SLTC/etools/poultry/receiving/03_live_hang.html#poor_lighting (last accessed November 30, 2011).

4. Public Justice Center, *Disposable Workforce*, 9; Russell Cobb, *Crying "Fowl" in Mississippi: The Use and Abuse of Social Security "No-Match Letters" in the Poultry Industry*, Report

of the Poultry Worker Justice Research Project, Inter-American Policy Studies Occasional Paper No. 2, sponsored by the Equal Justice Center, Austin, Tex., and the Inter-American Policy Studies Program, University of Texas at Austin, 2003, 4.

5. Striffler, "Inside a Poultry Processing Plant," 306.

6. Information from Tavia Wright and DeShaun Lowe, joint interview by author, March 11, 2006; Lena H. Sun, "On Chicken's Front Line: High Volume and Repetition Test Workers' Endurance," *Washington Post,* November 28, 1999.

7. Wright and Lowe, interview, March 11, 2006.

8. Goldoftas, "Inside the Slaughterhouse," 26.

9. West, interview, January 2, 2005.

10. Drayton, interview, November 7, 2004.

11. Wright and Lowe, interview, March 11, 2006.

12. Workers label broilers undergrade for a number of reasons, including bloody spots on the flesh or skin that does not cover all the flesh. Wright, interview, December 27, 2004.

13. Drayton, interview, November 7, 2004; Mays, electronic interview, September 27, 2011. A number of other women interviewed for this study spoke on the central role of women in the processing work, including Bella Dawes, Neysha Mallory, Lydia and Sylvia Martin, and Margie Young. In Stuesse's study an employee new to the plant exclaimed, "I had never seen so many women!" ("Globalization 'Southern Style,'" 265).

14. Michael J. Broadway and Donald D. Stull, "Killing Them Softly: Work in Meatpacking Plants and What It Does to Workers," in *Any Way You Cut It: Meat Processing and Small-Town America,* ed. Donald D. Stull, Michael J. Broadway, and David Griffith (Lawrence: University of Kansas Press, 1995), 61–84; U.S. Department of Labor, OSHA, 1997, *OSHA Survey of Poultry Processing Plants,* data summarized on the *OSHA Poultry Processing Industry eTool,* www. osha.gov/SLTC/etools/ poultry/statistics.html (last accessed November 30, 2011). According to OSHA, between 1975 and 2001 workers in this industry suffered injuries and illnesses at a rate of more than twice the national average.

15. Public Justice Center, *Disposable Workforce,* 30.

16. Hester J. Lipscomb et al., "Exploration of Work and Health Disparities among Black Women Employed in Poultry Processing in the Rural South," *Environmental Health Perspectives* 113, no. 12 (2005): 1834. Fogel discusses how the expansion of the poultry industry and its hiring of more black women workers drove down the wages of black workers in the meat industry (*Negro in the Meat Industry* 14, 65–66).

17. Linder, "I Gave My Employer a Chicken That Had No Bone," 59–60.

18. Linder, "I Gave My Employer a Chicken That Had No Bone," 59–60.

19. Striffler, *Chicken,* 115. Bob Hall of the Institute for Southern Studies agrees but adds that Latino men are also disproportionately represented in the industry's "high hazard" jobs ("The Kill Line: Facts of Life, Proposals for Change," in *Any Way You Cut It,* 220).

20. Drayton, interview, November 7, 2004; Mays, electronic interview, September 27, 2011; West, interview, January 2, 2005. Roger Horowitz notes a similar assignment of women to particularly unpleasant jobs in the meatpacking industry in "'Where Men Will Not Work': Gender, Power, Space, and the Sexual Division of Labor in America's Meatpacking Industry, 1890–1990," special issue on "Gender Analysis and the History of Technology," *Technology and Culture* 38, no. 1 (1997): 187–213.

21. Striffler calls the type of work that men did "auxiliary work" and explains that auxiliary workers "do not do the exact same series of movements with nearly the intensity as line workers" (*Chicken,* 115).

22. Young, interview, August 3, 2011; Lydia and Sylvia Martin, joint interview, August 7, 2011; Drayton, interview, November 7, 2004; Mallory, interview, August 3, 2011.

23. It is important to note that there were always men who worked on the lines, just not in large numbers.

24. Dawes, interview, August 4, 2011; West, interview, July 27, 2011; Mallory, interview, August 3, 2011.

25. Wright, interview, December 27, 2004. Wright was more accepting of the gendered division of labor than most of the women consulted for this study. This attitude was rooted in her belief that men and women should have different jobs to protect black women's status as "ladies." Of women's assignment to line work, she said: "I think that ladies are picked for it because of their gender. In a way maybe they are trying to respect us. Those tubs are thirty to forty pounds of meat. That would tear a lady's body down. Most of the time, I think they put the ladies on the line to save their body." She did not acknowledge in detail that line work, in fact, "tears a lady's body down," and she did not suffer from MSDs herself.

26. See, e.g., the discussions of the nature of black women's domestic labor throughout Gray-White, *Ar'n't I a Woman;* Jones's *Labor of Love, Labor of Sorrow,* esp. 127–34; Bridget Anderson, *Doing the Dirty Work? The Global Politics of Domestic Labor* (New York: St. Martin's Press, 2000), esp. 141–44; Nakano Glenn, "Cleaning Up / Kept Down"; Duffy, "Doing the Dirty Work," 313–36; Cheryl Townsend Gilkes, "'Liberated to Work like Dogs!' Labeling Black Women and Their Work," in *The Experience and Meaning of Work in Women's Lives,* ed. Hildreth Y. Grossman and Nia Lane Chester (London: Psychology Press, 1989), 165–88.

27. Nakano Glenn, "Cleaning Up / Kept Down," 1342; Gilkes, "'Liberated to Work like Dogs,'" 177–78. This issue is also discussed by Bridget Anderson in *Doing the Dirty Work.*

28. Horowitz, "Where Men Will Not Work," 197. Brattain also explores this racialized division of labor throughout *Politics of Whiteness.* For more on black women's "dirty" work in factories, see Robert Korstad, *Civil Rights Unionism: Tobacco Workers and the Struggle for Democracy in the Mid-Twentieth-Century South* (Chapel Hill: University of North Carolina Press, 2003); Deborah Fink, *Cutting into the Meatpacking Line: Workers and Change in the Rural Midwest* (Chapel Hill: University of North Carolina Press, 1998), esp. chap. 4; Beverly Jones, "Race, Sex, and Class: Black Female Tobacco Workers in Durham, North Carolina, 1920–1940, and the Development of Female Consciousness," *Feminist Studies* 10, no. 3 (1984): 441–51; Janiewski, *Sisterhood Denied;* Gilkes, "'Liberated to Work like Dogs,'" 171; Alice Kessler-Harris, "Where Are the Organized Women Workers?" *Feminist Studies* 3, no. 112 (1975): 238; Jones, *Labor of Love, Labor of Sorrow,* 134–42; Michael Honey, *Black Workers Remember: An Oral History of Segregation, Unionism and the Freedom Struggle* (Berkeley: University of California Press, 1999), chap. 3, esp. Honey's introduction and the interviews with Evelyn Bates and Irene Branch.

29. See Tucker, "Complex Bond" and *Telling Memories among Southern Women;* Sharpless, *Cooking in Other Women's Kitchens,* 66–67.

30. Tamara Beauboeuf-Lafontant, "Keeping Up Appearances, Getting Fed Up: The Embodiment of Strength among African American Women," *Meridians* 5, no. 2 (2005): 108. See also

See Melissa Harris-Lacewell, "No Place to Rest: African American Political Attitudes and the Myth of Black Women's Strength," *Women & Politics* 23, no. 3 (2001): 1–33; Joan Morgan, *When Chicken Heads Come Home to Roost: A Hip-Hop Feminist Breaks It Down* (New York: Simon & Schuster, 2000); Wallace, *Black Macho and the Myth of the Superwoman.*

31. The policy of excluding black women from clerical and/or "cleaner" work in the meat industry is well documented by Roger Horowitz and Rick Halpern. Walter Fogel also notes it about African Americans in general (105–8) and black women in particular (85, 109). He wrote, of the 1960s, that "there is probably little, if any, discrimination at present in the hiring of black women for manual jobs in the meat industry . . . But the white collar sector is another story. Informants frequently mentioned the complete or nearly complete exclusion of black women from clerical jobs" (*Negro in the Meat Industry,* 109).

32. Mays, electronic interview, September 27, 2011.

33. MSDs "are caused by too many uninterrupted repetitions of an activity or motion, unnatural or awkward motions such as twisting the arm or wrist, overexertion, incorrect posture, or muscle fatigue" (National Institutes of Health, National Institute of Neurological Disorders and Stroke, "Repetitive Motion Disorders Information Page," www.ninds.nih.gov/disorders/repetitive_motion/repetitive_motion.htm [last accessed November 30, 2011]). On the prevalence of black women in positions considered high risk for creating MSDs, Linder described a health hazard evaluation at a North Carolina plant that "found that 99% of participants in high-exposure positions were black and 86% were women" (36).

34. For more on the effects of line speed, see Human Rights Watch, "Blood, Sweat, and Fear: Workers' Rights in U.S. Meat and Poultry Plants," January 2005, 33–38, www.hrw.org/reports/2005/usa0105/usa0105.pdf (last accessed November 30, 2011).

35. West, interview, January 2, 2005.

36. West, interview, January 2, 2005.

37. Public Justice Center, *Disposable Workforce,* 9. The demand for further processed (value added) and more specialized cuts of chicken grew out of both consumer demand and poultry processing companies' attempts to keep their products relevant and cutting edge. After all, as Striffler notes, "chicken in its most basic form is simply not that profitable" (*Chicken,* 19). Similarly, Roger Horowitz argues that "product diversification" helped chicken "become a meat, and America's most popular one at that" (*Putting Meat on the American Table,* 121).

38. Joe Fahy, "All Pain, No Gain," *Southern Exposure,* Ruling the Roast: A Special Report on the Poultry Industry 17, no. 2 (1989): 35–38; St. Onge et al., "An Epidemic of Pain," *Charlotte Observer,* February 10, 2008.

39. St. Onge et al., "An Epidemic of Pain," *Charlotte Observer,* February 10, 2008; Fahy, "All Pain, No Gain," 35, 38; Bazemore, interview, 32; Stuesse, "Globalization 'Southern Style,'" 266.

40. Arkansas Department of Labor, Research and Statistics, *Meat Cutters in the Poultry Dressing Industry in Arkansas: A Special Report* (Little Rock: Arkansas Department of Labor, 1978), 15.

41. Fahy, "All Pain, No Gain," 37.

42. Strong, interview, 8 August 2005.

43. Line speeds increased noticeably after the USDA relaxed its inspection practices in the early 1980s. Simultaneously, large poultry firms bought up smaller processing plants and sped up their production. See Tom Devine, "The Fox Guarding the Henhouse," "Ruling the

Roost: A Special Report on the Poultry Industry," *Southern Exposure* 17, no. 2 (1989): 39–42; Goldoftas, "Inside the Slaughterhouse," 25–29.

44. Linder's article adroitly links the rise in line speeds to the rise in MSDs, as does Griffith in *Jones's Minimal,* 176–77. See also T. J. Armstrong et al., "Investigation of Cumulative Trauma Disorders in a Poultry Processing Plant," *American Industrial Hygiene Association Journal,* 43 (1982): 103–16; J. R. Schottland et al., "Median Nerve Latencies in Poultry Processing Workers: An Approach to Resolving the Role of Industrial 'Cumulative Trauma' in the Development of Carpal Tunnel Syndrome," *Journal of Occupational Medicine* 33, no. 5 (1991): 627–31; C. Vellala et al., "Analysis of Injuries and Illnesses in Poultry Processing Industries in Louisiana," in *Advances in Industrial Ergonomics and Safety VI,* ed. F. Aghazadeh (London: Taylor & Francis, 1994): 105; U.S. Department of Labor, OSHA, *Poultry Processing Industry E-Tool,* OSHA Survey, Examples and Statistics, hwww.osha.gov/SLTC/etools/poultry/statistics. html (last accessed November 30, 2011); H. J. Lipscomb et al., "Musculoskeletal Symptoms among Poultry Processing Workers and a Community Comparison Group: Black Women in Low-Wage Jobs in the Rural South," *American Journal of Industrial Medicine* 50, no. 5 (2007): 327–38. On Delmarva, one ergonomic consultant identified MSDs as the most common "work-related health problem experienced by poultry workers" (Public Justice Center, *Disposable Workforce,* 17).

45. Peter St. Onge, Franco Ordoñez, Kerry Hall, and Ames Alexander, "An Epidemic of Pain," *Charlotte Observer,* February 10, 2008. Although I focus primarily on musculoskeletal disorders in this work, poultry workers' descriptions of work-related injuries include burns, slips, falls, amputations, cuts, and the effects of exposure to chlorine (used for cleaning chickens) and ammonia (used for refrigeration).

46. Bazemore, interview, 32. Perdue Farms is a privately held, family-owned poultry company headquartered in Salisbury, Md. It is perhaps the most prominent processed poultry producer on the East Coast of the United States.

47. Striffler was interviewed for the article "An Epidemic of Pain." He also discusses the extent of injuries in his book *Chicken* (128–29).

48. Human Rights Watch, "Blood, Sweat, and Fear," 24.

49. Davis, interview, January 15, 2005.

50. Davis, interview, January 15, 2005.

51. At Perdue Farms, e.g., the July 1993 company letter fired injured workers who could not be reassigned (see "Kill Line," 219). Geraldine Baylor reports a similar experience at Holly Farms in Glen Allen, Va. (see "All Pain, No Gain," 35).

52. Pilgrim, *One Pilgrim's Progress,* 105.

53. Pilgrim, *One Pilgrim's Progress,* 91.

54. Statistic for 1994 from U.S. Department of Labor, Bureau of Labor Statistics, "Table 1: Nonfatal Occupational Injury and Illness Incidence Rates per 100 Full-Time Workers, by Industry, 1994," March 28, 1996, www.bls.gov/iif/oshwc/osh/os/ostb0169.txt (last accessed November 30, 2011); statistic for 2009 from U.S. Department of Labor, Bureau of Labor Statistics, "Table 1: Incidence Rates of Nonfatal Occupational Injuries and Illnesses by Industry and Case Types, 2009," October 21, 2010, www.bls.gov/iif/oshwc/osh/os/ostb2435.pdf (last accessed November 30, 2011). Quote from Workersafety.org, "Injury Rates," American Meat Institute, www.workersafety.org/ht/d/sp/i/26965/pid/26965 (last accessed November 30, 2011).

55. Pilgrim, *One Pilgrim's Progress,* 79.

56. For a description of changes made in the meat and poultry industry under "Voluntary Ergonomic Standards," see the American Meat Institute, "Fact Sheet: Worker Safety in the Meat and Poultry Industry," February 2009, www.meatami.com/ht/a/GetDocumentAction/i/47110 (last accessed November 30, 2011).

57. "The Cruelest Cuts," *Charlotte Observer,* February 10, 2008.

58. "Cruelest Cuts." This statistic is brought further into question in light of the fact that former president George W. Bush repealed federal ergonomics measures in 2001 ("Statement on Signing Legislation to Repeal Federal Ergonomics Regulations," *American Presidency Project,* March 20, 2001, www.presidency.ucsb.edu/ws/?pid=45790 [last accessed November 30, 2011]).

59. In a staff report the House Committee on Education and Labor noted that "low injury and illness rates decrease the chance of being inspected by OSHA." The report also listed other incentives for underreporting, including decreased workers' compensation expenses, the ability of businesses to earn bonuses from the state for low rates, and maintaining a favorable reputation with the public (U.S. Congress, House, Committee on Education and Labor, *Hidden Tragedy: Underreporting of Workplace Injuries and Illnesses,* a Majority Staff Report, 110th Cong., 2nd sess., June 2008, 14–15, www.gpo.gov/fdsys/pkg/CHRG-110hhrg42881/pdf/CHRG-110hhrg42881.pdf [last accessed November 30, 2011]).

60. *Safety in the Meat and Poultry Industry,* 4. In the aftermath of "The Cruelest Cuts" series, North Carolina's OSHA acknowledged the GAO's comment and issued a "directive [to establish] enforcement procedures to inspect the accuracy of the Occupational Injury and Illness Recording and Reporting Requirements for low rate establishments in selected industries," including poultry processing ("Subject: National Emphasis Program: Recordkeeping," No. 10-07, CPL 2, October 15, 2010, www.nclabor.com/osha/compliance/directives/CPL_02_10-07.pdf [last accessed November 30, 2011]).

61. The program is described in U.S. Department of Labor, OSHA, *Injury and Illness Recordkeeping National Emphasis Program,* Directive No. 09-08 (CPL 02), September 2009, www.osha.gov/OshDoc/Directive_pdf/CPL_02_09-08.pdf (last accessed November 30, 2011).

62. The House Committee on Education and Labor listed a number of ways companies' avoid lost time accidents: direct intimidation of workers, bringing seriously injured workers right back to work, discouraging appropriate medical attention, discouraging physicians from reporting injuries or diagnosing illnesses, "no-fault" absentee policies, safety incentive programs and games, manager incentives and bonuses, drug testing after every accident or injury, contractors and contracting out dangerous work, and misclassification of workers (U.S. Congress, *Hidden Tragedy.*)

63. Wright, interview; DeShaun Lowe, interview by author, Bernice, La.,, September 17, 2006; Johnson, interview, August 4, 2011. This behavior is also described by Mississippi poultry workers in Stuesse, "Globalization 'Southern Style,'" 261–62.

64. Deena Shine, interview by author, July 27, 2011.

65. Angela Goodwin et al. v. Con Agra Poultry Company and Pilgrim's Pride, Incorporated, Civil Action No. 03-1187 (U.S. District Court, Western District of Arkansas, El Dorado Division, 2003). This pattern is also noted by Stuesse, "Globalization 'Southern Style,'" 266–67.

66. Dawes, interview, August 4, 2011.

67. Stuesse, "Globalization 'Southern Style,'" 260.

68. Striffler, *Chicken*, 132. Linda Cromer also notes that "the company nurse was handing out Advil for everything from cut fingers to broken toes to carpal tunnel syndrome" ("Plucking Cargill," 19). This dynamic is also noted in the U.S. Congress's *Hidden Tragedy* report (17–19).

69. U.S. Department of Labor, OSHA, "Regulations (Standards-29 CFR) Part Number 1904: Recording and Reporting Occupational Injuries and Illness, Subpart C: Recordkeeping Forms and Recording Criteria, Standard Number 1904.7: General Recording Criteria," www.osha. gov/pls/oshaweb/owadisp.show_document?p_table=STANDARDS&p_id=9638 (last accessed November 30, 2011); U.S. Congress, *Hidden Tragedy*, 18.

70. Dawes, interview, August 4, 2011; Lydia and Sylvia Martin, joint interview, August 7, 2011.

71. Ames Alexander, "Judge Criticized Tyson Guidelines," *Charlotte Observer,* February 13, 2008, www.charlotteobserver.com/2008/09/30/223458/judge-criticized-tyson-guidelines. html#ixzz1axl8moQs (last accessed November 30, 2011). This delay is dangerous to workers' health, as doctors recommend treatment as soon as possible after the onset of symptoms to try to avoid permanent damage.

72. U.S. Congress, *Hidden Tragedy,* 19.

73. Stuesse, "Globalization 'Southern Style,'" 259.

74. Quoted in Stuesse, "Globalization 'Southern Style,'" 262.

75. Drayton, interview, November 7, 2004.

76. Griffith, *Jones's Minimal,* 93.

77. Moberg, "Puttin Down Ol' Massa," 298.

78. Wright, interview, December 27, 2004. In 1988 Barbara Goldoftas found that the wages at the Cargill plant in Buena Vista, Ga., while low, were the highest in the area. Goldoftas states that poultry processing tends to pay higher wages than unskilled jobs in convenience stores and fast food restaurants ("Inside the Slaughterhouse," 25). See also Sun, "On Chicken's Front Line," for similar findings in the areas on and around the Delmarva Peninsula.

79. Striffler, "Inside a Poultry Processing Plant," 306.

80. Gafford, interview, September 4, 2006.

81. It is important to note, however, that both these women worked second jobs. Earl eventually had support from her estranged husband, and Johnson had no children and lived with her mother.

82. David Griffith explores networks in plants in other areas in *Jones's Minimal* (esp. 159–63) and in "*Hay Trabajo:* Poultry Processing, Rural Industrialization, and the Latinization of Low-Wage Labor," in *Any Way You Cut It,* 141–43. In the same volume Mark Grey examines network recruitment among immigrant communities, in "Pork, Poultry, and Newcomers in Storm Lake, Iowa," as do Striffler, *Chicken;* and Fink, *Maya of Morganton.*

83. Strong, interview, August 8, 2005.

84. Lowe and Martin-Lowe, joint interview, March 21, 2005. Lydia and Sylvia Martin are Jackie Martin-Lowe's sisters.

85. Davis, interview, January 15, 2005. Griffith posits a number of reasons that employees engage in recruiting activities: it creates a more amenable social environment; employees feel the satisfaction of helping kin find work; employees improve their positions with plant management; network recruiting enriches the entire network; and having kin in the plant helps workers prepare and support excuses for missing work ("*Hay Trabajo,*" 146–47).

86. Griffith, *Jones's Minimal,* 180.

87. Pilgrim, *One Pilgrim's Progress,* 131–42.

88. Holloway, interview, 2011. She was speaking of the temporary idling of the plant in Farmerville, La. The plant was closed by Pilgrim's Pride. Louisiana's modern-day boosters intervened and helped bring Foster Farms to the area to run the plant. See Tim Morris, "Pilgrim's Pride to Idle Louisiana Chicken Plant," *NOLA.com,* February 27, 2009, www.nola .com/news/index.ssf/2009/02/pilgrims_pride_to_shut_operati.html (last accessed November 30, 2011); Mary Nash-Wood, "'Resurrected': Foster Farms Officially Takes Over Farmerville Poultry Plant," *Farmerville Gazette,* July 15, 2009, www.fgazette.com/news.php?id=998 (last accessed November 30, 2011); Foster Farms, "Foster Farms Earns Trade and Industry Development Magazine's CiCi Community Impact Award," press release, March 12, 2009, www.fosterfarms.com/about/press/press_release.asp?press_release_id=111 (last accessed November 30, 2011).

89. Dill, "'Means to Put My Children Through,'"; Hill Collins, *Black Feminist Thought,* chap. 3; Williams-Forson, *Building Houses;* and Sharpless, *Cooking in Other Women's Kitchens,* chap. 3, have all commented on how black women's work can simultaneously be a source of difficult, exploitative labor and the means by which black women can achieve some autonomy and subsistence for their families.

90. Stuesse, "Globalization 'Southern Style,'" 266.

91. J. T. Holleman, "In Arkansas Which Comes First, the Chicken or the Environment?" *Tulane Environmental Law Journal* 6, Tul. Envtl. L.J. 21 (1992): 22.

92. In June 2005 Oklahoma attorney general Drew Edmondson filed a suit against fourteen Arkansas poultry producers for polluting Oklahoma's waters. See Oklahoma Office of the Attorney General, "AG Sues Poultry Industry for Poultry Industry for Polluting Oklahoma Waters," press release, June 13, 2005, www.oag.state.ok.us/oagweb.nsf/srch/7DB11B73010B FF99862572B4006F60FB?OpenDocument (last accessed November 30, 2011); Juliet Eilperin, "Pollution in the Water, Lawsuits in the Air," *Washington Post,* August 28, 2006.

93. Michael J. Broadway, "From City to Countryside: Recent Changes in the Structure and Location of the Meat- and Fish-Processing Industries," in *Any Way You Cut It,* 35; and Denise Giardina and Eric Bates, "Fowling the Nest," "Ruling the Roost: A Special Report on the Poultry Industry," *Southern Exposure* 17, no. 2 (1989): 10–12.

94. Holleman, "In Arkansas Which Comes First."

95. David Griffith, Michael J. Broadway, and Donald D. Stull, "Introduction: Making Meat," in *Any Way You Cut It,* 4; Lourdes Gouveia and Donald D. Stull, "Dances with Cows: Beefpacking's Impact on Garden City, KS, and Lexington, NE," in *Any Way You Cut It,* 92.

96. Griffith, *Jones's Minimal,* 89; Robert A. Hackenberg, "Joe Hill Died for Your Sins: Empowering Minority Workers in the New Industrial Workforce," in *Any Way You Cut It,* 241–42; Horowitz and Miller, *Immigrants in the Delmarva Poultry Processing Industry,* 3.

97. Wright, interview, December 27, 2004. Anne Moody reported going to work in a processing plant, enticed by the wages, then deciding "it wasn't worth it" (163–68).

98. U.S. Department of Labor, *Poultry Processing Compliance Survey Fact Sheet, January 2001* (Washington, D.C.: GPO, 2001).

99. Workers filed a class action lawsuit against the company over this issue. The workers prevailed. See "In re: Pilgrim's Pride Fair Labor Standards Act Litigation, 1:07-cv-1832" (U.S. District Court, Western District of Arkansas, El Dorado Division, 2008).

100. Wright, interview, December 27, 2004.

101. Griffith, *Jones's Minimal,* 180–82. Brattain explores this process in early southern industrialization and similarly finds that kin recruitment could be a form of labor control, arguing that "the common southern practice of hiring entire families preserved and transplanted traditional rural hierarchies of gender and status into the world of wage work" (*Politics of Whiteness,* 40).

102. The Bureau of Labor Statistics reports that "food processing workers generally received typical benefits, including pension plans for union members or those employed by grocery stores. However, poultry workers rarely earned substantial benefits" (U.S. Department of Labor, Bureau of Labor Statistics, "Food Processing Occupations," in *Occupational Outlook Handbook, 2010–11 Edition,* www.bls.gov/ooh/ [last accessed November 30, 2011]).

103. Griffith, Broadway, and Stull, "Making Meat," 7–8; Griffith, *"Hay Trabajo,"* 146.

104. Griffith, Broadway, and Stull, "Making Meat," 7

105. Griffith, Broadway, and Stull, "Making Meat," 8; Griffith, *"Hay Trabajo,"* 146.

106. Bazemore, interview, 33.

107. Mallory, interview, August 3, 2011.

108. Striffler, *Chicken,* 123.

109. Lydia and Sylvia Martin, interview, August 7, 2011; Dawes, interview, August 4, 2011; Wright, interview, December 27, 2004.

110. "Fumes Kill 2 in Food Vat," *New York Times,* April 30, 1984, A12.

111. Fink, *Maya of Morganton.* The Interfaith Worker Justice project considers the condition of poultry processing workers one of its major issues (www.iwj.org/issues/poultry.html [last accessed March 25, 2007]). On November 15, 2000, the Catholic Bishops of the South issued a pastoral letter, "Voices and Choices," which focused on the lack of voices and choices that poultry processing workers have (www.americancatholic.org/News/PoultryPastoral/english. asp [last accessed November 30, 2011]).

112. The first, the Delmarva Poultry Justice Alliance, was founded in 1997 (Bussel, "Taking On 'Big Chicken,'" 2). Since then, a Georgia branch and a national PJA have been founded.

113. Rev. Jim Lewis, "Delmarva Poultry Justice Alliance," www.familyfarmer.org/ conference/lewis.html (last accessed November 30, 2011).

114. Rosalynn Evans Greshom, executive director of the GPJA, electronic interview by author, October 23, 2006. PJAs do receive some financial assistance from unions but list a variety of other organizations that support them—environmental groups, occupational health care, state departments of labor, community organizations, and individuals, to name a few. Former Equal Justice Center of Austin, Tex., had a similar Poultry Worker Justice Project (2004–6) with an objective of "achieving systemic reform in the poultry industry by working with poultry workers, their unions and other community allies to hold poultry companies accountable for worker safety, fair wages and just workplace practices." Three studies sponsored by the center, focusing on the industry in Mississippi, were consulted for this work.

115. Griffith, *Jones's Minimal,* 182.

116. Bazemore, interview, 33.

117. Harlan Joel Gradin, in an introduction to an interview with Donna (Bazemore) Latimer, *NC Crossroads,* a publication of the North Carolina Humanities Council, 9, no. 1 (April 2005): 3. Latimer describes her own experiences and the interconnectedness of the various forms of oppression poor women face in the same issue (5–8) and in a short

video on YouTube.com about the New Life Women's Leadership Project, www.youtube.com/watch?v=eEhswgB57xY (last accessed November 30, 2011). Stuesse also comments on female poultry processing workers' vulnerability as reflected in domestic violence and interpersonal sexual violence inside and outside the plants ("Globalization 'Southern Style,'" 243–45).

118. On the need for and possibilities of social justice unionism to transform and revive labor organizing in the United States, see Michael Schiavone, *Unions in Crisis? The Future of Organized Labor in America* (Westport, Conn.: Greenwood Publishing Group, 2008), esp. chaps. 5 and 6; and Bill Fletcher and Fernando Gaspain, *Solidarity Divided: The Crisis in Organized Labor and a New Path toward Social Justice* (Berkeley: University of California Press, 2008), pt. 5.

119. Lowe and Martin-Lowe, interview, March 21, 2005; George Williams v. ConAgra Poultry Co., Civil Action No. 03-2976 (U.S. Court of Appeals, Eighth Circuit, Arkansas, 2004). Lichtenstein suggests that this kind of individual rights consciousness is an outgrowth of civil rights legislation somewhat opposed to a union culture that emphasizes collective bargaining (*State of the Union,* 209–11).

120. The Eighth Circuit Court of appeals later reduced the award.

121. Evans Greshom, electronic interview, October 23, 2006.

122. Hill, quoted in Smothers, "Unions Try to Push Past Workers' Fear."

123. Angela Stuesse, *Poultry Processing, Industrial Restructuring, and Organizing in Transnational Mississippi: Challenges and Promises,* Report of the Poultry Worker Justice Research Project, Inter-American Policy Studies Occasional Paper No. 5, sponsored by the Equal Justice Center, Austin, Tex., and the Inter-American Policy Studies Program, University of Texas at Austin, 2003; Barb Kucera, "In Crisis, Union Office Becomes Community Center," *Workday Minnesota,* December 17, 2006, www.workdayminnesota.org/index.php?news_6_2810 (last accessed November 30, 2011).

124. Hill, quoted in Smothers, "Unions Try to Push Past Workers' Fear."

5. "THEY ARE ABOUT TO OUTNUMBER ALL THE DIFFERENT RACES"

The initial work on this manuscript began in 2003, well over a decade ago. Chapter 5, in particular, is a snapshot of a particular point in time in Bernice, La., roughly 2003–9. I acknowledge that the racial-ethnic dynamics of the region have continued to change and that Latino migrants, who were considered relatively "new" in the first decade of the twenty-first century, have created settled communities, are more integrated into the town's institutions, and they and their neighbors have developed relationships. Thus, chapter 5 is not meant to be read as a description of Bernice in 2014 but as one resource that gives the background of reactions to and reasons for the rise in the Latino population of the area and that helps contextualize the evolution of the community and interpersonal relationships within it.

1. Martha Brown and Barbara Chumley, "The Catholic Mexican Community of Bernice, LA," New Populations Project Field Report, furnished courtesy of Susan Roach, Louisiana Tech Folklife Program.

2. Some whites in high Latino growth areas such as Appalachian and southeastern United States towns have had similar perceptions of Latinos, but this chapter will focus on African Americans' perceptions.

3. Marrow, *New Destination Dreaming,* 8.

4. For historic tension between racial-ethnic groups over jobs and public spaces, see David Roediger, *The Wages of Whiteness: Race and the Making of the American Working Class* (New York: Verso, 1999); Noel Ignatiev, *How the Irish Became White* (New York: Routledge, 1995); Theodore Allen, *The Invention of the White Race,* vol. 1: *Racial Oppression and Social Control* (New York: Verso, 1994); Paul Gilje, *The Road to Mobocracy: Popular Disorder in New York City, 1763–1834* (Chapel Hill: University of North Carolina Press, 1987); Iver Bernstein, *The New York City Draft Riots: Their Significance for American Society and Politics in the Age of the Civil War* (New York: Oxford University Press, 1990); Brattain, *Politics of Whiteness;* Jones, *Labor of Love, Labor of Sorrow;* Bruce Nelson, "Class, Race and Democracy in the CIO: The New Labor History Meets the 'Wages of Whiteness,'" *International Review of Social History* 41, no. 3 (1996): 351–74; Janiewski, *Sisterhood Denied;* Robin D. G. Kelley, *Race Rebels: Culture, Politics, and the Black Working Class* (New York: Free Press, 1996); and Hill, "Problem of Race in American Labor History." On the tension between African Americans and Latinos, see Nicolas C. Vaca, *The Presumed Alliance: The Unspoken Conflict between Latinos and Blacks and What It Means for America* (New York: HarperCollins, 2004); Arnoldo de Leon, *Ethnicity in the Sunbelt: Mexican Americans in Houston* (College Station: Texas A&M Press, 2001), 164–65; Kenneth J. Meier et al., "Divided or Together? Conflict and Cooperation between African Americans and Latinos," *Political Research Quarterly* 57, no. 3 (2004): 399–409.

5. Jamie Winders, "Changing Politics of Race and Region: Latino Migration to the U.S. South," *Progress in Human Geography* 29, no. 6 (2005): 686; Vaca, *Presumed Alliance,* 6.

6. This is not to suggest that blacks wholeheartedly accept this association but that they are wary of losing these jobs when few alternatives are available. See also Stuesse, "Globalization 'Southern Style.'"

7. Rakesh Kochhar, Roberto Suro, and Sonya Tafoya, "The New Latino South: The Context and Consequences of Rapid Population Growth," report prepared for the Pew Hispanic Center, July 26, 2005, 1, http://pewhispanic.org/files/reports/50.pdf (last accessed November 30, 2011); Union Parish Chamber of Commerce, "Unemployment Falls—Earnings, Income Rise," *Chamber Newsletter* 1, no. 6 (November–December 2006): 1.

8. Other such industries are meat processing, carpet manufacturing, oil refining, and forestry. William Kandel and Emilio A. Parrado, "Hispanics in the American South and the Transformation of the Poultry Industry," in *Hispanic Spaces, Latino Places: Community and Cultural Diversity in Contemporary America,* ed. Daniel D. Arreola (Austin: University of Texas Press, 2004), 257; Katherine M. Donato, Carl L. Bankston, and Dawn T. Robinson, "Immigration and the Organization of the Onshore Oil Industry: Southern Louisiana in the Late 1990s," in *Latino Workers in the Contemporary South,* ed. Arthur D. Murphy, Colleen Blanchard, and Jennifer A. Hill (Athens: University of Georgia Press, 2001), 105–13.

9. Julie Weise, "Dispatches from the 'Viejo' New South: Historicizing Recent Latino Migrations," *Latino Studies* 10, nos. 1–2 (Spring 2012): 42; Julie Weise, "Mexican Nationalisms, Southern Racisms: Mexicans and Mexican Americans in the U.S. South, 1908–1939," *American Quarterly* 80, no. 3 (September 2008): 749–77. See also Néstor Rodríguez, "New Southern Neighbors: Latino Immigration and Prospects for Intergroup Relations between African-Americans and Latinos in the South," *Latino Studies* 10, nos. 1–2 (Spring 2012): 18–40.

10. Weise, "Mexican Nationalisms," 751.

11. Lisa Morales, interview by author, March 11, 2013.

12. Nonmetropolitan counties are counties that do not have an urbanized area of fifty thousand or more residents. Constance Newman, *Impacts of Hispanic Population Growth on Rural Wages*, U.S. Department of Agriculture, Agricultural Economic Report No. 826, September 2003, www.ers.usda.gov/publications/aer826/aer826.pdf (last accessed November 30, 2011).

13. Kandel and Parrado, "Hispanics in the American South," 257; Greig Guthey, "Mexican Places in Southern Spaces: Globalization, Work, and Daily Life in and around the North Georgia Poultry Industry," in *Latino Workers in the Contemporary South*, ed. Arthur D. Murphy, Colleen Blanchard, and Jennifer A. Hill (Athens: University of Georgia Press, 2001), 63–64.

14. Tony Horwitz, "9 to Nowhere: These Six Growth Jobs Are Dull, Dead-End, Sometimes Dangerous," *Wall Street Journal*, December 1, 1994. Looking back to the 1970s, in addition to increased consumption of various chicken products, William Kandel and Emilio Parrado also add the effects of "industry consolidation and vertical integration," "the location of production facilities in the Southeast," and "the attractiveness of meat-processing jobs" to the list of factors leading to the growth in the demand for labor within the industry ("Hispanics in the American South," 258–62).

15. Ruben Martinez, *Crossing Over: A Mexican Family on the Migrant Trail* (New York: Picador USA, 2002), 186.

16. Kandel and Parrado, "Hispanics in the American South," 264; Rogelio Saenz et al., "Latinos in the South: A Glimpse of Ongoing Trends and Research," *Southern Rural Sociology* 19, no. 2 (2003): 2; Guthey, "Mexican Places in Southern Spaces," 57.

17. Kandel and Parrado, "Hispanics in the American South," 257; Griffith and Runsten, "Impact of the 1986 Immigration Reform and Control Act," 118–30; Guthey, "Mexican Places in Southern Spaces," 61.

18. Jesse Katz, "1,000 Miles of Hope, Heartache," *Los Angeles Times*, November 10, 1996; Griffith, *Jones's Minimal*, 184–89.

19. Griffith, *Jones's Minimal*, 186; Griffith and Runsten, "Impact of the 1986 Immigration Reform and Control Act," 127; Guthey, "Mexican Places in Southern Spaces 64.

20. Griffith, *Jones's Minimal*, 184–85.

21. Brown and Chumley, "Catholic Mexican Community of Bernice," 1.

22. On I-9 forms the employer must verify the employment eligibility and identity documents presented by the employee and record the document information on the form (U.S. Citizenship and Immigration Services website, www.uscis.gov/files/form/i-9.pdf [last accessed November 30, 2011]). Lisa Magaña, *Straddling the Border: Immigration Policy and the INS* (Austin: University of Texas Press, 2003), 37–39.

23. Griffith and Runsten, "Impact of the 1986 Immigration Reform and Control Act," 123, 126; William Kandel and Emilio Parrado, "Restructuring of the U.S. Meat Processing Industry and New Hispanic Migrant Destinations," *Population and Development Review* 31, no. 3 (2005): 449.

24. House Committee on the Judiciary, Subcommittee on Immigration, Border Security, and Claims, *Illegal Immigration Enforcement and Social Security Protection Act of 2005: Hearing before the Subcommittee on Immigration, Border Security, and Claims,* 109th Cong., 1st sess., May 12, 2005 (Washington, D.C.: GPO, 2005), 1.

25. Franco Ordonez, Kerry Hall, and Ames Alexander, "Misery on the Line," *Charlotte Observer,* February 12, 2008.

26. U.S. Department of Justice, "INS Investigation of Tyson Foods, Inc. Leads to 36 Count Indictment for Conspiracy to Smuggle Illegal Aliens for Corporate Profit," press release, December 19, 2001, www.justice.gov/opa/pr/2001/December/01_crm_654.htm (last accessed November 30, 2011). Tyson, as a company, was cleared, but two managers pled guilty.

27. Mallory, interview, August 2011. If an employee quit or was fired for reasons such as excessive absences, she or he was required to wait six months before reapplying. If the employee was rehired, she or he had to start in live hanging or the back dock—usually regarded as the least desirable jobs (physically) in the plant. After six more months the employee was eligible to move back inside the plant. In the case of the man and woman he describes, Lowe believed they did wait eight months before reapplying, but because they had "new" names and social security numbers, they were able to return immediately to the line. Lowe, interview, September 17, 2006.

28. Lowe, interview, September 17, 2006.

29. Kandel and Parrado, "Restructuring of the U.S. Meat Processing Industry," 449.

30. Striffler, *Chicken,* 112.

31. Most white children from the area attend private and local Christian schools legally or the allegedly "better" public schools of Claiborne, Lincoln, and Ouachita parishes.

32. Randolph Capps et al., *A Profile of the Low-Wage Immigrant Workforce,* brief no. 4, "Immigrant Families and Workers: Facts and Perspectives Series," Urban Institute, October 2003, 5–6.

33. The 1996 Personal Responsibility and Work Opportunity Act (PRWORA), e.g., reiterated the exclusion of undocumented immigrants from programs such as AFDC (which became Temporary Assistance to Needy Families [TANF]) and food stamps but went further, barring them from housing assistance and their children from free immunizations and school lunches. The PRWORA also prohibited legal immigrants from obtaining food stamps and Supplemental Security Income. These provisions were an outcome of theories that U.S. welfare was a magnet "influencing immigrants' migration decisions" and leading to a "decline in the quality of new immigrants" (Stephen Bender, *Greasers and Gringos: Latinos, Law, and the American Imagination* [New York: New York University Press, 2003], 79; Michael Fix and Jeffrey Passel, "Assessing Welfare Reform's Immigrant Provisions," in *Welfare Reform: The Next Act,* ed. Alan Weil and Kenneth Finegold [Washington, D.C.: Urban Institute Press, 2002], 179).

34. Raymond A. Mohl, "Globalization, Latinization, and the Nuevo New South," *Journal of American Ethnic History* 22, no. 4 (2003): 41; Roger Waldinger, "Black/Immigrant Competition Re-Assessed: New Evidence from Los Angeles," *Sociological Perspectives* 40, no. 3 (1997): 365; Laura Helton, *Three Hundred Strangers Next Door: Native Mississippians Respond to Immigration,* Report of the Poultry Worker Justice Research Project, Inter-American Policy Studies Occasional Paper No. 4, sponsored by the Equal Justice Center, Austin, Tex., and the Inter-American Policy Studies Program, University of Texas at Austin, 14.

35. I focus on Latino men in Bernice because only 16 percent of Latinas over the age of sixteen who lived in Bernice in 1999 reported working outside the home.

36. Griffith and Runsten, "Impact of the 1986 Immigration Reform and Control Act," 127; Griffith, *Jones's Minimal,* 152–59; Fink, *Maya of Morganton,* 20. Fink notes that the personnel manager at the Morganton plant was so specific in his preferences that he rejected Mexican workers in favor of Guatemalan Mayas. Stuesse also discusses how management exploits conflict and tension between African Americans and Latinos in "Globalization 'Southern Style.'"

37. Griffith, *Jones's Minimal,* 170; Jennifer Gordon and R. A. Lenhardt, "Conflict and Solidarity between African American and Latino Immigrant Workers," prepared for the Chief Justice Earl Warren Institute on Race, Ethnicity, and Diversity, University of California, Berkeley Law School, November 30, 2007, www.nilc.org/dc_conf/wrkshp-materials-07/5-6_ solidarity_earlwarren.pdf (last accessed November 30, 2011), 8.

38. Griffith, "*Hay Trabajo,*" 147.

39. The third plant is in Arcadia, La., approximately thirty-seven miles southwest of Bernice.

40. Helton, *Three Hundred Strangers,* 14.

41. LaDonna Island, telephone interview by author, April 24, 2007. A number of black workers interviewed for this study shared that opinion. See also Stuesse, "Globalization 'Southern Style,'" 218–22; Gordon and Lenhardt, "Conflict and Solidarity," 8.

42. Marrow, *New Destination Dreaming,* 59–67.

43. Barbara Berry of Tyson Foods, from transcript of "Immigrant Influx," *News Hour with Jim Lehrer,* television broadcast, February 16, 1998, www.pbs.org/newshour/bb/race_rela-tions/jan-june98/arkansas_2–16.html (accessed November 30, 2011).

44. Mallory, interview, August 3, 2011.

45. "The Cruelest Cuts," *Charlotte Observer,* February 10, 2008.

46. Griffith and Runsten, "Impact of the 1986 Immigration Reform and Control Act," 127; Cobb, "Chicken Hangers." A more detailed version of Cobb's work is available as *Crying "Fowl" in Mississippi.*

47. Fink, *Maya of Morganton,* 165.

48. Guthey, "Mexican Places in Southern Spaces," 64–65.

49. Stuesse, "Globalization 'Southern Style,'" 238.

50. Jeffrey Passel, "Unauthorized Migrants: Numbers and Characteristics," report prepared for the Pew Hispanic Center, June 14, 2005, 29, http://pewhispanic.org/files/reports/46.pdf (last accessed April 11, 2007).

51. Cobb, "Chicken Hangers."

52. Wright, interview, December 27, 2004.

53. Stuesse, "Globalization 'Southern Style,'" 224.

54. Nelson Lim, "On the Backs of Blacks? Immigrants and the Fortunes of African Americans," in *Strangers at the Gates: New Immigrants in Urban America,* ed. Roger Waldinger (Berkeley: University of California Press, 2001), 204–18.

55. Gordon and Lenhardt, "Conflict and Solidarity"; Stuesse, "Globalization 'Southern Style.'"

56. Stuesse, "Globalization 'Southern Style,'" 236.

57. Lowe, interview, September 17, 2006; Mallory, interview, August 3, 2011; Shine, interview, July 27, 2011.

58. Miriam Jordan, "Blacks vs. Latinos at Work," *Wall Street Journal,* January 24, 2006; Waldinger, "Black/Immigrant Competition Re-Assessed," 365–86; Stephen Steinberg, "Immigration, African Americans and Race Discourse," in *Race and Labor Matters in the New U.S. Economy,* ed. Manning Marable, Immanuel Ness, and Joseph Wilson (Lanham, Md.: Rowman & Littlefield, 2006).

59. Massey et al., *Beyond Smoke and Mirrors* 120–21; Stuesse, "Globalization 'Southern Style,'" 10; Tina Susman, "New Orleans Cleanup Crews Remain Uncompensated," *Knight Ridder/Tribune Business News,* December 19, 2005.

60. U.S. Congress, *Hidden Tragedy,* 22.

61. Helton, *Three Hundred Strangers,* 13; Griffith, *Jones's Minimal,* 152–59.

62. Helton, *Three Hundred Strangers,* 13; Vaca, *Presumed Alliance,* 25; Stuesse, "Globalization 'Southern Style,'" 239–41.

63. This idea is noted repeatedly in much of the literature regarding immigration and the poultry processing industry, including works by Fink; Griffith; Guthey; and Kandel and Parrado.

64. Frank Fellone, "The Fate of the Chickens," *Arkansas Democrat-Gazette,* March 31, 1997.

65. Jessica Seid, "Debate over the Jobs Americans 'Just Won't Do,'" *CNNMoney.com,* May 1, 2006, http://money.cnn.com/2006/04/24/smbusiness/immigration_reform/ (last accessed November 30, 2011); and "Immigration Reform: No Ditches and Dirty Plates," *CNNMoney.com,* March 30, 2006, http://money.cnn.com/2006/03/30/smbusiness/immigration_reform/index.htm (last accessed November 30, 2011).

66. Office of the Press Secretary, "President Urges Senate to Pass Comprehensive Immigration Reform," April 5, 2006, http://georgewbush-whitehouse.archives.gov/news/releases/2006/04/20060405.html (last accessed November 30, 2011); and Office of the Press Secretary, "President Discusses Comprehensive Immigration Reform," April 24, 2006, http://georgewbush-whitehouse.archives.gov/news/releases/2006/04/20060424-2.html (last accessed November 30, 2011).

67. Pew Hispanic Center, "The State of American Public Opinion on Immigration in Spring 2006: A Review of Major Surveys," May 17, 2006, 6, www.pewhispanic.org/files/2011/10/18.pdf (last accessed November 30, 2011).

68. Gordon and Lenhardt, "Conflict and Solidarity," 8.

69. Seid, "Jobs Americans 'Just Won't Do'"; "Jobs Americans Won't Do," *Wall Street Journal,* April 7, 2006. Gordon and Lenhardt offer a similar conclusion, noting that African Americans are hesitant to do work that is "increasing abusive and poorly remunerated" ("Conflict and Solidarity," 9).

70. Helton, *Three Hundred Strangers,* 14, 18; Mohl, "Globalization, Latinization, and the Nuevo New South," 41.

71. Evan Perez and Corey Dade, "Reversal of Fortune: An Immigration Raid Aids Blacks," *Wall Street Journal,* January 17, 2007.

72. Daniel Hamermesh based this observation on the fact that black workers "are more likely to work at distinctly inferior times . . . they work in industries where the risk of injury is greater and the duration of industries is longer, and they are less likely to report a variety of job amenities than are members of other groups of native workers" ("Immigration and the Quality of Jobs," in *Help or Hindrance? The Economic Implications of Immigration for African Americans,* ed. Daniel Hamermesh and Frank Bean [New York: Russell Sage Foundation, 1998], 104).

73. In its November–December 2006 newsletter, e.g., the Union Parish Chamber of Commerce noted that the parish's unemployment rate of 3.8 percent was well below the national rate of 4.7 percent. See also Strausberg, *From Hills and Hollers,* 133; Kandel and Parrado, "Hispanics in the American South," 270; and Katz, "1,000 Miles of Hope, Heartbreak," 4.

74. Stuesse, "Globalization 'Southern Style,'" 136–37.

75. Kandel and Parrado, "Hispanics in the American South," 270; Newman, Impacts of Hispanic *Population Growth* 17–20; Mohl, "Globalization, Latinization, and the Nuevo New South," 47.

76. Horwitz, "9 to Nowhere," *Wall Street Journal,* January 24, 2006, 2. The lack of marketable skills is partially a result of what Griffith and Kandel call the deskilling of meat processing jobs. Brad Branan, "Blue-Collar Blues," *Arkansas Democrat-Gazette,* November 24, 2002.

77. George J. Borjas, "Do Blacks Gain or Lose from Immigration?" in *Help or Hindrance? The Economic Implications of Immigration for African Americans,* ed. Daniel Hamermesh and Frank Bean (New York: Russell Sage Foundation, 1998); James P. Smith and Barry Edmonson, eds., "Immigration's Effects on Jobs and Wages: First Principles," *The New Americans: Economic, Demographic and Fiscal Effects of Immigration* (Washington, D.C.: National Academy Press, 1997), 135–72.

78. George J. Borjas, Richard B. Freeman, and Lawrence F. Katz, "Searching for the Effect of Immigration on the Labor Market," *American Economic Review* 86, no. 2, Papers and Proceedings of the Hundredth and Eighth Annual Meeting of the American Economic Association, San Francisco, Calif., January 5–7, 1996, 246; Smith and Edmonson, "Immigration's Effects," 173–237; David Card, "The Impact of the Mariel Boatlift on the Miami Labor Market," *Industrial and Labor Relations Review* 43, no. 2 (1990): 245–57.

79. Steinberg, "Immigration, African Americans and Race Discourse," 180.

80. Gordon and Lenhardt, "Conflict and Solidarity," 5.

81. Stuesse, "Globalization 'Southern Style,'" 9. Stephen Steinberg and Nicolas Vaca both list occupations in which a once predominantly black workforce is now overwhelmingly Latino. Steinberg, "Immigration, African Americans and Race Discourse," 182–83; Vaca, *Presumed Alliance,* 6, 25–26.

82. Borjas, "Do Blacks Gain or Lose from Immigration," 69. Economists Steven Shulman and Robert C. Smith echo Borjas, noting that "the findings of negligible impact should not be taken at face value." Nevertheless, Borjas's theories have been the subject of much critique—Doug Henwood notes that Borjas and colleagues work with "heroic models with heroic assumptions about the mobility and substitutability of capital and labor—statistical systems that are always highly susceptible to assumptions." Of Borjas's findings that high school dropouts have taken a 4–8 percent wage hit because of immigration between 1980 and 2000, Henwood argues, "Missing from this analysis are the words 'union' and 'minimum wage,' making it incomplete and tendentious, since it's likely that union-busting and the eroding value of the minimum have had more effects than immigration ever could." Similarly, while journalist Roger Lowenstein refers to Borjas as the preeminent scholar in his field, he points out that "the consensus of most [economists] is that, on balance, immigration is good for the country" (Steven Shulman and Robert C. Smith, "Immigration and African Americans," in *African Americans in the U.S. Economy,* ed. Cecilia A. Conrad, et al. [Lanham, Md.: Rowman & Littlefield, 2005], 200; Doug Henwood, "A Nation of [Yesterday's] Immigrants," *Left Business Observer,* no. 113 [May 2006], www.leftbusinessobserver.com/Immigration.html [last accessed November 30, 2011]; Roger Lowenstein, "The Immigration Equation," *New York Times,* July 9, 2006).

83. Vernon Briggs most recently made this argument in *Mass Immigration and the National Interest: Policy Directions for the New Century* (Armonk, N.Y.: M. E. Sharpe, 2003), but he has supported this position for decades.

84. This quote is from a survey distributed to black and white Bernice residents to gauge their opinions about and responses to the growth of the Latino population in the town. I will refer to surveys by a number assigned to each. This quote comes from survey no. 23.

85. Kandel and Parrado, "Hispanics in the American South," 269; Striffler, *Chicken,* 112.

86. West, interview, January 2, 2005.

87. Wright, interview, December 27, 2004; Shine, interview, July 27, 2011.

88. Survey nos. 20, 9, and 30.

89. Survey no. 36.

90. U.S. Government Accountability Office, *Safety in the Meat and Poultry Industry, While Improving, Could Be Further Strengthened,* GAO-05-96, January 2005, www.gao.gov/new. items/d0596.pdf (last accessed November 30, 2011), 1.

91. Island, telephone interview, April 24, 2007.

92. Lowe, interview, September 17, 2006.

93. Mallory, interview, August 2011.

94. While this sentiment is expressed by both black and white southerners, Helton (*Three Hundred Strangers,* 15–16) and Vaca (*Presumed Alliance,* 24–26 and throughout the volume) suggest that blacks may be more likely to report feeling this way. I would suggest that the reason for the discrepancy lies in the facts that (1) whites know they are not in danger of losing their place at the top of the U.S. racial hierarchy and (2) it is blacks with whom Latinos have competed for everything from jobs to homes to "largest minority" status.

95. Deborah O. Erwin, "An Ethnographic Description of Latino Immigration in Rural Arkansas: Intergroup Relations and Utilization of Healthcare Services," *Southern Rural Sociology* 19, no. 1 (2003): 67. Some residents of rapid population growth areas believe local businesses sold their communities out by initiating and sustaining the growth in immigrant populations with little regard for those already living there. Greg Harton, "Shut Aliens Out," *Arkansas Democrat-Gazette,* June 8, 1997; Brian Grow, "A Body Blow to Illegal Labor?" *Businessweek Online,* www.businessweek.com/magazine/content/06_13/b3977087.htm (last accessed November 30, 2011); James Engstrom, "Industry and Immigration in Dalton, Georgia," in *Latino Workers in the Contemporary South,* ed. Arthur D. Murphy, Colleen Blanchard, and Jennifer A. Hill (Athens: University of Georgia Press, 2001).

96. Survey no. 5. Helton maintains that this type of observation is common: "Grocery stores turned out to be key spaces where longtime residents sought to understand . . . demographic changes" (*Three Hundred Strangers,* 6).

97. Survey no. 1.

98. Survey no. 29.

99. Roberto Suro, "Remittance Senders and Receivers: Tracking the Transnational Channels," report prepared for the Pew Hispanic Center, November 24, 2003, http://pewhispanic. org/files/reports/23.pdf (last accessed November 30, 2011); B. Lindsay Lowell and Rodolfo O. De La Garza, "The Developmental Role of Remittances in U.S. Latino Communities and in Latin American Countries," a project of the Inter-American Dialogue, June 2000, www .thedialogue.org/PublicationFiles/Final%20report.pdf (last accessed November 30, 2011).

100. Survey no. 45.

101. Erwin, "Ethnographic Description," 57. Laura Helton reported a similar story in Scott County, Miss. (*Three Hundred Strangers,* 10).

102. Survey no. 30.

103. Nayan Shah, *Contagious Divides: Epidemics and Race in San Francisco's Chinatown* (Berkeley: University of California Press, 2001); Arnold Shankman, "Black on Yellow: Afro-Americans View Chinese Americans 1850–1935," *Phylon* 39, no. 1 (1978): 3; Howard Markel

and Alexandra Minna Stern, "The Foreignness of Germs: The Persistent Association of Immigrants and Disease in American Society," *Millbank Quarterly* 80, no. 4 (2002): 765; M. Mark Stolarik, "From Field to Factory: The Historiography of Slovak Immigration to the United States," *International Migration Review* 10, no. 1 (1976): 96–97.

104. Cobb, "Chicken Hangers."

105. David L. Ostendorf, "Exploiting Immigrant Workers," *Christian Century* 116, no. 14 (1999): 492; Stuesse relates similar stories in "Globalization 'Southern Style'" (187–88).

106. Jesse Katz, "New Migrant Trails Take Latinos to Remote Towns," *Los Angeles Times*, November 12, 2006.

107. Katz, "New Migrant Trails."

108. Horowitz and Miller, *Immigrants in the Delmarva Poultry Processing Industry*, 8.

109. See Fink, *Maya of Morganton*, 18; Griffith, *Jones's Minimal*, 167, 180–81; Stuesse, "Globalization 'Southern Style,'" 180–90; and Helton, *Three Hundred Strangers*.

110. Mohl, "Globalization, Latinization, and the Nuevo New South," 31; Erwin, "Ethnographic Description," 49; Terrence W. Haverluk, "Hispanization of Hereford," in *Latino Workers in the Contemporary South*, ed. Arthur D. Murphy, Colleen Blanchard, and Jennifer A. Hill (Athens: University of Georgia Press, 2001). A resident of Rogers, Ark., a city whose Latino population grew from 460 in 1990 to 7,490 in 2000, noted, e.g., that many natives felt their way of life would be eroded (Harton).

111. Survey nos. 2, 12, and 29. "Natives" are also bothered because they do not understand Spanish and fear Spanish speakers may be making derogatory remarks or purposely excluding English-only speakers. Tatcho Mindiola Jr., Yolanda Flores Niemann, and Nestor Rodriguez, *Black-Brown Relations and Stereotypes* (Austin: University of Texas Press, 2002), 52.

112. Survey no. 12.

113. Frantz Fanon, *Black Skin, White Masks*, trans. Charles Lam Markmann (New York: Grove Press, 1991), 17.

114. Pastora San Juan Cafferty, "The Language Question," in *Hispanics in the United States*, ed. Pastora San Juan Cafferty and David W. Engstrom (New Brunswick: Transaction Publishers, 2000), 69–96; Mohl, "Globalization, Latinization, and the Nuevo New South," 51; Erwin, "Ethnographic Description," 49, 58; Bender, *Greasers and Gringos*, 82–103. Twenty-four states in all have declared English the official language since 1981 (ten of them southern), though the Alaska Supreme Court overturned that state's amendment (Deborah J. Schildkraut, "Official-English and the States: Influences on Declaring English the Official Language in the United States," *Political Research Quarterly* 54, no. 2 [2001]: 445–57).

115. Gary Gerstle, "Liberty, Coercion, and the Making of Americans," *Journal of American History* 84, no. 2 (1997): 530. See also Eileen H. Tamura, "The English Only Effort, the Anti-Japanese Campaign, and Language Acquisition in the Education of Japanese Americans in Hawaii, 1915–1940," *History of Education Quarterly* 33, no. 1 (1993): 37–58; Linda Gordon, "Family Violence, Feminism, and Social Control," *Feminist Studies* 12, no. 3 (1986): 452–78; Rivka Shpak Lissak, *Pluralism and Progressives: Hull House and the New Immigrants, 1890–1919* (Chicago: University of Chicago Press, 1989); and William G. Ross, *Forging New Freedoms: Nativism, Education and the Constitution, 1917–1927* (Lincoln: University of Nebraska Press, 1994).

116. Cafferty, "Language Question," 78; Pew Hispanic Center, "Hispanic Attitudes toward Learning English," fact sheet, June 7, 2006, www.pewtrusts.org/uploadedFiles/wwwpewtrusts

org/Fact_Sheets/Hispanics_in_America/PHC_fact_sheet_0606.pdf (last accessed November 30, 2011).

117. Teresa G. Labov, "English Acquisition by Immigrants to the United States at the Beginning of the Twentieth Century," *American Speech* 73, no. 4 (1998): 368, 392–93.

118. Brown and Chumley, "Catholic Mexican Community of Bernice," 2.

119. Ana Smith, electronic interview, December 6–7, 2006.

120. Quoted in Vaca, *Presumed Alliance,* 25.

121. Kochhar, Suro, and Tafoya, "New Latino South," 37.

122. Gafford, electronic interview, September 4, 2006.

123. Ana Smith, telephone interview by author, Farmerville, La., August 2, 2006.

124. Jordan Blum, "Union School Board Puts Out Feelers for Consolidation Blueprint," *Monroe NewsStar,* September 22, 2006.

125. Mike Rodman, "Northwest Wants Language Barrier to Add Up in School Formula," *Arkansas Democrat-Gazette,* June 2, 1994; Michael Leahy, "English Lessons," *Arkansas Democrat-Gazette,* March 26, 1997; Rose Ann Pearce, "Programs for Migrants Help Pupils Assimilate," *Arkansas Democrat-Gazette,* May 8, 2000.

126. Julian R. Betts, "Educational Crowding Out: Do Immigrants Affect the Educational Attainment of American Minorities?" in *Help or Hindrance? The Economic Implications of Immigration for African Americans,* ed. Daniel Hamermesh and Frank Bean (New York: Russell Sage Foundation, 1998), 255.

127. Survey no. 24.

128. Betts, "Educational Crowding Out," 254–55, 276–78.

129. This, too, is a repeated conflict in American history. In New York, e.g., there have been episodes of interethnic "fighting" over New York schools—notably between Protestants and Irish Catholics in the 1830s and between African Americans and Jews in the 1960s. See Diane Ravitch, *The Great School Wars, New York City, 1805–1973: A History of the Public Schools as Battlefields of Social Change* (New York: Basic Books, 1974). Parents also realized that a lack of control could mean that their children would be educated poorly or not at all. Guadalupe San Miguel argues that Mexican Americans also recognized this fact and pushed for some control over and equality with Anglos in their children's education. Guadalupe San Miguel, *"Let All of Them Take Heed": Mexican Americans and the Campaign for Educational Equality in Texas, 1910–1981* (Austin: University of Texas Press, 1987).

130. Survey no. 30.

131. Melissa Roderick, "Hispanics and Education," in *Hispanics in the United States,* ed. Pastora San Juan Cafferty and David W. Engstrom (New Brunswick: Transaction Publishers, 2000), 123–59; Valerie Martinez-Ebers, Luis Fraga, Linda Lopez, and Arturo Vega, "Latino Interest in Education, Health and Criminal Justice Policy," *Political Science and Politics* 33, no. 3 (2000): 547–54.

132. Bender, *Greasers and Gringos,* 110; Teresa Sullivan, "A Demographic Portrait," in *Hispanics in the United States,* ed. Pastora San Juan Cafferty and David W. Engstrom (New Brunswick: Transaction Publishers, 2000), 14–16.

133. Gafford, electronic interview by author, September 4, 2006; survey nos. 3, 29, and 17.

134. Gafford, electronic interview by author, April 25, 2007.

135. Marrow, *New Destination Dreaming,* throughout chap. 4, e.g., esp. 118–19.

136. Gafford, electronic interview by author, September 9, 2006.

137. Claudine Gay, "Seeing Difference: The Effect of Economic Disparity on Black Attitudes toward Latinos," *American Journal of Political Science* 50, no. 4 (2006): 982–97.

138. Island, telephone interview, April 24, 2007.

139. On racial distancing, see Neil Foley, *The White Scourge: Mexicans, Blacks, and Poor Whites in Texas Cotton Culture* (Berkeley: University of California Press, 1997); Claire Jean Kim, *Bitter Fruit: The Politics of Black-Korean Conflict in New York City* (New Haven: Yale University Press, 2000); Paula McClain et al., "Racial Distancing in a Southern City: Latino Immigrants' Views of Black Americans," *Journal of Politics* 68, no. 3 (2006): 571–84; Susan Koshy, "Morphing Race into Ethnicity: Asian Americans and Critical Transformations of Whiteness," *boundary 2* 28, no. 1 (2001): 173–80; Mindiola et al., *Black-Brown Relations,* 58–59; Jorge Duany, "Reconstructing Racial Identity: Ethnicity, Color, and Class among Dominicans in the United States and Puerto Rico," "Race and National Identity in the Americas," *Latin American Perspectives* 25, no. 3 (May 1998): 147–72. These studies suggest that while skin color differences may slow other groups' attainment of whiteness, these groups work toward the goal in other ways. Mexicanos, e.g., sought whiteness through land ownership and independence from landlords, accomplishments virtually impossible for black sharecroppers. In coastal cities Korean merchants have created a place that, while not equal to whites, places them as sort of a "middleman," acting as agents of the white establishment in black communities. Cubans in Miami and the Chinese who came to Mississippi in the early twentieth century employed similar strategies. Looking at the Chinese in Mississippi, Koshy asserts that they achieved honorary whiteness by accepting and emulating white cultural norms and by abandoning the social and business relationships they had cultivated with blacks.

140. Vaca, *Presumed Alliance.*

141. hooks, *Killing Rage, Ending Racism,* 198.

142. Toni Morrison, cited in hooks, *Killing Rage* 198 (originally in "On the Backs of Blacks," *Time* 142, no. 3 [Fall 1993]: 57).

143. Mindiola et al., *Black-Brown Relations,* 58–59.

144. Stuesse, "Globalization 'Southern Style,'" 329. According to Stuesse, "neoliberal" thought and language disguise today's more subtle racism and dismiss it by relying on concepts such as "economics, criminality, personal responsibility, and individual achievement" (29).

145. McClain et al., "Racial Distancing," 574; Stuesse, "Globalization 'Southern Style,'" 226.

146. Bender, *Greasers and Gringos,* 73; Jewelle Gibbs and Teiahsha Bankhead, *Preserving Privilege: California Politics, Propositions, and People of Color* (Westport, Conn.: Praeger, 2001): 73–93. Kitty Calavita posits that Californians, sensing a fiscal crisis and consumed by "balanced budget conservatism," blamed undocumented immigrants for excessive government spending and "insatiable social service needs" ("The New Politics of Immigration: 'Balanced Budget Conservatism' and the Symbolism of Proposition 187," *Social Problems* 43, no. 3 [1996]: 284–305).

147. Peter Brimelow, *Alien Nation: Common Sense about America's Immigration Disaster* (New York: Random House, 1995).

148. Bender, *Greasers and Gringos,* 79.

149. Fix and Passel, "Assessing Welfare Reform's Immigrant Provisions," in *Welfare Reform,* 179.

150. Gibbs and Bankhead focus their fifth chapter on Proposition 187 and the preceding "demonizing" of immigrants. Kitty Calavita locates the sentiment behind and victory of Proposition 187 in an era of new nativism. Elliott Barkan, who argues that California was not a leader of a neonativist movement, nonetheless admits, "For a time the climate of public opinion [regarding immigrants] became more overtly negative" ("Return of the Nativists? California Public Opinion and Immigration in the 1980s and 1990s," *Social Science History* 27, no. 2 [2003]: 261).

151. Michael Fix and Jeffrey Passel, with María E. Enchautegui and Wendy Zimmermann, *Immigration and Immigrants: Setting the Record Straight* (Washington, D.C.: Urban Institute, 1994); J. F. Perea, ed., *Immigrants Out! The New Nativism and the Anti-Immigrant Impulse in the United States* (New York: New York University Press, 1997). PRWORA did initially cut benefits to elderly immigrants receiving SSI, but the reality of leaving elderly people without any income created such negative publicity and real suffering that benefits were reinstated.

152. Fink, *Maya of Morgantown,* 28–31; Ostendorf, "Exploiting Immigrant Workers," 493; Lewis, "Grasshopper Power," in *Workers' Rights as Human Rights.*

153. See, e.g., Emilio Zamora, *The World of the Mexican Worker in Texas* (College Station: Texas A&M University Press, 1993), chap. 4; Vicki Ruiz, *From Out of the Shadows: Mexican Women in Twentieth Century America* (Oxford: Oxford University Press, 1998); Devra Weber's *Dark Sweat, White Gold: California Farm Workers, Cotton, and the New Deal* (Berkeley: University of California Press, 1994); Fink on burial and community associations in *Maya of Morganton,* chap. 3.

154. Weber, *Dark Sweat, White Gold,* 60.

155. Survey nos. 33, 13, and 14.

156. Survey no. 12. Social services agents are careful, however, only to give aid for the children. If, e.g., undocumented parents apply for food stamps for one eligible child, they will receive the amount allotted for one person, not three.

157. Mohl, "Globalization, Latinization, and the Nuevo New South," 41; Waldinger, "Black/Immigrant Competition Re-Assessed," 365; Helton, *Three Hundred Strangers,* 14.

158. Quoted in Stuesse, "Globalization 'Southern Style,'" 224.

159. See the description of black labor activist Charles Carney in Cobb, "Chicken Hangers"; and Stuesse's explanation of the goals and techniques of Workers' Centers in Mississippi in "Globalization 'Southern Style.'"

160. Wright, interview, December 27, 2004.

161. Survey no. 6.

CONCLUSION

1. "Pilgrim's Pride Completes Acquisition of Gold Kist," http://phx.corporate-ir.net/phoenix.zhtml?c=68228&p=irol-newsArticle&ID=948851&highlight= (last accessed October 21, 2011).

2. "Pilgrim's Pride Named to Fortune's 'Most Admired Companies' List for Fifth Consecutive Year," *Farmerville Gazette,* March 22, 2007; "The List of Industry Stars," *Fortune* 155, no. 5, March 19, 2007, http://money.cnn.com/magazines/fortune/fortune_archive/2007/03/19/8402372/index.htm (last accessed October 21, 2011).

3. From Pilgrim's Pride Corporation, "Proven Performance, Poised for Growth," Stephens, Inc. Conference, March 14, 2006, http://media.corporate-ir.net/media_files/irol/68/68228/pdfs/Stephens_Conference_March_13142006.pdf (last accessed January 20, 2014).

4. Cobb, *Selling of the South;* Brattain, *Politics of Whiteness;* Numan Bartley, *The New South, 1945–1980* (Baton Rouge: Louisiana State University Press, 1995).

5. Quote from Karl Raitz, "Advantages of Place as Perceived by Sunbelt Promoters," *Growth and Change* 19, no. 4 (1988): 14–29.

6. When, e.g., Louise Levy died, Louisiana, "based on morals and general welfare," denied that her children had a right to sue for wrongful death because they had been born out of wedlock. The Supreme Court overturned the Louisiana courts' decision (U.S. Supreme Court *Levy v. Louisiana,* 391 U.S. 68 [1968]).

7. Data from QT-P35, Poverty Status in 1999 of Families and Nonfamily Householders: 2000 Data Set: Census 2000 Summary File 3 (SF 3)—Sample Data Geographic Area: Bernice town, La.; QT-P10, Households and Families: 2000 Data Set: Census 2000 Summary File 2 (SF 2) 100-Percent Data Geographic Area: Bernice town, La., Racial or Ethnic Grouping: Black or African American alone; QT-P10, Households and Families: 2000 Data Set: Census 2000 Summary File 2 (SF 2) 100-Percent Data Geographic Area: Bernice town, La., www.census.gov.

8. Louisiana Department of Children and Family Services, *Temporary Assistance for Needy Families State Plan,* www.dcfs.louisiana.gov/assets/docs/searchable/OFS/TANF/TANFStatePlanAmended20112012.pdf (last accessed December 4, 2011).

9. M. A. Lee and Joachim Singlemann, "Welfare Reform amidst Chronic Poverty in the Mississippi Delta," in *Population Change and Rural Society,* ed. W. A. Kandel and D. L. Brown (Dordrecht, The Netherlands: Springer, 2006).

10. In fact, when former Louisiana governor Mike Foster established the Louisiana Commission on Marriage and Family, one of its stated purposes was to "propose and analyze initiatives, programs, policies, and/or incentives that would induce and/or encourage low-income couples and/or welfare recipients to marry" (Louisiana Division of Administration, *Executive Order MJF 01-19: Louisiana Commission on Marriage and Family,* April 6, 2001, http://doa.louisiana.gov/osr/other/mjf01-19.htm [last accessed December 4, 2011]). The push to incentivize marriage is partially rooted in the same stereotypes that have led to the denigration of black motherhood that I argued in chapter 2, particularly that black women are so immoral and deviant that they do not desire the "respectability" of marriage or do not ascribe to the same cultural norms as other women and thus must be "guided" into making better choices, and the assumption that marriage is a magic cure-all for female and child poverty, with little attention paid to underlying structural problems that sustain this poverty. On using welfare as a tool of "reform," see Thomas, "Race, Gender, and Welfare Reform"; Roberts, "Race, Gender, and the Value of Mothers' Work"; Mittelstadt, *From Welfare to Workfare;* and Chad Broughton, "Reforming Poor Women: The Cultural Politics and Practices of Welfare Reform," *Qualitative* Sociology 26, no. 1 (Spring 2003): 35–51. Throughout their work scholars such as Gwendolyn Mink and Dorothy Roberts argue that welfare actually offered some autonomy and self-sufficiency to women. Similarly, Linda Gordon suggests that social control institutions such as welfare help some women empower themselves by undermining patriarchal systems and securing maintenance and child support payments ("Family Violence, Feminism, and Social Control"). Gordon and Nancy Fraser argue that it has been the framing,

paltriness, and stigmatization of welfare and the notion of "dependency" that makes welfare such an unpopular program ("Dependency Demystified"). Mimi Abramovitz also explores the shortcomings and stigmatization of ADC in *Regulating the Lives of Women.*

11. Louisiana Department of Education, Division of Standards, Assessments, and Accountability, *Fall 2006 School Report Cards and Accountability Reports,* www.doe.state.la.us/lde/saa/2394.asp (last accessed April 13, 2007).

12. Tre Bischof, "Union Voters Crush Consolidation Plan," *Farmerville Gazette,* March 31, 2007.

13. In 2011–12 the school was for kindergarten through sixth grade; in 2013–14, the final year it was open, it was for kindergarten through fifth grade.

14. Susan Thomson, "El Dorado Hopes the Promise Brings Back the Golden Days," *Regional Economist* (January 2009), www.stlouisfed.org/publications/re/articles/?id=1318 (last accessed September 16, 2013).

15. Jason Wiest, "Pilgrim's Pride Considering El Dorado Plant Closure; 1,620 Could Lose Jobs," *Arkansas News Bureau,* April 11, 2008.

16. Stacey Roberts, "Pilgrim's Pride Closing El Dorado Site," *Arkansas Democrat-Gazette,* February 28, 2009.

17. Roberts, "Pilgrim's Pride Closing El Dorado Site."

18. Thomson, "El Dorado Hopes the Promise Brings Back the Golden Days."

19. Quote from the "Economic Development" page of the GoEldorado.com website,www.goeldorado.com/ (last accessed April 1, 2011).

20. Top pay was reached after one year of work. Starting pay was $7.25 per hour. "Agreement between United Food and Commercial Workers Union, Local 2008 and Pilgrim's Pride Corporation, El Dorado, AR."

21. Strausberg, *From Hills and Hollers,* 133–38.

22. Compa, *Blood, Sweat, and Fear,* 37.

23. Compa, *Blood, Sweat, and Fear,* 37–38. On government responsibility for line speed and resultant injuries, see also Gail Eisnitz, *Slaughterhouse: The Shocking Story of Greed, Neglect, and Inhumane Treatment inside the U.S. Meat Industry,* esp. 167–68; and Linder, "I Gave My Employer a Chicken That Had No Bone."

24. Kitty Calavita, "The Demise of the Occupational Safety and Health Administration: A Case Study in Symbolic Action," *Social Problems* 30, no. 4 (1983): 437–48. On the ineffectiveness of OSHA, see Kerry Hall and Ames Alexander, "He Says His Agency Is at Fault," *Charlotte Observer,* February 2008, www.charlotteobserver.com/2008/09/30/223430/he-says-his-agency-is-at-fault.html (last accessed December 4, 2011). Eisnitz, *Slaughterhouse,* pt. 4; Linder, "I Gave My Employer a Chicken That Had No Bone"; and Scott Bronstein, "USDA Eases Up on Plant Six Times—On-Line Inspectors Can't Slow Production," *Atlanta Journal-Constitution,* May 26, 1991.

25. Howard, *The Death of Common Sense: How Law Is Suffocating America* (New York: Random House, 1994). On the ongoing lack of oversight and related problems, see also "Needed: A Watchdog," *CharlotteObserver.com,* June 25, 2010, www.charlotteobserver.com/2008/09/30/223518/needed-a-watchdog.html#.UqItUaVW7wI. (last accessed January 20, 2014).

26. Striffler, *Chicken,* 164.

27. David Smith, "USDA Closes Unclean ConAgra Plant," *Arkansas Democrat-Gazette,* August 24, 2001.

28. Steven Reinberg, "Salmonella Common in U.S. Poultry," *U.S. News and World Report,*

January 23, 2009, http://health.usnews.com/health-news/family-health/childrens-health/articles/2009/01/23/salmonella-common-in-us-poultry (last accessed December 4, 2011); Teresa Lostroh and Rachel Albin, "Laws Haven't Kept Deadly Pathogens Out of Meat, Poultry," *News21,* http://foodsafety.news21.com/2011/safety/inspection (last accessed December 4, 2011). Even the U.S. Government Accounting Office expressed skepticism about the USDA's plans to effectively leave the foxes guarding the henhouses (*Food Safety: Weaknesses in Meat and Poultry Inspection Pilot Should Be Addressed before Implementation,* Report to the Committee on Agriculture, Nutrition, and Forestry, U.S. Senate, December 2001, www.gao.gov/products/GAO-02-59 [last accessed December 4, 2011]; Eisnitz, *Slaughterhouse,* chap. 13).

29. On the ineffectiveness of the USDA in the aftermath of deregulation, see Bronstein, "Chicken—How Safe? First of Two Parts," *Atlantic Journal-Constitution,* May 26, 1991. On the fate of USDA inspectors who have challenged poultry processors, see Kerry Hall, Ames Alexander, and Franco Ordoñez, "Fight and Might," *Charlotte Observer,* February 11, 2008, www.charlotteobserver.com/2008/09/30/223442/fight-and-might.html (last accessed December 4, 2011); Eisnitz, *Slaughterhouse,* 173–76.

30. Strong, interview, August 8, 2005.

31. Anita Grabowski, *Organizing for Change: Labor Organizers and Latin American Poultry Workers,* report of the Poultry Worker Justice Research Project Inter-American Policy Studies Occasional Paper No. 3, sponsored by the Equal Justice Center, Austin, Tex., and the Inter-American Policy Studies Program, University of Texas at Austin, 2003, 9.

32. On the role of Latino immigrant workers in successful unionization, see Christopher David Ruiz Cameron, "Labryinth of Solidarity: Why the Future of the American Labor Movement Depends on Latino Workers," *University of Miami Law Review* 53, no. 1089 (July 1999): 1098–1114; Vanessa Tait, *Poor Workers' Unions: Rebuilding Labor from Below* (Boston: South End Press, 2005), esp. chap. 5; essays in Ruth Milkman, ed., *Organizing Immigrants: The Challenge for Unions in Contemporary California* (Ithaca, N.Y.: Cornell University Press, 2000).

33. Gloria Anzaldúa, "Speaking in Tongues: A Letter to Third World Women Writers," in *Women Writing Resistance,* ed. Jennifer Browdy de Hernandez (Cambridge, Mass.: South End Press, 2005), 83–84.

34. Audre Lorde, "The Transformation of Silence into Language and Action," *Sister Outsider: Essays and Speeches* (Berkeley, Calif.: Crossing Press, 2007), 42.

35. Lorde, "Learning from the 60s," *Sister Outsider,* 137.

BIBLIOGRAPHY

PRIMARY SOURCES
Interviews by Author

Biles, Delores. Bernice, La., August 8, 2011.
Davis, Natalie. Bernice, La., January 15, 2005, and July 26, 2006.
Dawes, Bella. Bernice, La., August 4, 2011.
Drayton, Kenya. Houston, Tex., November 7, 2004.
———. Bernice, La., August 4, 2011.
Earl, Janae. Bernice, La., August 4, 2011, and October 14, 2012.
Evans Greshom, Rosalynn. Electronic interview. October 23, 2006.
Gafford, Lillian. Electronic interview. September 4 and 9, 2006.
———. Bernice, La., September 3, 2011.
Holloway, Eleanor. Bernice, La., August 3, 2011.
Island, LaDonna. Electronic interview. October 22, 2005, and September 27, 2011.
James, Ruth. Bernice, La., November 19, 2005, and August 4, 2011.
Johnson, LeeAnn. Bernice, La., August 4, 2011.
Jones, Aarica. Bernice, La., July 7, 2012.
Lowe, DeShaun. Bernice, La., March 21, 2005, and September 17, 2006.
Lowe, DeShaun, and Jackie Martin-Lowe. Bernice, La., March 21, 2005.
Mallory, Neysha. Bernice, La., August 3, 2011.
Martin, Lydia, and Sylvia Martin. Joint interview. Bernice, La., August 7, 2011.
Mays, Trinity. Electronic interview. April 4, 2007, and October 14, 2012.
Morales, Lisa. Bernice, La., March 11, 2013.
Shine, Deena. Bernice, La., July 27, 2011.
Smith, Ana. Farmerville, La., August 2, 2006.

———. Electronic interview. December 6–7, 2006.

Strong, Janet. El Dorado, Ark., August 8, 2005.

Tyler, Geeta. Bernice, La., August 8, 2011.

West, Vivian. Bernice, La., January 2, 2005, and July 27, 2011.

Wright, Tavia. Bernice, La., December 27, 2004, and November 24, 2005.

———. Telephone interview. Bernice, La., October 1, 2011, and October 14, 2012.

Wright, Tavia, and DeShaun Lowe. Bernice, La., March 11, 2006.

Young, Margie. Bernice, La., August 3, 2011.

Other Interviews

Bazemore, Donna. Interview by Bob Hall. Published in "I Feel What Women Feel." *Southern Exposure* 17, no. 2 (Summer 1989): 30–33.

Carter, Sherry. Interview by Videssa Morris-Owens. Bernice, La., November 24, 2012.

Carter, Timothy. Interview by Videssa Morris-Owens. Bernice, La., November 24, 2012.

Foster, Ella. Interview by Videssa Morris-Owens. Bernice, La., August 31, 2012.

Merkle, Jess. Interview by the University of Arkansas–Fayetteville Center of Excellence for Poultry Science. May 1987.

Monroe, Faith. Interview by Videssa Morris-Owens. Bernice, La., August 31, 2012.

Thomas, Lizzie. Interview by Videssa Morris-Owens. Bernice, La., August 31, 2012.

Archives

Amalgamated Meatcutters and Butcher Workmen of North America Records, 1903–80. Reels 138, 181, 478–80. Wisconsin Historical Society Archives, Madison.

Bailey Collection (O. C. and Marjorie Bailey). Riley-Hickingtham Library, Ouchita Baptist University.

Bernice Historical Society Collection (No. M248). Department of Special Collections, Manuscripts, and Archives, Prescott Memorial Library, Louisiana Tech University, Ruston.

International Association of Machinists and Aerospace Workers Records, 1901–74. Reel 40. Wisconsin Historical Society Archives, Madison.

"Poultry." Eighth Drawer, Vertical Files. Archives at Torreyson Library, University of Central Arkansas, Conway.

"Poultry Industry." Vertical File. Special Collections, Mullins Library, University of Arkansas, Fayetteville.

"Jess Merkle." Vertical File. Special Collections, Mullins Library, University of Arkansas, Fayetteville.

Louisiana Collection. State Library of Louisiana, Baton Rouge.

Papers of the Chicken-of-Tomorrow Contest." Special Collections, Mullins Library, University of Arkansas, Fayetteville.

Papers of the Greater El Dorado Committee. Housed at the El Dorado Chamber of Commerce, El Dorado, Ark.

Papers of Orval Faubus (MC F27 301). Special Collections, Mullins Library, University of Arkansas, Fayetteville.

Papers of Richard Twedell. Accession Nos. AR259 and AR264. Special Collections, Central Library, University of Texas at Arlington.

Papers of Samuel Twedell. Accession No. AR44. Special Collections, Central Library, University of Texas at Arlington.

Government Documents

Arkansas. Department of Labor. Research and Statistics Division. *Meat Cutters in the Poultry Dressing Industry in Arkansas: A Special Report.* Little Rock, 1978.

Bobo, James R., and Harris S. Segal, eds. *Statistical Abstracts of Louisiana,* 6th ed. New Orleans: University of New Orleans College of Business Administration, 1977.

Louisiana. Department of Education, Division of Standards, Assessments, and Accountability. *Fall 2006 School Report Cards and Accountability Reports.* www. doe.state.la.us/ lde/saa/2394.asp (last accessed April 13, 2007).

——. Department of Public Welfare, Mary Evelyn Parker, Commissioner, to Parish and Area Staffs, "News Release," State of Louisiana, from Accession No. P 1995-17, Social Service Publications, 1941–1969, Records of the Louisiana Department of Welfare, State Archives of Louisiana, Baton Rouge.

——. Department of Public Works. Union Parish Development Board. *Union Parish Resources and Facilities.* Baton Rouge, 1954.

——. Department of Social Services. *Temporary Assistance for Needy Families State Plan.* www.dss.state.la.us/Documents/OFS/TANF_State_Plan_Amen.pdf (last accessed April 13, 2007).

——. Division of Administration. *Executive Order MJF 01-19: Louisiana Commission on Marriage and Family.* April 6, 2001. http://doa.louisiana.gov/osr/other/mjf01–19.htm (last accessed April 13, 2007).

National Institutes of Health, National Institute of Neurological Disorders and Stroke. "Repetitive Motion Disorders Information Page." www.ninds.nih.gov/disorders/repetitive_motion/repetitive_motion.htm (last accessed November 30, 2011).

National Labor Relations Board. "Decision and Order in the Matter of Fairmont Creamery Company and Amalgamated Meat Cutters and Butcher Workmen of North America, Local No. 142 A. F. of L." Case No. 18-C-1085, November 15, 1945.

——. "Decision and Order in the Matter of Tyson Foods, Inc. and United Food and Commercial Workers, Local 425, AFL-CIO." Cases 26-CA-14731 and 26-CA-14821, May 28, 1993.

Office of Economic Opportunity Information Center. *Community Profile: Union Parish, Louisiana.* 1966.

Oklahoma. Office of the Attorney General. "AG Sues Poultry Industry for Poultry Industry for Polluting Oklahoma Waters." Press Release, June 13, 2005. www .oag.state.ok.us/oagweb.nsf/9a798028e1753ff786256c16005d5855/2448aafc29ac 39668625701f0067edbe?OpenDocument (last accessed March 30, 2007).

Ollinger, Michael, Sang Nguyen, Donald Blayney, Bill Chambers, and Ken Nelson. *Structural Change in the Meat, Poultry, Dairy, and Grain Processing Industries.* Economic Research Service. Economic Research Report No. 3. www.ers.usda. gov/publications/err3/err3.pdf (last accessed April 11, 2007).

University of Arkansas Industrial Research and Extension Center. *Potential Broiler Production in Southwest Arkansas.* Fayetteville: University of Arkansas, 1957.

U.S. Commission on Civil Rights. *Report of the United States Commission on Civil Rights, 1959.* Washington, D.C.: GPO, 1959.

U.S. Congress. *Congressional Record.* 85th Cong., 1st sess., 1957. Vol. 103, pts. 7, 10.

——. *Congressional Record.* 86th Cong., 2nd sess., 1960. Vol. 106, pt. 4.

——. House Committee on Education and Labor. *Hidden Tragedy: Underreporting of Workplace Injuries and Illnesses.* Majority Staff Report. 110th Cong., 2nd sess., June 2008, 14–15. www.gpo.gov/fdsys/pkg/CHRG-110hhrg42881/pdf/ CHRG-110hhrg42881.pdf (last accessed November 30, 2011).

——. House Committee on Education and Labor, Subcommittee on Labor-Management Relations. *Hearing on H.R. 3368, Whistleblower Protection Act.* 101st Cong., 1st sess., November 16, 1989, 42.

——. House Committee on the Judiciary, Subcommittee on Immigration, Border Security and Claims. *Illegal Immigration Enforcement and Social Security Protection Act of 2005: Hearing before the Subcommittee on Immigration, Border Security, and Claims.* 109th Cong., 1st sess., May 12, 2005. Washington, D.C.: GPO, 2005.

U.S. Court of Appeals for the Eighth Circuit. George Williams v. ConAgra Poultry Company. Case No. 03-2976.

U.S. Department of Agriculture. National Commission on Small Farms. *A Time to Act: A Report of the USDA National Commission on Small Farms.* January 1998. www.csrees.usda.gov/nea/ag_systems/pdfs/time_to_act_1998.pdf (last accessed October 18, 2011).

——. Newman, Constance. *Impacts of Latino Population Growth on Rural Wages.* Agricultural Economic Report No. 826. September 2003. www.ers.usda.gov/ publications/aer826/aer826.pdf (last accessed April 11, 2007).

———. Ollinger, Michael, James McDonald, and Milton Madison. *Structural Changes in U.S. Chicken and Turkey Slaughter.* Economic Research Service. Economic Report No. 787. Washington, D.C.: GPO, September 2000.

———. Packers and Stockyards Administration. *The Broiler Industry: An Economic Study of Structure, Practices, and Problems.* Washington, D.C.: GPO, August 1967.

———. Rural Electrification Administration. "Comprehensive Survey of Claiborne, Webster, and Union Parishes in Power, Fuel, Agricultural Products, Water, Skilled Labor, Etc.

———. *The U.S. Broiler Industry,* by Harold Jones, Edward Easterling, and Lee Christensen. Economic Research Service. Agricultural Economic Report No. 591. Washington, D.C.: GPO, 1988.

———. *The U.S. Poultry Industry: Changing Economics and Structure,* by Floyd Lasley. Economic Research Service. Agricultural Economic Report No. 502. Washington, D.C.: GPO, 1983.

U.S. Department of Commerce. Bureau of the Census. *U.S. Census of Agriculture: Final Report.* Vol. 1: Parishes, pt. 35: Louisiana. Washington, D.C.: GPO, 1961.

U.S. Department of Homeland Security. Federal Emergency Management Agency. U.S. Fire Administration. *Chicken Processing Plant Fires: Hamlet, North Carolina and North Little Rock, Arkansas.* Report 57 of the Major Fires Investigation Project. www.usfa.dhs.gov/downloads/pdf/publications/tr-057.pdf (last accessed April 11, 2007).

U.S. Department of Justice. "INS Investigation of Tyson Foods, Inc. Leads to 36 Count Indictment for Conspiracy to Smuggle Illegal Aliens for Corporate Profit." Press Release, December 19, 2001. *www.justice.gov/opa/pr/2001/December/01_crm_654.htm* (last accessed January 20, 2014).

U.S. Department of Labor. Bureau of Labor Statistics. "Food Processing Occupations." In *Occupational Outlook Handbook, 2006–7. www.bls.gov/ooh/production/food-processing-occupations.htm* (last accessed January 20, 2014).

———. Bureau of Labor Statistics. *Table 1: Incidence Rates of Nonfatal Occupational Injuries and Illnesses by Industry and Case Types, 2005.* October 19, 2006. www.bls.gov/iif/oshwc/osh/os/ostb1619.txt (last accessed April 20, 2007).

———. Bureau of Labor Statistics. *Table 1: Nonfatal Occupational Injury and Illness Incidence Rates per 100 Full-Time Workers, by Industry, 1994.* March 28, 1996. www.bls.gov/iif/oshwc/osh/os/ostb0169.txt (last accessed April 20, 2007).

———. Occupational Safety and Health Administration. *1997 OSHA Survey of Poultry Processing Plants.* Data summarized on the *OSHA Poultry Processing Industry eTool.* www.osha.gov/SLTC/etools/poultry/statistics.html (last accessed November 30, 2011).

———. Occupational Safety and Health Administration. *Injury and Illness Record-keeping National Emphasis Program.* Directive No. 09-08 (CPL 02), September

2009. www.osha.gov/OshDoc/Directive_pdf/CPL_02_09–08.pdf (last accessed November 30, 2011).

———. Occupational Safety and Health Administration. "Regulations (Standards-29 CFR) Part Number 1904: Recording and Reporting Occupational Injuries and Illness, Subpart C: Recordkeeping Forms and Recording Criteria, Standard Number 1904.7: General Recording Criteria." *www.osha.gov/pls/oshaweb/* owadisp.show_ document?p_table=STANDARDS&p_id=9638 (last accessed November 30, 2011).

———. Office of Policy Planning and Research. "The Negro Family: The Case for National Action," March 1965. www.dol.gov/oasam/programs/history/webid-meynihan.htm (last accessed September 24, 2011).

———. *Poultry Processing Compliance Survey Fact Sheet.* Washington, D.C.: GPO, 2001.

U.S. Federal Emergency Relief Administration, Division of Research, Statistics, and Finance. "The Western Cotton Growing Area: Union Parish, LA." *Rural Problem Areas Survey Report No. 65,* January 14, 1935, 4.

U.S. General Accounting Office. *Meat and Poultry Better USDA Oversight and Enforcement of Safety Rules Needed to Reduce Risk of Foodborne Illnesses.* GAO-02-902. August 2002. www.gao.gov/new.items/d02902.pdf (last accessed April 11, 2007).

U.S. Government Accountability Office. *Safety in the Meat and Poultry Industry, While Improving, Could Be Further Strengthened.* GAO-05-96. January 2005. www.gao.gov/new.items/d0596.pdf (last accessed April 13, 2007).

U.S. District Court. Angela Goodwin, et al. v. Con Agra Poultry Company and Pilgrim's Pride, Incorporated. Civil Action No. 03-1187. Western District of Arkansas, El Dorado Division, 2003.

U.S. Supreme Court. Levy v. Louisiana, 391 U.S. 68 (1968).

White House, Office of the Press Secretary. "President Discusses Comprehensive Immigration Reform." April 24, 2006. www.whitehouse.gov/news/releases/2006/04/20060424–2.html (last accessed April 11, 2007).

———. "President Urges Senate to Pass Comprehensive Immigration Reform." April 5, 2006. www.whitehouse.gov/news/releases/2006/04/print/20060405 .html (last accessed April 11, 2007).

NEWSPAPERS AND MAGAZINES

Ames, Alexander. "Judge Criticized Tyson Guidelines." *Charlotte Observer,* February 13, 2008. www.charlotteobserver.com/2008/09/30/223458/judge-criticized-tyson-guidelines.html#ixzz1axl8moQs (last accessed November 30, 2011).

Behar, Richard. "Arkansas Pecking Order." *Time* 140, no. 17, October 26, 1992, 52–54.

Bischof, Tre. "Union Voters Crush Consolidation Plan." *Farmerville Gazette,* March 31, 2007.

Blum, Jordan. "Union School Board Puts Out Feelers for Consolidation Blueprint." *Monroe NewsStar,* September 22, 2006.

Bronstein, Scott. "USDA Eases Up on Plant Six Times—On-Line Inspectors Can't Slow Production." *Atlanta Journal-Constitution,* May 26, 1991.

———. "Chicken-How Safe? First of Two Parts." *Atlantic Journal-Constitution,* May 26, 1991.

Eilperin, Juliet. "Pollution in the Water, Lawsuits in the Air." *Washington Post,* August 28, 2006.

Fellone, Frank. "The Fate of the Chickens." *Arkansas Democrat-Gazette,* March 31, 1997.

"Firm Opens New Office." *El Dorado Evening Times,* June 12, 1964.

"Fumes Kill 2 in Food Vat." *New York Times,* April 30, 1984. A12.

Graff, E. J., and Evelyn Murphy. "The Skinny Pink Paycheck Syndrome." *Los Angeles Times,* February 12, 2006.

Grow, Brian. "A Body Blow to Illegal Labor?" *Businessweek* Online. www.businessweek.com/magazine/content/06_13/b3977087.htm (last accessed April 12, 2007).

Hall, Kerry, and Ames Alexander. "He Says His Agency Is at Fault." *Charlotte Observer,* June 25, 2010. www.charlotteobserver.com/2008/09/30/223430/he-says-his-agency-is-at-fault.html (last accessed December 4, 2011).

Hall, Kerry, Ames Alexander, and Franco Ordoñez. "The Cruelest Cuts." *Charlotte Observer,* February 10, 2008.

———. "Fight and Might." *Charlotte Observer,* February 11, 2008. www.charlotteobserver.com/2008/09/30/223442/fight-and-might.html (last accessed December 4, 2011).

Harton, Greg. "Shut Aliens Out." *Arkansas Democrat-Gazette,* June 8, 1997.

Horwitz, Tony. "9 to Nowhere: These Six Growth Jobs Are Dull, Dead-End, Sometimes Dangerous." *Wall Street Journal,* December 1, 1994.

Jordan, Miriam. "Blacks vs. Latinos at Work." *Wall Street Journal,* January 24, 2006.

"'Judge Coty' Is Given a Five-Year Sentence." *Farmerville Gazette,* April 11, 1934.

Katz, Jesse. "1000 Miles of Hope, Heartache." *Los Angeles Times,* November 10, 1996.

———. "New Migrant Trails Take Latinos to Remote Towns." *Los Angeles Times,* November 12, 2006.

"Local Poultry Plant Leased to Two Chicago Businessmen." *Town Talk,* October 23, 1954.

Leahy, Michael. "English Lessons." *Arkansas Democrat-Gazette.* March 26, 1997.

"The List of Industry Stars." *Fortune* 155, no. 5, March 19, 2007. http://money.cnn.com/magazines/fortune/fortune_archive/2007/03/19/8402372/index.htm (last accessed April 13, 2007).

Lostroh, Teresa, and Rachel Albin. "Laws Haven't Kept Deadly Pathogens Out of Meat, Poultry." *News21.* http://foodsafety.news21.com/2011/safety/inspection (last accessed December 4, 2011).

Morris, Tim. "Pilgrim's Pride to Idle Louisiana Chicken Plant." *NOLA.Com,* February 27, 2009. www.nola.com/news/index.ssf/2009/02/pilgrims_pride_to_shut_operati.html (last accessed November 30, 2011).

Morrison, Toni. "On the Backs of Blacks." *Time* 142, no. 3, December 2, 1993, 57.

Nash-Wood, Mary. "'Resurrected': Foster Farms Officially Takes Over Farmerville Poultry Plant." *Farmerville (Ark.) Gazette* July 15, 2009. www.fgazette.com/news.php?id=998 (last accessed November 30, 2011).

"Negro Killed by Officers When He Makes Resistance." *Farmerville Gazette,* November 22, 1933.

Ordoñez, Franco, Kerry Hall, and Ames Alexander. "Misery on the Line." *Charlotte Observer,* February 12, 2008.

Pearce, Rose Ann. "Programs for Migrants Help Pupils Assimilate." *Arkansas Democrat- Gazette,* May 8, 2000.

Perez, Evan, and Corey Dade. "Reversal of Fortune: An Immigration Raid Aids Blacks." *Wall Street Journal,* January 17, 2007.

"Pilgrim's Pride Completes Acquisition of Gold Kist." http://phx.corporate-ir.net/phoenix.zhtml?c=68228&p=irol-newsArticle&ID=948851&highlight= (last accessed April 13, 2007).

"Pilgrim's Pride Named to Fortune's 'Most Admired Companies' List for Fifth Consecutive Year." *Farmerville Gazette,* March 22, 2007.

Reinberg, Steven. "Salmonella Common in U.S. Poultry." *U.S. News and World Report,* January 23, 2009. http://health.usnews.com/health-news/family-health/childrens-health/articles/2009/01/23/salmonella-common-in-us-poultry (last accessed December 4, 2011).

Roberts, Stacey. "Pilgrim's Pride Closing El Dorado Site." *Arkansas Democrat Gazette,* February 28, 2009.

Rodman, Mike. "Northwest Wants Language Barrier to Add Up in School Formula." *Arkansas Democrat-Gazette,* June 2, 1994.

"Ruston Misses Poultry Plant Which Would Have Hired 75; Paid Growers $2 ¼ Million," *Ruston Daily Leader,* March 1, 1956.

Seid, Jessica. "Debate over the Jobs Americans 'Just Won't Do.'" CNNMoney.com, May 1, 2006.

Seid, Jessica. "Immigration Reform: No Ditches and Dirty Plates." CNNMoney.com, March 30, 2006.

Shiras, Tom. "Eggs by the Barrel." *Arkansas Gazette,* August 9, 1942.

"Simmons Celebrates 50 Years." *Partners,* University of Arkansas, Division of Agriculture, Center of Excellence for Poultry Science, 7, no. 2 (1999): 6.

Smith, David. "USDA Closes Unclean ConAgra Plant." *Arkansas Democrat-Gazette,* August 24, 2001.

"Sovereignty Commission Lists Aims." *Farmerville Gazette,* September 1, 1960.

St. Onge, Peter, Franco Ordoñez, Kerry Hall, and Ames Alexander. "An Epidemic of Pain." *Charlotte Observer,* February 10, 2008.

"State among Top Broiler Producers." *Arkansas Democrat,* June 24, 1951.

Stern, Mort. "Federal Poultry Chief Declares U of A Setting Pace in Research." *Arkansas Gazette,* June 17, 1951.

Sun, Lena H. "On Chicken's Front Line: High Volume and Repetition Test Workers' Endurance." *Washington Post,* November 28, 1999.

Susman, Tina. "New Orleans Cleanup Crews Remain Uncompensated." *Knight Ridder/Tribune Business News.* December 19, 2005.

"Sweetheart Terms." *Time* 71, no. 21, May 26, 1958. www.time.com/time/magazine/ article/0,9171,936895,00.html (last accessed April 11, 2007).Thames, Rick. "Poultry Series Exposes an New, Silent Subclass." *Charlotte Observer,* February 10, 2008.

Wiest, Jason. "Pilgrim's Pride Considering El Dorado Plant Closure; 1,620 Could Lose Jobs." *Arkansas News Bureau,* April 11, 2008.

OTHER PRIMARY SOURCES

"Agreement between United Food and Commercial Workers Union, Local 2008, and Pilgrim's Pride Corporation, El Dorado, AR." March 1, 2004.

Berry, Barbara of Tyson Foods from Transcript of "Immigrant Influx." *News Hour with Jim Lehrer.* Broadcast, February 16, 1998. www.pbs.org/newshour/bb/ race_relations/jan-june98/arkansas_2-16.html (accessed November 30, 2011).

Capps, Randolph, Michael E. Fix, Jeffrey S. Passel, Jason Ost, and Dan Perez-Lopez. *A Profile of the Low-Wage Immigrant Workforce.* Brief No. 4: *Immigrant Families and Workers: Facts and Perspectives Series,* Urban Institute, October 2003, 5–6.

Catholic Bishops of the South. "Voices and Choices: A Pastoral Letter from the Catholic Bishops of the South." November 15, 2000. *www.americancatholic.org/ News*/PoultryPastoral/english.asp (last accessed April 11, 2007).

City of El Dorado, Arkansas, Chamber of Commerce. "An Economy That Manufactures Growth, among Other Things," http://boomtown.org/work.aspx (last accessed April 15, 2007).

El Dorado League of Women Voters. *El Dorado: Where Oil Flows and Soft Pine Grows.* N.p.: 1958.

Foster Farms. "Foster Farms Earns Trade and Industry Development Magazine's CiCi Community Impact Award." Press Release, March 12, 2009. www.fosterfarms

.com/about/press/press_release.asp?press_release_id=111 (last accessed November 30, 2011).

Gordon, Jennifer, and R. A. Lenhardt. "Conflict and Solidarity between African American and Latino Immigrant Workers." Prepared for the Chief Justice Earl Warren Institute on Race, Ethnicity, and Diversity. University of California, Berkeley, School of Law, November 30, 2007. https://www.law.berkeley.edu/files/GordonLenhardtpaperNov30.pdf (last accessed November 20, 2014).

Human Rights Watch. "Blood, Sweat, and Fear: Workers' Rights in U.S. Meat and Poultry Plants." January 2005. www.hrw.org/reports/2005/usa0105/usa0105.pdf (last accessed October 18, 2011).

Jones, Jean W., ed. *I Remember Life in Union Parish, 1910–1960.* Farmerville, La.: Union Parish Council on Aging, 2004.

Kochhar, Rakesh. "Growth in the Foreign-Born Workforce and Employment of the Native Born." Report for the Pew Hispanic Center, August 10, 2006. http://pewhispanic.org/files/ reports/69.pdf (last accessed April 12, 2007).

Kockhar, Rakesh, Roberto Suro, and Sonya Tafoya. "The New Latino South: The Context and Consequences of Rapid Population Growth." Report prepared for the Pew Hispanic Center, 26 July 2005. http://pewhispanic.org/files/reports/50.pdf (last accessed April 11, 2007).

Lewis, Jim. "Delmarva Poultry Justice Alliance." www.familyfarmer.org/conference/lewis.html (last accessed August 21, 2013).

———. "Grasshopper Power." In *Workers' Rights as Human Rights,* edited by James Gross. Ithaca, N.Y.: ILR Press, 2003.

Lord, Linda. Interviews by Cedric Chatterley and Stephen Cole. In *"I Was Content and Not Content": The Story of Linda Lord and the Closing of Penobscot Poultry,* by Cedric N. Chatterley and Alicia J. Rouverol, with Stephen A. Cole. Carbondale: Southern Illinois University Press, 2000.

LSUAgCenter.com. "Louisiana Poultry Industry Major Economic Factor." www.lsuagcenter.com/en/crops_livestock/livestock/poultry/Broiler+Production/Louisiana+Poultry+Industry+Major+Economic+Factor.htm (last accessed September 26, 2011).

Mabry, R. B. Interview by J. T. Baldwin. In "'Three Apples for a Dime,' and Other Recollections of the Early Days of Bernice." *North Louisiana Historical Association Journal* 4, no. 2 (Winter 1973): 64–68.

Malakoff, Robert. *Arkansas' Strike Record, 1947–57 . . . with National and Regional Comparisons.* University of Arkansas, College of Business, Administration, Industrial Research and Extension Center, 1959.

McNeil, John, and Felix Stanley. *Organizational Problems on Small Farms in North Louisiana Upland Cotton Area.* Department of Agricultural Economics and Agribusiness, Louisiana State University and Agricultural and Mechanical

College, Lithographed Circular No. 147. Baton Rouge: Louisiana State University Press, 1953.

Moody, Anne. *Coming of Age in Mississippi.* New York: Dell, 1968.

Moody, Kim. *An Injury to All: The Decline of American Trade Unionism.* London: Verso, 1988.

National Planning Association (NPA). *New Industry Comes to the South.* NPA Committee of the South Reports, Report No. 1. Washington, D.C.: National Publishing Co., 1949.

Passel, Jeffrey. "Unauthorized Migrants: Numbers and Characteristics." Report prepared for the Pew Hispanic Center, June 14, 2005. http://pewhispanic.org/files/reports/46.pdf (last accessed April 11, 2007).

Pew Hispanic Center. "Hispanic Attitudes toward Learning English." Fact Sheet, June 7, 2006. http://pewhispanic.org/files/ factsheets/20.pdf (last accessed April 12, 2007).

———. "The State of American Public Opinion on Immigration in Spring 2006: A Review of Major Surveys." May 17, 2006.http://pewhispanic.org/files/factsheets/18.pdf (last accessed April 12, 2007).

Pilgrim, Bo. *One Pilgrim's Progress: How to Build a World-Class Company and Who to Credit.* Nashville: Thomas Nelson Publishers, 2005.

Pilgrim's Pride. "Continuous Improvement." www.pilgrimspride.com/aboutus/continuousimprovement.aspx (last accessed April 13, 2007).

Pilgrim's Pride Corporation. *Pilgrim's Pride: Shared Values and Behaviors.* Pittsburg, Tex.: Pilgrim's Pride Corp., 2005.

Public Justice Center. *The Disposable Workforce: A Worker's Perspective—A Documentation Study of Working Conditions in Delmarva Poultry Processing Plants.* Report. Baltimore, Md., n.d. *www.upc-online.org/workers/Poultrystudy.pdf* (January 22, 2014).

Suro, Roberto. "Remittance Senders and Receivers: Tracking the Transnational Channels." Report prepared for the Pew Hispanic Center, November 24, 2003. *http://pewhispanic* .org/files/reports/23.pdf (last accessed April 12, 2007).

Wales, Don. "History of Pilgrim's Pride—El Dorado Complex." Speech presented to the El Dorado Chamber of Commerce. El Dorado, Ark., April 2005.

West's *Louisiana Statutes Annotated.* Revised Statutes. LSA-R.S. 14:1 and 45:1131–46:970. *www.legis.state.la.us/.*

SECONDARY SOURCES

Abramovitz, Mimi. *Regulating the Lives of Women: Social Welfare Policy from Colonial Times to the Present.* Rev. ed. Boston: South End Press, 1996.

Ahmed, Z. Z., and Mark Sieling. "Two Decades of Productivity Growth in Poultry Dressing and Processing." *Monthly Labor Review* 110 (April 1987): 34–39.

Aho, Paul, and Allan Rahn. "Broilers in the Midwest?" *Broiler Industry* (January 1989): 75.

Alexander, Charles C. *The Ku Klux Klan in the Southwest.* Norman: University of Oklahoma Press, 1995.

Allen, Theodore. *The Invention of the White Race.* Vol. 1: *Racial Oppression and Social Control.* New York: Verso, 1994.

Anderson, Bridget. *Doing the Dirty Work? The Global Politics of Domestic Labor.* New York: St. Martin's Press, 2000.

Anderson, Eugene, and Steven Shugan. "Repositioning for Changing Preferences: The Case of Beef versus Poultry." *Journal of Consumer Research* 18 (1991): 219–32.

Anderson, Karen Tucker. "Last Hired, First Fired: Black Women Workers during World War II." *Journal of American History* 69 (1982): 82–97.

Anzaldúa, Gloria. "Speaking in Tongues: A Letter to Third World Women Writers." In *Women Writing Resistance,* edited by Jennifer Browdy de Hernandez, 83–84. Cambridge, Mass.: South End Press, 2005.

Armstrong, T. J., J. A. Foulke, B. S. Joseph, and S. A. Goldstein. "Investigation of Cumulative Trauma Disorders in a Poultry Processing Plant." *American Industrial Hygiene Association Journal* 43 (1982): 103–16.

Arnesen, Eric. "A. Philip Randolph, Black Anticommunism, and the Race Question." In *Rethinking U.S. Labor History: Essays on the Working-Class Experience, 1756–2009,* edited by Donna T. Haverty-Stacke and Daniel J. Walkowitz, 137–67. New York: Continuum, 2010.

———. "Following the Color Line of Labor: Black Workers and the Labor Movement before 1930." *Radical History Review* 55 (1993): 53–87.

Arnold, George, and Shea Hutchens Wilson. *Then and Now: A Guide to Historic Union County.* El Dorado: News-Times Publishing Co., 1994.

Baldwin, Jack, and Winnie Baldwin. "The Old Shiloh Black School: A One-Room Landmark." Collection No. M248, box 1, folder 2, LTU Special Collections.

Barbash, Jack. "Trade Unionism from Roosevelt to Reagan." *Annals of the American Academy of Political and Social Science: The Future of American Unionism* 473 (1984): 11–22.

Barkan, Elliott. "Return of the Nativists? California Public Opinion and Immigration in the 1980s and 1990s." *Social Science History* 27, no. 2 (2003): 229–83.

Barrett, James R., and David R. Roediger. "The Irish and the 'Americanization' of the 'New Immigrants' in the Streets and in the Churches of the Urban United States, 1900–1930." *Journal of American Ethnic History* 24 (2005): 4–33.

Barry, John. "After the Deluge." *Smithsonian* 36, no. 8 (2005): 114–21.

———. *Rising Tide: The Great Mississippi Flood of 1927 and How It Changed America.* New York: Simon & Schuster, 1997.

Bartley, Numan. *The New South, 1945–1980.* Baton Rouge: Louisiana State University Press, 1995.

Bates, Beth Tompkins. *Pullman Porters and the Rise of Protest Politics in Black America, 1925–1945.* Chapel Hill: University of North Carolina Press, 2001.

Bell, Winifred. *Aid to Dependent Children.* New York: Columbia University Press, 1963.

Bender, Stephen. *Greasers and Gringos: Latinos, Law, and the American Imagination.* New York: New York University Press, 2003.

Bennett, D. Gordon. "Population Change and Mobility A Case Study of an Arkansas State Economic Area." *Land Economics* 46 (1970): 206–8.

Beauboeuf-Lafontant, Tamara. "Keeping Up Appearances, Getting Fed Up: The Embodiment of Strength among African American Women." *Meridians* 5 (2005): 108.

Berk, Sarah. *The Gender Factory: The Apportionment of Work in American Households.* New York: Plenum Press, 1985.

Bernstein, Iver. *The New York City Draft Riots: Their Significance for American Society and Politics in the Age of the Civil War.* New York: Oxford University Press, 1990.

Betts, Julian R. "Educational Crowding Out: Do Immigrants Affect the Educational Attainment of American Minorities?" In *Help or Hindrance? The Economic Implications of Immigration for African Americans,* edited by Daniel Hamermesh and Frank Bean, 253–81. New York: Russell Sage Foundation, 1998.

Blevins, Brook. *Hill Folks: A History of Arkansas Ozarkers and Their Image.* Chapel Hill: University of North Carolina Press, 2002.

Bolton, S. Charles. "Turning Point: World War II and the Economic Development of Arkansas." *Arkansas Historical Quarterly,* 61, no. 2 (2002): 123–51.

Borjas, George J. "Do Blacks Gain or Lose from Immigration?" In *Help or Hindrance? The Economic Implications of Immigration for African Americans,* edited by Daniel Hamermesh and Frank Bean, 51–74. New York: Russell Sage Foundation, 1998.

Borjas, George J., Richard B. Freeman, and Lawrence F. Katz. "Searching for the Effect of Immigration on the Labor Market." *American Economic Review,* Papers and Proceedings of the Hundredth and Eighth Annual Meeting of the American Economic Association, San Francisco, January 5–7, 1996, 86, no. 2 (1996): 246–51.

Boyd, William. "Science, Technology, and American Poultry Production." *Technology and Culture* 42 (2001): 631–64.

Boyd, William, and Michael Watts. "Agro-Industrial Just-in-Time: The Chicken Industry and Post War American Capitalism." In *Globalising Food: Agrarian Questions and Global Restructuring,* edited by David Goodman and Michael Watts, 192–225. New York: Routledge, 1997.

Branch, Enobong Hannah. *Opportunity Denied: Limiting Black Women to Devalued Work.* New Brunswick, N.J.: Rutgers University Press, 2011.

Brattain, Michelle. *The Politics of Whiteness: Race, Workers, and Culture in the Modern South.* Princeton: Princeton University Press, 2001.

Briggs, Vernon. *Mass Immigration and the National Interest: Policy Directions for the New Century.* Armonk, N.Y.: M. E. Sharpe, 2003.

Brimelow, Peter. *Alien Nation: Common Sense about America's Immigration Disaster.* New York: Random House, 1995.

Broadway, Michael J. "From City to Countryside: Recent Changes in the Structure and Location of Meat- and Fish-Processing Industries." In *Any Way You Cut It: Meat Processing and Small Town America,* edited by Donald D. Stull, Michael J. Broadway, and David Griffith, 17–40. Lawrence: University Press of Kansas, 1995.

Broadway, Michael J., and Donald D. Stull. "Killing Them Softly: Work in Meatpacking Plants and What It Does to Workers." In *Any Way You Cut It: Meat Processing and Small-Town America,* edited by Donald D. Stull, Michael J. Broadway, and David Griffith, 61–84. Lawrence: University of Kansas Press, 1995.

Brody, David. *The Butcher Workmen: A Study of Unionization.* Cambridge: Harvard University Press, 1964.

———. *Labor Embattled: History. Power. Rights.* Urbana: University of Illinois Press, 2005.

Broughton, Chad. "Reforming Poor Women: The Cultural Politics and Practices of Welfare Reform." *Qualitative Sociology 26* (Spring 2003): 35–51.

Brown, Elsa Barkley. "Womanist Consciousness: Maggie Lena Walker and the Independent Order of St. Luke." *Signs* 14 (1989): 610–33.

Browne, Irene, ed. *Latinas and African American Women at Work: Race Gender and Economic Inequality.* New York: Russell Sage Foundation, 1999.

Brown, Irene, and Ivy Kennelly. "Stereotypes and Realities: Images of Black Women in the Labor Market." In *Latinas and African American Women at Work: Race Gender and Economic Inequality,* edited by Irene Brown, 302–26. New York: Russell Sage Foundation, 1999.

Buckalew, A. R., and R. B. Buckalew. "The Discovery of Oil in South Arkansas: 1920–1924." *Arkansas Historical Quarterly* 33 (Fall 1974): 195–238.

Buhle, Paul. *Taking Care of Business: Samuel Gompers, George Meany, Lane Kirkland, and the Tragedy of American Labor.* New York: Monthly Review Press, 1999

Bussel, Robert. "Taking on 'Big Chicken': The Delmarva Poultry Justice Alliance." *Labor Studies Journal* 28 (2003): 1–24.

Cable, C. Curtis. *Growth of the Arkansas Broiler Industry.* Arkansas Agricultural Experiment Station, Bulletin 520. Fayetteville: University of Arkansas, April 1952.

Cafferty, Pastora San Juan. "The Language Question." In *Hispanics in the United States: An Agenda for the 21st Century,* edited by Pastora San Juan Cafferty and David W. Engstrom, 69–96. New Brunswick, N.J.: Transaction Publishers, 2000.

Calavita, Kitty. "The Demise of the Occupational Safety and Health Administration: A Case Study in Symbolic Action." *Social Problems* 30 (1983): 437–48.

———. "The New Politics of Immigration: 'Balanced Budget Conservatism' and the Symbolism of Proposition 187." *Social Problems* 43 (1996): 284–305.

Cameron, Christopher David Ruiz. "Labryinth of Solidarity: Why the Future of American Labor Movement Depends on Latino Workers." 53 *University of Miami Law Review* 1089 (1999).

Capps, Randolph, Michael E. Fix, Jeffrey S. Passel, Jason Ost, and Dan Perez-Lopez. *A Profile of the Low-Wage Immigrant Workforce*. Brief No. 4. *Immigrant Families and Workers: Facts and Perspectives Series*. Urban Institute. October 2003, 5–6.

Card, David. "The Impact of the Mariel Boatlift on the Miami Labor Market." *Industrial and Labor Relations Review* 43, no. 2 (1990): 245–57.

Carroll, Thomas. "Right-to-Work Laws Do Matter." *Southern Economic Journal* 50 (1983): 494–509.

Cash, W. J. *The Mind of the South*. New York: Vintage Books, 1941.

Cayton, Horace R., and George S Mitchell. *Black Workers and the New Unions*. Chapel Hill: University of North Carolina Press, 1939.

Chamberlain, Charles. *Victory at Home: Manpower and Race in the American South during World War II*. Athens: University Press of Georgia, 2003.

Chiswick, Barry R., and Michael E. Hurst. "Hispanics in the American Labor Market." In *Hispanics in the United States: An Agenda for the 21st Century*, edited by Pastora San Juan Cafferty and David W. Engstrom, 175–94. New Brunswick, N.J.: Transaction Publishers, 2000.

Cobb, James C. *The Selling of the South: The Southern Crusade for Industrial Development, 1936–1980*. 2nd ed. Urbana: University of Illinois Press, 1993.

Cobb, Russell. "The Chicken Hangers." *In the Fray*, February 1, 2004. www.inthe fray.com/html/article.php?sid=208 (last accessed November 14, 2011).

Cobble, Dorothy Sue. *The Other Women's Movement: Workplace Justice and Social Rights in Modern America*. Princeton: Princeton University Press, 2004.

———. "Rethinking Troubled Relations between Women and Unions: Craft Unions and Female Activism." *Feminist Studies* 16 (1990): 519–48.

Cohen, Lizabeth. *Making a New Deal: Industrial Workers in Chicago, 1919–1939*. New York: Cambridge University Press, 1990.

Cook, Alice, with Val R. Lorwin and Arlene Kaplan Daniels. *The Most Difficult Revolution: Women and Trade Unions*. Ithaca, N.Y.: ILR Press, 1992.

Cordell, Anna Harmon. *Dates and Data of Union County Arkansas, 1541–1948*. Monroe, La.: Century Printing & Publishing, 1984.

———. "El Dorado: Place of Riches." *Arkansas State Magazine* (Spring 1967): 32–37.

Crain, Marion, and Ken Matheny. "Labor's Identity Crisis." *California Law Review* 89 (2001): 1767–1846.

Cromer, Linda. "Plucking Cargill: The RWDSU in Georgia." *Labor Research Review* 9 (1990): 15–23.

Daniel, Pete. *Breaking the Land: The Transformation of Cotton, Tobacco, and Rice Cultures since 1880*. Urbana: University of Illinois Press, 1985.

——. *Lost Revolutions: The South in the 1950s.* Chapel Hill: University of North Carolina Press, 2000.

Daniels, Roger. *Guarding the Golden Door: American Immigration Policy and Immigrants since 1882.* New York: Hill & Wang, 2004.

Davis, Angela. "Reflections on the Black Woman's Role in the Community of Slaves." *Black Scholar* 3 (1971): 3–15.

Davis, Mike. *Prisoners of the American Dream: Politics and Economy in the History of the U.S. Working Class.* London k: Verso, 1986.

De Jong, Greta. *A Different Day: African American Struggles for Justice in Rural Louisiana, 1900–1970.* Chapel Hill: University of North Carolina Press, 2002.

De Leon, Arnoldo. *Ethnicity in the Sunbelt: Mexican Americans in Houston.* College Station: Texas A&M Press, 2001.

Devine, Tom. "The Fox Guarding the Henhouse." "Ruling the Roost: A Special Report on the Poultry Industry." *Southern Exposure* 17 (1989): 39–42.

Dill, Bonnie Thornton. "'The Means to Put My Children Through': Child-Rearing Goals and Strategies among Black Female Domestic Servants." In *The Black Woman,* edited by LaFrances Rodgers-Rose, 107–23. Beverly Hills, Calif.: Sage Publications, 1980.

Donato, Katherine M., Carl L. Bankston, and Dawn T. Robinson. "Immigration and the Organization of the Onshore Oil Industry: Southern Louisiana in the Late 1990s." In *Latino Workers in the Contemporary South,* edited by Arthur D. Murphy, Colleen Blanchard, and Jennifer A. Hill, 105–13. Athens,: University of Georgia Press, 2001.

Douglass, Harrison. "Farm Practices in Animal Husbandry among Negro Farmers in Union Parish, Louisiana." Master's thesis, Iowa State College, 1942.

Douty, Esther. "FERA and the Rural Negro." *Survey* 70, no. 7 (1934): 215–16.

Draper, Alan. "Brown v. Board of Education and Organized Labor in the South." *Historian* 57 (1994): 75–88.

——. *Conflict of Interests: Organized Labor and the Civil Rights Movements in the South, 1954–1968.* Ithaca, N.Y.: ILR Press, 1994.

Duany, Jorge. "Reconstructing Racial Identity: Ethnicity, Color, and Class among Dominicans in the United States and Puerto Rico." *Latin American Perspectives* 25 (May 1998): 147–72.

Duffy, Mignon, "Doing the Dirty Work: Gender, Race, and Reproductive Labor in Historical Perspective." *Gender and Society* 21 (2007): 313–36.

Ellwood, David, and Glenn Fine. "The Impact of Right-to-Work Laws on Union Organizing." *Journal of Political Economy* 95 (1987): 250–73.

Engstrom, David. "Hispanic Immigration at the New Millennium." In *Hispanics in the United States,* edited by Pastora San Juan Cafferty and David W. Engstrom, 31–68. New Brunswick, N.J.: Transaction Publishers, 2000.

Engstrom, James. "Industry and Immigration in Dalton, Georgia." In *Latino Workers in the Contemporary South,* edited by Arthur D. Murphy, Colleen Blanchard, and Jennifer A. Hill, 44–56. Athens: University of Georgia Press, 2001.

Erwin, Deborah O. "An Ethnographic Description of Latino Immigration in Rural Arkansas: Intergroup Relations and Utilization of Healthcare Services." *Southern Rural Sociology* 19 (2003): 46–72.

Evans, Dennis. "A Study of Relative Quality of Life in Selected Louisiana Parishes." Ed.D. diss., Louisiana State University, 1974.

Fahy, Joe. "All Pain, No Gain." "Ruling the Roost: A Special Report on the Poultry Industry." *Southern Exposure* 17 (1989): 34–38.

Fairclough, Adam. *Race and Democracy: The Civil Rights Struggle in Louisiana, 1915–1972.* Athens: University of Georgia Press, 1995.

Fanon, Frantz. *Black Skin, White Masks.* Translated by Charles Lam Markmann. New York: Grove Press, 1991.

Fantasia, Rick, and Kim Voss. *Hard Work: Remaking the American Labor Movement.* Berkeley: University of California Press, 2004.

Faue, Elizabeth. *Community of Suffering and Struggle: Women, Men, and the Labor Movement in Minneapolis, 1915–1945.* Chapel Hill: University of North Carolina Press, 1991.

Fehn, Bruce. "African-American Women and the Struggle for Equality in the Meatpacking Industry, 1940–1960." *Journal of Women's History* 10 (1998): 45–69.

———. "Chickens Come Home to Roost: Industrial Reorganization, Seniority, and Gender Conflict in the United Packinghouse Workers of America, 1956–1966." *Labor History* 34 (1993): 324–41.

Fenton, John. "The Negro Voter in Louisiana." *Journal of Negro Education* 26 (1957): 319–28.

Fineman, Martha L. "Images of Mothers in Poverty Discourses," *Duke Law Journal,* no. 2 (April 1991): 274–95.

Fink, Deborah. *Cutting into the Meatpacking Line: Workers and Change in the Rural Midwest.* Chapel Hill: University of North Carolina Press, 1998.

Fink, Leon. *The Maya of Morganton: Work and Community in the Nuevo New South.* Chapel Hill: University of North Carolina Press, 2003.

Fite, Gilbert. *Cotton Fields No More: Southern Agriculture, 1985–1980.* Lexington: University Press of Kentucky, 1984.

Fix, Michael, and Jeffrey Passel. "Assessing Welfare Reform's Immigrant Provisions." In *Welfare Reform: The Next Act,* edited by Alan Weil and Kenneth Finegold, 179–202. Washington, D.C.: Urban Institute Press, 2002.

Fix, Michael, and Jeffrey Passel, with María E. Enchautegui and Wendy Zimmermann. *Immigration and Immigrants: Setting the Record Straight.* Washington, D.C.: Urban Institute, 1994.

Fletcher, Bill, and Fernando Gaspain. *Solidarity Divided: The Crisis in Organized Labor and a New Path toward Social Justice.* Berkeley: University of California Press, 2008.

Foley, Neil. *The White Scourge: Mexicans, Blacks, and Poor Whites in Texas Cotton Culture.* Berkeley: University of California Press, 1997.

Foner, Philip. *Organized Labor and the Black Worker, 1619–1981.* 2nd ed. New York: International Publishers, 1982.

Fraser, Nancy, and Linda Gordon. "'Dependency Demystified': Inscriptions of Power in a Keyword of the Welfare State." *Social Politics* 1(1994): 4–31.

Frystak, Shannon. *Our Minds on Freedom: Women and the Struggle for Black Equality in Louisiana, 1924–1967.* Baton Rouge: Louisiana State University Press, 2009.

Gay, Claudine. "Seeing Difference: The Effect of Economic Disparity on Black Attitudes toward Latinos." *American Journal of Political Science* 50 (2006): 982–97.

Gentry, Jonathan. "'Christ Is Out, Communism Is On': Opposition to the Congress of Industrial Organizations' 'Operation Dixie' in South Carolina, 1946–1951." *Proceedings of the South Carolina Historical Association,* 2003.

Gerstle, Gary. "Liberty, Coercion, and the Making of Americans." *Journal of American History* 84 (1997): 524–58.

———. *Working-Class Americanism: The Politics of Labor in a Textile City, 1914–1960.* New York: Cambridge University Press, 1989.

Giardina, Denise, and Eric Bates. "Fowling the Nest." "Ruling the Roost: A Special Report on the Poultry Industry." *Southern Exposure* 17 (1989): 10–12.

Gibbs, Jewelle, and Teiahsha Bankhead. *Preserving Privilege: California Politics, Propositions, and People of Color.* Westport, Conn.: Praeger, 2001.

Giddings, Paula. *When and Where I Enter: The Impact of Black Women on Race and Sex in America.* New York: Morrow, 1984.

Gilje, Paul. *The Road to Mobocracy: Popular Disorder in New York City, 1763–1834.* Chapel Hill: University of North Carolina Press, 1987.

Gilkes, Cheryl Townsend. "'Liberated to Work like Dogs!' Labeling Black Women and Their Work." In *The Experience and Meaning of Work in Women's Lives,* edited by Hildreth Y. Grossman and Nia Lane Chester, 165–88. London: Psychology Press, 1989.

Gilmore, Glenda. *Gender and Jim Crow: Women and the Politics of White Supremacy in North Carolina, 1896–1920.* Chapel Hill: University of North Carolina Press, 1996.

Gisolfi, Monica. "From Cotton Farmers to Poultry Growers: The Rise of Industrial Agriculture in Upcountry Georgia, 1914–1960." Ph.D. diss., Columbia University, 2007.

———. "From Crop Lien to Contract Farming: The Roots of Agribusiness in the American South, 1929–1939." *Agricultural History* 80 (April 2006): 167–89.

———. "Leaving the Farm to Save the Farm: The Poultry Industry and the Problem of 'Public Work': 1950–1970." In *Migration and the Transformation of the South-*

ern Workplace since 1945, edited by Robert Cassanello and Colin Davis, 64–79. Gainesville: University Press of Florida, 2009.

Goldfield, David. *Cotton Fields and Skyscrapers: Southern City and Region, 1607–1980.* Baton Rouge: Louisiana State University Press, 1982.

Goldoftas, Barbara. "Inside the Slaughterhouse." "Ruling the Roost: A Special Report on the Poultry Industry." *Southern Exposure* 17 (1989): 25–29.

Gordon, Linda. "Family Violence, Feminism, and Social Control." *Feminist Studies* 12 (1986): 452–78.

———. *Pitied but Not Entitled: Single Mothers and the History of Welfare.* Cambridge: Harvard University Press, 1994.

Gouveia, Lourdes. "Global Strategies and Local Linkages: The Case of the U.S. Meatpacking Industries." In *From Columbus to ConAgra: The Globalization of Agriculture and Food,* edited by Alessandro Bonanno, Lawrence Busch, William H. Friedland, Lourdes Gouveia, and Enzo Mingione, 125–48. Lawrence: University Press of Kansas, 1994.

Gouveia, Lourdes, and Donald D. Stull. "Dances with Cows: Beefpacking's Impact on Garden City, KS and Lexington, NE." In *Any Way You Cut It: Meat Processing and Small Town America,* edited by Donald D. Stull, Michael J. Broadway, and David Griffith, 85–108. Lawrence: University Press of Kansas, 1995.

Grabowski, Anita. *Organizing for Change: Labor Organizers and Latin American Poultry Workers.* A Report of the Poultry Worker Justice Research Project Inter-American Policy Studies Occasional Paper No. 3. Sponsored by the Equal Justice Center, Austin, Tex., and the Inter-American Policy Studies Program, University of Texas at Austin, 2003.

Gray-White, Deborah. *Ar'n't I a Woman? Female Slaves in the Plantation South.* Rev. ed. New York: Norton, 1999.

———. *Too Heavy a Load: Black Women in Defense of Themselves, 1894–1994.* New York: Norton, 1999.

Green, George N. "The Texas 'Sick Chicken' Strike, 1950s." *East Texas Historical Association* 26 (1988): 14–30.

Green, James. *World of the Worker.* New York: Hill & Wang, 1980.

Grey, Mark. "Pork, Poultry, and Newcomers in Storm Lake, Iowa." In *Any Way You Cut It: Meat Processing and Small Town America,* edited by Donald D. Stull, Michael J. Broadway, and David Griffith, 109–28. Lawrence: University Press of Kansas, 1995.

Griffith, Barbara. *The Crisis of American Labor: Operation Dixie and the Defeat of the CIO.* Philadelphia: Temple University Press, 1988.

Griffith, David. "*Hay Trabajo:* Poultry Processing, Rural Industrialization, and the Latinization of Low-Wage Labor." In *Any Way You Cut It: Meat Processing and Small Town America,* edited by Donald D. Stull, Michael J. Broadway, and David Griffith, 129–52. Lawrence: University Press of Kansas, 1995.

———. *Jones's Minimal: Low-Wage Labor in the United States.* Albany: State University of New York Press, 1993.

Griffith, David, and David Runsten. "The Impact of the 1986 Immigration Reform and Control Act on the U.S. Poultry Industry: A Comparative Analysis." *Policy Studies Review* 11 (1992): 118–30.

Griffith, David, Michael J. Broadway, and Donald D. Stull. "Introduction: Making Meat." In *Any Way You Cut It: Meat Processing and Small Town America,* edited by Donald D. Stull, Michael J. Broadway, and David Griffith, 1–16. Lawrence: University Press of Kansas, 1995.

Gross, Leonard. "Are We Paying an Illegitimacy Bonus?" *Saturday Evening Post,* January 30, 1960, 30.

Grubbs, Donald. *Cry from the Cotton: The Southern Tenant Farmers' Union and the New Deal.* Chapel Hill: University of North Carolina Press, 1971.

Guthey, Greig. "Mexican Places in Southern Spaces: Globalization, Work, and Daily Life in and around the North Georgia Poultry Industry." In *Latino Workers in the Contemporary South,* edited by Arthur D. Murphy, Colleen Blanchard, and Jennifer A. Hill, 57–67. Athens: University of Georgia Press, 2001.

Hackenberg, Robert A. "Joe Hill Died for Your Sins: Empowering Minority Workers in the New Industrial Workforce." In *Any Way You Cut It: Meat Processing and Small Town America,* edited by Donald D. Stull, Michael J. Broadway, and David Griffith, 231–64. Lawrence: University Press of Kansas, 1995.

Hall, Bob. "Chicken Empires." *Southern Exposure* 17 (1989): 15.

———. "The Kill Line: Facts of Life, Proposals for Change." In *Any Way You Cut It: Meat Processing and Small Town America,* edited by Donald D. Stull, Michael J. Broadway, and David Griffith, 213–30. Lawrence: University Press of Kansas, 1995.

Halpern, Rick. *Down on the Killing Floor: Black and White Workers in Chicago's Packinghouses, 1904–1954.* Urbana: University of Illinois Press, 1997.

———. "Organized Labor, Black Workers, and the Twentieth Century South: The Emerging Revision." In *Race and Class in the American South since 1890,* edited by Melvyn Stokes and Rick Halpern, 43–76. Oxford: Berg Publishers, 1994.

Halpern, Rick and Roger Horowitz. *Meatpackers: An Oral History of Black Packinghouse Workers and Their Struggle for Racial and Economic Equality.* New York: Twayne Publishers, 1996.

Hamermesh, Daniel. "Immigration and the Quality of Jobs." In *Help or Hindrance? The Economic Implications of Immigration for African Americans,* edited by Daniel Hamermesh and Frank Bean, 75–106. New York: Russell Sage Foundation, 1998.

Hamilton, C. H. "The Sociology of a Changing Agriculture." *Social Forces* 37 (1958): 1–7.

Harley, Sharon. "For the Good of Family and Race: Gender, Work, and Domestic Roles in the Black Community, 1880–1930." *Signs* 15 (1990): 336–49.

———. "When Your Work Is Not Who You Are: The Development of Working Class Consciousness among Afro-American Women." In *Gender, Class, Race and Re-*

form in the Progressive Era, edited by Noralee Frankel and Nancy Dye, 42–55. Lexington: University Press of Kentucky, 1991.

———. "'Working for Nothing but for a Living': Black Women in the Underground Economy." In *Sister Circle: Black Women and Work,* edited by Sharon Harley and the Black Women and Work Collective, 48–66. New Brunswick, N.J.: Rutgers University Press, 2002.

Harris-Lacewell, Melissa. "No Place to Rest: African American Political Attitudes and the Myth of Black Women's Strength." *Women & Politics* 23 (2001): 1–33.

Harris-Perry, Melissa V. *Sister Citizen: Shame, Stereotypes, and Black Women in America.* New Haven: Yale University Press, 2011.

Harris, William H. "Federal Intervention in Union Discrimination: FEPC and West Coast Shipyards during World War II." *Labor History* 22 (1981): 325–47.

Hartwell, Albion. "The Need of Social and Unemployment Insurance for Negroes." *Journal of Negro Education* 5 (1936): 79–87.

Harvey, David. *Justice, Nature, and the Geography of Difference.* Cambridge, Mass.: Blackwell Publishers, 1996.

Hattam, Victoria. *Labor Visions and State Power: The Origins of Business Unionism in the United States.* Princeton: Princeton University Press, 1993.

Haverluk, Terrence W. "Hispanization of Hereford." In *Latino Workers in the Contemporary South,* edited by Arthur D. Murphy, Colleen Blanchard, and Jennifer A. Hill, 277–91. Athens: University of Georgia Press, 2001.

Heffernan, William D. "Constraints in the U.S. Poultry Industry." *Research in Rural Sociology and Development* 1 (1984): 237–60.

Heffernan, William D., and Douglas H. Constance. "Transnational Corporations and the Globalization of the Food System." In *From Columbus to ConAgra: The Globalization of Agriculture and Food,* edited by Alessandro Bonanno, Lawrence Busch, William H. Friedland, Lourdes Gouveia, and Enzo Mingione, 29–51. Lawrence: University Press of Kansas, 1994.

Helton, Laura. *Three Hundred Strangers Next Door: Native Mississippians Respond to Immigration.* A Report of the Poultry Worker Justice Research Project, Inter-American Policy Studies Occasional Paper No. 4. Sponsored by the Equal Justice Center, Austin, Tex., and the Inter-American Policy Studies Program, University of Texas at Austin, 2003.

Henwood, Doug. "A Nation of (Yesterday's) Immigrants." *Left Business Observer,* no. 113 (2006). www.leftbusinessobserver.com/Immigration.html (last accessed April 12, 2007).

Herndon, Dallas T. *Centennial History of Arkansas.* Vol. 2. Chicago: S. J. Clarke, 1922.

Hessing, Melody. "More than Clockwork: Women's Time Management in Their Combined Workloads." *Sociological Perspectives* 37 (1994): 611–33.

Higginbotham, Evelyn. *Righteous Discontent: The Women's Movement in the Black Baptist Church, 1880–1920.* Cambridge: Harvard University Press, 1993.

Higham, John. *Strangers in the Land: Patterns of American Nativism.* 2nd ed. New Brunswick, N.J.: Rutgers University Press, 1988.

Hill, Herbert. "Anti-Oriental Agitation and the Rise of Working-Class Racism." *Society* 10 (1973): 43–54.

———. "The Problem of Race in American Labor History." *Reviews in American History* 24 (1996): 189–208.

———. "Recent Effects of Racial Conflict on Southern Industrial Development." *Phylon Quarterly* 20 (1959): 319–26.

Hill Collins, Patricia. *Black Feminist Thought: Knowledge, Consciousness, and the Politics of Empowerment.* 2nd ed. New York: Routledge, 2000.

Hine, Darlene Clark. "Rape and the Inner Lives of Black Women: Thoughts on the Culture of Dissemblance." In *Hine Sight: Black Women and the Re-Construction of American History.* Brooklyn: Carlson Publishing, 1994.

Hobson, Janell. *Venus in the Dark: Blackness and Beauty in Popular Culture.* New York: Routledge, 2005.

Holleman, J. T. "In Arkansas, Which Comes First, the Chicken or the Environment?" *Tulane Environmental Law Journal* 6, no. 21 (1992).

Holley, Donald. "Leaving the Land of Opportunity: Arkansas and the Great Migration." *Arkansas Historical Quarterly* 64 (2005): 245–61.

———. *The Second Great Emancipation: The Mechanical Cotton Picker, Black Migration, and How They Shaped the Modern South.* Fayetteville: University of Arkansas Press, 2000.

———. "The Second Great Emancipation: The Rust Cotton Picker and How It Changed Arkansas." *Arkansas Historical Quarterly* 52 (1993): 44–77.

Holt, Marilyn Irvin. *Linoleum, Better Babies and the Modern Farm Woman, 1890–1930.* Albuquerque: University of New Mexico Press, 1995.

Honey, Michael. *Black Workers Remember: An Oral History of Segregation, Unionism and the Freedom Struggle.* Berkeley: University of California Press, 1999.

———. "Industrial Unionism and Racial Justice in Memphis." In *Organized Labor in the Twentieth Century South,* edited by Robert H. Zieger, 152. Knoxville: University of Tennessee Press, 1991.

———. *Southern Labor and Black Civil Rights: Organizing Memphis Workers.* Urbana: University of Illinois Press, 1993.

hooks, bell. *Feminist Theory: From Margin to Center.* Boston: South End Press, 1984.

———. *Killing Rage, Ending Racism.* New York: Henry Holt, 1995.

Horowitz, Roger. *"Negro and White, Unite and Fight!" A Social History of Industrial Unionism in Meatpacking, 1930–90.* Urbana: University of Illinois Press, 1997.

———. *Putting Meat on the American Table: Taste, Technology, Transformation.* Baltimore: Johns Hopkins University Press, 2005.

———. "'Where Men Will Not Work': Gender, Power, Space, and the Sexual Division of Labor in America's Meatpacking Industry, 1890–1990." *Technology and Cul-*

ture 38, Special Issue: Gender Analysis and the History of Technology (1997): 187–213.

Horowitz, Roger, and Mark Miller. *Immigrants in the Delmarva Poultry Processing Industry: The Changing Face of Georgetown, Delaware and Environs.* Occasional Paper No. 37, *Latino Studies Series,* Julian Samora Research Institute, January 1999.

Howard, Philip. *The Death of Common Sense: How Law Is Suffocating America.* New York: Random House, 1994.

Humphreys, Hubert. "In a Sense Experimental: The Civilian Conservation Corps in Louisiana." *Louisiana History* 5 (1964): 345–67.

Hunter, Tera. *To 'Joy My Freedom: Southern Black Women's Lives and Labor after the Civil War.* Cambridge: Harvard University Press, 1997.

Ignatiev, Noel. *How the Irish Became White.* New York: Routledge, 1995.

Janiewski, Dolores. *Sisterhood Denied: Race, Gender, and Class in a New South Community.* Philadelphia: Temple University Press, 1985.

Jewell, K. Sue. *From Mammy to Miss America and Beyond: Cultural Images and the Shaping of U.S. Policy.* London: Routledge, 1993.

Johnson, Ben. *Arkansas in Modern America, 1930–1999.* Fayetteville: University of Arkansas Press, 2000.

Johnson, Phillip J. "Confronting the Dilemma: Charles S. Johnson's Study of Louisiana's Black Schools." *Louisiana History: The Journal of the Louisiana Historical Association* 38 (Spring 1997): 133–55.

Jones, Beverly. "Race, Sex, and Class: Black Female Tobacco Workers in Durham, North Carolina, 1920–1940, and the Development of Female Consciousness." *Feminist Studies* 10 (1984): 441–51.

Jones, Clarisse, and Kumea Shorter-Gooden. *Shifting: The Double Lives of Black Women in America.* New York: HarperCollins, 2003.

Jones, Jacqueline. *Labor of Love, Labor of Sorrow: Black Women, Work, and the Family from Slavery to the Present.* New York: Basic Books, 1983.

Jones, Jean W., ed. *I Remember Life in Union Parish, 1910–1960: A Collection of Personal Remembrances.* Farmerville, La.: Union Parish Council on Aging, 2004.

Jones, Lu Ann. *Mama Learned Us to Work: Farm Women in the New South.* Chapel Hill: University of North Carolina Press, 2002.

Jones, William P. "Black Workers and the CIO's Turn toward Racial Liberalism: Operation Dixie and the North Carolina Lumber Industry, 1946–1953." *Labor History* 41 (2000): 279–306.

Jordan-Zachery, and Julia Sheron. *Black Women, Cultural Images, and Social Policy.* New York: Routledge, 2009.

Kandel, William, and Emilio A. Parrado. "Latinos in the American South and the Transformation of the Poultry Industry." In *Hispanic Spaces, Latino Places:*

Community and Cultural Diversity in Contemporary America, edited by Daniel D. Arreola, 255–76. Austin: University of Texas Press, 2004.

Kaufman, Jacob J. "Farm Labor during World War II." *Journal of Farm Economics* 31 (1949): 131–42.

Kelley, Robin D. G. *Hammer and Hoe: Alabama Communists during the Great Depression.* Chapel Hill: University of North Carolina Press, 1990.

———. *Race Rebels: Culture, Politics, and the Black Working Class.* New York: Free Press, 1996.

Kessler-Harris, Alice. "Where Are the Organized Women Workers?" *Feminist Studies* 3 (1975): 92–110.

Kim, Chul-Kyoo, and James Curry. "Fordism, Flexible Specialization, and Agri-industrial Restructuring: The Case of the U.S. Broiler Industry." *Sociologia Ruralis* 33 (1993): 61–80.

Kim, Claire Jean. *Bitter Fruit: The Politics of Black-Korean Conflict in New York City.* New Haven: Yale University Press, 2000.

Kinnucan, Henry, Hui Xiao, Chung-Jen Hsia, and John D. Jackson. "Effects of Health Information and Generic Advertising on U.S. Meat Demand." *American Journal of Agricultural Economics* 79 (1997): 13–23.

Kirby, Jack. *Rural Worlds Lost: The American South, 1920–1960.* Baton Rouge: Louisiana State University Press, 1987.

Korstad, Robert. *Civil Rights Unionism: Tobacco Workers and the Struggle for Democracy in the Mid-Twentieth-Century South.* Chapel Hill: University of North Carolina Press, 2003.

Korstad, Robert, and Nelson Lichtenstein. "Opportunities Found and Lost: Labor, Radicals, and the Early Civil Rights Movement." *Journal of American History* 75 (1988): 786–811.

Koshy, Susan. "Morphing Race into Ethnicity: Asian Americans and Critical Transformations of Whiteness." *Boundary 2* 28 (2001): 173–80.

Kucera, Barb. "In Crisis, Union Office Becomes Community Center." *Workday Minnesota,* December 17, 2006. www.workdayminnesota.org/articles/crisis-union-office-becomes-community-center (last accessed January 20, 2014).

Labov, Teresa G. "English Acquisition by Immigrants to the United States at the Beginning of the Twentieth Century." *American Speech* 73 (1998): 368–98.

Lawrence, Ken, and Anne Braden. "The Long Struggle." *Southern Exposure* 11 (1983): 85–89.

Lee, M. A., and Joachim Singlemann. "Welfare Reform amidst Chronic Poverty in the Mississippi Delta." In *Population Change and Rural Society,* edited by W. A. Kandel and D. L. Brown, 381–403. Dordrecht, The Netherlands: Springer, 2006.

Lester, Jim. *A Man for Arkansas: Sid McMath and the Southern Reform Tradition.* Little Rock, Ark.: Rose Publishing Co., 1976.

Levenstein, Lisa. "From Innocent Children to Unwanted Migrants and Unwed Moms: Two Chapters in Public Discourse on Welfare in the United States 1960–1961." *Journal of Women's History* 11 (2000): 10–33.

Lichtenstein, Nelson. *State of the Union: A Century of American Labor.* Princeton: Princeton University Press, 2002.

Lichtman, Allan. "The Federal Assault against Voting Discrimination in the Deep South, 1957–1967." *Journal of Negro History* 54, no. 4 (1969): 346–67.

Lim, Nelson. "On the Backs of Blacks? Immigrants and the Fortunes of African Americans." In *Strangers at the Gates: New Immigrants in Urban America,* edited by Roger Waldinger, 186–227. Berkeley: University of California Press, 2001.

Linder, Marc. "I Gave My Employer a Chicken that Had No Bone: Joint Firm-State Responsibility for Line-Speed-Related Occupational Injuries." *Case Western Reserve Law Review* 46 (1995): 33–143.

Lindhorst, Taaryn, and Leslie Leighninger. "'Ending Welfare as We Know It' in 1960: Louisiana's Suitable Home Law." *Social Service Review* 77 (2003): 564–84.

Lipscomb, Hester J., et al. "Exploration of Work and Health Disparities among Black Women Employed in Poultry Processing in the Rural South." *Environmental Health Perspectives* 113, no. 12 (2005): 1834.

Lipscomb, Hester J., et al. "Musculoskeletal Symptoms among Poultry Processing Workers and a Community Comparison Group: Black Women in Low-Wage Jobs in the Rural South." *American Journal of Industrial Medicine* 50, no. 5 (2007): 327–38.

Lisenby, Foy. "Winthrop Rockefeller and the Arkansas Image." *Arkansas Historical Quarterly* 43 (1984): 143–52.

Lissak, Rivka Shpak. *Pluralism and Progressives: Hull House and the New Immigrants, 1890–1919.* Chicago: University of Chicago Press, 1989.

Litwack, Leon. *Trouble in Mind: Black Southerners in the Age of Jim Crow.* New York: Knopf, 1988.

Lorde, Audre. "Learning from the 60's." In *Sister Outsider: Essays and Speeches.* Berkeley, CA: Crossing Press, 2007, 137.

———. "The Transformation of Silence into Language and Action." In *Sister Outsider: Essays and Speeches.* Berkeley, CA: Crossing Press, 2007, 42.

Lowell, B. Lindsay, and Rodolfo O. De La Garza. "The Developmental Role of Remittances in U.S. Latino Communities and in Latin American Countries." A Project of the Inter-American Dialogue, June 2000. www.iadialog.org/publications/pdf/lowell.pdf (last accessed April 12, 2007).

Magana, Lisa. *Straddling the Border: Immigration Policy and the INS.* Austin: University of Texas Press, 2003.

Markel, Howard, and Alexandra Minna Stern. "The Foreignness of Germs: The Persistent Association of Immigrants and Disease in American Society." *Millbank Quarterly* 80 (2002): 757–88.

Marrow, Helen B. *New Destination Dreaming: Immigration, Race, and Legal Status in the American South.* Stanford, Calif.: Stanford University Press, 2011.

Martinez, Ruben. *Crossing Over: A Mexican Family on the Migrant Trail.* New York: Picador USA, 2002.

Martinez-Ebers, Valerie, Luis Fraga, Linda Lopez, and Arturo Vega. "Latino Interest in Education, Health and Criminal Justice Policy." *Political Science and Politics* 33 (2000): 547–54.

Massey, Douglas, Jorge Durand, and Nolan J. Malone. *Beyond Smoke and Mirrors: Mexican Immigration in an Era of Economic Integration.* New York: Russell Sage Foundation, 2002.

May, Martha. "Bread before Roses: American Workingmen, Labor Unions and the Family Wage." In *Women, Work and Protest: A Century of U.S. Women's Labor History,* edited by Ruth Milkman, 1–21. Boston: Routledge & Kegan Paul, 1985.

McClain, Paula, et al. "Racial Distancing in a Southern City: Latino Immigrants' Views of Black Americans." *Journal of Politics* 68 (2006): 571–84.

Meier, Kenneth, Paula McClain, J. L. Polinard, and Robert D. Wrinkle. "Divided or Together? Conflict and Cooperation between African Americans and Latinos." *Political Research Quarterly* 57 (2004): 399–409.

Minchin, Timothy. *Fighting against the Odds: A History of Southern Labor since World War II.* Gainesville: University of Florida Press, 2005.

Mindiola, Tatcho, Jr., Yolanda Flores Niemann, and Nestor Rodriguez. *Black-Brown Relations and Stereotypes.* Austin: University of Texas Press, 2002.

Mink, Gwendolyn. "The Lady and the Tramp (II): Feminist Welfare Politics, Poor Single Mothers, and the Challenge of Welfare Justice." *Feminist Studies* 24, no. 1 (Spring 1998): 55–64.

——. *Welfare's End.* Ithaca, N.Y.: Cornell University Press, 1998.

——. *Whose Welfare?* Ithaca, N.Y.: Cornell University Press, 1999.

Misra, Joya, Stephanie Moller, and Marina Karides. "Envisioning Dependency: Changing Media Depictions of Welfare in the 20th Century." *Social Problems* 50 (November 2003): 482–504.

Mittelstadt, Jennifer. *From Welfare to Workfare: The Unintended Consequence of Welfare Reform, 1945–1965.* Chapel Hill: University of North Carolina Press, 2005.

Mohl, Raymond A. "Globalization, Latinization, and the Nuevo New South." *Journal of American Ethnic History* 22 (2003): 31–66.

Moberg, David. "Puttin' Down Ol' Massa: Laurel, Mississippi, 1979." In *Working Lives: The* Southern Exposure *History of Labor in the South,* edited by Marc S. Miller, 291–301. New York: Pantheon Books, 1980.

Moneyhon, Carl. *Arkansas and the New South: 1874–1929.* Fayetteville: University of Arkansas Press, 1997.

Moore, William J., and Robert J. Newman. "The Effects of Right-to-Work Laws: A Review of the Literature." *Industrial and Labor Relations Review* 38 (1985): 571–85.

Moreno, Paul. *Black Americans and Organized Labor: A New History.* Baton Rouge: Louisiana State University Press, 2006.

Morgan, Joan. *When Chicken Heads Come Home to Roost: A Hip-Hop Feminist Breaks It Down.* New York: Simon & Schuster, 2000.

Morris, Aldon. *The Origins of the Civil Rights Movement: Black Communities Organizing for Change.* New York: Free Press, 1984.

Munro, Anne. *Women, Work, and Trade Unions.* New York: Mansell, 2000.

Murphy, Angela. "Abolition, Irish Freedom, and Immigrant Citizenship: American Slavery and the Rise and Fall of the American Associations for Irish Repeal." Ph.D. diss., University of Houston, 2006.

Nakano Glenn, Evelyn. "From Servitude to Service Work: Historical Continuities in the Racial Division of Paid Reproductive Labor." *Signs* 18 (1992): 1–43.

———. "Cleaning Up / Kept Down: A Historical Perspective on Racial Inequality in 'Women's Work.'" *Stanford Law Review* 43 (1999): 1333–56.

Nelson, Barbara. "The Origins of the Two-Channel Welfare State: Workman's Compensation and Mothers' Aid." In *Women, the State, and Welfare,* edited by L. Gordon, 123–51. Madison: University of Wisconsin Press, 1990.

Nelson, Bruce. "Class, Race and Democracy in the CIO: The New Labor History Meets the 'Wages of Whiteness.'" *International Review of Social History* 41 (1996): 351–74.

Norrell, Robert. "Caste in Steel: Jim Crow Careers in Birmingham, Alabama." *Journal of American History* 73 (1986): 669–94.

Norwood, Stephen. "Bogalusa Burning: The War against Biracial Unionism in the Deep South, 1919." *Journal of Southern History* 63 (1997): 591–628.

———. *Strikebreaking and Intimidation: Mercenaries and Masculinity in Twentieth Century.* Chapel Hill: University of North Carolina Press, 2002.

Ostendorf, David L. "Exploiting Immigrant Workers." *Christian Century* 116 (1999): 492–93.

Palmer, Phyllis. *Domesticity and Dirt: Housewives and Domestic Servants in the United States, 1920–1945.* Philadelphia: Temple University Press, 1989.

———. "Outside the Law: Agricultural and Domestic Workers Under the Fair Labor Standards Act." *Journal of Policy History* 7 (1995): 416–40.

Parker, James S. *A Deeper History: The Oil Boom of the 1920s in Union County Arkansas.* Fayetteville: University of Arkansas Press, 2000.

Parker, J. Scott. "A Changing Landscape: Environmental Conditions and Consequences of the 1920s Union County Oil Booms." *Arkansas Historical Quarterly* 60 (2001): 30–52.

Payne, Charles. *I've Got the Light of Freedom: The Organizing Tradition and the Mississippi Freedom Struggle.* Berkeley: University of California Press, 1995.

Perea, J. F., ed. *Immigrants Out! The New Nativism and the Anti-Immigrant Impulse in the United States.* New York: New York University Press, 1997.

Bibliography

Peterson, John. "News and Notes: University of Arkansas Industrial Research and Extension Center." *Industrial and Labor Relations Review* 12 (1959): 325.

Quadagno, Jill. *The Color of Welfare: How Racism Undermined the War on Poverty.* New York: Oxford University Press, 1994.

———. "Social Movements and State Transformation: Labor Unions and Racial Conflict in the War on Poverty." *American Sociological Review* 57 (1992): 616–34.

Rafferty, Milton D. *The Ozarks: Land and Life.* Fayetteville: University of Arkansas Press, 2001.

Ragsdale, John G. *As We Were in South Arkansas.* Little Rock, Ark.: August House Publishers, 1995.

Raitz, Karl. "Advantages of Place as Perceived by Sunbelt Promoters." *Growth and Change* 19 (1988): 14–29.

Ravitch, Diane. *The Great School Wars, New York City, 1805–1973: A History of the Public Schools as Battlefields of Social Change.* New York: Basic Books, 1974.

Reese, Ellen. *Backlash against Welfare Mothers: Past and Present.* Berkeley: University of California Press, 2005.

Riffel, Brent. "The Feathered Kingdom: Tyson Foods and the Transformation of American Land, Labor, and Law, 1930–2005." Ph.D. diss., University of Arkansas, 2008.

Roberts, Dorothy. *Killing the Black Body: Race, Reproduction, and the Meaning of Liberty.* New York: Pantheon Books, 1997.

———. "Race, Gender, and the Value of Mother's Work." *Social Politics* 2, no. 2 (1995): 195–207.

———. *Shattered Bonds: The Color of Child Welfare.* New York: Basic Books, 2002.

———. "Welfare's Ban on Poor Motherhood." In *Whose Welfare?* edited by Gwendolyn Mink, 152–70. Ithaca, N.Y.: Cornell University Press, 1999.

Roderick, Melissa. "Hispanics and Education." *Hispanics in the United States: An Agenda for the 21st Century,* edited by Pastora San Juan Cafferty and David W. Engstrom, 123–73. New Brunswick, N.J.: Transaction Publishers, 2000.

Rodriguez, Nestor. "New Southern Neighbors: Latino Immigration and Prospects for Intergroup Relations between African-Americans and Latinos in the South." *Latino Studies* 10 (Spring 2012): 18–40.

Roediger, David. *The Wages of Whiteness: Race and the Making of the American Working Class.* New York: Verso, 1999.

Rollins, Judith. *Between Women: Domestics and Their Employers.* Philadelphia: Temple University Press, 1987.

Ross, William G. *Forging New Freedoms: Nativism, Education, and the Constitution, 1917– 1927.* Lincoln: University of Nebraska Press, 1994.

Rosswurm, Steve, ed. *The CIO's Left-Led Unions.* New Brunswick, N.J.: Rutgers University Press, 1992.

Ruiz, Vicki L. *Cannery Women, Cannery Lives: Mexican Women, Unionization, and the California Food Processing Industry, 1930–1950.* Albuquerque: University of New Mexico Press, 1987.

———. *From Out of the Shadows: Mexican Women in Twentieth-Century America.* Oxford: Oxford University Press, 1998.

Sachs, Carolyn. *Gendered Fields: Rural Women, Agriculture, and Environment.* Boulder, Colo.: Westview Press, 1996.

Saenz, Rogelio, Katharine Donato, Lourdes Gouveia, and Cruz Torres. "Latinos in the South: A Glimpse of Ongoing Trends and Research." *Southern Rural Sociology* 19 (2003): 1–19.

San Miguel, Guadalupe. *"Let All of Them Take Heed": Mexican Americans and the Campaign for Educational Equality in Texas, 1910–1981.* Austin: University of Texas Press, 1987.

Sawyer, Gordon. *The Agribusiness Poultry Industry: A History of Its Development.* Jericho, N.Y.: Exposition Press, 1971.

Schiavone, Michael. *Unions in Crisis? The Future of Organized Labor in America.* Westport, Conn.: Greenwood Publishing Group, 2008.

Schiele, Jerome, and Ellarwee Gadsen. "Racial Control and Resistance among African Americans in the Aftermath of the Welfare Reform Act of 1996." In *Social Welfare Policy: Regulation and Resistance among People of Color,* edited by Jerome H. Schiele, 91–110. Thousand Oaks, Calif.: Sage Publications, 2011.

Schildkraut, Deborah J. "Official-English and the States: Influences on Declaring English the Official Language in the United States." *Political Research Quarterly* 54 (June 2001): 445–57.

Schlosser, Eric. *Fast Food Nation: The Dark Side of the All-American Meal.* Boston: Houghton Mifflin, 2001.

Schmitt, John, and Ben Zipperer. "Dropping the Ax: Illegal Firings during Union Election Campaigns." Center for Economic and Policy Research. January 2007. www.cepr.net/documents/publications/unions_2007_01.pdf (last accessed March 25, 2007).

Schottland, J. R., G. J. Kirschberg, R. Fillingim, U. P. Davis, and F. Hogg. "Median Nerve Latencies in Poultry Processing Workers: An Approach to Resolving the Role of Industrial 'Cumulative Trauma' in the Development of Carpal Tunnel Syndrome." *Journal of Occupational Medicine* 33 (1991): 627–31.

Schulman, Bruce. *From Cotton Belt to Sunbelt: Federal Policy, Economic Development, and the Transformation of the South, 1938–1980.* New York: Oxford University Press, 1991.

Schwartz, Martin. *Tyson: From Farm to Market.* Fayetteville: University of Arkansas Press, 1991.

Shah, Nayan. *Contagious Divides: Epidemics and Race in San Francisco's Chinatown.* Berkeley: University of California Press, 2001.

Shankman, Arnold. "Black on Yellow: Afro-Americans View Chinese Americans 1850–1935." *Phylon* 39 (1978): 1–17.

Sharpless, Rebecca. *Cooking in Other Women's Kitchens: Domestic Workers in the South, 1865–1960.* Chapel Hill: University of North Carolina Press, 2010.

Shaw, Stephanie. *What a Woman Ought to Be and Do: Black Professional Women Workers during the Jim Crow Era.* Chicago: University of Chicago Press, 1996.

Shulman, Steven, and Robert C. Smith. "Immigration and African Americans." In *African Americans in the U.S. Economy,* edited by Cecilia A. Conrad, John Whitehead, Patrick Mason, and James Stewart, 149–53. Lanham, Md.: Rowman and Littlefield, 2005.

Sidel, Ruth. *Keeping Women and Children Last: America's War on the Poor.* New York: Penguin Books, 1998.

Silver, Beverly. *Forces of Labor: Workers' Movements and Globalization since 1870.* Cambridge: Cambridge University Press, 2003.

Smith, Anna Marie. *Welfare Reform and Sexual Regulation.* New York: Cambridge University Press, 2007.

Smith, James P., and Barry Edmonston. "Immigration's Effects on Jobs and Wages: First Principles." In *The New Americans: Economic, Demographic and Fiscal Effects of Immigration,* edited by James P. Smith and Barry Edmonston, 135–72. Washington, D.C.: National Academy Press, 1997.

Solinger, Rickie. *Wake Up, Little Susie: Single Pregnancy and Race before Roe v. Wade.* New York: Routledge, 2000.

Spaights, Ernest, and Ann Whitaker. "Black Women in the Workforce: A New Look at an Old Problem." *Journal of Black Studies* 25 (1995): 283–96.

Spalding, Sophie. "The Myth of the Classic Slum: Contradictory Perceptions of Boyle Heights Flats, 1900–1991." *Journal of Architectural Education* 45 (1992): 107–19.

Starobin, Robert S. "Privileged Bondsmen and the Process of Accommodation: The Role of Houseservants and Drivers as Seen in Their Own Letters." *Journal of Social History* 5 (Fall 1971): 52.

Steinberg, Stephen. "Immigration, African Americans and Race Discourse." In *Race and Labor Matters in the New U.S. Economy,* edited by Manning Marable, Immanuel Ness, and Joseph Wilson, 175–92. Lanham, Md.: Rowman and Littlefield, 2006.

Stepan-Norris, Judith, and Maurice Zeitlin. *Left Out: Reds and America's Industrial Unions.* Cambridge: Cambridge University Press, 2003.

Stolarik, M. Mark. "From Field to Factory: The Historiography of Slovak Immigration to the United States." *International Migration Review* 10 (1976): 81–102.

Strausberg, Stephen. *A Century of Research: Centennial History of the Arkansas Agricultural Experiment Station.* Fayetteville: Arkansas Agricultural Experiment Station, 1989.

——. *From Hills and Hollers: Rise of the Poultry Industry in Arkansas.* Arkansas Agricultural Experiment Station, Special Report No. 170. Fayetteville: University of Arkansas: Arkansas Agricultural Experiment Station, 1995.

Striffler, Steve. *Chicken: The Dangerous Transformation of America's Favorite Food.* New Haven, Conn.: Yale University Press, 2005.

——. "Inside a Poultry Processing Plant: An Ethnographic Portrait." *Labor History* 43 (2002): 305–13.

Stuesse, Angela Christine. "Globalization 'Southern Style': Transnational Migration, the Poultry Industry, and Implications for Organizing Workers across Difference." Ph.D. diss., University of Texas at Austin, 2008. www.lib.utexas.edu/etd/d/2008/stuessed98532/stuessed98532.pdf (last accessed November 15, 2011).

——. *Poultry Processing, Industrial Restructuring, and Organizing in Transnational Mississippi: Challenges and Promises.* A Report of the Poultry Worker Justice Research Project, Inter-American Policy Studies Occasional Paper No. 5. Sponsored by the Equal Justice Center, Austin, Tex., and the Inter-American Policy Studies Program. University of Texas at Austin, 2003.

Sullivan, Teresa. "A Demographic Portrait." In *Hispanics in the United States: An Agenda for the 21st Century,* edited by Pastora San Juan Cafferty and David W. Engstrom, 1–29. New Brunswick, N.J.: Transaction Publishers, 2000.

Tait, Vanessa. *Poor Workers' Unions: Rebuilding Labor from Below.* Cambridge, Mass.: South End Press, 2005.

Tamura, Eileen H. "The English Only Effort, the Anti-Japanese Campaign, and Language Acquisition in the Education of Japanese Americans in Hawaii, 1915–1940." *History of Education Quarterly* 33 (1993): 37–58.

Taylor, Laval Franklin. "Development of Public Education in Union Parish." Master's thesis, Louisiana State University, 1939.

Thomas, Charles E. *Jelly Roll: A Black Neighborhood in a Southern Mill Town.* Little Rock, Ark.: Rose Publishing, 1986.

Thomas, Susan L. "Race, Gender, and Welfare Reform: The Antinatalist Response." *Journal of Black Studies* 28 (March 1998): 419–46.

Thomson, Susan C. "El Dorado Hopes the Promise Brings Back the Golden Days." *Regional Economist* (January 2009). www.stlouisfed.org/publications/re/articles/?id=1318 (last accessed September 16, 2013).

Thornhill, Margaret. "Problems of Repeated Out-of-Wedlock Pregnancies." *Child Welfare* (June 1959): 1–4.

Tomlinson, Sylvia. *Plucked and Burned.* Victoria, Tex.: Redbud Publishing, 2003.

Tucker, Susan. "A Complex Bond: Southern Black Domestic Workers and Their White Employers." Special issue on "Women in the American South." *Frontiers* 9, no. 3 (1987): 6–13.

——. *Telling Memories among Southern Women: Domestic Workers and Their Employers in the Segregated South.*

Vaca, Nicolas. *The Presumed Alliance: The Unspoken Conflict between Latinos and Blacks and What It Means for America.* New York: HarperCollins, 2004.

Valk, Anne, and Leslie Brown, eds. *Living with Jim Crow: African American Women and Memories of the Segregated South.* Interviews of Ila J. Blue and Vermelle Ely. New York: Palgrave Macmillan, 2010.

Various authors. "Ruling the Roost: A Special Report on the Poultry Industry." Special Edition, *Southern Exposure* 17 (1989).

Vellala, C., F. Aghazadeh, John C. Pine, and Brian D. Marx. "Analysis of Injuries and Illnesses in Poultry Processing Industries in Louisiana." In *Advances in Industrial Ergonomics and Safety VI,* edited by F. Aghazadeh. London: Taylor & Francis, 1994.

Venkataramani, M. S. "Norman Thomas, Arkansas Sharecroppers and the Roosevelt Agricultural Policies, 1933–1937." *Mississippi Valley Historical Review* 47 (1960): 225–46.

Volanto, Keith J. "The AAA Cotton Plow-Up Campaign in Arkansas." *Arkansas Historical Quarterly* 59 (2000): 388–406.

Waldinger, Roger. "Black/Immigrant Competition Re-Assessed: New Evidence from Los Angeles." *Sociological Perspectives* 40 (1997): 365–86.

Walker, Melissa. *All We Knew Was to Farm: Rural Women in the Upcountry South, 1919–1941.* Revisiting Rural America Series. Baltimore: Johns Hopkins University Press, 2000.

———. "The Changing Character of Farm Life: Rural Southern Women." In *Southern Women at the Millennium: A Historical Perspective,* edited by Melissa Walker, Jeanette R. Dunn, and Joe P. Dunn, 145–75. Columbia: University of Missouri Press, 2003.

Wallace, Michele. *Black Macho and the Myth of the Superwoman.* New York: Dial Press, 1979.

Weber, Devra. *Dark Sweat, White Gold: California Farm Workers, Cotton, and the New Deal.* Berkeley: University of California Press, 1994.

Wehrwein, George. "Changes in Farm and Farm Tenure 1930–1935." *Journal of Land and Public Utility Economics* 12 (1936): 200–205.

Weise, Julie. "Dispatches from the 'Viejo' New South: Historicizing Recent Latino Migrations." *Latino Studies* 10 (Spring 2012): 42.

———. "Mexican Nationalisms, Southern Racisms: Mexicans and Mexican Americans in the U.S. South, 1908–1939." *American Quarterly* 80 (September 2008): 749–77.

West, Truett. "Union Parish Conspiracy of 1933." *North Louisiana Historical Association Journal* 20 (1989): 79–94.

Westbrook, Lawrence. "Farm Tenancy: A Program." *Nation* 144, January 9, 1937, 39–41.

Whayne, Jennie. *A New Plantation South: Land, Labor, and Federal Favor in Twentieth Century Arkansas.* Charlottesville: University Press of Virginia, 1996.

Whitaker-Green, Juanita. *The History of Union County Arkansas.* Reproduced from author's typewritten copy, 1954.

Wiggins, Daphne. *Righteous Content: Black Women's Perspectives of Church and Faith.* New York: New York University Press, 2005.

Williams-Forson, Psyche A. *Building Houses Out of Chicken Legs: Black Women, Food, and Power.* Chapel Hill: University of North Carolina Press, 2006.

Winders, Jamie. "Changing Politics of Race and Region: Latino Migration to the U.S. South." *Progress in Human Geography* 29 (2005): 683–99.

Witwer, David. "The Scandal of George Scalise: A Case Study in the Rise of Labor Racketeering in the 1930s." *Journal of Social History* 36 (2003): 917–40.

Wolf, Jerome. *Ferment in Labor.* Beverly Hills, Calif.: Glencoe Press, 1968.

Wollett, Donald. "Race Relations." *Louisiana Law Review* 21 (1960–61): 85–108.

Woodruff, Nan Elizabeth. *As Rare as Rain: Federal Relief in the Great Southern Drought of 1930–1931.* Urbana: University of Illinois Press, 1985.

———. "The Failure of Relief during the Arkansas Drought of 1930–1931." *Arkansas Historical Quarterly* 39 (1980): 301–13.

———. "Pick or Fight: The Emergency Farm Labor Program in the Arkansas and Mississippi Deltas during World War II." *Agricultural History* 64 (1990): 74–85.

Woody, Bette. *Black Women in the Workplace: Impacts of Structural Change in the Economy.* New York: Greenwood Press, 1992.

Yeoman, Barry. "Don't Count Your Chickens." *Southern Exposure* 17 (1989): 21–24.

Zamora, Emilio. *The World of the Mexican Worker in Texas.* College Station: Texas A&M University Press, 1993.

Zellar, Gary. "H. C. Ray and Racial Politics in the African American Extension Service Program in Arkansas, 1915–1929." *Agricultural History* 72 (1998): 429–45.

Zieger, Robert, and Gilbert J. Gall. *American Workers, American Unions.* 2nd ed. Baltimore: Johns Hopkins University Press, 1994.

Zook, Kristal Brent. "Dreaming in the Delta: A Memoir Essay." *Meridians* 3, no. 2 (2003): 278–88.

INDEX

Aaron Poultry and Egg Company, 21
Abou-Karr, Nadia, 160
AFL-CIO, 12, 96, 124–25
Agricultural Adjustment Act (AAA), 6, 7
agriculture. *See* farmers and agriculture
Aho, Paul, 36
Aid to Dependent Children program (ADC), 8, 52–55, 59. *See also* welfare benefits
Alexandria, LA, 19–20
Amalgamated Meatcutters and Butcher Workmen of North America (AMBW): Brody on, 11; contract negotiations, 206n106; inspection system and, 157; leftist purge and, 90; Local 425, 98–99, 100, 101, 208n124; merger into UFCW, 100; pragmatism of, 93–94; race and, 94–95; on wages, 198n130
American Federation of Labor (AFL), 90
Anderson, Karen, 8
Anzaldúa, Gloria, 160
Apollon, Dominique, 64, 174n41
A&P Supermarkets, 28
Arkansas: industrial financing laws, 183n110; Latinos in, 131; population decline in, 182n87; right-to-work law, 39, 40. *See also* El Dorado (AR)

Arkansas Agricultural Experiment Station, 21–22, 25
"Arkansas Broilers," 21
Arkansas Division of Agriculture and Industry (AIDC), 181n87, 182n90
Arkansas Economic Council, 31
Arkansas Industrial Development Act, 31
Arkansas Industrial Development Commission (AIDC), 31
Arkansas Poultry Federation (APF), 28
Arkansas Poultry Improvement Association, 25
Arkansas Resources and Development Commission, 31, 182n90

Bailey, Marjorie, 176n5
Bankhead, Teiahsha, 229n150
Barkan, Elliott, 229n150
Barker, Shirley, 93, 157
bathroom breaks, restriction of, 88–89, 203n64
Bazemore, Donna, 61, 70, 78, 81–82, 83, 106, 112, 121, 123–24, 196n114, 203n64, 217n117
Beauboeuf-Lafontant, Tamara, 110
Bell, Winifred, 193n81, 195n95

benefits, 118, 121, 217n102

Bernice (LA): chicken processing boosterism, 60–61; garment factories and health-care work in, 60; Latinos in, 127, 132, 138; poultry workers drawn to El Dorado from, 43–44, 61; racial divisions in, 126–27; timber and agriculture in, 45–46. *See also* Pilgrim's Pride; Union Parish (LA)

Biles, DeLores (pseud.), 87, 149, 163

bilingual education, 145–48

black women: control of sexuality and fertility of, 187n6; current status of, 155; "dirty work"" and, 109–10; exclusion from clerical jobs, 212n31; labor history of, 5–9; shaming and stigmatization of, 55–56; stereotypical characterization of, 51–52; vulnerability of, 4, 40–42, 123. *See also specific people and topics*

Blue, Ila J., 23

Bolton, Charles S., 182n87, 182n90

boosterism: in Bernice, 60–61; in El Dorado, 30–33; paternalism, racism, and, 39–40

Boris, Eileen, 8

Borjas, George, 138, 224n82

Braden, Anne, 12–13, 93

Bradford, Fannie, 186n157

Brattain, Michelle, 39, 173n18, 217n101

breaks, restriction of, 88–89, 203n64

breeding, 27–28

Briggs, Vernon, 138, 224n83

Brimelow, Peter, 151

Brody, David, 11, 89–90, 95, 99

Brooks, Gwendolyn, 62

Brown, Elsa Barkley, 207n117

Brown, Keisha, 149

Browne, Irene, 61

Buckalew, A. R., 30

Buckalew, R. B., 30

Buhle, Paul, 96

Burnside, Houston, 47, 189n26

Burnside, Walter, 47, 189n26

Burnside conspiracy, 47–48, 189n26

Bush, George W., 136

Byrd, Harry, 48–49

Cable, C. Curtis, 37–38, 179n43, 179n45

Calavita, Kitty, 228n146, 229n150

carpal tunnel syndrome (CTS), 111–13

Carroll, Thomas, 204n83

Carter, Sherry (pseud.), 72, 73, 76–77, 163

Carter, Timothy (pseud.), 163

Catholic Bishops of the South, 217n111

Center for Women's Economic Alternatives (CWEA), 83, 123–24

Change to Win (CtW) coalition, 125

Chicken of Tomorrow contest, 28

childcare, 66, 68

children. *See* families and children; motherhood and mothering

Chitwood, Mrs. Hoyt, 24

church involvement, 152, 160, 199n149

Citizens' Councils, 49, 189n32

Civil Rights Act (1957), 49–50

civil rights movement, 48–50, 196n115. *See also* segregationism and Jim Crow

Clark, Richard, 21

class action suit (2003), 79, 81

Clayton, Pressie, 88

Clinton, Bill, 96, 206n108

Clymer, Ray, 98

Cobb, James, 30, 40, 171n6

Cobble, Dorothy Sue, 206n99

collective action, 77, 122. *See also* unions and unionization

Commission on Civil Rights, 49–50

Committee for Justice in Mississippi, 96

common law marriage, criminalization of, 56

communism and unions, 90–91, 94–95, 205n97, 206n100

community building in the plant, 84–85

Compa, Lance, 157

ConAgra: El Dorado and, 20; lawsuits against, 124; Pilgrim's Pride compared to, 67; policies of, 199n148

Congress of Industrial Organizations (CIO), 91, 94–95, 205nn97–98

consumer demand for poultry, 27, 34, 212n37

contract growing system, 37–38, 185n142

cooperative spirit, 121–22

Cordell, Anna, 29, 30, 33

"core" workers, 121

Corn Belt Hatchery, 32

cotton farmers, 24–25, 26, 60

Craig, Bill, 181n81

Crain, Marion, 207n110

credit arrangements, 37–38

Cromer, Linda, 13, 98

"The Cruelest Cuts" series (*Charlotte Observer*), 10, 16, 83, 114, 115

Curry, James, 37

Daniel, Pete, 25

Davis, Jimmie, 59, 60, 195n98

Davis, Natalie (pseud.), 73, 112–13, 118, 139, 163

Dawes, Bella (pseud.), 79–80, 81, 86, 109, 115, 116, 122, 164, 199n148

death of workers, 85–87, 122

debt of small farmers, 37–38

De Jong, Greta, 47

Delmarva Poultry Industries, 143

demand for poultry, 27, 34, 212n37

Denison Poultry (Center, TX), 93–94, 97, 98, 208n122

Department of Public Welfare (LA), 58–59, 195n93

deskilling, 120

Dingell, John, 50

"disposable workforce," 83–84

dissembling, 63

domestic service: denial of womanhood in, 172n9; "dirty work" and, 109–10; history of, 5, 8, 172n8; poultry work compared to, 62–64; power relations in, 62–63; social insurance, exclusion from, 53, 191n55, 191n57

Douglass, Harrison, 188n12

Drayton, Kenya (pseud.), 42, 68–69, 74–75, 77, 79, 82, 83, 84, 85, 87, 88, 101–2, 106–7, 108, 117, 139, 164

Du Bois, W.E.B., 52

Duffy, Mignon, 63

Earl, Janae (pseud.), 66, 70, 118, 147, 164, 215n81

Eason, Rita, 87

Eastex Company (Center, TX), 93–94, 97, 208n122

economic and social vulnerability, connection between, 4

education: bilingual, 145–48; black children and, 46, 66–67, 188n17; status of, 155–56; white children and, 221n31

El Dorado (AR): black resistance and demonstrations in, 196n115; boosterism in, 30–33; economic plight of, 156–57; industrial complex in, 40; Latino workers in, 140; oil industry in, 29–30, 176n7; population explosion in, 29–30; railroads and timber in, 29; workers drawn from Bernice, 43–44, 61. *See also specific people and topics*

El Dorado Chamber of Commerce, 31

El Dorado Poultry By-Products Company, 32

El Dorado poultry industry, history of: overview, 19–20; black women and, 40–42; booster efforts, 30–33; consumer demand and, 27, 34; early poultry raising, growth of, 21–28; government policies and, 38–39; industrial development of timber and oil, 28–30; location and southern labor climate and, 35–42; paternalism, racism, and, 39–40; related businesses, 32; vertical integration and, 34–35

Ellender, Allen, 50

Ellwood, David, 92, 204n83

emotional labor, domestic service and, 62–63

English and Spanish, 139–40, 143–47, 226n111, 226n114

eugenics, 193n77

Evans-Greshom, Rosalynn, 164

evisceration process, 44, 106, 111

Executive Order 8802 (1941), 7

Fair Employment Practices Committee (FEPC), 7–8, 173nn18–19

Fair Labor Standard Act, 93, 120

families and children: domestic work and subordination of, 63; elderly parents, 71–72; kin recruitment, 118, 120, 215n85, 217n101; as reason to stay, 119; segregated communities and, 76; work-life balance issues and, 65–72

Fanon, Frantz, 144

Fantasia, Rick, 99

farmers and agriculture: black women on farms, 5–6; conditions in 1920s and 1930s and, 24–25; contract growing system and debt of, 37–38, 185n142; relief, denial of, 47; run off their land, 48; small farms in the South, 35–36; social insurance, exclusion from, 53, 191n55, 191n57; in Union Parish, 45–46, 60, 188n12

Farmerville, LA, 17, 47, 117, 139, 175n45

Fast Food Nation (Schlosser), 10

Faubus, Orval, 32, 33, 182n90

Faue, Elizabeth, 96

fear, 78, 82–83

Federal Emergency Relief Agency (FERA), 45

Fields, Ella, 41, 53–54, 57

Fine, Glenn, 92, 204n83

Fink, Leon, 11, 12, 67, 202n48, 221n36

Flemming, Arthur, 59, 195n98

Fogel, Walter A., 94, 95, 204n89, 206n106, 210n16, 212n31

food preparation and people of color, 63–64

Food Safety Inspection Service (FSIS), 158

food system, 64, 174n41

Forestier, Pablo, 112

Forthner, Verlina, 92

Foster, Ron, 17

Foster Farms, 17

Franklin, Benjamin, 144

Fraser, Nancy, 56, 230n10

Fullbright, Jay, 21

Gafford, Lillian (pseud.), 66–67, 79, 117, 146, 148–49, 164

gender: dangerous work and gendered division of labor, 107–10, 210n20; early poultry growing and, 22–24, 177n23; El Dorado industrial complex and, 40; men on the lines, 211n23; paternalism, 39–40; patriarchy and paternalism, 39–40, 47, 77–79, 191n54; race issues, false separation from, 9; structural sexism, 108; unions and sexism, 96–97; vertical integration and, 37

Georgia Poultry Justice Alliance, 123, 124

Gerstle, Gary, 144

Gibbs, Jewelle, 229n150

Gilkes, Cheryl, 110

Gisolfi, Monica, 12, 24, 38

Glover, J. J., 21

Goldoftas, Barbara, 215n78

Goolsby, O. B., Jr., 154

Gordon, Jennifer, 136, 138, 223n69

Gordon, Linda, 56, 191n54, 192n65, 230n10

Gorman, Patrick, 99, 100, 101

Gouveia, Lourdes, 183n110

grading, 107

Graff, E. J., 207n116

Great Depression, 25–26, 30. *See also* New Deal

Greater El Dorado Committee (GEC), 19, 31–32, 33

Great Flood of 1927, 39, 178n38

Green, George, 97

Green, James, 8

Green, Tommy, 41

Griffith, Barbara, 205n98

Griffith, David, 10, 12, 118, 174n38, 215n85

Halpern, Rick, 9, 94, 95, 206n99

Hamermesh, Daniel, 223n72

Harrell, Rose, 111

Harris, Pearl Adams, 46

Harris-Perry, Melissa, 52, 55

Hartwell, Albion, 191n57

Harvey, David, 2, 10

Heffernan, William, 38

Helton, Laura, 225n94, 225n96

Henwood, Doug, 224n82

hierarchy, gendered and racial, 64–65, 78–79

Hill, Herbert, 124, 205n98

Hispanic workers. *See* Latino immigrants and workers

"Hispanization," 143
Hobson, Janell, 51
Holley, Donald, 181n87
Holloway, Eleanor (pseud.), 67, 74, 119, 164
Holly Farms (Glen Allen, VA), 98, 213n51
Honey, Michael, 90–91, 205n97
Hoover, Herbert, 25
Horowitz, Roger, 9, 94, 95, 178n37, 187n4, 202n48, 206n99, 210n20, 212n37
House of Raeford, 78, 130–31
housing, Latinos and, 142–43
Howard, Philip, 158
Hudson Foods, 142
humanity of workers, denial of, 86–88

illegitimacy laws, 56–57, 59, 230n10
illegitimacy rhetoric, 55–56
immigrants. *See* Latino immigrants and workers
Immigration and Customs Enforcement (ICE) agency, 131
Immigration and Naturalization Service (INS), 130
Immigration Reform and Control Act (IRCA), 130, 135
Imperial Foods "cook plant" fire (Hamlet, NC), 9–10
industrial development corporations (IDCs), 31–32
injuries and illness: being fired for, 113; company nurses and, 114–16, 215n68; deaths, 85–87, 122; dehumanization and, 104–5; efforts for safer workplace, 116–17; gendered division of labor and dangerous work, 107–10; "light duty" and, 114–15; musculoskeletal disorders (MSDs), 110–13, 212n33; never stopping the line and, 85–87; other types of injury, 213n45; public expense of, 119; subcontracting and, 135; underreporting of, 113–15, 214n59
inspections, 157–58, 208n122, 212n43
Interfaith Worker Justice (IWJ), 122, 217n111
International Chemical Workers' Union, 96

intimidation, atmosphere of, 78
Island, LaDonna (pseud.), 70–71, 82, 139–40, 149, 164

Jackson, Jesse, 84
James, Ruth (pseud.), 69, 73, 101, 105, 164, 199n149
Jewell, K. Sue, 56, 192n66
Jim Crow. *See* segregationism and Jim Crow
Jindal, Bobby, 16–17, 175n45
J-M Poultry Packing Company: arrival in El Dorado, 19–20; black women from Louisiana and, 61; GEC and, 32; growth of, 32; unionization and, 100; vertical integration and, 35; women, hiring of, 40. *See also specific people and topics, such as* working conditions
Johnican, John, 124
Johnson, Ben, 29, 31, 34, 39
Johnson, Charles Spurgeon, 192n59
Johnson, Herb, 19, 28
Johnson, LeeAnn (pseud.), 80, 114, 118, 165, 215n81
Joint Legislative Committee to Maintain Segregation (LA), 49
Jones, Aarica (pseud.), 54, 58, 73, 165
Jones, Jacqueline, 8, 23, 65, 72, 84, 92, 178n28
Jones, Lewis, 28
Jones, LuAnn, 22
Jones, William, 205n98
Jordan, Gloria, 78, 81, 82

Kandel, William, 220n14
Kennelly, Ivy, 61
Kim, Chul-Kyoo, 36–37
King, Martin Luther, Jr., 18
King Chicken Day (El Dorado), 33
kin networks: recruitment through, 118, 120, 215n85, 217n101; support from, 74. *See also* families and children
Korstad, Robert, 206n99

labor, organized. *See* unions and unionization

Laborers' International Union of North America (LIUNA), 11, 94
labor feminists, 206n99, 209n135
labor history of black women, 5–9
labor pool and climate, southern, 36–42
"labor shortages," 129, 136–37
language issues, 139–40, 143–47, 226n111, 226n114
Latimer, Donna. *See* Bazemore, Donna
Latino immigrants and workers: black anti-Latino hostility, 140–43; black perception of racial dynamics, 148–50; black supervisors and, 80; effects on nonimmigrant workers, 137–40; employer manipulation of inter-group tensions, 135; growth in numbers of, 127, 128–29, 131; jobs "Americans won't do" and, 136–37; Maya of Morganton (NC), 11, 94, 133; positive relationship with African Americans, 152–53; recruitment of, 129–30, 134–35; shift of poultry jobs from black women to Latino men, 132–34; social service provision and, 150–52, 221n33; Spanish vs. English and bilingual education, 143–48; subcontracting and, 135; supervisors, 201n20; undocumented workers, 130–31; unions and, 158–59
Lawrence, Ken, 12–13, 93
lawsuits, 79, 81, 124
leftist purge by unions, 90–91, 94–95, 205n97, 206n100
Leighninger, Leslie, 58, 195n95
Lenhardt, Robin, 136, 138, 223n69
Levenstein, Lisa, 195n95
Levy, Louise, 230n6
Lewis, Jim, 3, 83–84
Lichtenstein, Nelson, 204n77
light duty, 114–15
Linder, Marc, 108
Lindhorst, Taaryn, 58, 195n95
line work: evisceration process, 44, 106, 111, 187n4; as hellaceous, 1; never stopping the line, 85–87; process along the line, 105–7; speed of, 2, 88, 110–11, 212n43.

See also poultry processing work; working conditions
Lion Oil Company, 30, 181n81
Lisenby, Foy, 182n90
Liu, Yvonne Yen, 64, 174n41
live hang, 106
Lloyd, Thomas, 101
Long, Russell, 50, 155, 195n99
Lorde, Audre, 160
Louisiana Commission on Marriage and Family, 230n10
Louisiana state legislature: illegitimacy and "suitable home" laws, 56–58, 193n81; voting restriction laws, 57, 189n32; welfare "reform," 155
Lowe, DeShaun (pseud.), 82, 114, 124, 131, 134, 140, 165
Lowenstein, Roger, 224n82
lumber industry, 29, 45

Mallory, Neysha (pseud.), 65, 67–68, 83, 84, 86, 88, 109, 111, 121, 131, 133–34, 138–42, 165
"marginal" workers, 121
Marrow, Helen, 10–11, 12, 127
Martin, Lydia (pseud.), 70, 74, 86, 116, 165
Martin, Sylvia (pseud.), 65, 66, 74, 86, 87, 109, 121, 165
Martin-Lowe, Jackie (pseud.), 118, 139, 165
Matheny, Ken, 207n110
Maya of Morganton (NC), 11, 94, 133
Mays, Trinity (pseud.), 69, 72–73, 80–81, 107, 108, 110, 139, 165
McGuire, Danielle, 18
McMath, Sid, 31
meat processing industry, black workers in, 9. *See also* Amalgamated Meatcutters and Butcher Workmen of North America (AMBW)
mechanization, 111, 119–20
Meet Your Meat (film), 104
men. *See* gender
mentoring, informal, 85
Merkle, Jess, 19, 28, 32, 33, 35, 40

middle-class black women, 69

Mink, Gwendolyn, 230n10

Mississippi Poultry Workers' Union
(MPWU), 12–13

Moneyhon, Carl, 25

Monroe, Faith (pseud.), 165, 199n146

Montgomery, L. M., 53, 192n59

Morales, Lisa, 128–29

Morganton (NC), Maya of, 11, 94, 133

Morrison, Toni, 150

motherhood and mothering: devaluing of
black mothering, 51–52; single mothers,
70–71, 155, 192n65, 200n160; value
placed on, 69. *See also* families and
children

Moynihan Report (1965), 52

Munro, Anne, 207n116

Murphy, Evelyn, 207n116

Murphy Oil Corp., 157

musculoskeletal disorders (MSDs), 110–13,
212n33

Musgrove, Alice, 65

Nakano Glenn, Evelyn, 63, 64, 110, 198n132,
204n88

National Committee on Household Employment, 5

National Labor Relations (Wagner) Act, 6, 7

National Labor Relations Board (NLRB),
90, 91–92, 98, 208n124

National Planning Association (NPA) Committee of the South on the Location of
Industry, 36–37

negotiation: contract negotiations, 101–2,
157, 158, 206n106, 208n124; by domestic
workers, 63, 172n8; individual skills in,
4–5; with supervisors for time off, 73

Nelson, Bruce, 205n98

New Deal, 6, 7, 46, 47

New Life Women's Leadership Project, 123

night shifts, 73

Norrell, Robert, 205n98

Northwest Arkansas Broiler Show, 27

nurses, company, 114–16, 215n68

Occupational Safety and Health Administration (OSHA), 107, 112, 115, 116, 157–58,
214nn59–60

Office of Price Administration, 27

oil industry in El Dorado, 29–30, 176n7

"Operation Dixie" (CIO), 91

Orange, James, 153

overtime pay, 120

Ozark Poultry and Egg Company, 21

Packinghouse Workers' Organizing
Committee (PWOC), 94–95, 206n101

Pagan, Enrique, 201n17

Palmer, Phyllis, 53

Parker, J. Scott, 30

Parker, Mary Evelyn, 59

Parker, Robert, 98

Parrado, Emilio, 220n14

patriarchy and paternalism: boosters and,
39–40; company benevolence, façade
of, 77–79; relief denial and, 47; welfare
benefits and, 191n54

Payne, Charles, 207n118

Perdue Farms (Salisbury, MD), 213n46,
213n51

Perez, Luis, 148, 153

Personal Responsibility and Universal
Engagement Act (LA), 155

Personal Responsibility and Work Opportunity Reconciliation Act (PRWORA),
151–52, 155, 221n33, 229n151

Pilgrim, Bo, 16, 77–78, 79, 87–88, 113,
118–19, 154

Pilgrim's Pride: El Dorado and, 20; façade
of benevolence in, 77–78; Gold Kist
acquisition, 154; human life, devaluing
of, 86–87; injury rate and, 113; plant
closure, 156; point system, 67–68; as
"savior," 16–17. *See also specific people
and topics, such as* working conditions

plantation model of labor, 38

planter class, 38, 185n145; relief, denial
of, 47

Pluss, Frank, 2

point system at Pilgrim's Pride, 67–68
pollution, 119
Poultry Justice Alliances (PJA), 122–23, 124–25, 217n114
poultry processing industry: antiunion tactics, 97–99; cook plants vs. kill plants, 64; exposés and studies on, 9–13; inspection, mandatory, 208n122; "noble mission" of, 16–17, 118–19; production levels in Arkansas, 27, 183n103; shift from hiring white women to black women, 187n4; status of, 157. *See also* El Dorado poultry industry, history of
poultry processing work: as alternative for women in Bernice, 61; domestic service compared to, 62–64; family-work balance and motherhood issues, 65–74; Latinos and, 129–37; live hanging process, 187n4; racial/gender hierarchy and, 64–65; self-definition and, 74–75; status of, 157; violent nature of, 77. *See also* line work; working conditions
poultry scientists, 24, 25
power relations: American Business, power of, 99; civil rights and, 49; in domestic service, 62–63; farmers and, 38; fear of job loss and, 82–83; gendered division of labor and, 108; Latinos and, 140; patriarchy and paternalism, 39–40, 47, 77–79, 191n54
Price, M. L., 21
price of chicken, 34
property values, 141–42
Proposition 187 (CA), 151, 229n150
protests and demonstrations in El Dorado, 196n115

Quadagno, Jill, 172n16

race: gender issues, false separation from, 9; legacy of racial etiquette, 78; racial distancing, 149–50; unions and, 95–96, 205n98; welfare visions, racialized, 191n54; whiteness, attainment of, 148–50, 228n139; whites, hesitancy to

trust, 82. *See also* Latino immigrants and workers
racism: boosters and, 39–40; hostile work atmosphere, racial, 81–83; structural problems of, 108
Ragsdale, John, 30
Rahn, Allan, 36
Rainach, Willie, 49
Raitz, Karl, 155
Reagan, Ronald, 157–58
recruitment: kin-based, 118, 120, 215n85, 217n101; of Latinos, 129–30, 137
Reese, Ellen, 53, 59
remittances, 141
Retail, Wholesale and Department Store Union (RWDSU), 13
Reynolds, Thomas, 31–32
Riffel, Brent, 12, 21
right-to-work laws: Arkansas, 39, 40; effects of, 204n83; spread of, 204n82; unions and, 92
Roberts, Dorothy, 51, 230n10
Rockefeller, Winthrop, 31, 182n90
Rollins, Judith, 62
Roosevelt, Franklin D., 53
Ruth, Robert, 78

Sachs, Carolyn, 22–23, 41
Sanderson, Joe, 78
Sanderson Farms, 13, 78–79, 88
San Miguel, Guadalupe, 227n129
Schlosser, Eric, 10
segregationism and Jim Crow: children shielded from racism within, 76; LA state sovereignty commission, 59–60; Louisiana laws, 56–59; shaming and stigmatization of black Louisianans, 55–56; voter purges and, 49–50. *See also* civil rights movement
self-definition, 74–75
sex discrimination, 108–10. *See also* gender
sexual harassment and exploitation, 80–81
shaming, 55
sharecropper system, 6
Sharpless, Rebecca, 62, 63

Sheppard, Essie Mae, 100, 101, 209n135
"shifting," 63
Shine, Deena (pseud.), 84, 85, 102, 114–15, 116, 134, 138, 165
Shulman, Steven, 224n82
Sidel, Ruth, 200n160
Simmons, Mark, 2
singing while working, 84
single mothers, 70–71, 155, 192n65, 200n160
slavery, 51, 80
smell of the plant, 105
Smith, Ana (pseud.), 145, 146, 165
Smith, Anna Marie, 57
Smith, Robert C., 224n82
social and economic vulnerability, connection between, 4
social justice issues, 122–24
Social Security Act (1935), 6, 7, 52–53. *See also* welfare benefits
social services. *See* Aid to Dependent Children program (ADC); welfare benefits
Solinger, Rickie, 55, 56
Sonderegger, V. H., 47
the South: El Dorado location and Southern labor climate, 35–42; exploitation of vulnerable workers, 8–9; factors encouraging industry in, 3, 36–37; Latino history in, 128–29; as "Sunbelt," 155; unions, hostility toward, 39, 90, 91, 203n76. *See also* segregationism and Jim Crow
Southern Exposure, 9, 115
Spanish and English, 139–40, 143–47, 226n111, 226n114
speaking out, 73
speed of the line, 2, 88, 110–11, 212n43
Steinberg, Stephen, 137–38
Strategies to Empower People (STEP) program, 155
Strausberg, Stephen, 22, 119, 179n43
strength stereotypes, 110
Striffler, Steve, 11, 12, 98, 106, 108, 112, 115, 117, 121, 211n21, 212n37
strikes: for bathroom breaks, 203n64; Center, TX, 93–94, 97–98, 208n122;

Forest, MS, 12–13; strikebreaking, 92; Taft-Hartley restrictions on, 91–92
Strong, Angela, 112
Strong, Janet (pseud.), 17–18, 100, 102, 118, 158, 160–61, 166
Stuesse, Angela, 10, 61, 79, 80, 116, 119, 133, 134, 149, 150, 203n64, 221n36, 228n144
subcontracting, 135
subsidization of illegitimacy myth, 55–56
suitable home laws, 57–58, 193n81
supervisors: black, 79–80, 201n22; Latino, 201n20; nastiness of, 76; paternalism and, 79
Swift Company, 93

Taft-Hartley Act (1947), 90, 91–92, 205n97
temperatures in the plant, 106–7
testimony, role of, 18, 160–61
Thames, Rick, 83
Thomas, Floyd, 196n115
Thomas, Lizzie (pseud.), 166
Thomas, Norman, 185n144
Thompson, Jewell, 122
Thomson, Susan, 156
Thornhill, Margaret, 55
timber industry, 29, 45
Tureaud, A. P., 189n27
Twedell, Richard, 99
Tyler, Geeta (pseud.), 166
Tyson, John, 26, 27, 28
Tyson Foods: antiunion tactics, 98–99, 208n124; expansion of, 28; "generosity" to employees, 79; injury and, 116; Latino workers and, 133; Riffel on, 12; undocumented workers and, 130; vertical integration and, 34

unemployment benefits, denial of, 172n14
unemployment rates, 137, 223n73
Union Parish (LA): bilingual education in, 145–48; Burnside conspiracy, 47–48; timber and farming in, 45–46, 188n12; unemployment rate in, 223n73; welfare benefits, denial of, 46, 60. *See also* Bernice (LA)

Union Parish Welfare Board, 53–54

unions and unionization: Change to Win (CtW) coalition, 125; closed shops and racial exclusion in, 7; company tactics against, 90, 97–99; current status of, 158; defeatist attitudes and pragmatism in, 93–94; disillusionment with, 99–103; distrust of, 92–93; dues, 99; importance of, 124–25; Latino workers and, 158–59; legislative barriers, 90, 91–92; race issues and, 95–96, 205n98; sexism and, 96–97; southern hostility toward, 39, 90, 91, 203n76; suppression of radicals and, 90–91, 94–95, 206n100. *See also specific unions*

United Food and Commercial Workers (UFCW): Change to Win coalition and, 124–25; dismay with, 4; formation of, 100; Local 2008, 100, 102, 158–59, 209n139; on sex discrimination, 108

United Packinghouse Workers of America (UPWA), 9, 94–95, 97, 206n101

United States Employment Service, 172n14, 172n16

University of Arkansas–Fayetteville, 28

U.S. Department of Agriculture (USDA), 107, 116, 157–58

U.S. Department of Health, Education, and Welfare (HEW), 59, 195n98

Vaca, Nicolas, 149, 225n94

vertical integration, 34–35, 37

violence of work, 77

Voss, Kim, 99

voting restrictions and purges, 49–50, 57, 189n32

wages and earnings: benefits, 118, 121, 217n102; at Cargill, 215n78; current status of, 157; as enticement to stay, 117–18; Latino workers and, 133, 137–39, 224n82; poverty wages, 198n130; underpayment and denied overtime, 120

Wagner (National Labor Relations) Act, 6, 7

Walker, Melissa, 22, 23, 176n14, 178n26

Wallace, Michele, 51

Watley, John Quincy, 46

Weise, Julie, 128

welfare benefits: denial of, 53–54; foster care and adoption services, 192n59; growth of, 54–55; Latinos and, 150–52; patriarchal and racialized notions of, 191n54; PRWORA and, 151–52, 155, 221n33, 229n151; restrictions and denial of, 46; stereotypical characterization of black women and, 51–52; subsidization of illegitimacy myth, shaming, and suitable home laws, 55–58; terminations of, 58–59, 60; two-tier system and, 52–53; white widows vs. other single mothers, 192n65. *See also* Aid to Dependent Children program (ADC)

West, Truett, 46

West, Vivian (pseud.), 43–44, 66, 74, 78, 81, 89, 101, 102–3, 109, 166, 199n149

White, Marion, 83

White, Sarah, 203n64

White, Willie Earl, 122

whiteness and Latinos, 148–50, 228n139

Williams, George, 124

Williams, L. C., 206n99

Williams-Forson, Psyche, 23, 62

Wollett, Donald, 193n78

womanhood, traditional ideology of, 69

women. *See* black women; gender

Women's Bureau, 172n14

Woodruff, Nan, 24, 38

work-family balance issues, 65–74

working conditions: bathroom breaks, restriction of, 88–89, 203n64; community-building efforts within, 84–85; "disposable workforce" and, 83–84; fear of job loss, 82–83; humanity, denial of, 87–88; paternalism and façade of benevolence, 77–79; racially hostile atmosphere, 81–82; reasons for staying, 117–21; resistance, forms of, 121–25; sexual harassment and exploitation, 80–81; sickness or death of workers, and line never stopping, 85–87; supervisor paternalism and hostility, 79–80; temperatures in the plant, 106–7. *See also* injuries and illness

Works Progress Administration, 26

World War II and postwar labor, 6–9, 27

Wright, Skelly, 50

Wright, Tavia (pseud.), 41, 67, 68–69, 71–72, 73–74, 80, 81, 84–88, 101–2, 109, 114, 117, 120, 122, 134, 138, 153, 158, 166, 199n149, 211n25

Young, Margie (pseud.), 84, 102, 109, 166

Young Women's Christian Association (TWCA), 5